C-313   CAREER EXAMINATION SERIES

This is your
PASSBOOK for...

General Contractor

Test Preparation Study Guide
Questions & Answers

NATIONAL LEARNING CORPORATION®

COPYRIGHT NOTICE

This book is SOLELY intended for, is sold ONLY to, and its use is RESTRICTED to individual, bona fide applicants or candidates who qualify by virtue of having seriously filed applications for appropriate license, certificate, professional and/or promotional advancement, higher school matriculation, scholarship, or other legitimate requirements of education and/or governmental authorities.

This book is NOT intended for use, class instruction, tutoring, training, duplication, copying, reprinting, excerption, or adaptation, etc., by:

1) Other publishers
2) Proprietors and/or Instructors of "Coaching" and/or Preparatory Courses
3) Personnel and/or Training Divisions of commercial, industrial, and governmental organizations
4) Schools, colleges, or universities and/or their departments and staffs, including teachers and other personnel
5) Testing Agencies or Bureaus
6) Study groups which seek by the purchase of a single volume to copy and/or duplicate and/or adapt this material for use by the group as a whole without having purchased individual volumes for each of the members of the group
7) Et al.

Such persons would be in violation of appropriate Federal and State statutes.

PROVISION OF LICENSING AGREEMENTS – Recognized educational, commercial, industrial, and governmental institutions and organizations, and others legitimately engaged in educational pursuits, including training, testing, and measurement activities, may address request for a licensing agreement to the copyright owners, who will determine whether, and under what conditions, including fees and charges, the materials in this book may be used them. In other words, a licensing facility exists for the legitimate use of the material in this book on other than an individual basis. However, it is asseverated and affirmed here that the material in this book CANNOT be used without the receipt of the express permission of such a licensing agreement from the Publishers. Inquiries re licensing should be addressed to the company, attention rights and permissions department.

All rights reserved, including the right of reproduction in whole or in part, in any form or by any means, electronic or mechanical, including photocopying, recording, or by any information storage and retrieval system, without permission in writing from the Publisher.

Copyright © 2025 by
National Learning Corporation

212 Michael Drive, Syosset, NY 11791
(516) 921-8888 • www.passbooks.com
E-mail: info@passbooks.com

PASSBOOK® SERIES

THE *PASSBOOK® SERIES* has been created to prepare applicants and candidates for the ultimate academic battlefield – the examination room.

At some time in our lives, each and every one of us may be required to take an examination – for validation, matriculation, admission, qualification, registration, certification, or licensure.

Based on the assumption that every applicant or candidate has met the basic formal educational standards, has taken the required number of courses, and read the necessary texts, the *PASSBOOK® SERIES* furnishes the one special preparation which may assure passing with confidence, instead of failing with insecurity. Examination questions – together with answers – are furnished as the basic vehicle for study so that the mysteries of the examination and its compounding difficulties may be eliminated or diminished by a sure method.

This book is meant to help you pass your examination provided that you qualify and are serious in your objective.

The entire field is reviewed through the huge store of content information which is succinctly presented through a provocative and challenging approach – the question-and-answer method.

A climate of success is established by furnishing the correct answers at the end of each test.

You soon learn to recognize types of questions, forms of questions, and patterns of questioning. You may even begin to anticipate expected outcomes.

You perceive that many questions are repeated or adapted so that you can gain acute insights, which may enable you to score many sure points.

You learn how to confront new questions, or types of questions, and to attack them confidently and work out the correct answers.

You note objectives and emphases, and recognize pitfalls and dangers, so that you may make positive educational adjustments.

Moreover, you are kept fully informed in relation to new concepts, methods, practices, and directions in the field.

You discover that you are actually taking the examination all the time: you are preparing for the examination by "taking" an examination, not by reading extraneous and/or supererogatory textbooks.

In short, this PASSBOOK®, used directedly, should be an important factor in helping you to pass your test.

GENERAL CONTRACTOR

DUTIES
Performs building services for property owners in the construction of new residential and commercial buildings, as well as the alteration of existing buildings. Hires subcontractors and works with architects and owners in the performance of his duties.

SCOPE OF THE WRITTEN TEST
The written test will be designed to test for knowledge, skills, and/or abilities in such areas as:
1. Principles and practices of building construction;
2. Building trades; and
3. Contract documents.

HOW TO TAKE A TEST

I. YOU MUST PASS AN EXAMINATION

A. *WHAT EVERY CANDIDATE SHOULD KNOW*

Examination applicants often ask us for help in preparing for the written test. What can I study in advance? What kinds of questions will be asked? How will the test be given? How will the papers be graded?

As an applicant for a civil service examination, you may be wondering about some of these things. Our purpose here is to suggest effective methods of advance study and to describe civil service examinations.

Your chances for success on this examination can be increased if you know how to prepare. Those "pre-examination jitters" can be reduced if you know what to expect. You can even experience an adventure in good citizenship if you know why civil service exams are given.

B. *WHY ARE CIVIL SERVICE EXAMINATIONS GIVEN?*

Civil service examinations are important to you in two ways. As a citizen, you want public jobs filled by employees who know how to do their work. As a job seeker, you want a fair chance to compete for that job on an equal footing with other candidates. The best-known means of accomplishing this two-fold goal is the competitive examination.

Exams are widely publicized throughout the nation. They may be administered for jobs in federal, state, city, municipal, town or village governments or agencies.

Any citizen may apply, with some limitations, such as the age or residence of applicants. Your experience and education may be reviewed to see whether you meet the requirements for the particular examination. When these requirements exist, they are reasonable and applied consistently to all applicants. Thus, a competitive examination may cause you some uneasiness now, but it is your privilege and safeguard.

C. *HOW ARE CIVIL SERVICE EXAMS DEVELOPED?*

Examinations are carefully written by trained technicians who are specialists in the field known as "psychological measurement," in consultation with recognized authorities in the field of work that the test will cover. These experts recommend the subject matter areas or skills to be tested; only those knowledges or skills important to your success on the job are included. The most reliable books and source materials available are used as references. Together, the experts and technicians judge the difficulty level of the questions.

Test technicians know how to phrase questions so that the problem is clearly stated. Their ethics do not permit "trick" or "catch" questions. Questions may have been tried out on sample groups, or subjected to statistical analysis, to determine their usefulness.

Written tests are often used in combination with performance tests, ratings of training and experience, and oral interviews. All of these measures combine to form the best-known means of finding the right person for the right job.

II. HOW TO PASS THE WRITTEN TEST

A. NATURE OF THE EXAMINATION

To prepare intelligently for civil service examinations, you should know how they differ from school examinations you have taken. In school you were assigned certain definite pages to read or subjects to cover. The examination questions were quite detailed and usually emphasized memory. Civil service exams, on the other hand, try to discover your present ability to perform the duties of a position, plus your potentiality to learn these duties. In other words, a civil service exam attempts to predict how successful you will be. Questions cover such a broad area that they cannot be as minute and detailed as school exam questions.

In the public service similar kinds of work, or positions, are grouped together in one "class." This process is known as *position-classification*. All the positions in a class are paid according to the salary range for that class. One class title covers all of these positions, and they are all tested by the same examination.

B. FOUR BASIC STEPS

1) Study the announcement

How, then, can you know what subjects to study? Our best answer is: "Learn as much as possible about the class of positions for which you've applied." The exam will test the knowledge, skills and abilities needed to do the work.

Your most valuable source of information about the position you want is the official exam announcement. This announcement lists the training and experience qualifications. Check these standards and apply only if you come reasonably close to meeting them.

The brief description of the position in the examination announcement offers some clues to the subjects which will be tested. Think about the job itself. Review the duties in your mind. Can you perform them, or are there some in which you are rusty? Fill in the blank spots in your preparation.

Many jurisdictions preview the written test in the exam announcement by including a section called "Knowledge and Abilities Required," "Scope of the Examination," or some similar heading. Here you will find out specifically what fields will be tested.

2) Review your own background

Once you learn in general what the position is all about, and what you need to know to do the work, ask yourself which subjects you already know fairly well and which need improvement. You may wonder whether to concentrate on improving your strong areas or on building some background in your fields of weakness. When the announcement has specified "some knowledge" or "considerable knowledge," or has used adjectives like "beginning principles of..." or "advanced ... methods," you can get a clue as to the number and difficulty of questions to be asked in any given field. More questions, and hence broader coverage, would be included for those subjects which are more important in the work. Now weigh your strengths and weaknesses against the job requirements and prepare accordingly.

3) Determine the level of the position

Another way to tell how intensively you should prepare is to understand the level of the job for which you are applying. Is it the entering level? In other words, is this the position in which beginners in a field of work are hired? Or is it an intermediate or advanced level? Sometimes this is indicated by such words as "Junior" or "Senior" in the class title. Other jurisdictions use Roman numerals to designate the level – Clerk I, Clerk II, for example. The word "Supervisor" sometimes appears in the title. If the level is not indicated by the title, check the description of duties. Will you be working under very close supervision, or will you have responsibility for independent decisions in this work?

4) Choose appropriate study materials

Now that you know the subjects to be examined and the relative amount of each subject to be covered, you can choose suitable study materials. For beginning level jobs, or even advanced ones, if you have a pronounced weakness in some aspect of your training, read a modern, standard textbook in that field. Be sure it is up to date and has general coverage. Such books are normally available at your library, and the librarian will be glad to help you locate one. For entry-level positions, questions of appropriate difficulty are chosen – neither highly advanced questions, nor those too simple. Such questions require careful thought but not advanced training.

If the position for which you are applying is technical or advanced, you will read more advanced, specialized material. If you are already familiar with the basic principles of your field, elementary textbooks would waste your time. Concentrate on advanced textbooks and technical periodicals. Think through the concepts and review difficult problems in your field.

These are all general sources. You can get more ideas on your own initiative, following these leads. For example, training manuals and publications of the government agency which employs workers in your field can be useful, particularly for technical and professional positions. A letter or visit to the government department involved may result in more specific study suggestions, and certainly will provide you with a more definite idea of the exact nature of the position you are seeking.

III. KINDS OF TESTS

Tests are used for purposes other than measuring knowledge and ability to perform specified duties. For some positions, it is equally important to test ability to make adjustments to new situations or to profit from training. In others, basic mental abilities not dependent on information are essential. Questions which test these things may not appear as pertinent to the duties of the position as those which test for knowledge and information. Yet they are often highly important parts of a fair examination. For very general questions, it is almost impossible to help you direct your study efforts. What we can do is to point out some of the more common of these general abilities needed in public service positions and describe some typical questions.

1) General information

Broad, general information has been found useful for predicting job success in some kinds of work. This is tested in a variety of ways, from vocabulary lists to questions about current events. Basic background in some field of work, such as sociology or economics, may be sampled in a group of questions. Often these are principles which have become familiar to most persons through exposure rather than through formal training. It is difficult to advise you how to study for these questions; being alert to the world around you is our best suggestion.

2) Verbal ability

An example of an ability needed in many positions is verbal or language ability. Verbal ability is, in brief, the ability to use and understand words. Vocabulary and grammar tests are typical measures of this ability. Reading comprehension or paragraph interpretation questions are common in many kinds of civil service tests. You are given a paragraph of written material and asked to find its central meaning.

3) Numerical ability

Number skills can be tested by the familiar arithmetic problem, by checking paired lists of numbers to see which are alike and which are different, or by interpreting charts and graphs. In the latter test, a graph may be printed in the test booklet which you are asked to use as the basis for answering questions.

4) Observation

A popular test for law-enforcement positions is the observation test. A picture is shown to you for several minutes, then taken away. Questions about the picture test your ability to observe both details and larger elements.

5) Following directions

In many positions in the public service, the employee must be able to carry out written instructions dependably and accurately. You may be given a chart with several columns, each column listing a variety of information. The questions require you to carry out directions involving the information given in the chart.

6) Skills and aptitudes

Performance tests effectively measure some manual skills and aptitudes. When the skill is one in which you are trained, such as typing or shorthand, you can practice. These tests are often very much like those given in business school or high school courses. For many of the other skills and aptitudes, however, no short-time preparation can be made. Skills and abilities natural to you or that you have developed throughout your lifetime are being tested.

Many of the general questions just described provide all the data needed to answer the questions and ask you to use your reasoning ability to find the answers. Your best preparation for these tests, as well as for tests of facts and ideas, is to be at your physical and mental best. You, no doubt, have your own methods of getting into an exam-taking mood and keeping "in shape." The next section lists some ideas on this subject.

IV. KINDS OF QUESTIONS

Only rarely is the "essay" question, which you answer in narrative form, used in civil service tests. Civil service tests are usually of the short-answer type. Full instructions for answering these questions will be given to you at the examination. But in case this is your first experience with short-answer questions and separate answer sheets, here is what you need to know:

1) Multiple-choice Questions

Most popular of the short-answer questions is the "multiple choice" or "best answer" question. It can be used, for example, to test for factual knowledge, ability to solve problems or judgment in meeting situations found at work.

A multiple-choice question is normally one of three types—
- It can begin with an incomplete statement followed by several possible endings. You are to find the one ending which *best* completes the statement, although some of the others may not be entirely wrong.
- It can also be a complete statement in the form of a question which is answered by choosing one of the statements listed.

- It can be in the form of a problem – again you select the best answer.

Here is an example of a multiple-choice question with a discussion which should give you some clues as to the method for choosing the right answer:

When an employee has a complaint about his assignment, the action which will *best* help him overcome his difficulty is to
- A. discuss his difficulty with his coworkers
- B. take the problem to the head of the organization
- C. take the problem to the person who gave him the assignment
- D. say nothing to anyone about his complaint

In answering this question, you should study each of the choices to find which is best. Consider choice "A" – Certainly an employee may discuss his complaint with fellow employees, but no change or improvement can result, and the complaint remains unresolved. Choice "B" is a poor choice since the head of the organization probably does not know what assignment you have been given, and taking your problem to him is known as "going over the head" of the supervisor. The supervisor, or person who made the assignment, is the person who can clarify it or correct any injustice. Choice "C" is, therefore, correct. To say nothing, as in choice "D," is unwise. Supervisors have and interest in knowing the problems employees are facing, and the employee is seeking a solution to his problem.

2) True/False Questions

The "true/false" or "right/wrong" form of question is sometimes used. Here a complete statement is given. Your job is to decide whether the statement is right or wrong.

SAMPLE: A roaming cell-phone call to a nearby city costs less than a non-roaming call to a distant city.

This statement is wrong, or false, since roaming calls are more expensive.

This is not a complete list of all possible question forms, although most of the others are variations of these common types. You will always get complete directions for answering questions. Be sure you understand *how* to mark your answers – ask questions until you do.

V. RECORDING YOUR ANSWERS

Computer terminals are used more and more today for many different kinds of exams.

For an examination with very few applicants, you may be told to record your answers in the test booklet itself. Separate answer sheets are much more common. If this separate answer sheet is to be scored by machine – and this is often the case – it is highly important that you mark your answers correctly in order to get credit.

An electronic scoring machine is often used in civil service offices because of the speed with which papers can be scored. Machine-scored answer sheets must be marked with a pencil, which will be given to you. This pencil has a high graphite content which responds to the electronic scoring machine. As a matter of fact, stray dots may register as answers, so do not let your pencil rest on the answer sheet while you are pondering the correct answer. Also, if your pencil lead breaks or is otherwise defective, ask for another.

Since the answer sheet will be dropped in a slot in the scoring machine, be careful not to bend the corners or get the paper crumpled.

The answer sheet normally has five vertical columns of numbers, with 30 numbers to a column. These numbers correspond to the question numbers in your test booklet. After each number, going across the page are four or five pairs of dotted lines. These short dotted lines have small letters or numbers above them. The first two pairs may also have a "T" or "F" above the letters. This indicates that the first two pairs only are to be used if the questions are of the true-false type. If the questions are multiple choice, disregard the "T" and "F" and pay attention only to the small letters or numbers.

Answer your questions in the manner of the sample that follows:

32. The largest city in the United States is
    A. Washington, D.C.
    B. New York City
    C. Chicago
    D. Detroit
    E. San Francisco

1) Choose the answer you think is best. (New York City is the largest, so "B" is correct.)
2) Find the row of dotted lines numbered the same as the question you are answering. (Find row number 32)
3) Find the pair of dotted lines corresponding to the answer. (Find the pair of lines under the mark "B.")
4) Make a solid black mark between the dotted lines.

VI. BEFORE THE TEST

Common sense will help you find procedures to follow to get ready for an examination. Too many of us, however, overlook these sensible measures. Indeed, nervousness and fatigue have been found to be the most serious reasons why applicants fail to do their best on civil service tests. Here is a list of reminders:

- Begin your preparation early – Don't wait until the last minute to go scurrying around for books and materials or to find out what the position is all about.
- Prepare continuously – An hour a night for a week is better than an all-night cram session. This has been definitely established. What is more, a night a week for a month will return better dividends than crowding your study into a shorter period of time.
- Locate the place of the exam – You have been sent a notice telling you when and where to report for the examination. If the location is in a different town or otherwise unfamiliar to you, it would be well to inquire the best route and learn something about the building.
- Relax the night before the test – Allow your mind to rest. Do not study at all that night. Plan some mild recreation or diversion; then go to bed early and get a good night's sleep.
- Get up early enough to make a leisurely trip to the place for the test – This way unforeseen events, traffic snarls, unfamiliar buildings, etc. will not upset you.
- Dress comfortably – A written test is not a fashion show. You will be known by number and not by name, so wear something comfortable.

- Leave excess paraphernalia at home – Shopping bags and odd bundles will get in your way. You need bring only the items mentioned in the official notice you received; usually everything you need is provided. Do not bring reference books to the exam. They will only confuse those last minutes and be taken away from you when in the test room.
- Arrive somewhat ahead of time – If because of transportation schedules you must get there very early, bring a newspaper or magazine to take your mind off yourself while waiting.
- Locate the examination room – When you have found the proper room, you will be directed to the seat or part of the room where you will sit. Sometimes you are given a sheet of instructions to read while you are waiting. Do not fill out any forms until you are told to do so; just read them and be prepared.
- Relax and prepare to listen to the instructions
- If you have any physical problem that may keep you from doing your best, be sure to tell the test administrator. If you are sick or in poor health, you really cannot do your best on the exam. You can come back and take the test some other time.

VII. AT THE TEST

The day of the test is here and you have the test booklet in your hand. The temptation to get going is very strong. Caution! There is more to success than knowing the right answers. You must know how to identify your papers and understand variations in the type of short-answer question used in this particular examination. Follow these suggestions for maximum results from your efforts:

1) Cooperate with the monitor

The test administrator has a duty to create a situation in which you can be as much at ease as possible. He will give instructions, tell you when to begin, check to see that you are marking your answer sheet correctly, and so on. He is not there to guard you, although he will see that your competitors do not take unfair advantage. He wants to help you do your best.

2) Listen to all instructions

Don't jump the gun! Wait until you understand all directions. In most civil service tests you get more time than you need to answer the questions. So don't be in a hurry. Read each word of instructions until you clearly understand the meaning. Study the examples, listen to all announcements and follow directions. Ask questions if you do not understand what to do.

3) Identify your papers

Civil service exams are usually identified by number only. You will be assigned a number; you must not put your name on your test papers. Be sure to copy your number correctly. Since more than one exam may be given, copy your exact examination title.

4) Plan your time

Unless you are told that a test is a "speed" or "rate of work" test, speed itself is usually not important. Time enough to answer all the questions will be provided, but this does not mean that you have all day. An overall time limit has been set. Divide the total time (in minutes) by the number of questions to determine the approximate time you have for each question.

5) Do not linger over difficult questions

If you come across a difficult question, mark it with a paper clip (useful to have along) and come back to it when you have been through the booklet. One caution if you do this – be sure to skip a number on your answer sheet as well. Check often to be sure that you have not lost your place and that you are marking in the row numbered the same as the question you are answering.

6) Read the questions

Be sure you know what the question asks! Many capable people are unsuccessful because they failed to *read* the questions correctly.

7) Answer all questions

Unless you have been instructed that a penalty will be deducted for incorrect answers, it is better to guess than to omit a question.

8) Speed tests

It is often better NOT to guess on speed tests. It has been found that on timed tests people are tempted to spend the last few seconds before time is called in marking answers at random – without even reading them – in the hope of picking up a few extra points. To discourage this practice, the instructions may warn you that your score will be "corrected" for guessing. That is, a penalty will be applied. The incorrect answers will be deducted from the correct ones, or some other penalty formula will be used.

9) Review your answers

If you finish before time is called, go back to the questions you guessed or omitted to give them further thought. Review other answers if you have time.

10) Return your test materials

If you are ready to leave before others have finished or time is called, take ALL your materials to the monitor and leave quietly. Never take any test material with you. The monitor can discover whose papers are not complete, and taking a test booklet may be grounds for disqualification.

VIII. EXAMINATION TECHNIQUES

1) Read the general instructions carefully. These are usually printed on the first page of the exam booklet. As a rule, these instructions refer to the timing of the examination; the fact that you should not start work until the signal and must stop work at a signal, etc. If there are any *special* instructions, such as a choice of questions to be answered, make sure that you note this instruction carefully.

2) When you are ready to start work on the examination, that is as soon as the signal has been given, read the instructions to each question booklet, underline any key words or phrases, such as *least, best, outline, describe* and the like. In this way you will tend to answer as requested rather than discover on reviewing your paper that you *listed without describing*, that you selected the *worst* choice rather than the *best* choice, etc.

3) If the examination is of the objective or multiple-choice type – that is, each question will also give a series of possible answers: A, B, C or D, and you are called upon to select the best answer and write the letter next to that answer on your answer paper – it is advisable to start answering each question in turn. There may be anywhere from 50 to 100 such questions in the three or four hours allotted and you can see how much time would be taken if you read through all the questions before beginning to answer any. Furthermore, if you come across a question or group of questions which you know would be difficult to answer, it would undoubtedly affect your handling of all the other questions.

4) If the examination is of the essay type and contains but a few questions, it is a moot point as to whether you should read all the questions before starting to answer any one. Of course, if you are given a choice – say five out of seven and the like – then it is essential to read all the questions so you can eliminate the two that are most difficult. If, however, you are asked to answer all the questions, there may be danger in trying to answer the easiest one first because you may find that you will spend too much time on it. The best technique is to answer the first question, then proceed to the second, etc.

5) Time your answers. Before the exam begins, write down the time it started, then add the time allowed for the examination and write down the time it must be completed, then divide the time available somewhat as follows:
    - If 3-1/2 hours are allowed, that would be 210 minutes. If you have 80 objective-type questions, that would be an average of 2-1/2 minutes per question. Allow yourself no more than 2 minutes per question, or a total of 160 minutes, which will permit about 50 minutes to review.
    - If for the time allotment of 210 minutes there are 7 essay questions to answer, that would average about 30 minutes a question. Give yourself only 25 minutes per question so that you have about 35 minutes to review.

6) The most important instruction is to *read each question* and make sure you know what is wanted. The second most important instruction is to *time yourself properly* so that you answer every question. The third most important instruction is to *answer every question*. Guess if you have to but include something for each question. Remember that you will receive no credit for a blank and will probably receive some credit if you write something in answer to an essay question. If you guess a letter – say "B" for a multiple-choice question – you may have guessed right. If you leave a blank as an answer to a multiple-choice question, the examiners may respect your feelings but it will not add a point to your score. Some exams may penalize you for wrong answers, so in such cases *only*, you may not want to guess unless you have some basis for your answer.

7) Suggestions
    a. Objective-type questions
        1. Examine the question booklet for proper sequence of pages and questions
        2. Read all instructions carefully
        3. Skip any question which seems too difficult; return to it after all other questions have been answered
        4. Apportion your time properly; do not spend too much time on any single question or group of questions

5. Note and underline key words – *all, most, fewest, least, best, worst, same, opposite*, etc.
6. Pay particular attention to negatives
7. Note unusual option, e.g., unduly long, short, complex, different or similar in content to the body of the question
8. Observe the use of "hedging" words – *probably, may, most likely,* etc.
9. Make sure that your answer is put next to the same number as the question
10. Do not second-guess unless you have good reason to believe the second answer is definitely more correct
11. Cross out original answer if you decide another answer is more accurate; do not erase until you are ready to hand your paper in
12. Answer all questions; guess unless instructed otherwise
13. Leave time for review

b. Essay questions
1. Read each question carefully
2. Determine exactly what is wanted. Underline key words or phrases.
3. Decide on outline or paragraph answer
4. Include many different points and elements unless asked to develop any one or two points or elements
5. Show impartiality by giving pros and cons unless directed to select one side only
6. Make and write down any assumptions you find necessary to answer the questions
7. Watch your English, grammar, punctuation and choice of words
8. Time your answers; don't crowd material

8) Answering the essay question

Most essay questions can be answered by framing the specific response around several key words or ideas. Here are a few such key words or ideas:

M's: manpower, materials, methods, money, management
P's: purpose, program, policy, plan, procedure, practice, problems, pitfalls, personnel, public relations

a. Six basic steps in handling problems:
1. Preliminary plan and background development
2. Collect information, data and facts
3. Analyze and interpret information, data and facts
4. Analyze and develop solutions as well as make recommendations
5. Prepare report and sell recommendations
6. Install recommendations and follow up effectiveness

b. Pitfalls to avoid
1. *Taking things for granted* – A statement of the situation does not necessarily imply that each of the elements is necessarily true; for example, a complaint may be invalid and biased so that all that can be taken for granted is that a complaint has been registered

2. *Considering only one side of a situation* – Wherever possible, indicate several alternatives and then point out the reasons you selected the best one
3. *Failing to indicate follow up* – Whenever your answer indicates action on your part, make certain that you will take proper follow-up action to see how successful your recommendations, procedures or actions turn out to be
4. *Taking too long in answering any single question* – Remember to time your answers properly

IX. AFTER THE TEST

Scoring procedures differ in detail among civil service jurisdictions although the general principles are the same. Whether the papers are hand-scored or graded by machine we have described, they are nearly always graded by number. That is, the person who marks the paper knows only the number – never the name – of the applicant. Not until all the papers have been graded will they be matched with names. If other tests, such as training and experience or oral interview ratings have been given, scores will be combined. Different parts of the examination usually have different weights. For example, the written test might count 60 percent of the final grade, and a rating of training and experience 40 percent. In many jurisdictions, veterans will have a certain number of points added to their grades.

After the final grade has been determined, the names are placed in grade order and an eligible list is established. There are various methods for resolving ties between those who get the same final grade – probably the most common is to place first the name of the person whose application was received first. Job offers are made from the eligible list in the order the names appear on it. You will be notified of your grade and your rank as soon as all these computations have been made. This will be done as rapidly as possible.

People who are found to meet the requirements in the announcement are called "eligibles." Their names are put on a list of eligible candidates. An eligible's chances of getting a job depend on how high he stands on this list and how fast agencies are filling jobs from the list.

When a job is to be filled from a list of eligibles, the agency asks for the names of people on the list of eligibles for that job. When the civil service commission receives this request, it sends to the agency the names of the three people highest on this list. Or, if the job to be filled has specialized requirements, the office sends the agency the names of the top three persons who meet these requirements from the general list.

The appointing officer makes a choice from among the three people whose names were sent to him. If the selected person accepts the appointment, the names of the others are put back on the list to be considered for future openings.

That is the rule in hiring from all kinds of eligible lists, whether they are for typist, carpenter, chemist, or something else. For every vacancy, the appointing officer has his choice of any one of the top three eligibles on the list. This explains why the person whose name is on top of the list sometimes does not get an appointment when some of the persons lower on the list do. If the appointing officer chooses the second or third eligible, the No. 1 eligible does not get a job at once, but stays on the list until he is appointed or the list is terminated.

X. HOW TO PASS THE INTERVIEW TEST

The examination for which you applied requires an oral interview test. You have already taken the written test and you are now being called for the interview test – the final part of the formal examination.

You may think that it is not possible to prepare for an interview test and that there are no procedures to follow during an interview. Our purpose is to point out some things you can do in advance that will help you and some good rules to follow and pitfalls to avoid while you are being interviewed.

What is an interview supposed to test?

The written examination is designed to test the technical knowledge and competence of the candidate; the oral is designed to evaluate intangible qualities, not readily measured otherwise, and to establish a list showing the relative fitness of each candidate – as measured against his competitors – for the position sought. Scoring is not on the basis of "right" and "wrong," but on a sliding scale of values ranging from "not passable" to "outstanding." As a matter of fact, it is possible to achieve a relatively low score without a single "incorrect" answer because of evident weakness in the qualities being measured.

Occasionally, an examination may consist entirely of an oral test – either an individual or a group oral. In such cases, information is sought concerning the technical knowledges and abilities of the candidate, since there has been no written examination for this purpose. More commonly, however, an oral test is used to supplement a written examination.

Who conducts interviews?

The composition of oral boards varies among different jurisdictions. In nearly all, a representative of the personnel department serves as chairman. One of the members of the board may be a representative of the department in which the candidate would work. In some cases, "outside experts" are used, and, frequently, a businessman or some other representative of the general public is asked to serve. Labor and management or other special groups may be represented. The aim is to secure the services of experts in the appropriate field.

However the board is composed, it is a good idea (and not at all improper or unethical) to ascertain in advance of the interview who the members are and what groups they represent. When you are introduced to them, you will have some idea of their backgrounds and interests, and at least you will not stutter and stammer over their names.

What should be done before the interview?

While knowledge about the board members is useful and takes some of the surprise element out of the interview, there is other preparation which is more substantive. It *is* possible to prepare for an oral interview – in several ways:

1) Keep a copy of your application and review it carefully before the interview

This may be the only document before the oral board, and the starting point of the interview. Know what education and experience you have listed there, and the sequence and dates of all of it. Sometimes the board will ask you to review the highlights of your experience for them; you should not have to hem and haw doing it.

2) Study the class specification and the examination announcement

Usually, the oral board has one or both of these to guide them. The qualities, characteristics or knowledges required by the position sought are stated in these documents. They offer valuable clues as to the nature of the oral interview. For example, if the job involves supervisory responsibilities, the announcement will usually indicate that knowledge of modern supervisory methods and the qualifications of the candidate as a supervisor will be tested. If so, you can expect such questions, frequently in the form of a hypothetical situation which you are expected to solve. NEVER go into an oral without knowledge of the duties and responsibilities of the job you seek.

3) Think through each qualification required

Try to visualize the kind of questions you would ask if you were a board member. How well could you answer them? Try especially to appraise your own knowledge and background in each area, *measured against the job sought*, and identify any areas in which you are weak. Be critical and realistic – do not flatter yourself.

4) Do some general reading in areas in which you feel you may be weak

For example, if the job involves supervision and your past experience has NOT, some general reading in supervisory methods and practices, particularly in the field of human relations, might be useful. Do NOT study agency procedures or detailed manuals. The oral board will be testing your understanding and capacity, not your memory.

5) Get a good night's sleep and watch your general health and mental attitude

You will want a clear head at the interview. Take care of a cold or any other minor ailment, and of course, no hangovers.

What should be done on the day of the interview?

Now comes the day of the interview itself. Give yourself plenty of time to get there. Plan to arrive somewhat ahead of the scheduled time, particularly if your appointment is in the fore part of the day. If a previous candidate fails to appear, the board might be ready for you a bit early. By early afternoon an oral board is almost invariably behind schedule if there are many candidates, and you may have to wait. Take along a book or magazine to read, or your application to review, but leave any extraneous material in the waiting room when you go in for your interview. In any event, relax and compose yourself.

The matter of dress is important. The board is forming impressions about you – from your experience, your manners, your attitude, and your appearance. Give your personal appearance careful attention. Dress your best, but not your flashiest. Choose conservative, appropriate clothing, and be sure it is immaculate. This is a business interview, and your appearance should indicate that you regard it as such. Besides, being well groomed and properly dressed will help boost your confidence.

Sooner or later, someone will call your name and escort you into the interview room. *This is it.* From here on you are on your own. It is too late for any more preparation. But remember, you asked for this opportunity to prove your fitness, and you are here because your request was granted.

What happens when you go in?

The usual sequence of events will be as follows: The clerk (who is often the board stenographer) will introduce you to the chairman of the oral board, who will introduce you to the other members of the board. Acknowledge the introductions before you sit down. Do not be surprised if you find a microphone facing you or a stenotypist sitting by. Oral interviews are usually recorded in the event of an appeal or other review.

Usually the chairman of the board will open the interview by reviewing the highlights of your education and work experience from your application – primarily for the benefit of the other members of the board, as well as to get the material into the record. Do not interrupt or comment unless there is an error or significant misinterpretation; if that is the case, do not hesitate. But do not quibble about insignificant matters. Also, he will usually ask you some question about your education, experience or your present job – partly to get you to start talking and to establish the interviewing "rapport." He may start the actual questioning, or turn it over to one of the other members. Frequently, each member undertakes the questioning on a particular area, one in which he is perhaps most competent, so you can expect each member to participate in the examination. Because time is limited, you may also expect some rather abrupt switches in the direction the questioning takes, so do not be upset by it. Normally, a board member will not pursue a single line of questioning unless he discovers a particular strength or weakness.

After each member has participated, the chairman will usually ask whether any member has any further questions, then will ask you if you have anything you wish to add. Unless you are expecting this question, it may floor you. Worse, it may start you off on an extended, extemporaneous speech. The board is not usually seeking more information. The question is principally to offer you a last opportunity to present further qualifications or to indicate that you have nothing to add. So, if you feel that a significant qualification or characteristic has been overlooked, it is proper to point it out in a sentence or so. Do not compliment the board on the thoroughness of their examination – they have been sketchy, and you know it. If you wish, merely say, "No thank you, I have nothing further to add." This is a point where you can "talk yourself out" of a good impression or fail to present an important bit of information. Remember, *you close the interview yourself.*

The chairman will then say, "That is all, Mr. _____, thank you." Do not be startled; the interview is over, and quicker than you think. Thank him, gather your belongings and take your leave. Save your sigh of relief for the other side of the door.

How to put your best foot forward

Throughout this entire process, you may feel that the board individually and collectively is trying to pierce your defenses, seek out your hidden weaknesses and embarrass and confuse you. Actually, this is not true. They are obliged to make an appraisal of your qualifications for the job you are seeking, and they want to see you in your best light. Remember, they must interview all candidates and a non-cooperative candidate may become a failure in spite of their best efforts to bring out his qualifications. Here are 15 suggestions that will help you:

1) **Be natural – Keep your attitude confident, not cocky**

If you are not confident that you can do the job, do not expect the board to be. Do not apologize for your weaknesses, try to bring out your strong points. The board is interested in a positive, not negative, presentation. Cockiness will antagonize any board member and make him wonder if you are covering up a weakness by a false show of strength.

2) **Get comfortable, but don't lounge or sprawl**

Sit erectly but not stiffly. A careless posture may lead the board to conclude that you are careless in other things, or at least that you are not impressed by the importance of the occasion. Either conclusion is natural, even if incorrect. Do not fuss with your clothing, a pencil or an ashtray. Your hands may occasionally be useful to emphasize a point; do not let them become a point of distraction.

3) **Do not wisecrack or make small talk**

This is a serious situation, and your attitude should show that you consider it as such. Further, the time of the board is limited – they do not want to waste it, and neither should you.

4) Do not exaggerate your experience or abilities

In the first place, from information in the application or other interviews and sources, the board may know more about you than you think. Secondly, you probably will not get away with it. An experienced board is rather adept at spotting such a situation, so do not take the chance.

5) If you know a board member, do not make a point of it, yet do not hide it

Certainly you are not fooling him, and probably not the other members of the board. Do not try to take advantage of your acquaintanceship – it will probably do you little good.

6) Do not dominate the interview

Let the board do that. They will give you the clues – do not assume that you have to do all the talking. Realize that the board has a number of questions to ask you, and do not try to take up all the interview time by showing off your extensive knowledge of the answer to the first one.

7) Be attentive

You only have 20 minutes or so, and you should keep your attention at its sharpest throughout. When a member is addressing a problem or question to you, give him your undivided attention. Address your reply principally to him, but do not exclude the other board members.

8) Do not interrupt

A board member may be stating a problem for you to analyze. He will ask you a question when the time comes. Let him state the problem, and wait for the question.

9) Make sure you understand the question

Do not try to answer until you are sure what the question is. If it is not clear, restate it in your own words or ask the board member to clarify it for you. However, do not haggle about minor elements.

10) Reply promptly but not hastily

A common entry on oral board rating sheets is "candidate responded readily," or "candidate hesitated in replies." Respond as promptly and quickly as you can, but do not jump to a hasty, ill-considered answer.

11) Do not be peremptory in your answers

A brief answer is proper – but do not fire your answer back. That is a losing game from your point of view. The board member can probably ask questions much faster than you can answer them.

12) Do not try to create the answer you think the board member wants

He is interested in what kind of mind you have and how it works – not in playing games. Furthermore, he can usually spot this practice and will actually grade you down on it.

13) Do not switch sides in your reply merely to agree with a board member

Frequently, a member will take a contrary position merely to draw you out and to see if you are willing and able to defend your point of view. Do not start a debate, yet do not surrender a good position. If a position is worth taking, it is worth defending.

14) Do not be afraid to admit an error in judgment if you are shown to be wrong

The board knows that you are forced to reply without any opportunity for careful consideration. Your answer may be demonstrably wrong. If so, admit it and get on with the interview.

15) Do not dwell at length on your present job

The opening question may relate to your present assignment. Answer the question but do not go into an extended discussion. You are being examined for a *new* job, not your present one. As a matter of fact, try to phrase ALL your answers in terms of the job for which you are being examined.

Basis of Rating

Probably you will forget most of these "do's" and "don'ts" when you walk into the oral interview room. Even remembering them all will not ensure you a passing grade. Perhaps you did not have the qualifications in the first place. But remembering them will help you to put your best foot forward, without treading on the toes of the board members.

Rumor and popular opinion to the contrary notwithstanding, an oral board wants you to make the best appearance possible. They know you are under pressure – but they also want to see how you respond to it as a guide to what your reaction would be under the pressures of the job you seek. They will be influenced by the degree of poise you display, the personal traits you show and the manner in which you respond.

ABOUT THIS BOOK

This book contains tests divided into Examination Sections. Go through each test, answering every question in the margin. We have also attached a sample answer sheet at the back of the book that can be removed and used. At the end of each test look at the answer key and check your answers. On the ones you got wrong, look at the right answer choice and learn. Do not fill in the answers first. Do not memorize the questions and answers, but understand the answer and principles involved. On your test, the questions will likely be different from the samples. Questions are changed and new ones added. If you understand these past questions you should have success with any changes that arise. Tests may consist of several types of questions. We have additional books on each subject should more study be advisable or necessary for you. Finally, the more you study, the better prepared you will be. This book is intended to be the last thing you study before you walk into the examination room. Prior study of relevant texts is also recommended. NLC publishes some of these in our Fundamental Series. Knowledge and good sense are important factors in passing your exam. Good luck also helps. So now study this Passbook, absorb the material contained within and take that knowledge into the examination. Then do your best to pass that exam.

EXAMINATION SECTION

EXAMINATION SECTION
TEST 1

DIRECTIONS: Each question or incomplete statement is followed by several suggested answers or completions. Select the one that BEST answers the question or completes the statement. *PRINT THE LETTER OF THE CORRECT ANSWER IN THE SPACE AT THE RIGHT.*

1. The most common approach used by a prime contractor to hold its subcontractors to their initial bids is the doctrine of promissory estoppel. In order to bind a subcontractor to its bid price, the prime contractor must prove each of the following EXCEPT that the

    A. prime contractor relied on the subcontractor's offer when making its own bid
    B. subcontractor submitted a clear and definite offer
    C. subcontractor's bid was formally accepted by the prime contractor
    D. subcontractor could have expected the prime contractor to rely on the subcontractor's offer when making its own bid

1.____

2. Which type of specification in a construction contract is intended to invite the greatest amount of competition?

    A. Base bid   B. Closed
    C. Open   D. Bidder's choice

2.____

3. Written or graphic instruments issued prior to the execution of a contract, which modify or interpret the bidding documents by additions, deletions, clarifications, or corrections, are generally referred to as

    A. contract modifications   B. addenda
    C. reference documents   D. supplementary conditions

3.____

4. What type of warranty is used to limit the manufacturer's responsibility in a construction contract?

    A. Service agreement   B. Correction of work
    C. Limited term   D. Material-only

4.____

5. Which of the following statements represents the most important difference between drawings and specifications?

    A. Specifications constitute one of the contract documents.
    B. Specifications segregate information in order to aid in forming subcontracts.
    C. Drawings are used to show which materials are to be used.
    D. Drawings name the quantity of materials to be used.

5.____

6. The usual fidelity bond arrangement used in construction contracts is used to protect the contractor against

    A. loss, damage or excessive wear of rented equipment
    B. catastrophic damage to completed elements of the construction project
    C. dishonest acts of an employee such as theft, forgery or embezzlement
    D. bid stability of subcontractors

6.____

7. Each of the following is a common purpose of an agreement in construction contract documents EXCEPT to

    A. state the work to be done and the price to be paid for it
    B. specifically formalize the construction contract
    C. act as a single instrument that brings together all of the contract segments by reference
    D. list the technical specifications that must be adhered to in the construction project

8. Which of the following is an attribute that might be considered for the ceiling subsystem in a performance specification?

    A. Maximum claim spread 25
    B. Fire safety
    C. Smoke development shall not exceed 75
    D. ASTM E84

9. Of the following types of hold-harmless clauses, _____ indemnification used in construction contracts indemnifies the owner and/or architect engineer even when the party indemnified is solely responsible for the loss.

    A. limited-form   B. intermediate-form
    C. broad-form   D. omnibus

10. Unit kitchens are an item that would be described under the _____ Division heading in the CSI Masterformat of specifications.

    A. Equipment   B. Special Construction
    C. Furnishings   D. Specialties

11. Which of the following information is usually described in contract specifications?

    A. Test and code requirements
    B. Size of component parts
    C. Overall dimensions
    D. Schedules of finishes, windows, and doors

12. The PRIMARY advantage associated with unit-price construction contracts is

    A. open competition on projects involving quantities of work that cannot be accurately forecast at the time of bidding or negotiation
    B. fully completed drawings and specifications at the time of bidding or negotiation
    C. greater-than-usual flexibility with regard to special reimbursable costs
    D. flexibility in negotiating a unit price for agreed-upon work items

13. Which of the following information is typically shown by drawings?

    A. Methods of fabrication, installation, and erection
    B. Alternates and unit prices
    C. Interrelation of materials, equipment, and space
    D. Gages of manufacturer's equipment

14. Which of the following is/are typical purposes of a changed-condition clause in a construction contract?
    I. To protect the owner from unforeseen increases in project costs
    II. To reduce the contractor's liability for the unexpected
    III. To alleviate the need for including large contingency sums in the bid
    The CORRECT answer is:

    A. I only   B. II only   C. I, II   D. II, III

15. In construction contracts, a special warranty most frequently applies to the work of a(n)

    A. architect
    B. subcontractor
    C. engineer
    D. contractor

16. The MAIN advantage associated with the use of bid bonds as security for submitted proposals is that they

    A. will hold subcontractors accountable for their subbids
    B. don't require an annual service charge
    C. are estimated according to the minimum bid price
    D. don't immobilize appreciable sums of a contractor's money

17. Under most statutes governing construction contract law, a prime contractor may be relieved from its bid at any time after the opening of bids by the *doctrine of mistake*. Which of the following are conditions that would support an argument for applying the doctrine of mistake?
    The
    I. mistake relates to a material feature of the contract
    II. mistake is one of judgment, rather than fact
    III. owner is put in a status quo position, to the extent that he suffers no serious prejudice except the loss of his bargain
    IV. mistake is of a mechanical or clerical nature
    The CORRECT answer is:

    A. I only   B. III only   C. II, IV   D. I, III, IV

18. Which of the following is NOT typically a disadvantage associated with the use of retainage arrangements in construction contracts?

    A. Reduced bidding competition
    B. Higher construction costs for owners
    C. Tends to sacrifice workmanship for speed of completion
    D. Cash-flow problems for contractors

19. What is the term for a detailed compilation of the quantity of each elementary work item that is called for on the project?

    A. Specification
    B. Takeoff
    C. Bid invitation
    D. Summary sheet

20. Which of the following is NOT one of the general types of specifications used in construction contracts?

    A. Proprietary
    B. Surety
    C. Descriptive
    D. Performance

21. When negotiating a cost-plus contract, the owner and contractor must pay particular attention to each of the following considerations EXCEPT

    A. a list of job costs to be reimbursable to the contractor
    B. a common understanding regarding the accounting methods to be used
    C. the number of work units to be performed in executing the project
    D. a definite and mutually agreeable subcontract-letting procedure

22. According to construction contract law, what is the term for a promise by a party called the guarantor to make good the mistake, debt, or default of another party?

    A. Guaranty   B. Warranty   C. Guarantee   D. Surety

23. In a technical section that has been written according to the CSI standard format, which of the following descriptions would be sequenced FIRST?

    A. Warranty   B. Summary
    C. Project/site conditions D. Maintenance

24. In a construction contract, addendum changes to _____ are typically sequenced first.

    A. drawings   B. bid form
    C. prior addenda D. general conditions

25. Which of the following is typically added to a construction contract as a means of providing financial protection to a contractor?
    I.   Value engineering clause
    II. Escalation clause
    III. Escape clause
    The CORRECT answer is:

    A. I only   B. I, II   C. I, III   D. II, III

KEY (CORRECT ANSWERS)

1. C
2. C
3. B
4. D
5. B

6. C
7. D
8. B
9. C
10. A

11. A
12. A
13. C
14. D
15. B

16. D
17. D
18. C
19. B
20. B

21. C
22. A
23. B
24. C
25. D

TEST 2

DIRECTIONS: Each question or incomplete statement is followed by several suggested answers or completions. Select the one that BEST answers the question or completes the statement. *PRINT THE LETTER OF THE CORRECT ANSWER IN THE SPACE AT THE RIGHT.*

1. Which type of specification is most commonly used for public work? 1.____

    A. Open
    B. Closed
    C. Restricted
    D. Bidder's choice

2. Changes in the general conditions of a contract are expressed in the form of 2.____

    A. contract modifications
    B. change orders
    C. supplementary conditions
    D. addenda

3. The listing of subcontractors is often troublesome for contractors when it comes to bidding on projects with 3.____

    A. unbalanced bids
    B. alternates
    C. contract bonds
    D. unit pricing

4. Of the following, it is NOT a typical right assigned to an owner under the terms of a construction contract to 4.____

    A. inspect the work as it proceeds
    B. terminate the contract for cause
    C. intervene in the direction and control of the work
    D. retain a specified portion of the contractor's periodic payments

5. In most states, oral purchase agreements are NOT enforceable when 5.____

    A. they are carried out without the knowledge or consent of the prime contractor
    B. the price of goods is $500 or more
    C. the seller has not been approved by the owner
    D. the seller is not required under the agreement to deliver the goods to the site

6. Which of the following elements of a project manual is NOT usually included under the Sample Forms heading? 6.____

    A. Bid bond
    B. Supplementary conditions
    C. Performance and payment bonds
    D. Agreement

7. As part of a construction contract, a retainage arrangement can substantially serve an owner in each of the following ways EXCEPT 7.____

    A. protection against a contractor's failure to remedy defective work
    B. collection of damages from the contractor for late completion
    C. protection against breach of contract
    D. protection against damages to others caused by the contractor's performance

8. In general, the submission of *qualified* bids by a contractor is not permissible in public bidding because it

    A. is considered to be an arbitrary and unfair practice.
    B. will make the bid subject to rejection
    C. avoids fixing a total cost for the project
    D. is an illegal practice

9. Which of the following bonds is given by a self-insured contractor to the state to guarantee payment of statutory benefits to injured employees?

    A. Union wage bond
    B. License bond
    C. Workman's compensation bond
    D. Fidelity bond

10. The Divisions of the CSI Masterformat of specifications are based on four major categories. Which of the following is NOT one of these categories?

    A. Trades
    B. Levels of specialization
    C. Place relationships
    D. Materials

11. In construction contract law, what is the term for the promise that certain facts are true as represented and that they will remain so?

    A. Guaranty   B. Guarantee   C. Surety   D. Warranty

12. An owner may occasionally want a contractor to start construction operations before the formalities associated with the signing of the contract can be completed. In this case, a(n) _____ should be conveyed to authorize the start of work.

    A. letter of intent
    B. escape clause
    C. proviso of estoppel
    D. writ of mediation

13. In performance specifying, the term *criterion* refers to a(n)

    A. set of physical measurements of the materials specified
    B. qualitative statement of the desired performance
    C. evaluative procedure to assure compliance with the standard
    D. quantitative statement of the desired performance

14. A construction contract may be terminated on the grounds of the doctrine of impossibility of performance. Which of the following would be most likely to be interpreted as constituting impossibility of performance?

    A. Prolonged infirmity of prime contractor
    B. Withdrawal of subbids that make the execution of construction too costly to be profitable
    C. Unexpected site conditions found that make the construction impracticable
    D. One party finds it an economic burden to continue

15. Which of the following contracts is NOT typically defined in a contractual liability insurance policy that is included in a construction contract?

    A. Hold-harmless agreements
    B. Lease of premises
    C. Easement agreements
    D. Sidetrack agreements

16. For a contractor, the main disadvantage associated with lump-sum contracts is that 16.____

    A. they increase the likelihood of impossibility of performance
    B. the total amount of payment will be unknown until project completion
    C. they make it more difficult to hold subcontractors to their subbids
    D. adverse changes in the contractor's project costs will not be compensated

17. When a bidder's list of substitutions is used in the specifications of a construction contract, each of the following is generally true EXCEPT 17.____

    A. the bid must include the net difference in cost if the substitutions are accepted
    B. each bidder is free to submit any substitution
    C. it is the best method for achieving pure competition
    D. each of the bidders is unaware of the substitution his competitor may offer

18. In a(n) _____ contract, it is especially important that the work must be of such a nature that it can be fairly well-defined and a reasonably good estimate of cost can be approximated at the time of negotiations. 18.____

    A. incentive   B. cost-plus-fixed-fee
    C. progress payment   D. cost-plus-percentage

19. In a typical surety bond arrangement written into a construction contract, the principal is the 19.____

    A. owner   B. surety company
    C. contractor   D. architect/engineer

20. When several prime contracts are desired in a construction project, the limits of each prime contract will usually be established in the 20.____

    A. specifications   B. general conditions
    C. agreement   D. bidding requirements

21. Under the terms of a *liquidated damages* bid bond, the surety agrees to pay the _____ as damages for a contractor's default on a bid. 21.____

    A. entire bond amount
    B. difference between the contractor's defaulted low bid and the price the owner must pay to the next lowest responsible bidder
    C. agreed-upon percentage, usually 5 to 10 percent, of the minimum bid price
    D. amount of the initial progress payment plus a penalty

22. Which of the following descriptions in a technical section would appear in Part 3, according to the CSI standard fornat? 22.____

    A. Manufacturers   B. Installation
    C. Definitions   D. Accessories

23. Before a contract award is made, the bids must be carefully studied and evaluated by the owner and architect-engineer, a process which is typically referred to as 23.____

    A. prepping   B. polling
    C. canvassing   D. bonding

24. On small projects, office functions are usually carried out in a contractor's main office and particular items of office overhead are difficult to establish. If the contractor is working such a project on a cost-plus basis, it is common practice to
    A. agree with the owner upon a disinterested third party who will estimate the total office overhead costs of the project, and incorporate this figure into the contract
    B. eliminate office overhead altogether as a reimbursed cost and increase the contractor's fee by a reasonable amount
    C. agree in advance with the owner upon an estimated percentage of total job costs that will be named as office overhead in the accounting of the contract
    D. agree in advance with the owner upon a fixed amount that will be named as office overhead in the accounting of the contract

25. In the absence of any clause in a construction contract that addresses the point of excusable delay by a contractor, the contractor may only expect relief from delays with specified causes. Which of the following is NOT one of these causes?
    A. The architect-engineer
    B. The law
    C. Subcontractors
    D. The owner

KEY (CORRECT ANSWERS)

1.	A		11.	D
2.	C		12.	A
3.	B		13.	D
4.	C		14.	C
5.	B		15.	A
6.	B		16.	D
7.	C		17.	C
8.	B		18.	B
9.	C		19.	C
10.	B		20.	A

21. A
22. B
23. C
24. B
25. C

EXAMINATION SECTION
TEST 1

DIRECTIONS: Each question or incomplete statement is followed by several suggested answers or completions. Select the one that BEST answers the question or completes the statement. *PRINT THE LETTER OF THE CORRECT ANSWER IN THE SPACE AT THE RIGHT.*

1. A significant difference between ordinary contract law and construction contract law is that under most construction contracts,

    A. *breach of contract* is interpreted more widely
    B. a prime contractor's bid proposal is normally considered to be irrevocable after the bid opening and during the acceptance period prescribed in the bidding documents
    C. a subcontractor's bid is normally considered to be irrevocable even if the acceptance period is extended without his knowledge or consent
    D. an owner is not bound by oral agreements regarding the materials or workmanship of a project

2. Most negotiated construction contracts are on a _____ basis.

    A. cost-plus-fee B. lump-sum
    C. unit-price D. fee simple

3. When a specifier states outright the actual make, model, and catalog number of a product or the installation instructions of a manufacturer, he has written a _____ specification into the contract.

    A. reference B. descriptive
    C. proprietary D. performance

4. The written documents in a construction contract that describe the work to be done — including materials, equipment, construction systems, standards, and workmanship — requirements are commonly referred to as

    A. reference documents B. drawings
    C. general conditions D. specifications

5. According to the CSI Masterformat for specifications, each of the following would be listed in the General Requirements division of the specifications EXCEPT

    A. alternates B. bonds and certificates
    C. maintenance D. summary of work

6. In construction contract documents, invitations to bid are typically bound in the

    A. agreement B. general conditions
    C. specifications D. addenda

7. When substantial completion of a project has been achieved, it is customary for an inspection to be held to determine items that require completion or correction. The record of these items is known as a(n)

    A. supplementary condition B. punch list
    C. escalator clause D. change order

8. The manner in which construction contracts are most commonly terminated is by

   A. full and satisfactory performance by both parties
   B. proving impossibility of performance
   C. breach of contract by either party
   D. mutual agreement of both parties

9. On a unit-price project, a bid in which each bid item includes its own direct project cost plus its pro rata share of the project overhead, markup, bond, and tax is referred to as

   A. balanced   B. bonded
   C. weighted   D. cost-plus-percentage

10. Extensions of time in construction contracts are typically formalized by an instrument known as a(n)

    A. change order   B. squinter
    C. supplementary condition   D. easement

11. Under the terms of most cost-plus contracts, a common contract provision is for

    A. weekly or biweekly reimbursement of payrolls, and monthly reimbursement of all other costs, including a pro rata share of the contractor's fee
    B. monthly reimbursement of all costs including payroll and a pro rata share of the fee
    C. weekly reimbursement of all costs including payroll, and a monthly pro rata installment of the contractor's fee
    D. weekly or biweekly reimbursement of payrolls, and monthly reimbursement of all other costs except any portion of the contractor's fee, which is paid in full upon substantial completion

12. When open bidding is being used, it is necessary to include a prepared proposal form with the contract documents, because it

    A. helps in itemizing unbalanced bids
    B. exposes the different unit prices used by competing bidders
    C. is required by law
    D. ensures that all bids will be prepared and evaluated on the same basis

13. Where several different kinds or classes of similar materials are used, they should be described in a manner that permits some materials to be specified for every part of the building. This technique is a system known as the

    A. residuary legatee   B. subdivision
    C. criterion reference   D. variable proviso

14. A physical aspect of a construction site that differs materially from that indicated by the contract documents, or that is of an unusual nature and differs materially from the environment normally encountered, is described in the contract as a(n)

    A. supplementary condition   B. bid point
    C. changed condition   D. estoppel

15. Which of the following is a performance specification?

    A. Ceilings will be 2' x 2' lay-in acoustical panels.
    B. The heating system shall use #6 oil and shall be a hot water system.

C. Doors and other interior woodwork will have a natural finish.
D. Contractors shall install four inch ceramic tile throughout bathroom floor area.

16. Which of the following are generally TRUE of construction contract documents?
    I. Specific provisions prevail over general provisions.
    II. The handwritten version prevails over the typewritten version.
    III. In the event that inconsistencies exist where numbers are expressed in words and figures, the numbers govern.
    IV. If a conflict exists between drawings and specifications, the drawings usually take precedence.

    The CORRECT answer is:

    A. I, II
    B. III, IV
    C. I, II, IV
    D. II, III, IV

17. For very large construction projects, an insurance program is sometimes used which combines all the interests involved in a construction project for insurance purposes with one insurer chosen by either the owner or the contractor. This type of arrangement is known as

    A. comprehensive general liability insurance
    B. umbrella excess liability coverage
    C. wrap-up insurance policy
    D. subrogation

18. In a cost-incentive contract, the most common share of savings awarded to a contractor is _____ percent.

    A. 40
    B. 50
    C. 60
    D. 75

19. In the CSI Masterformat for specifications, which of the following items would be described and listed in Division 9?

    A. Carpet
    B. Insulation
    C. Rough carpentry
    D. Pest control

20. The submission of a complimentary bid by a contractor is generally thought to be an acceptable practice when it is done for any of the following reasons EXCEPT to

    A. fix prices and make the bidding process less competitive
    B. keep the goodwill of the owner or engineer who solicits the bid
    C. please an owner-client
    D. obtain the refund of plan deposits

21. Which of the following specifications is most effectively written?

    A. Each joint must be filled solid with mortar.
    B. Each joint is to be filled solid with mortar.
    C. Each joint shall be filled solid with mortar.
    D. Fill each joint solid with mortar.

22. Which of the following is a duty of an architect-engineer under the terms of a typical construction contract?

    A. Authorizing a contractor's periodic payments
    B. Ensuring that workmanship and materials fulfill the requirements of drawings and specifications
    C. Issuing direct instructions as to the method or procedures used in construction operations
    D. Conducting property surveys that describe the project site

23. In a technical section of a construction contract, tests for soil compaction would be described in a subparagraph under the heading of

    A. materials/equipment
    B. fabrication
    C. field quality control
    D. project/site conditions

24. Which of the following is a form that authorizes a contractor to proceed with work until a formal change order can be processed?

    A. Writ of mandamus
    B. Field order
    C. Presentment
    D. Letter of intent

25. When included in a construction contract, completed operations insurance is a liability contract that covers which of the following damages?
    I. Injuries to persons
    II. Damage to property attributed to the operation
    III. Damage to the completed work itself
    The CORRECT answer is:

    A. I only
    B. III only
    C. I, II
    D. II, III

KEY (CORRECT ANSWERS)

1. B
2. A
3. C
4. D
5. B

6. C
7. B
8. A
9. A
10. A

11. A
12. D
13. A
14. C
15. B

16. A
17. C
18. B
19. A
20. A

21. D
22. B
23. C
24. B
25. C

TEST 2

DIRECTIONS: Each question or incomplete statement is followed by several suggested answers or completions. Select the one that BEST answers the question or completes the statement. *PRINT THE LETTER OF THE CORRECT ANSWER IN THE SPACE AT THE RIGHT.*

1. Design decisions and special project requirements recorded at the end of the design-development phase of document preparation are included in the

    A. addendum
    B. project manual
    C. outline specification
    D. supplementary conditions

    1.____

2. The greatest apparent drawback to using product approval standards in the bidding of a construction project is that

    A. competition is limited
    B. the bidding period is extended
    C. bidders assume a greater risk in accepting products other than those specified
    D. relatively less flexibility

    2.____

3. The general clauses of a construction contract are composed of each of the following EXCEPT

    A. specifications
    B. supplementary conditions
    C. provisions of the agreement
    D. general conditions

    3.____

4. In specifications writing, the most common form of duplication is the use of a heading titled

    A. Work of Other Sections
    B. Scope of Work
    C. Work Not Included
    D. Duplication-Repetition

    4.____

5. A common provision of construction contracts is that final payment is due the contractor

    A. 30 days after substantial completion
    B. at the end of the warranty period
    C. at the stated end of the contract period
    D. upon final completion

    5.____

6. The MAIN advantage of the bidder's choice specification over the base bid specification is that

    A. product selection rests entirely with the architect or engineer
    B. greater competition is invited
    C. bid shopping is eliminated
    D. specifications are generally shorter

    6.____

7. Sometimes, an owner will require that a contractor include in his bid a listing of the subcontractors whose bids were used in the preparation of the prime contractor's proposal. The subcontractor listing requirement is primarily used by the owner for the purpose of

    A. estimating unit prices
    B. keeping the subcontractors subject to the owners' approval
    C. determining the percentage for a cost-plus-percentage contract
    D. discouraging bid shopping by the prime contractor

    7.____

13

8. Special warranties that are written into construction contracts typically extend a term to

    A. 1 to 5 years
    B. 5 to 10 years
    C. 2 to 20 years
    D. 2 to lifetime

9. Of the following, which most clearly is considered a general release in full by a contractor of all claims against the owner arising out of or in consequence of the work?

    A. Agreement to terminate the contract
    B. Submission to binding arbitration
    C. Acceptance of final payment
    D. Completion of the work specified in the contract

10. A project manual is typically recorded toward the final review of the _____ phase of document preparation.

    A. construction documents
    B. schematic design
    C. design-development
    D. evaluation

11. Which of the following Division headings appears EARLIEST in the CSI Masterformat of specifications?

    A. Wood and plastics
    B. Thermal and moisture protection
    C. Sitework
    D. Concrete

12. In a typical technical section, the criteria by which the subcontractor determines that the substrates to receive his work are sound, proper, and free of defects are included in the subparagraphs under the heading of

    A. examination
    B. preparation
    C. field quality control
    D. mixes

13. For a contractor, each of the following is a potential disadvantage associated with granting an extension for the owner's acceptance period EXCEPT

    A. the potential for rises in labor wages
    B. the forfeiture of bid bonds
    C. the delaying of material orders by price advances
    D. a subcontractor or supplier's unwillingness to stand by earlier price quotes

14. What is the term for bidding requirements, contract forms, contract conditions, and specifications all bound collectively?

    A. Project manual
    B. Conditions
    C. Contract forms
    D. Master documents

15. Which of the following descriptions would NOT appear in Part 1 of a technical section that follows the CSI standard format?

    A. Submittals
    B. Equipment
    C. Delivery, storage, and handling
    D. Schedules

16. Which of the following is a disadvantage associated with the cost-plus-percentage contract?　　16.____

    A. There are no direct incentives for the contractor to minimize construction costs.
    B. It is not suitable for work whose scope and nature are poorly defined at the outset of operations.
    C. It is considered unsuitable for public projects.
    D. It does not offer much flexibility in handling emergency situations.

17. In construction contracts, the term of the general warranty typically does not exceed　　17.____

    A. 90 days　　B. 6 months　　C. 1 year　　D. 2 years

18. In a construction contract, what is the term for a word description of a basic trade or material installation which outlines the quality of material to be used and the quality of workmanship to be practiced in its installation?　　18.____

    A. Annotated drawing　　B. Technical section
    C. Standard reference　　D. Specification division

19. When an addendum is added to a construction contract, which of the following elements is typically included FIRST?　　19.____

    A. Date of addendum
    B. Opening remarks and instructions
    C. Addendum and addendum number
    D. Name of architect/engineer or issuing agency

20. The main DISADVANTAGE associated with the use of alternates in the bidding process is that they　　20.____

    A. decrease the security of individual bids
    B. complicate the bidding process and may increase inaccuracies
    C. are only effective when they are subtractive, rather than additive
    D. do not give the owner a clear idea of how to minimize costs

21. In a technical section written to conform to the CSI standard format, Part 2 would include descriptions of　　21.____

    A. preparation　　B. references
    C. field quality control　　D. materials

22. In a typical project manual, which of the following elements appears FIRST?　　22.____

    A. Bid bond　　B. Schedule of drawings
    C. Agreement　　D. General conditions

23. The insurance considerations of a construction contract, especially those governing liability, are typically incorporated into the　　23.____

    A. agreement　　B. general conditions
    C. specifications　　D. addenda

24. Written or graphic instruments issued after the execution of a contract, which alter contract documents by additions, deletions, or corrections, are known specifically as

    A. contract modifications
    B. change orders
    C. addenda
    D. supplementary conditions

25. When a progress payments are part of a construction contract, it is common for a contractor to apply for a payment
    I. when a prescribed amount of quantified construction costs have been expended
    II. on completion of designated phases of the work
    III. a prescribed number of days before it is due under the payment schedule written into the contract

    The CORRECT answer is:

    A. II only
    B. I or III
    C. II or III
    D. I, II, or III

KEY (CORRECT ANSWERS)

1. C
2. B
3. A
4. B
5. A

6. B
7. D
8. C
9. C
10. A

11. C
12. A
13. B
14. A
15. D

16. A
17. C
18. B
19. D
20. B

21. D
22. C
23. B
24. A
25. C

EXAMINATION SECTION
TEST 1

DIRECTIONS: Each question or incomplete statement is followed by several suggested answers or completions. Select the one that BEST answers the question or completes the statement. *PRINT THE LETTER OF THE CORRECT ANSWER IN THE SPACE AT THE RIGHT.*

1. It is generally recommended that bid security in a construction contract should NOT be less than _____ percent of the amount of the bid.

    A. 5   B. 10   C. 15   D. 20

2. Which of the following is NOT a Division 4 item according to the CSI Masterformat for specifications?

    A. Concrete
    B. Stone
    C. Masonry restoration and cleaning
    D. Refractories

3. What is the term for the written documents which describe the rights, responsibilities, and relationships of the contracting parties?

    A. Contract documents   B. General conditions
    C. Standard documents   D. Specifications

4. Which of the following is most likely to be covered under a contractor's comprehensive general liability insurance policy?

    A. Injury to the contractor's own employees
    B. Damage to underground utilities
    C. Damage to property under the care, custody or control of the contractor
    D. Bodily injury to visitors of the construction site

5. Generally, which of the following types of contracts presents the fewest difficulties in dealing with change orders?

    A. Unit-price   B. Cost-plus-fee
    C. Lump-sum   D. Cost-plus-award

6. Which of the following performance characteristics is associated with fire safety in construction specifications?

    A. Air infiltration   B. Thermal expansion
    C. Toxicity   D. Water vapor transmission

7. The acceptance period most commonly used in the bidding process of construction projects is a period of _____ days.

    A. 10   B. 30   C. 60   D. 90

8. Each of the following is an advantage associated with the use of product approval standards in construction contract specifications EXCEPT

A. the architect has control over the products used
B. it discourages bid peddling or shopping
C. complete flexibility in contracting the arrangement
D. it limits the number of products that can be specified

9. If a retainage arrangement has been made part of a construction contract, what percent is usually held by the owner until final payment is made?

   A. 5   B. 10   C. 25   D. 50

10. Of the following construction specifications, which is most effectively written?

    A. Install glass panels on both sides of main entrance
    B. Glass panels shall be installed on both sides of main entrance
    C. Glass panels shall be installed on either side of main entrance
    D. Glass panels shall be installed by a licensed workman on both sides of main entrance

11. In general, the use of a subcontractor listing requirement in the bidding process is favored by each of the following:
    I. Owners
    II. Prime contractors
    III. Subcontractors

    The CORRECT answer is:

    A. I only   B. II only   C. III only   D. I, III

12. A base bid specification used in a construction contract

    A. specifies only one brand name or proprietary make for each individual material, piece of equipment or product
    B. is written without reference to brand names or proprietary makes
    C. names two or more brand names or proprietary makes for each item the architect or engineer wishes to use
    D. includes a list of substitutions

13. Which of the following statements is true concerning the use of the double form of bonds as surety regarding a construction contract?

    A. It presents a potential conflict of interest between the owner and persons furnishing labor and materials.
    B. The premium cost of the bond protection is higher than the single form.
    C. It covers separately the interests of the owner and of subcontractors, material suppliers, and workmen.
    D. The face value of the bond can be consumed entirely by the owner, since the owner's interest takes priority.

14. Each of the following is an element that is typically included in an Invitation to Bid EXCEPT

    A. acknowledgement
    B. guarantee bonds
    C. time and place for receipt of bids
    D. examination and procurement of documents

15. Under most construction contracts, an owner will have a right of action against a contractor beyond the warranty period if the

   A. contractor's inadequate performance is a result of insufficient plans and specifications that were not prepared by the contractor or with the contractor's guarantee of adequacy
   B. contractor's inadequate performance is latent in nature and could not have been detected by the owner during ordinary use and maintenance of the structure
   C. nature of the contractor's inadequate performance is not specifically named in the terms of the performance bond
   D. contractor has been grossly negligent

16. In performance specifying, what is the term for a qualitative statement of the desired performance?

   A. Requirement   B. Criterion
   C. Test   D. Standard

17. Which of the following is a nontechnical paragraph that would appear in a technical section that is included in a book of specifications?

   A. Workmanship
   B. Samples and shop drawings
   C. Schedules
   D. General requirements

18. In cases where the courts are consulted to grant a contractor relief from a bid that was submitted in error, the most likely result is that the contractor

   A. must forfeit the entire amount of bid security to the owner
   B. is permitted to submit a corrected bid without penalty
   C. is permitted only to withdraw the bid without penalty
   D. is permitted to submit a corrected bid after forfeiting a nominal amount of bid security

19. Which of the following is least likely to result in a claim dispute between the contractor and an owner?

   A. Rejection of subcontractor
   B. Changed conditions
   C. Acceleration
   D. Rejection of *or-equal* substitutions

20. Which of the following is MOST likely to be considered an excusable cause of delay by the contractor under the terms of a construction contract?

   A. Adverse weather
   B. Labor strike
   C. Insufficient estimate of required materials
   D. Insufficient labor pool

21. In the bidding documents of a construction contract, which of the following elements would typically appear in the Instructions to Bidders?

    A. Agreement to accept contract
    B. Bid schedule
    C. Project identification
    D. Reform of bid

22. Target estimates are not typically involved in the negotiation or bidding of _____ contracts.

    A. cost-plus-fixed-fee
    B. lump-sum
    C. cost-plus-percentage
    D. unit-price

23. A _____ bond is given by a developer to a public body to guarantee construction of all necessary improvements and utilities.

    A. subdivision
    B. license
    C. fidelity
    D. discharge

24. Of the following, which Division heading would appear latest in the CSI Masterformat of construction specifications?

    A. Furnishings
    B. Special Construction
    C. Electrical
    D. Equipment

25. Each of the following is typically included in a contract's bidding requirements EXCEPT

    A. bid forms
    B. specifications
    C. instructions to bidders
    D. information available to bidders

KEY (CORRECT ANSWERS)

1.	A	11.	D
2.	A	12.	A
3.	B	13.	C
4.	D	14.	A
5.	B	15.	B
6.	C	16.	A
7.	B	17.	B
8.	D	18.	C
9.	B	19.	A
10.	A	20.	B

21. D
22. B
23. A
24. C
25. B

TEST 2

DIRECTIONS: Each question or incomplete statement is followed by several suggested answers or completions. Select the one that BEST answers the question or completes the statement. *PRINT THE LETTER OF THE CORRECT ANSWER IN THE SPACE AT THE RIGHT.*

1. Each of the following is a common motivation for a contractor's submission of an unbalanced bid on a project EXCEPT to

    A. distribute fixed costs properly over the true quantities of work when errors are perceived in the quantities listed on the proposal form
    B. increase the percentage in a cost-plus-percentage project
    C. increase profit, especially on quantities that have been underestimated by the owner
    D. make early progress payments large enough to minimize the contractor's initial costs

2. When specifications in construction contracts are written without reference to brand names or proprietary makes, they are known as _____ specifications.

    A. open
    B. base bid
    C. bidder's choice
    D. alternate listing

3. Of the following types of hold-harmless clauses, _____ indemnification used in construction contracts holds the owner and architect-engineer harmless against any claims caused by the negligence of the prime contractor or subcontractor.

    A. exclusive
    B. limited-form
    C. intermediate-form
    D. broad-form

4. In the CSI Masterformat of specifications, plumbing is a construction item that is described under the heading of

    A. metals
    B. mechanical
    C. specialties
    D. special construction

5. Which of the following are generally true of unit-price contracts?
    I. Units of work are estimated before project operations begin and are not allowed to vary thereafter.
    II. The unit costs of items in the contract documents are indeterminable until the project is completed.
    III. The total sum of money paid to the contractor for each work item remains indeterminable until completion of the project.

    The CORRECT answer is:

    A. I only
    B. III only
    C. I, II
    D. II, III

6. Which of the following phrases appearing in construction specifications is most potentially troublesome?

    A. Contractor shall
    B. Free of defect
    C. Guaranteed
    D. Or equal

7. For a contractor to bind a subcontractor to its initial subbid on the basis that the contractor relied on this bid in submitting its own project proposal, the contractor should have

   A. asked the subcontractor to verify the subbid's correctness in advance
   B. located evidence that the subcontractor has submitted unresponsive bids in the past
   C. delayed accepting the subcontractor's bid after its own bid is accepted by the owner
   D. announced a *freeze* on subcontractor bids before submitting its own bid proposal

8. Typically, the preliminary project description, a written document that records early decisions about major project elements, is recorded during the _____ phase of document preparation.

   A. schematic design
   B. bidding
   C. design-development
   D. construction documents

9. In the bidding documents of a typical construction contract, which of the following elements is included in the Bid Form?

   A. Conditions under which bids can be rejected
   B. Guarantee bonds
   C. Alternates
   D. The procedure under which the award to contract will be made

10. Under the terms of a typical construction project, the contractor may be held to guarantee that the completed project
    I. is free of defects in design
    II. has been executed with the quality of workmanship and materials specified in the contract documents
    III. will accomplish the intended purpose
    The CORRECT answer is:

    A. I only   B. II only   C. III only   D. II, III

11. Which of the following descriptions would appear LAST in a technical section that is written according to the CSI standard format?

    A. Examination
    B. Summary
    C. Schedules
    D. Definitions

12. _____ clauses are used in construction contracts to eliminate or modify contract provisions that add cost to a project but are not necessary to the structure's required performance, safety, appearance, or maintenance.

    A. Escape
    B. Changed-conditions
    C. Value engineering
    D. Escalation

13. Standard documents which are incorporated by citation in the bidding and contract documents are known as

    A. general conditions
    B. specifications
    C. reference documents
    D. drawings

14. If addenda to a construction contract are included in a project manual, they usually appear

    A. at the very beginning, after the title page
    B. between the table of contents and the bidding requirements
    C. between the conditions of the contract and the schedule of drawings
    D. at the very end

15. Which of the following would most likely be included in a *changed-conditions* clause in a construction contract?

    A. Subsurface soil conditions
    B. Conditions resulting from drought
    C. Conditions resulting from flood
    D. Nonphysical conditions

16. What type of specification refers to a standard established for either a material, a test method or an insulation procedure?

    A. Proprietary   B. Descriptive
    C. Performance   D. Reference

17. In a contract bond arrangement, the _____ is the obligee.

    A. owner   B. surety company
    C. architect-engineer D. contractor

18. Specifications that are written into a construction contract should usually be formatted in the _____ style.

    A. indented   B. modified block
    C. block   D. centered

19. When several alternates are listed on the base bid for a lump-sum project submitted by a contractor, it may be possible for an owner to juggle acceptance of the alternates so that a preferred contractor receives the contract. The best way to safeguard against this possibility is for the bidding documents to

    A. prohibit the use of alternatives altogether
    B. state the order of acceptance of the alternatives
    C. limit the use of alternates to scope of construction, rather than methods or materials
    D. limit the use of alternates to materials

20. Which of the following is NOT an *XCU* exclusion from property damage liability coverage under the terms of most construction contracts?

    A. Damage caused by flooding
    B. Underground damage caused by and occurring during the use of mechanical equipment
    C. Collapse or structural damage to any building or structure
    D. Explosion or blasting

21. In the CSI Masterformat of specifications, the item *window treatments* would be described under which of the following headings?   21.____

    A. Specialties
    B. Thermal and moisture protection
    C. Furnishings
    D. Doors and windows

22. In writing construction specifications, each of the following performance characteristics is associated with compatibility EXCEPT   22.____

    A. chemical interaction
    B. dimensional stability
    C. differential thermal movement
    D. galvanic interaction

23. When the drawings and specifications are not complete at the time of negotiation of a cost-plus contract, the owner and contractor negotiate what is commonly called a(n)   23.____

    A. encumbrance   B. adhesion contract
    C. scope contract   D. arbitration

24. In a typical *Invitation to Bid*, which of the following elements would typically appear first?   24.____

    A. Bid security   B. Type of contract
    C. Project description   D. Identification of Principals

25. Each of the following is a responsibility bestowed upon the owner in typical construction contracts EXCEPT   25.____

    A. securing and paying for necessary easements
    B. assuming liability for negligent acts committed by the contractor in the course of operations
    C. furnishing property surveys that describe and locate project site
    D. providing certain types of insurance

KEY (CORRECT ANSWERS)

1. B	11. C	21. C
2. A	12. C	22. B
3. B	13. C	23. C
4. B	14. B	24. D
5. B	15. A	25. B
6. D	16. D	
7. A	17. A	
8. A	18. C	
9. C	19. B	
10. B	20. A	

EXAMINATION SECTION
TEST 1

DIRECTIONS: Each question or incomplete statement is followed by several suggested answers or completions. Select the one that BEST answers the question or completes the statement. *PRINT THE LETTER OF THE CORRECT ANSWER IN THE SPACE AT THE RIGHT.*

1. Management by exception (MBE) is

    A. designed to locate bottlenecks
    B. designed to pinpoint superior performance
    C. a form of index locating
    D. a form of variance reporting

2. In managerial terms, gap analysis is useful primarily in

    A. problem solving B. setting standards
    C. inventory control D. locating bottlenecks

3. ABC analysis involves

    A. problem solving B. indexing
    C. brainstorming D. inventory control

4. The Federal Discrimination in Employment Act as amended in 1978 prohibits job discrimination based on age for persons between the ages of

    A. 35 and 60   B. 40 and 65   C. 45 and 65   D. 40 and 70

5. Inspectors should be familiar with the contractor's CPM charts for a construction job primarily to determine if

    A. the job is on schedule
    B. the contractor is using the charts correctly
    C. material is on hand to keep the job on schedule
    D. there is a potential source of delay

6. The value engineering approach is frequently found in public works contracts. Value engineering is

    A. an effort to cut down or eliminate extra work payments
    B. a team approach to optimize the cost of the project
    C. to insure that material and equipment will perform as specified
    D. to insure that insurance costs on the project can be minimized

7. Historically, most costly claims have been either for

    A. unreasonable inspection requirements or unforeseen weather conditions
    B. unreasonable specification requirements or unreasonable completion time for the contract
    C. added costs due to inflation or unavailability of material
    D. delays or alleged changed conditions

8. A claim is a

   A. dispute that cannot be resolved
   B. dispute arising from ambiguity in the specifications
   C. dispute arising from the quality of the work
   D. recognition that the courts are the sole arbiters of a dispute

9. Disputes arising between a contractor and the owning agency are

   A. the result of inflexibility of either or both parties to the dispute
   B. mainly the result of shortcomings in the design
   C. the result of shortcomings in the specifications
   D. inevitable

Questions 10-13.

DIRECTIONS: Questions 10 through 13, inclusive, refers to the array of numbers listed below.

16, 7, 9, 5, 10, 8, 5, 1, 2

10. The mean of the numbers is

    A. 2   B. 5   C. 7   D. 8

11. The median of the numbers is

    A. 2   B. 5   C. 7   D. 8

12. The mode of the numbers is

    A. 2   B. 5   C. 7   D. 8

13. In statistical measurements, a subgroup that is representative of the entire group is a

    A. commutative group   B. sample
    C. central index   D. Abelian group

14. Productivity is the ratio of

    A. $\dfrac{\text{product costs}}{\text{labor costs}}$

    B. $\dfrac{\text{cost of final product}}{\text{cost of materials}}$

    C. $\dfrac{\text{outputs}}{\text{inputs}}$

    D. $\dfrac{\text{outputs cost}}{\text{time needed to product the output}}$

15. Downtime is the time a piece of equipment is

    A. idle waiting for other equipment to become available
    B. not being used for the purpose it was intended

C. being used inefficiently
D. unavailable for use

16. Index numbers 16._____

    A. relates to the cost of a product as material costs vary
    B. allows the user to find the variation from the norm
    C. are a way of comparing costs of different approaches to a problem
    D. a way of measuring and comparing changes over a period of time

17. The underlying idea behind Management by Objectives is to provide a mechanism for managers to 17._____

    A. coordinate personal and departmental plans with organizational goals
    B. motivate employees by having them participate in job decisions
    C. motivate employees by training them for the next higher position
    D. set objectives that are reasonable for the employees to attain, thus improving self-esteem among the employees

18. The ultimate objective of the project manager in planning and scheduling a project is to 18._____

    A. meet the completion dates of the project
    B. use the least amount of labor on the project
    C. use the least amount of material on the project
    D. prevent interference between the different trades

19. Scheduling with respect to the critical path method usually does not involve 19._____

    A. cost allocation
    B. starting and finishing time
    C. float for each activity
    D. project duration

20. When CPM is used on a construction project, updates are most commonly made 20._____

    A. weekly   B. every two weeks
    C. monthly   D. every two months

Questions 21-24.

DIRECTIONS: Questions 21 through 24 refer to the following network.

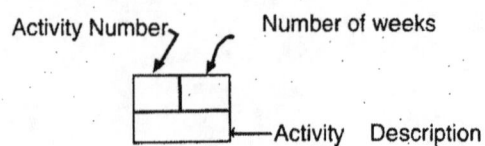

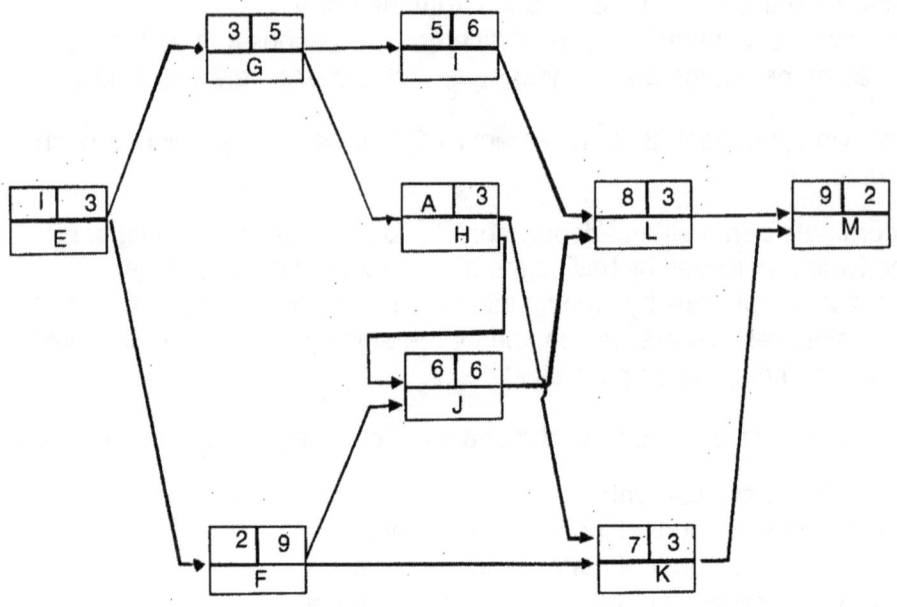

Activity Number	Activity Description	Duration in Weeks	Early Start	Early Finish	Late Start	Late Finish	Total Slack
1	E	3					
2	F	9					
3	G	5					
4	H	3					
5	I	6					
6	J	6					
7	K	3					
8	L	3					
9	M	2					

21. The critical path is

    A. E G H J L M B. E G I L M
    C. E F J L M   D. E G H K M

22. The minimum time needed to complete the job is, in weeks,

    A. 19   B. 21   C. 22   D. 23

23. The slack time in J is, in weeks,

    A. 0   B. 1   C. 2   D. 3

24. The slack time in K is, in weeks,

    A. 4   B. 5   C. 6   D. 7

25. Of the following, the primary objective of CPM is to 25.____
    A. eliminate duplication of work
    B. overcome obstacles such as bad weather
    C. spot potential bottlenecks
    D. save on the cost of material

KEY (CORRECT ANSWERS)

1.	D	11.	C
2.	A	12.	B
3.	D	13.	B
4.	D	14.	C
5.	A	15.	D
6.	B	16.	D
7.	D	17.	A
8.	A	18.	A
9.	D	19.	A
10.	C	20.	C

21. C
22. D
23. A
24. C
25. C

TEST 2

DIRECTIONS: Each question or incomplete statement is followed by several suggested answers or completions. Select the one that BEST answers the question or completes the statement. *PRINT THE LETTER OF THE CORRECT ANSWER IN THE SPACE AT THE RIGHT.*

1. Gantt refers to   1.____
   - A. bar charts
   - B. milestone charts
   - C. PERT networks
   - D. Management by Objectives

2. PERT is an abbreviation for   2.____
   - A. Progress Evaluation in Real Time
   - B. Preliminary Evaluation of Running Time
   - C. Program Evaluation Review Techniques
   - D. Program Estimation and Repair Times

3. In project management terms, slack is equivalent to   3.____
   - A. tare
   - B. off time
   - C. delay
   - D. float

4. The FIRST step in planning and programming a roadway pavement management system is to evaluate   4.____
   - A. priorities for the work to be done
   - B. the condition of your equipment
   - C. the condition of the roads in the system
   - D. the storage and maintenance facilities

5. Managers accomplish their work in an ever changing environment by integrating three time-tested approaches. The one of the following that is NOT a time-tested approach is   5.____
   - A. scientific adaptation
   - B. scientific management
   - C. behavior management
   - D. management sciences

6. The most effective managers manage for optimum results. This means that the manager is seeking to _____ a given situation.   6.____
   - A. get the maximum results from
   - B. get the most favorable results from
   - C. get the most reasonable results from
   - D. satisfy the conflicting interests in

7. If a manager believes that an employee is irresponsible, the employee, in subtle response to the manager's assessment, will in fact prove to be irresponsible. This is an example of a(n)   7.____
   - A. conditioned reflex
   - B. self-fulfilling prophesy
   - C. Freudian response
   - D. automatic reaction

8. Perhaps nothing distinguishes the younger generation from the older so much as the value placed on work. The older generation was generally raised to believe in the Protestant work ethic.   8.____
   This ethic holds primarily that

A. people should try to get the highest salary possible
B. work should help people to advance
C. work should be well done if it is interesting
D. work is valuable in itself and the person who does it focuses on his work

9. The standard method currently in use in inspecting bituminous paving is to inspect each activity in detail as the paving work is being installed. In recent years some agencies use a different method of inspection known as a(n)

A. as-built quality control method
B. statistically controlled quality assurance method
C. data based history of previous contracts of this type
D. performance evaluation of the completed paving contract

10. Aggregates for use in bituminous pavements should be tested for grading,

A. abrasion, soundness, and specific gravity
B. type of rock, abrasion, and specific gravity
C. abrasion, soundness, and deleterious material
D. specific gravity, chemical composition of the aggregate, and deleterious material

11. Of the following, the one that is LEAST likely to be a test for asphalt is

A. specific gravity
C. viscosity
B. flashpoint
D. penetration

12. According to the AASHO, for bituminous pavements PSI is an abbreviation for _____ Index.

A. Present Serviceability
C. Pavement Serviceability
B. Pavement Smoothness
D. Present Smoothness

13. According to the AASHO, a bituminous pavement that is in extremely poor condition will have a PSI

A. above 5.5
C. below 3.5
B. above 3.5
D. below 1.5

14. The U.S. Federal Highway Administration defines asphalt maintenance as including work designed primarily for rejuvenation or protection of existing surfaces less than _____ inch minimum thickness.

A. 1/4   B. 1/2   C. 3/4   D. 1

15. The maintenance phase of a highway management system includes the establishment of a program and schedule of work based largely on budget considerations, the actual operations of crack filling, patching, etc. and

A. inspection of completed work
B. planning of future operations
C. upgrading existing pavements
D. acquisition and processing of data

16. In a bituminous asphalt pavement, the progressive separation of aggregate particles in a pavement from the surface downward or from the edges inward is the definition of   16.____

    A. alligatoring   B. raveling
    C. scaling   D. disintegration

17. The bituminous pavement condition for the purpose of overlay design includes ride quality, structural capacity, skid resistance, and   17.____

    A. durability   B. age of the pavement
    C. CBR value   D. surface distress

18. An asphalt mix is being transferred from an asphalt truck to the hopper of the paving machine. Blue smoke rises from the material being emptied into the hopper of the paving machine.   18.____
Your conclusion should be that

    A. this is normal and is to be expected
    B. the mix is overheated
    C. the mix is too cold
    D. the mix is being transferred too rapidly

19. Polished aggregate in an asphalt pavement are aggregate particles that have been rounded and polished smooth by traffic. This is a   19.____

    A. *good* condition as it allows a smooth ride
    B. *good* condition as it preserves tires
    C. *poor* condition as it promotes skidding
    D. *poor* condition as it tends to break the bond between the asphalt and the aggregate

20. A slippery asphalt surface requires a skid-resistant surfacing material. Of the following, the cover that would be most appropriate is a(n)   20.____

    A. asphalt tack coat
    B. fog seal
    C. layer of sand rolled into the asphalt surface
    D. asphalt emulsion slurry seal

21. The maximum size of aggregate in a hot mix asphalt concrete surfacing and bases allowed by the Federal Highway Administration Grading A is _____ inch(es).   21.____

    A. 3/4   B. 1   C. 1 1/4   D. 1 1/2

22. Wet sand weighs 132 pounds per cubic foot and contains 8% moisture. The dry weight of a cubic foot of sand is _____ pounds.   22.____

    A. 122.2   B. 122.0   C. 121.7   D. 121.4

23. A very light spray application of 551h emulsified asphalt diluted with water is used on existing pavement as a seal to minimize raveling and to enrich the surface of a dried-out pavement is known as a(n)   23.____

    A. prime coat   B. tack coat
    C. fog seal   D. emulsion seal

24. 90 kilometers per hour is equivalent to _____ miles per hour. 24.____

    A. 49　　　　B. 54　　　　C. 59　　　　D. 64

25. In a table of pavement distress manifestations is a column broadly titled *Density of Pavement Distress*. 25.____
    This is equivalent to _____ of the defects.

    A. average depth
    B. average area
    C. extent of occurrence
    D. seriousness

KEY (CORRECT ANSWERS)

1. A		11. A
2. A		12. A
3. D		13. D
4. C		14. C
5. A		15. D
6. B		16. B
7. B		17. D
8. D		18. B
9. B		19. C
10. C		20. D

21. D
22. A
23. C
24. B
25. C

EXAMINATION SECTION
TEST 1

DIRECTIONS: Each question or incomplete statement is followed by several suggested answers or completions. Select the one that BEST answers the question or completes the statement. *PRINT THE LETTER OF THE CORRECT ANSWER IN THE SPACE AT THE RIGHT.*

1. A percentage of the payment for a contract is held back until the job is completed for one year.
   The MAIN reason for this practice is to insure that the

   A. city doesn't overpay the contractor for the job
   B. contractor will return to correct defective work after the job is completed
   C. contractor will not make unwarranted claims against the city
   D. contractor will pay all his subcontractors

   1.____

2. There are four separate major contracts on a certain building construction project.
   The MAJOR disadvantage of this practice, as compared to the practice of having a single contract, is

   A. the difficulty in coordinating the work
   B. the low level of productivity of the tradesman
   C. cost of the material going into the building is greater
   D. the difficulty in finding competent bidders on the contracts

   2.____

3. Of the following, the PREFERRED way to authorize a contractor to perform work other than required by the contract is by a

   A. T & M order   B. unit price order
   C. lump sum modification D. change order

   3.____

4. A contract requires that the prime contractor do a certain minimum percentage of the work with his own forces.
   Of the following, the BEST reason for this requirement is to

   A. insure good work
   B. discourage bidders who may not have the ability to do the job
   C. encourage more people to bid the job, thus lowering the bid price
   D. freeze out incompetent subcontractors

   4.____

5. In computing an extra based on the actual cost of work done, the THREE MAJOR items that go into the cost are

   A. taxes, labor, and material
   B. time, taxes, and material
   C. labor, material, and equipment
   D. taxes, labor, and equipment

   5.____

6. A contractor is to be penalized if he exceeds a certain completion date. There is a major strike lasting a month that shuts down all construction.
   Under these conditions, the completion date should be

   6.____

A. held unchanged
B. made two weeks later than the original date
C. made one month later than the original date
D. made six weeks later than the original completion date

7. The one of the following that refers to a Federal safety program in construction is

   A. OSHA   B. AISC   C. AIEE   D. UL

8. With regard to the placing of concrete, the contractor is GENERALLY

   A. limited to a specific method by the contract
   B. not permitted to rent equipment to place the concrete
   C. not permitted to pump the concrete into place
   D. permitted to choose his own method of placing the concrete

9. The MOST practical control the inspector or resident engineer has over the contractor when the inspector is not satisfied with the quality of the work is to

   A. discuss withholding payment on that part of the work that is unsatisfactory
   B. threaten to have the contractor thrown off the job
   C. request that the contractor fire the men responsible for the unsatisfactory work
   D. call the owner of the company and explain the situation to him

10. The MOST practical method of being sure that the architect will be satisfied with the appearance of the exterior brick work for a building is to

    A. build a sample wall section, for the architect's approval, with the brick that is delivered to the job site
    B. send the architect to the plant supplying the brick to insure that the color and tone of the brick is satisfactory
    C. have the architect's representative on the job while the brick work is being erected to be sure the finished product is satisfactory
    D. put a damage clause in the contract penalizing the contractor if the brick work is not satisfactory to the architect

11. Of the following, the MOST frequent problem that will arise during the construction of a building is

    A. inability to fit all the reinforcing steel in the space allotted to it
    B. interference in piping and ductwork
    C. inability to keep walls level
    D. settling of the foundation as the load comes on the building

12. To find the number of reinforcing bars that should be in a slab, the inspector SHOULD refer to the

    A. architect's plan
    B. reinforcing steel design drawings
    C. standard detail drawings
    D. reinforcing steel detail drawings

13. The specifications for a building state that a certain brick type shall be *Stark Brick type XX or equal.*
The BEST reason for inserting the *or equal* clause is to

    A. permit other companies to compete in supplying the brick
    B. allow other companies to submit their product to determine which is best
    C. limit the suppliers only to those companies whose product is superior to that produced by Stark
    D. allow Stark Brick Company to set the standard for the industry

14. In the absence of a formal training program for inspectors, the BEST of the following ways to train a new man who is to do inspection work is to

    A. give him the literature on the subject so that he can learn what he has to know
    B. have him accompany an inspector as the inspector does his work so that he can learn by observing
    C. assign him the job and let him learn on his own
    D. tell him to go to a school at night that specializes in this field so that he will gain the necessary background

15. Of the following, the safety practice that is REQUIRED on the construction job site is

    A. safety shoes must be worn by all workers
    B. safety goggles must be worn by all workers
    C. safety helmets must be worn by all workers
    D. all workers must have a safety kit in their possession

16. Safety on the job is the concern of

    A. the individual workman only
    B. the contractor only
    C. all parties on the job
    D. the insuring company only

17. Frequently, payments due the contractor are delayed many months because of a backlog of work in the agency.
This practice is considered

    A. *good* because the city saves money by delaying payment
    B. *poor* because the contractors will raise their bids in the future to compensate for the added cost
    C. *poor* because it becomes difficult to compute payments
    D. *good* because it forces the contractor to do good work in order to be sure that he will receive payment

18. Provisions are made in a contract for payment for certain items when delivered to the job before installation.
The MAIN reason for this practice is to

    A. enable better inspection of the items
    B. prevent bottlenecks during construction
    C. give the contractor a quick profit on the items
    D. allow the contractor more time to shop for the items

19. The agency that approves payments to building contractors is the

   A. Corporation Counsel
   B. Comptroller's Office
   C. Board of Estimate
   D. City Planning Commission

20. The bond that the contractor puts up to insure that he will start work is the

   A. Bid Bond
   B. Payment Bond
   C. Performance Bond
   D. Liability Insurance

21. Of the following, the BEST practice to follow in order to minimize claims of damage to adjacent buildings during the construction of a building is to

   A. take out special insurance against such claims
   B. make a detailed survey of the condition of the nearby buildings before construction begins
   C. make a payment to adjacent property owners in advance so that they waive claims of damage to their property
   D. have the buildings underpinned

22. The four MAJOR contracts on a building project are:

   A. General Construction, Electrical, Plumbing and Drainage, Heating, Ventilating and Air Conditioning
   B. Plumbing, Heating and Ventilating, Air Conditioning, and General Construction
   C. Foundations, Superstructure, Mechanical, and Electrical
   D. Air Conditioning, Electrical, Mechanical, and Structural

23. Oil tanks, when set in place inside a building, are frequently filled with water.
The BEST reason for this practice is

   A. to prevent them from floating off their foundation if water fills the room
   B. to enable them to be lifted up more easily
   C. to prevent them from becoming rusted
   D. for emergency use in case of fire

24. The filing system used in the field for correspondence is required to be uniform for all jobs.
The BEST reason for this requirement is that

   A. there is only one good way of setting up the filing system
   B. the standardized system is compact, thereby saving space
   C. other interested parties such as engineers from the main office will be able to use the files
   D. the contractor's forces will understand the filing system and will be able to extract necessary correspondence

25. Upon excavation to the subgrade of a footing to be placed on piles, the inspector finds that the soil is very poor.
Of the following, the PROPER action for the inspector to take is to

   A. do nothing
   B. add 20% to the number of piles
   C. notify the engineer's office of this condition
   D. order the contractor to keep excavating until he hits better soil

26. The general contractor is required to submit a progress schedule before starting work. Of the following, the BEST reason for this requirement is to

   A. determine if the contractor intends to complete the job
   B. enable the inspector to determine whether the contractor is on schedule
   C. enable the inspector to estimate monthly payments
   D. check minority hiring

27. If a contractor is falling behind schedule, the FIRST thing to check if the inspector is looking for the cause of this condition is the

   A. number of men he has on the job
   B. efficiency of his crew
   C. availability of equipment needed to do the job
   D. availability of the latest drawings needed by the contractor

28. The critical path method is a method for

   A. finding the best material needed for a specific use
   B. determining the best arrangement of equipment
   C. determining the best time to replace a piece of machinery
   D. scheduling work

29. The contractor states to the inspector that a given structural detail is undersized and unsafe.
    Of the following, the BEST action for the inspector to take in this situation is to

   A. ignore the complaint since the contractor is not an engineer
   B. change the detail by issuing a change order
   C. notify your superiors of the contractor's statements
   D. allow the contractor to modify the detail since it is his responsibility

30. The contractor proposes to use an additive to the concrete to accelerate its set. He asks you, the inspector, for permission to use it.
    Of the following, the FIRST action to take in response to his request is to

   A. check if the use of the additive is permitted by the specifications
   B. tell him to put the request in writing
   C. ask your superior if the use of the additive is acceptable
   D. deny him permission since additives to concrete are not permitted

KEY (CORRECT ANSWERS)

1.	B		16.	C
2.	A		17.	B
3.	D		18.	B
4.	B		19.	B
5.	C		20.	A
6.	C		21.	B
7.	A		22.	A
8.	D		23.	A
9.	A		24.	C
10.	A		25.	A
11.	B		26.	B
12.	D		27.	A
13.	A		28.	D
14.	B		29.	C
15.	C		30.	A

EXAMINATION SECTION
TEST 1

DIRECTIONS: Each question or incomplete statement is followed by several suggested answers or completions. Select the one that BEST answers the question or completes the statement. *PRINT THE LETTER OF THE CORRECT ANSWER IN THE SPACE AT THE RIGHT.*

1. Concrete with a slump of 2 inches would *most likely* be used for

   A. floors
   B. thin wall sections
   C. columns
   D. deep beams

   1.____

2. The structure above the roof of a building which encloses a stairway is called a

   A. scuttle
   B. bulkhead
   C. penthouse
   D. shaft

   2.____

3. A #4 reinforcing bar has a diameter, in inches, of *approximately*

   A. 1/4   B. 3/8   C. 1/2   D. 5/8

   3.____

4. A spandrel beam will usually be found

   A. at the wall
   B. around stairs
   C. at the peak of a roof
   D. underneath a column

   4.____

5. Oil is applied to the inside surfaces of concrete forms to

   A. prevent loss of water from the concrete
   B. obtain smoother concrete surfaces
   C. make stripping easier
   D. prevent honeycombing

   5.____

6. A retaining wall is built with a batter.
   Of the following conditions, the one which *most likely* applies to the wall is

   A. it is out of plumb
   B. it is thinner at top than at bottom
   C. neither surface is vertical
   D. both surfaces are vertical

   6.____

7. Two cubic yards of sand and four cubic yards of broken stone are to be used to make 1:2:4 concrete.
   If all the aggregate is used, the number of bags of cement that would be required is

   A. 1   B. 9   C. 18   D. 27

   7.____

8. A rectangular plot is 30 feet wide by 60 feet long. The length of the diagonal, in feet, is *most nearly*

   A. 68   B. 67   C. 66   D. 65

   8.____

9. Wood floor joists are supported on masonry walls which have a clear spacing of 17'0". The number of rows of cross-bridging required is

   A. 4   B. 3   C. 2   D. 1

   9.____

10. When painting wood, the puttying of nail holes and cracks should be done

    A. *after* the priming coat is dry
    B. *before* the priming coat is applied
    C. *while* the priming coat is still wet
    D. *after* the finish coat is applied

11. The material that would normally be used to make a corbel in a brick wall is

    A. brick   B. wood   C. steel   D. concrete

12. Headers and trimmers are used in the construction of

    A. footings   B. walls   C. floors   D. arches

13. In the design of stairs, the designer should consider

    A. maximum height of riser only
    B. minimum width of tread only
    C. product of riser height by tread width only
    D. all of the above

14. A reduction in the required number of columns in a building can be made by using one of the following types of beam. Which one?

    A. floor   B. girder   C. cantilever   D. jack

15. Doors sheathed in metal are known as _____ doors.

    A. kalamein   B. tin-clad   C. bethlehem   D. flemish

16. A coat of plaster which is scratched deliberately would *most likely* be

    A. used in two-coat work only
    B. the first coat placed
    C. the second coat placed
    D. condemned by the inspector

17. A concealed draft opening is

    A. *good* because it improves the appearance of a room
    B. *bad* because it might be accidentally blocked up
    C. *good* because it can be used to regulate the flow of fresh air
    D. *bad* because it is a fire hazard

18. A groove is cut in the underside of a stone sill. This is done to

    A. keep rain water from running down the wall
    B. allow the insertion of dowels
    C. improve the mortar bond
    D. reduce the weight of the sill

19. Of the following, the one which would LEAST likely be used in conjunction with the others is

    A. rafter
    B. collar beam
    C. ridgeboard
    D. tail beam

20. The dimensions of a 2 x 4 when dressed are, *most nearly,*

    A. 2 x 4
    B. 1 1/2 x 3 1/2
    C. 1 5/8 x 3 5/8
    D. 1 3/4 x 3 1/2

21. The story heights of a building could be MOST readily determined from

    A. a plan view
    B. an elevation view
    C. a plot map
    D. all of the above

22. Honeycombing in concrete is *most likely* to occur

    A. if the forms are vibrated
    B. near the top of the forms
    C. if the mix is stiff
    D. if the concrete is well-spaded

23. A weather joint in brick work is one in which the mortar is

    A. flush with the face of the lower brick and slopes inward
    B. flush with the face of the upper brick and slopes inward
    C. recessed a fixed distance behind the face of the brick
    D. flush with the face of upper and lower brick but curves inward between the two bricks

24. A 12 inch brick wall is constructed using stretchers only.
    The PRINCIPAL objection to such a wall is with

    A. appearance
    B. construction difficulties
    C. bond
    D. dimensional problems

25. To prevent sagging joists from damaging a brick wall in the event of a fire, it is BEST to

    A. anchor the joists firmly in the wall
    B. make a bevel cut on the end of the joists
    C. use bridal irons to support the joists
    D. box out the wall for the joists

26. Flashing would *most likely* be found in a

    A. footing   B. floor   C. ceiling   D. parapet

27. Vermiculite is used in plaster to

    A. reduce weight
    B. permit easier cleaning
    C. give architectural effects
    D. reduce the mixing water required

28. The volume in cubic feet of a room 8'6" wide by 10'6" long by 8'8" high is *most nearly*

    A. 770 B. 774 C. 778 D. 782

29. A slab of concrete is 2'0" by 3'0" by 8" thick.
    The weight of the slab is, in pounds, *most nearly*

    A. 450 B. 500 C. 550 D. 600

30. Wainscoting is USUALLY found on

    A. floors B. walls C. ceilings D. roofs

31. A piece of wood covering the plaster below the stool of a window is called a(n)

    A. apron B. sill C. coping D. trimmer

32. English bond is used in

    A. plastering B. papering C. roofing D. bricklaying

33. In plastering, coves would *most likely* be found where

    A. wall meets ceiling
    C. wall meets floor
    B. one wall meets another
    D. wall meets column

34. Fire stopping is usually accomplished by

    A. installing self-closing doors
    B. bricking up the space between furring at floors
    C. installing wire glass
    D. using fire resistive materials throughout the building

35. A Class 1 (fireproof structure) building has floor sleepers of wood. This is

    A. *not permitted*
    B. *permitted*
    C. *permitted* if the space between sleepers is filled with incombustible material
    D. *permitted* if a wearing surface similar to asphalt tile is applied to the wooden flooring

KEY (CORRECT ANSWERS)

1.	A	16.	B
2.	B	17.	D
3.	C	18.	A
4.	A	19.	D
5.	C	20.	C
6.	B	21.	B
7.	D	22.	C
8.	B	23.	A
9.	C	24.	C
10.	A	25.	B
11.	A	26.	D
12.	C	27.	A
13.	D	28.	B
14.	C	29.	D
15.	A	30.	B

31. A
32. D
33. A
34. B
35. C

TEST 2

DIRECTIONS: Each question or incomplete statement is followed by several suggested answers or completions. Select the one that BEST answers the question or completes the statement. *PRINT THE LETTER OF THE CORRECT ANSWER IN THE SPACE AT THE RIGHT.*

1. Joints on interior surfaces of brick walls are usually flush joints EXCEPT when the walls are to be   1.____

    A. painted
    B. plastered
    C. waterproofed
    D. dampproofed

2. The headers in a brick veneer wall serve   2.____

    A. both a structural and an architectural purpose
    B. a structural purpose only
    C. an architectural purpose only
    D. NO structural or architectural purpose

3. Of the following, the one which is NOT usually classified as interior wood trim is   3.____

    A. apron   B. ribbon   C. jamb   D. base mold

4. Single-strength glass would *most likely* be found in   4.____

    A. single light sash
    B. doors in fire walls
    C. doors in fire partitions
    D. multi-light sash

5. The one of the following items that is LEAST related to the others is   5.____

    A. newel   B. riser   C. nosing   D. sill

6. In a plastered room, grounds for plaster are LEAST likely to be used   6.____

    A. at baseboards
    B. around windows
    C. around doors
    D. at the top of wainscoting

7. Of the following types of walls, the type which is *most likely* an interior wall is _____ wall.   7.____

    A. curtain   B. faced   C. panel   D. fire

8. *Boxing* is *most likely* to be performed by a   8.____

    A. mason
    B. plasterer
    C. plumber
    D. painter

9. Linseed oil is classified as a   9.____

    A. vehicle
    B. thinner
    C. drying oil
    D. pigment

10. Curing of concrete would be MOST critical when the temperature and humidity are, respectively,

    A. 75° and 80%
    B. 80° and 90%
    C. 85° and 10%
    D. 90° and 95%

11. Of the following items, the item which is LEAST related to the others is

    A. putty
    B. sash weight
    C. glazier's points
    D. lights

12. Assume that a wood-frame house has studs of 2 x 4's.
    Placing the studs so that the wider dimension is parallel to the wall is

    A. *good* because it provides a wider nailing surface for sheathing and lathing
    B. *bad* because it reduces the open space available for windows
    C. *good* because it stiffens the frame
    D. *bad* because it reduces the load-carrying capacity of the studs

13. Government anchors are used in one of the following types of construction. Which one?

    A. Wood frame
    B. Steel beams supported on masonry bearing walls
    C. Wooden joists on masonry bearing walls
    D. Steel frame with steel joists

14. When rivet holes in structural steel fail to match up by an eighth of an inch, the BEST thing to do is

    A. ignore the mismatch and force the rivet into the hole
    B. enlarge the holes with a drift pin
    C. ream the holes to a larger diameter
    D. use a smaller sized rivet

15. The BEST way to use two angles to make a lintel is

16. A single channel section would *most likely* be used for a

    A. floor beam
    B. girder
    C. spandrel beam
    D. column

17. An oil-base paint is usually thinned with

    A. linseed oil
    B. turpentine
    C. a drying oil
    D. a resin

18. Red lead is often used as a pigment in metal priming paints PRIMARILY because it

    A. provides good coverage
    B. presents a good appearance
    C. makes painting easier
    D. is a rust inhibitor

19. Knots in wood that is to be painted

   A. require no special treatment
   B. should be painted with the priming paint before the priming paint is applied to the rest of the wood
   C. should be coated with linseed oil before any painting is done
   D. should be coated with shellac before any painting is done

20. A dove-tail anchor would *most likely* be used to bond brick veneer with a _____ wall.

   A. brick   B. concrete   C. wood frame   D. concrete block

21. A rafter is MOST similar in function to a

   A. joist   B. stud   C. sill   D. girder

22. In steel construction, it is usually MOST important to mill the ends of

   A. beams   B. girders   C. columns   D. lintels

23. Furring tile is usually set so that the air spaces in the tile are

   A. continuous in a vertical direction
   B. continuous in a horizontal direction
   C. closed off at the ends of each tile
   D. set at random

24. When plastering a wall surface of glazed tile, it is MOST important that the tile

   A. be wet
   B. be dry
   C. be scored
   D. joints be raked

25. In a peaked roof, the run of a rafter is

   A. less than the length of the rafter
   B. greater than the length of the rafter
   C. equal to the length of the rafter
   D. dependent upon the slope of the rafter

26. Construction of a dormer window does NOT usually involve

   A. cut rafters
   B. rafter headers
   C. trimmer rafters
   D. hip rafters

27. In a four-ply slag roof,

   A. there is no overlap of the roofing felt
   B. a uniform coating of pitch or asphalt is placed on top of the top layer of felt
   C. slag is placed between the layers of felt
   D. there is no need to use flashing

28. Copper wire basket strainers would *most likely* be used by a

   A. carpenter   B. plumber   C. painter   D. roofer

29. Splices of columns in steel construction are usually made 29.____

    A. at floor level
    B. two feet above floor level
    C. two feet below floor level
    D. midway between floors

30. In plumbing, a lead bend is usually used in the line from a 30.____

    A. slop sink   B. shower
    C. water closet   D. kitchen sink

31. The location of leaks in gas piping may be BEST detected by use of a 31.____

    A. match   B. heated filament
    C. soapy water solution   D. guinea pig

32. The one of the following items that would be MOST useful in eliminating water hammer from a water system is a 32.____

    A. magnesium anode   B. surge tank
    C. clean out   D. quick-closing valve

33. The MAIN purpose of a fixture trap is to 33.____

    A. catch small articles that may have accidentally dropped in the fixture
    B. prevent back syphonage
    C. make it easier to repair the fixture
    D. block the passage of foul air

34. In a certain district, the area of a building may be no longer than 55% of the area of the lot on which it stands. On a rectangular lot 75 ft. by 125 ft., the maximum permissible area of building is, in square feet, *most nearly* 34.____

    A. 5148   B. 5152   C. 5156   D. 5160

35. The allowable tensile stress in steel is 18,000 pounds per square inch. The maximum permissible tensile load in a 1-inch diameter steel bar is, in pounds, *most nearly* 35.____

    A. 13,500   B. 13,800   C. 14,100   D. 14,400

KEY (CORRECT ANSWERS)

1.	B		16.	C
2.	C		17.	B
3.	B		18.	D
4.	D		19.	D
5.	D		20.	B
6.	D		21.	A
7.	D		22.	C
8.	D		23.	B
9.	A		24.	C
10.	C		25.	A
11.	B		26.	D
12.	D		27.	B
13.	B		28.	D
14.	C		29.	B
15.	A		30.	C

31. C
32. B
33. D
34. C
35. C

TEST 3

DIRECTIONS: Each question or incomplete statement is followed by several suggested answers or completions. Select the one that BEST answers the question or completes the statement. *PRINT THE LETTER OF THE CORRECT ANSWER IN THE SPACE AT THE RIGHT.*

1. The ends of a joist in a brick building are cut to a bevel. This is done PRINCIPALLY to prevent damage to

    A. joist   B. floor   C. sill   D. wall

2. Of the following, the wood that is MOST commonly used today for floor joists is

    A. long leaf yellow pine
    B. douglas fir
    C. oak
    D. birch

3. Quarter sawed lumber is preferred for the best finished flooring PRINCIPALLY because it

    A. has the greatest strength
    B. shrinks the least
    C. is the easiest to nail
    D. is the easiest to handle

4. Of the following, the MAXIMUM height that would be considered acceptable for a stair riser is

    A. 6 1/2"   B. 7 1/2"   C. 8 1/2"   D. 9 1/2"

5. The part of a tree that will produce the DENSEST wood is the _____ wood.

    A. spring   B. summer   C. sap   D. heart

6. Lumber in quantity is ordered by

    A. cubic feet
    B. foot board measure
    C. lineal feet
    D. weight and length

7. A *chase* in a brick wall is a

    A. pilaster   B. waterstop   C. recess   D. corbel

8. *Parging* refers to

    A. increasing the thickness of a brick wall
    B. plastering the back of face brickwork
    C. bonding face brick to backing blocks
    D. leveling each course of brick

9. In brickwork, muriatic acid is commonly used to

    A. increase the strength of the mortar
    B. etch the brick
    C. waterproof the wall
    D. clean the wall

53

10. Cement mortar can be made easier to work by the addition of a small quantity of

   A. lime   B. soda   C. litharge   D. plaster

11. Joints in brick walls are tooled

   A. immediately after each brick is laid
   B. after the mortar has had its initial set
   C. after the entire wall is completed
   D. 28 days after the wall has been built

12. If cement mortar has begun to set before it can be used in a wall, the BEST thing to do is to

   A. use the mortar immediately as is
   B. add a small quantity of lime
   C. add some water and mix thoroughly
   D. discard the mortar

13. The BEST flux to use when soldering galvanized iron is

   A. killed acid   B. sal-ammoniac
   C. muriatic acid   D. resin

14. The type of solder that would be used in *hard soldering* is _____ solder.

   A. bismuth   B. wiping   C. 50-50   D. silver

15. Roll roofing material is usually felt which has been impregnated with

   A. cement   B. mastic   C. tar   D. latex

16. The purpose of flashing on roofs is to

   A. secure roofing materials to the roof
   B. make it easier to lay the roofing
   C. prevent leaks through the roof
   D. insulate the roof from excessive heat

17. The type of chain used with sash weights is _____ link.

   A. flat   B. round
   C. figure-eight   D. basketweave

18. The material that would be used to seal around a window frame is

   A. oakum   B. litharge   C. grout   D. calking

19. The function of a window sill is *most nearly* the same as that of a

   A. jamb   B. coping   C. lintel   D. buck

20. Lightweight plaster would be made with

   A. sand   B. cinders   C. potash   D. vermiculite

21. The FIRST coat of plaster to be applied on a three-coat plaster job is the _____ coat.

   A. brown   B. scratch   C. white   D. keene

22. The FIRST coat of plaster over rock lath should be a _____ plaster. 22.____

    A. gypsum   B. lime
    C. Portland cement   D. pozzolan cement

23. The PRINCIPAL reason for covering a concrete sidewalk with straw or paper after the 23.____
    concrete has been poured is to

    A. prevent people from walking on the concrete while it is still wet
    B. impart a rough, non-slip surface to the concrete
    C. prevent excessive evaporation of water in the concrete
    D. shorten the length of time it would take for the concrete to harden

24. Concrete is *rubbed* with a(n) 24.____

    A. emery wheel   B. carborundum brick
    C. sandstone   D. alundum stick

25. To prevent concrete from sticking to forms, the forms should be painted with 25.____

    A. oil   B. kerosene   C. water   D. lime

26. One method of measuring the consistency of a concrete mix is by means of a _____ 26.____
    test.

    A. penetration   B. flow
    C. slump   D. weight

27. A chemical that is sometimes used to prevent the freezing of concrete in cold weather is 27.____

    A. alum   B. glycerine
    C. calcium chloride   D. sodium nitrate

28. The one of the following that is LEAST commonly used for columns is 28.____

    A. wide flange beams   B. angles
    C. concrete-filled pipe   D. "I" beams

29. Fire protection of steel floor beams is MOST frequently accomplished by the use of 29.____

    A. gypsum block   B. brick
    C. rock wool fill   D. vermiculite gypsum plaster

30. A *Pittsburgh lock* is a(n) 30.____

    A. emergency door lock   B. sheet metal joint
    C. elevator safety   D. boiler valve

31. Of the following items, the one which is NOT used in making fastenings to masonry or 31.____
    plaster walls is a(n)

    A. lead shield   B. expansion bolt
    C. rawl plug   D. steel bushing

32. The term *bell and spigot* USUALLY refers to 32.____

    A. refrigerator motors   B. cast iron pipes
    C. steam radiator outlets   D. electrical receptacles

33. In plumbing work, a valve which allows water to flow in one direction only is commonly known as a _____ valve.

    A. check   B. globe   C. gate   D. stop

34. A pipe coupling is BEST used to connect two pieces of pipe of

    A. the same diameter in a straight line
    B. the same diameter at right angles to each other
    C. different diameters at a 45° angle
    D. different diameters in a 1/8th bend

35. One method of testing fuses is to connect a pair of test lamps in the circuit in such a manner that the test lamp will light up if the fuse is good and will remain dark if the fuse is bad. In the illustration, 1 and 2 are fuses. In order to test if fuse 1 is bad, test lamps should be connected between

    A. A and B   B. B and D   C. A and D   D. C and B

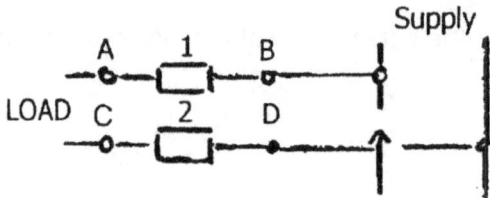

36. Operating an incandescent electric light bulb at less than its rated voltage will result in

    A. shorter life and brighter light
    B. longer life and dimmer light
    C. brighter light and longer life
    D. dimmer light and shorter life

37. In order to control a lamp from two different positions, it is necessary to use

    A. two single pole switches
    B. one single pole switch and one four-way switch
    C. two three-way switches
    D. one single pole switch and one four-way switch

38. The PRINCIPAL reason for the grounding of electrical equipment and circuits is to

    A. prevent short circuits   B. insure safety from shock
    C. save power   D. increase voltage

39. The ordinary single-pole flush wall type switch must be connected

    A. across the line
    B. in the "hot" conductor
    C. in the grounded conductor
    D. in the white conductor

40. A strike plate is MOST closely associated with a

    A. lock   B. sash   C. butt   D. tie rod

41. A room is 7'6" wide by 9'0" long, with a ceiling height of 8'0". One gallon of flat paint will cover approximately 400 square feet of wall.
The number of gallons of this paint required to paint the walls of this room, making no deductions for windows or doors, is *most nearly* _____ gallon.

    A. 1/4   B. 1/3   C. 3/4   D. 1

41.____

42. The cost of a certain job is broken down as follows:
    Materials $375
    Rental of equipment   120
    Labor   315

    The percentage of the total cost of the job that can be charged to materials is *most nearly*

    A. 40%   B. 42%   C. 44%   D. 46%

42.____

43. By trial, it is found that by using two cubic feet of sand, a 5 cubic foot batch of concrete is produced. Using the same proportions, the amount of sand required to produce 2 cubic yards of concrete is *most nearly* _____ cubic feet.

    A. 20   B. 22   C. 24   D. 26

43.____

44. It takes four men six days to do a certain job. Working at the same speed, the number of days it will take three men to do this job is

    A. 7   B. 8   C. 9   D. 10

44.____

45. The cost of rawl plugs is $2.75 per gross. The cost of 2,448 rawl plugs is

    A. $46.75   B. $47.25   C. $47.75   D. $48.25

45.____

KEY (CORRECT ANSWERS)

1.	D	11.	B	21.	B	31.	D	41.	C
2.	B	12.	D	22.	A	32.	B	42.	D
3.	B	13.	C	23.	C	33.	A	43.	B
4.	B	14.	D	24.	B	34.	A	44.	B
5.	D	15.	C	25.	A	35.	C	45.	A
6.	B	16.	C	26.	C	36.	B		
7.	C	17.	A	27.	C	37.	C		
8.	B	18.	D	28.	B	38.	B		
9.	D	19.	B	29.	D	39.	B		
10.	A	20.	D	30.	B	40.	A		

EXAMINATION SECTION
TEST 1

DIRECTIONS: Each question or incomplete statement is followed by several suggested answers or completions. Select the one that BEST answers the question or completes the statement. *PRINT THE LETTER OF THE CORRECT ANSWER IN THE SPACE AT THE RIGHT.*

Questions 1-5.

DIRECTIONS: For Questions 1 through 5, inclusive, Column I lists frequently used construction terms. Column II lists some of the building trades. For each item listed in Column I, enter in the appropriate space at the right the capital letter in front of the trade listed in Column II that is MOST closely associated with the item. Each trade may be used more than once or not at all.

COLUMN I	COLUMN II
1. Bed	A. Plumbing
2. Wiping	B. Plastering
3. Brown	C. Carpentry
4. Key	D. Masonry
5. Bridging	E. Painting
	F. Steelwork
	G. Roofing

1.____
2.____
3.____
4.____
5.____

6. A *cricket* would be found

    A. on a roof
    B. at a structural steel connection
    C. supporting reinforcing steel
    D. over a window

6.____

7. *Cutting in* is done when

    A. trimming a stud to size
    B. fitting a bat in a brick wall
    C. painting in tight corners
    D. trimming tallow for a wiped joint

7.____

8. *Corbeling* results in

    A. strengthening a concrete column
    B. waterproofing a foundation wall
    C. anchoring a steel girder to a bearing wall
    D. increasing the thickness of a brick wall

8.____

9. Solder used for copper gutters is MOST frequently

   A. 30-70   B. 40-60   C. 50-50   D. 60-40

10. A jack rafter runs from

    A. plate to ridge
    B. hip to ridge
    C. plate to hip
    D. plate to plate

11. The one of the following items that is LEAST related to the others is

    A. sill   B. joist   C. sole   D. newel

12. A *fire cut* is made on

    A. timber posts
    B. rafters
    C. floor joists
    D. lathing

13. The one of the following items that is LEAST related to the others is

    A. joist hanger
    B. pintle
    C. bridle iron
    D. stirrup

14. The PROPER order of nailing sub-flooring and bridging is

    A. top of bridging, bottom of bridging, sub-flooring
    B. bottom of bridging, sub-flooring, top of bridging
    C. top of bridging, sub-flooring, bottom of bridging
    D. bottom of bridging, top of bridging, sub-flooring

15. Sleepers would be found in

    A. walls   B. doors   C. footings   D. floors

16. The one of the following woods that is MOST commonly used for finish flooring is

    A. hemlock   B. cypress   C. larch   D. oak

17. Spacing of studs in a stud partition is MOST frequently _____" o.c.

    A. 12   B. 14   C. 16   D. 18

18. A hollow masonry wall should be used in preference to a solid masonry wall when the characteristic MOST desired is

    A. insulation
    B. strength
    C. beauty
    D. durability

19. The arrangement of headers and stretchers in brickwork is known as the

    A. bond   B. stringer   C. lacing   D. stile

20. Of the following, the reason that is LEAST likely to justify pointing brickwork is that pointing _____ the wall.

    A. improves the appearance of
    B. helps prevent cracking of
    C. increases the useful life of
    D. helps waterproof

21. The purpose of flashing is to 21._____

    A. keep water out   B. speed the set of mortar
    C. anchor a cornice   D. cover exposed joists

22. The one of the following classes of wall that would LEAST likely be the outside wall of a building is a 22._____

    A. spandrel   B. fire   C. curtain   D. parapet

23. Lime is added to mortar USUALLY to 23._____

    A. increase the strength of the mortar
    B. make the mortar water resistant
    C. make it easier to apply the mortar
    D. improve the appearance of the mortar joint

24. Efflorescence on the face of a brick wall is BEST removed by scrubbing with a solution of 24._____

    A. muriatic acid   B. sodium silicate
    C. oxalic acid   D. calcium oxide

25. The one of the following that is NOT a defect in painting is 25._____

    A. chalking   B. checking
    C. alligatoring   D. waning

26. The one of the following ingredients of a paint that would be called the *vehicle* is 26._____

    A. white lead   B. turpentine
    C. linseed oil   D. pigment

27. The one of the following that is used as a rust preventative in the prime coat for painting steel is 27._____

    A. aluminum   B. red lead
    C. titanium dioxide   D. carbon black

28. *Boxing*, with reference to paint, means 28._____

    A. thinning   B. mixing   C. spreading   D. drying

29. When painting new wood, filling of nail holes and cracks with putty should be done 29._____

    A. 24 hours before priming
    B. immediately before priming
    C. after priming and before the second coat
    D. after the second coat and before the finish coat

30. The one of the following that is the size of a reinforcing rod MOST commonly used in reinforced concrete construction is 30._____

    A. 1 3/4" ⌀   B. 18 gauge   C. #9   D. 2 ST3

31. Honeycombing in concrete is USUALLY caused by 31._____

    A. too plastic a mix   B. high fall of concrete
    C. mixing too long   D. inadequate vibration

32. A concrete mix is indicated as 1:2:3 1/2 mix. The number 2 refers to the proportion by volume of

   A. water B. cement C. gravel D. sand

33. Specifications for concrete mixes frequently call for the use of dry sand. The reason for this is that the additional water in wet sand will

   A. make it more difficult to place the concrete
   B. decrease the strength of the concrete
   C. cause the sand and stone to segregate
   D. increase the cost of waterproofing

34. Curing of concrete serves PRIMARILY to

   A. prevent freezing of the concrete
   B. permit early removal of forms
   C. delay setting of the concrete
   D. prevent evaporation of moisture

35. The MAIN reason that forms for concrete work are oiled is to

   A. *permit* easy removal of forms
   B. *prevent* rust marks on the concrete
   C. *prevent* bleeding of water
   D. *permit* easier vibration of the concrete

36. The one of the following terms that is LEAST related to the others is

   A. 5-ply B. mastic
   C. vapor barrier D. flashing

37. Before quicklime can be used for plaster, it must be

   A. slaked B. burned C. floated D. glazed

38. When a hard plaster is required, as in halls, the one of the following that would MOST likely be used is

   A. lime B. Keene's cement
   C. stucco D. marbling

39. To give plaster a hard finish, hydrated lime is mixed with

   A. white cement B. linseed oil putty
   C. white lead D. plaster of paris

40. The purpose of a ground in plaster work is to

   A. provide a key for the plaster
   B. help the plasterer make an even wall
   C. prevent the plasterer's scaffold from slipping
   D. hold the loose plaster before it is placed

41. When a lightweight plaster is required, the one of the following fine aggregates that is MOST likely to be used is

    A. cinders
    B. sand
    C. talc
    D. vermiculite

42. Of the following fireproofing materials, the one which would be MOST frequently used to fireproof steel columns in a fireproof building is

    A. sheet rock
    B. vermiculite plaster
    C. brick
    D. rock lath

43. The one of the following items that is LEAST related to the others is

    A. rock wool
    B. wall board
    C. sheet rock
    D. rock lath

44. The first layer of plaster placed in a 3-coat plaster job is called the _____ coat.

    A. brown   B. scratch   C. hard   D. white

45. The one of the following symbols that represents a steel section which is MOST similar in appearance to a W section is

    A. U   B. L   C. I   D. Z

46. A plate used to connect two steel angles in a roof truss is known as a(n)

    A. angle iron
    B. gusset plate
    C. bearing plate
    D. tie bar

47. Steel beams are COMMONLY anchored to brick walls by

    A. government anchors
    B. tie rods
    C. eye bars
    D. anchor bolts

48. Rivet holes are lined up with a

    A. set screw
    B. ginnywink
    C. drift pin
    D. trivet

49. A sewer that carries BOTH storm water and sewage is called a _____ sewer.

    A. sanitary   B. flush   C. combined   D. mixed

50. A fresh air inlet for a house drainage system would be connected to the system

    A. just ahead of the house trap
    B. at each horizontal branch line
    C. at the top of the stack through the roof
    D. at the trap of each water closet

KEY (CORRECT ANSWERS)

1. D	11. D	21. A	31. D	41. D
2. A	12. C	22. B	32. D	42. B
3. B	13. B	23. C	33. B	43. A
4. B	14. C	24. A	34. D	44. B
5. C	15. D	25. D	35. A	45. C
6. A	16. D	26. C	36. C	46. B
7. C	17. C	27. B	37. A	47. A
8. D	18. A	28. B	38. B	48. C
9. C	19. A	29. C	39. D	49. C
10. C	20. B	30. C	40. B	50. A

TEST 2

DIRECTIONS: Each question or incomplete statement is followed by several suggested answers or completions. Select the one that BEST answers the question or completes the statement. *PRINT THE LETTER OF THE CORRECT ANSWER IN THE SPACE AT THE RIGHT.*

Questions 1-5.

DIRECTIONS: Column I consists of a list of trades, and Column II lists tools used in those trades. In the space at the right, opposite the number of the trade in Column I, write the letter preceding the tool of the trade in Column II.

COLUMN I		COLUMN II	
1. Carpenter	A.	Mop	1.____
2. Plumber	B.	Hawk	2.____
3. Plasterer	C.	Miter box	3.____
4. Bricklayer	D.	Shave-hook	4.____
5. Roofer	E.	Jointing tool	5.____

Questions 6-7.

DIRECTIONS: Questions 6 and 7 refer to the mortar joints shown below.

6. The mortar joint MOST frequently used on common brickwork is   6.____
   A. 1   B. 2   C. 3   D. 4

7. The mortar joint which would NOT usually be made unless an outside scaffold was used is   7.____
   A. 1   B. 2   C. 3   D. 4

8. A rectangular yard is 50'0" long by 8'6" wide.   8.____
   The area of the yard is, in square feet,
   A. 420.0   B. 422.5   C. 425.0   D. 427.5

9. A rectangular court is 23'0" long by 9'6" wide.
   The length of the diagonal is MOST NEARLY

   A. 24'8"   B. 24'10"   C. 25'2"   D. 25'6"

10. Concrete weighs 150 pounds per cubic foot.
    A slab of concrete 6'0" long by 3'6" wide by 1'4" thick weighs MOST NEARLY _____ pounds.

    A. 4150   B. 4200   C. 4250   D. 4300

11. A building 32'0" by 65'0" occupies a lot 60'0" by 110'0". The ratio of building area to lot area is MOST NEARLY

    A. 0.32   B. 0.33   C. 0.34   D. 0.35

12. When painting wood, puttying of nail holes and cracks is done

    A. before any painting is started
    B. after the priming coat is applied
    C. after the finish coat is applied
    D. at any stage in the painting

13. The process of pouring paint from one container to another in order to mix it is known as

    A. bleeding   B. boxing   C. cutting   D. stirring

14. Paint is *thinned* with

    A. linseed oil   B. turpentine
    C. varnish   D. gasoline

15. A wood screw which can be tightened by a wrench is known as a _____ screw.

    A. lag   B. Philips   C. carriage   D. monkey

16. To permit easy removal of forms from concrete, the inside surfaces of the forms are often coated with

    A. paint   B. oil   C. water   D. asphalt

17. Sixteen pieces of 2 x 4 lumber, each 10'6" long, contain a total of _____ FBM.

    A. 110   B. 111   C. 112   D. 113

18. The consistency of concrete is measured with a

    A. Vicat needle   B. slump cone
    C. hook gage   D. bourdon gage

19. End-matched lumber would MOST likely be used for

    A. sheathing   B. roofing   C. flooring   D. siding

20. A post or shore is to be placed midway between columns to support the formwork for a reinforced concrete girder. The post should be cut

    A. short, so that wedging is required
    B. to exact length

C. long, so that it will have to be driven into place
D. in two pieces, to permit jackknifing into place

21. Batter boards are set by a

    A. mason B. plumber C. roofer D. surveyor

22. Of the following terms, all of which refer to tools, the one which is LEAST related to the others is

    A. back B. box-end C. cross-cut D. rip

23. Of the following tools, the one which is LEAST like the others is

    A. brace and bit B. draw-knife
    C. plans D. spoke-shave

24. When wood splits easily, it is advisable to drill a hole for each nail. The hole for the nail should be _____ the nail.

    A. larger in diameter than
    B. smaller in diameter than
    C. exactly the same diameter as
    D. less than one-quarter the length of

25. The length of a 10-penny nail, in inches, is

    A. $2\frac{1}{2}$ B. 3 C. $3\frac{1}{2}$ D. 4

26. The decimal equivalent of 31/64 of an inch is MOST NEARLY

    A. 0.45 B. 0.46 C. 0.47 D. 0.48

27. Of the following, the one which is BEST classified as an abrasive is

    A. a saw B. a chisel C. graphite D. sandpaper

28. Of the following construction materials, the one which would MOST likely be stored directly on the ground is

    A. brick B. cement C. steel D. wood

29. The strength of brick walls is based upon the type of mortar used.
    The relative strength of the various types of mortar, in descending order, is

    A. cement, lime, cement-lime
    B. lime, cement-lime, cement
    C. cement-lime, cement, lime
    D. cement, cement-lime, lime

30. Coating reinforcing rods with oil before placing them in the forms is

    A. *good* practice, because it prevents rusting
    B. *poor* practice, because it makes the rods difficult to handle
    C. *good* practice if the forms are oiled
    D. *poor* practice, because it destroys the bond between the concrete and the rods

31. If the mixing plant should break down after one-half the concrete has been mixed for a floor, the BEST thing to do would be to
    A. take the concrete out of the forms and throw it away
    B. spread the available concrete evenly over the floor area
    C. block off one-half of the floor area and place the available concrete in the blocked-off area
    D. keep mixing the concrete in the forms with shovels until the plant is repaired

32. Splicing of reinforcing bars is accomplished by
    A. using wire ties
    B. underlapping the bars
    C. hooking the bars
    D. using metal clips

33. A sanitary sewer carries
    A. storm water only
    B. sewage only
    C. sewage and storm water
    D. the discharge from a sewage plant

34. A neat line
    A. is the result of good workmanship
    B. is used in concrete construction only
    C. defines an outer limit of a structure
    D. defines an outer limit of excavation for a structure

35. Continued trowelling of a cement-finish floor for a building is
    A. *good* practice, because it provides a smooth floor
    B. *poor* practice, because it produces a slippery floor
    C. *poor* practice, because it brings the fines to the surface
    D. *good* practice, because it insures proper mixing of the cement finish

36. In reinforced concrete form work, a beveled chamfer strip is used to
    A. reinforce the outside of the forms
    B. reinforce the inside of the forms
    C. seal leaks in the forms
    D. do none of the foregoing

37. Cracks in lumber due to contraction along annual rings are known as
    A. checks
    B. wanes
    C. pitch pockets
    D. dry rot

38. Honeycombing is MOST likely to occur in construction involving
    A. steel   B. concrete   C. wood   D. masonry

39. Floor beams are sometimes crowned to
    A. provide arch action
    B. eliminate deflection
    C. strengthen the floor
    D. provide a more nearly level floor than would be provided by straight beams

40. In brickwork, a rowlock course consists of

    A. headers
    B. stretchers
    C. bricks laid on edge
    D. bricks laid so that the longest dimension is vertical

41. The term *bond,* as used in bricklaying, refers to

    A. structure only
    B. pattern only
    C. structure and pattern
    D. color and finish of individual bricks

42. Concrete is a mixture of cement,

    A. fine aggregate, coarse aggregate, and water
    B. sand, and water
    C. stone, and water
    D. sand, and stone

43. Consistency, when used in connection with concrete, refers to the

    A. seven-day strength
    B. twenty-eight day strength
    C. initial set before forms are removed
    D. plasticity of freshly mixed concrete

44. Brick may be used for the facing material in both faced walls and veneered walls. The distinction between the two types of walls relates to

    A. bonding or lack of bonding between facing and backing
    B. type of material in facing and backing
    C. relative thickness of facing and backing
    D. the type of mortar used

45. A plaster *key* is NOT formed on _____ lath.

    A. wood   B. metal
    C. expanded metal D. gypsum

46. Of the following, the BEST tool to use to make a hole in a coping stone is a

    A. star drill   B. coping saw
    C. pneumatic grinder D. diamond wheel dresser

47. Roughing refers to work performed by a

    A. carpenter   B. bricklayer
    C. plumber   D. roofer

48. A post supporting a handrail is known as a

    A. tread   B. riser   C. newel   D. bevel

49. The live load on a floor is 40 pounds per square foot. The floor joists are on a 14'0" span and are spaced 2'6" on centers.
    The maximum live load carried by a joist, in pounds, is MOST NEARLY

    A. 700 B. 933 C. 1167 D. 1400

50. Of the following terms, the one LEAST related to the others is

    A. ground
    C. rafter
    B. purlin
    D. ridge board

KEY (CORRECT ANSWERS)

1. C	11. A	21. D	31. C	41. C
2. D	12. B	22. B	32. A	42. A
3. B	13. B	23. A	33. B	43. D
4. E	14. B	24. B	34. C	44. A
5. A	15. A	25. B	35. C	45. D
6. C	16. B	26. D	36. D	46. A
7. A	17. C	27. D	37. A	47. C
8. C	18. B	28. A	38. B	48. C
9. B	19. C	29. D	39. D	49. D
10. B	20. A	30. D	40. C	50. A

EXAMINATION SECTION
TEST 1

DIRECTIONS: Each question or incomplete statement is followed by several suggested answers or completions. Select the one that BEST answers the question or completes the statement. *PRINT THE LETTER OF THE CORRECT ANSWER IN THE SPACE AT THE RIGHT.*

1. A _____ would MOST likely be used to estimate the cost of additional yards of concrete, or additional lengths of piling.

    A. quantity survey
    B. lump-sum amount
    C. cost-per-square-foot estimate
    D. unit cost estimate

    1._____

2. How many studs are usually required for 10 linear feet of wall, excluding openings and plates?

    A. 1   B. 5   C. 10   D. 12

    2._____

3. What is represented by the mechanical symbol ⊠ shown at the right?

    A. Supply duct   B. Gauge
    C. Exhaust duct   D. Floor drain

    3._____

4. The excavation of compacted sand or gravel will require an angle of repose (slope) of 1 ft. vertical to _____ ft. horizontal.

    A. 3/4   B. 1   C. 1 1/2   D. 2

    4._____

5. Which of the following types of tile for resilient flooring would be LEAST expensive?

    A. Pure vinyl   B. Asphalt
    C. Cork   D. Rubberized marbleized

    5._____

6. What is the typical estimate (in linear feet) for two laborers' output per day of regular chain-link fencing?

    A. 50   B. 100   C. 150   D. 200

    6._____

7. What is used between the ridge and valley rafters of a roof construction?

    A. Fascia   B. Hip rafter
    C. Packing   D. Jack rafter

    7._____

8. Approximately how many square feet of surface area can be covered by 1 gallon of adhesive for resilient flooring sheet material?

    A. 75   B. 125   C. 200   D. 250

    8._____

9. Water piping is NOT typically made of

    A. copper   B. cast iron
    C. galvanized steel D. plastic

    9._____

10. What is represented by the electrical symbol shown at the right?

    A. Buzzer
    B. Clock receptacle
    C. Electric motor
    D. Circuit breaker

11. Approximately how many linear feet of 1/4" copper pipe can be installed in a typical work day?

    A. 35-40   B. 50-60   C. 65-75   D. 85-100

12. What is the term for short studs required beneath window framing, and at similar locations?

    A. Scrap   B. Cripple   C. Hash   D. Hips

13. For MOST brick work, scaffolding is required at intervals of about _____ feet.

    A. 4   B. 6   C. 8   D. 10

14. What type of concrete masonry unit is represented by the drawing shown at the right?

    A. Header
    B. Stretcher
    C. Channel
    D. Bull nose

15. The movable portion of a window that contains the glass is the

    A. cornice   B. sash   C. scale   D. pane

16. Approximately how many hours of labor will be required for the installation of 100 square feet of countertop ceramic tile and a 6" back splash?

    A. 3   B. 5   C. 8   D. 12

17. Which of the following types of wall constructions will be LEAST able to dampen the transmission of sound?

    A. Single-stud gypsum board
    B. Metal-stud plaster on lath
    C. Single-stud plaster on gypsum board
    D. Staggered-stud gypsum board

18. What is represented by the mechanical symbol shown at the right?

    A. Return duct
    B. Shower
    C. Corner tub
    D. Water or fuel tank

19. Which of the following types of aluminum windows would be MOST expensive to install?

    A. Horizontal sliding
    B. Casement
    C. Double-hung
    D. Projected vent

20. Generally, an adequate interest or profit return from a construction job must be more than _____ %.

    A. 3-5 B. 7-10 C. 12-22 D. 24-45

21. Which of the following types of doors would be LEAST expensive?

    A. Hollow core, birch-veneer face
    B. Solid-core, walnut-faced
    C. Hollow core, hardboard-faced
    D. Solid-core, birch-veneer face

22. What is represented by the architectural symbol shown at the right?

    A. Shingle roofing   B. Aluminum
    C. Structural metal   D. Cast iron

23. Approximately how many hours should be estimated for the trimming of a door blank (3'x7' wood door), plus the installation of frame and trim?

    A. 1 B. 2 C. 4 D. 6

24. Which of the following types of wire enclosures is NOT currently in use?

    A. Romex   B. Conduit
    C. Flexible cable D. Knob-in-tube

25. If precut granite block is used for curbs, the cost will be roughly _____ % more than the cost for using concrete.

    A. 10 B. 30 C. 50 D. 70

KEY (CORRECT ANSWERS)

1. D
2. C
3. A
4. C
5. B

6. C
7. D
8. C
9. B
10. C

11. B
12. B
13. A
14. B
15. B

16. D
17. A
18. D
19. B
20. B

21. C
22. D
23. C
24. D
25. C

TEST 2

DIRECTIONS: Each question or incomplete statement is followed by several suggested answers or completions. Select the one that BEST answers the question or completes the statement. *PRINT THE LETTER OF THE CORRECT ANSWER IN THE SPACE AT THE RIGHT.*

1. In an average work day, approximately how many cubic yards of earth can be excavated by means of a tractor shovel with a 1-yard bucket?   1.____

    A. 10 B. 75 C. 350 D. 500

2. Mesh reinforcing material is MOST commonly used in   2.____

    A. vertical walls B. supports
    C. slabs D. footings

3. What is represented by the architectural symbol shown at the right?   3.____

    A. Cut stone B. Concrete block
    C. Rubble stone D. Fire brick

4. Which of the following does NOT require an external trap that connects the sewer line?   4.____

    A. Kitchen sink B. Toilet
    C. Lavatory D. Tub

5. In one hour, a typical caisson boring machine will be able to bore _____ linear feet.   5.____

    A. 75 B. 125 C. 200 D. 250

6. Most bath accessories require about _____ to install.   6.____

    A. 15 minutes B. 45 minutes
    C. 1 hour D. 14 hours

7. What is represented by the electrical symbol shown at the right?   7.____

    A. Electric motor B. Bell
    C. Paging system D. Street light and bracket

8. Which of the following plumbing (pipe) materials would be MOST expensive to install?   8.____

    A. 3" galvanized steel B. 1/4" galvanized steel
    C. 1/4" copper tubing D. High-strength PVC plastic

9. The horizontal band of material directly beneath a cornice, and above the siding, is known as the   9.____

    A. gable B. section C. perimeter D. frieze

10. Approximately how many hours are typically required for carpenter labor to install 1,000 square feet of plywood floor sheathing?   10.____

    A. 1-3 B. 3-4 C. 5-6 D. 7-8

11. The generally accepted method for figuring *in-place* costs for small accessories such as doorbells, smoke alarms, and garage door openers is to multiply the material cost by

    A. 4   B. 2   C. 3   D. 4

12. A _____ is represented by the mechanical symbol shown at the right.

    A. diaphragm valve   B. lock and shield valve
    C. gate valve   D. check valve

13. What is used to join lengths of galvanized steel pipe?

    A. Molten solder   B. Threaded ends and sealer
    C. Elbows   D. Lead-and-oakum seal

14. Approximately how much plumber's labor would be required for the installation of a single chrome-plated faucet set?

    A. 15 minutes   B. 30 minutes
    C. 1 hour   D. 1 1/2 hours

15. Each of the following roof flashing materials takes about the same amount of time to install EXCEPT

    A. aluminum   B. galvanized steel
    C. zinc alloy   D. stainless steel

16. What is the MOST commonly used grade of asphalt tile used for resilient flooring?

    A. A   B. B   C. C   D. D

17. Which of the following plastic pipe materials is usable for hot water lines?

    A. DWV   B. ABS   C. PVC   D. PVDC

18. Approximately how many linear feet of gutter material can be installed by one person in an average work day?

    A. 80   B. 120   C. 150   D. 175

19. What is represented by the electrical symbol shown at the right?

    A. Junction box   B. Blanked outlet
    C. Television outlet   D. Buzzer

20. When estimating the cost of resilient flooring material, how much floor tile and base should be calculated as waste?

    A. 5%   B. 10%   C. 20%   D. 30%

21. Most fire codes suggest that wall surfaces within _____ of a fireplace unit be covered with a fire-retardant surface.

    A. 8 inches B. 16 inches C. 4 feet   D. 8 feet

22. Wood, gypsum board, or expanded metal used as a base for plaster finish is known as 22.____
    A. parging B. lath C. chord D. aggregate

23. Approximately how many linear feet of sewer pipe can be installed in an average work day? 23.____
    A. 25 B. 50 C. 75 D. 100

24. Approximately how many square feet of board floor sheathing can be installed by a crew in a normal work day? 24.____
    A. 250 B. 500 C. 750 D. 1,000

25. A _____ line is represented by the mechanical _____ symbol shown at the right. 25.____
    A. soil
    B. refrigerant
    C. cold water
    D. hot water

KEY (CORRECT ANSWERS)

1. C
2. C
3. C
4. B
5. B

6. A
7. B
8. A
9. D
10. D

11. B
12. A
13. B
14. C
15. A

16. C
17. D
18. B
19. D
20. B

21. A
22. B
23. B
24. C
25. D

TEST 3

DIRECTIONS: Each question or incomplete statement is followed by several suggested answers or completions. Select the one that BEST answers the question or completes the statement. *PRINT THE LETTER OF THE CORRECT ANSWER IN THE SPACE AT THE RIGHT.*

1. Which of the following plumbing (pipe) materials would be LEAST expensive to install? 1.____

   A. 1/4" galvanized steel
   B. 1" copper pipe
   C. 1/4" copper tubing
   D. High-strength PVC plastic

2. Which of the following roof flashing materials would take the GREATEST amount of time to install? 2.____

   A. Aluminum
   B. Stainless steel
   C. Zinc alloy
   D. Copper

3. Approximately how many square feet of *Venetian* blind window accessory can be installed by a worker in an average day? 3.____

   A. 50   B. 100   C. 225   D. 450

4. What is the term for a short length of pipe threaded at each end and used to connect fittings? 4.____

   A. Joist   B. Nipple   C. ABS   D. Elbow

5. Approximately how many square yards of metal lathing work can be installed for a ceiling in a typical work day? 5.____

   A. 30-40   B. 50-60   C. 60-80   D. 85-100

6. The approximate weight specification for a 20-year bonded flat roof is _____ pounds per square foot of roof area. 6.____

   A. 3   B. 6   C. 9   D. 12

7. Approximately how many linear feet of PVC pipe can be installed in a typical work day? 7.____

   A. 35-40   B. 50-60   C. 65-75   D. 85-100

8. Each of the following is a primary factor in the pricing of finishing hardware EXCEPT 8.____

   A. finish   B. size   C. quality   D. use

9. What is the nominal length, in inches, of most ordered studs? 9.____

   A. 48   B. 60   C. 72   D. 96

10. The bottom member of a window assembly, which forms the sill, is the 10.____

    A. stringer   B. riser   C. slump   D. stool

11. For how many hours should a *D label* fire door be able to withstand continuous fire exposure? 11.____

    A. 3/4   B. 1   C. 1 1/2   D. 3

12. What type of window frame is anodized?

    A. Steel   B. Aluminum   C. Bronze   D. Wood

13. On average, the cost of materials for a job will be about _____ % of the total job cost.

    A. 15   B. 35   C. 55   D. 85

14. Each of the following means is used to secure vertical metal studs to wall plates EXCEPT

    A. sheet metal screws   B. spot welding
    C. tie wire   D. soldering

15. How much time should be estimated for the installation of a fire door and frame?

    A. 30 minutes   B. 1 hour
    C. 2 hours   D. 4 hours

16. Which of the following would NOT be a color of grade A asphalt tile?

    A. Black   B. Green   C. Yellow   D. Brown

17. Concrete for on-grade floor installations should typically have an aggregate size of not more than _____ inch.

    A. 1/4   B. 1/2   C. 3/4   D. 1

18. Which type of estimate is MOST often used with change orders?

    A. Quantity survey
    B. Lump-sum amount
    C. Cost-per-square-foot estimate
    D. Unit cost estimate

19. Which of the following types of glass will be LEAST expensive?

    A. Grade B sheet
    B. 1/4" wire glass
    C. Mirror
    D. 1/8" patterned *obscure* glass

20. According to established finish-designation standards, which of the following finish materials would be ranked at the HIGHEST grade?

    A. Chromium-plated   B. Bright bronze
    C. Stainless steel   D. Lacquered satin aluminum

21. What is represented by the mechanical symbol shown at the right?

    A. Door   B. Scale trap
    C. Strainer   D. T connection

22. Most metal roofs require a waterproof underlayment that weighs about _____ pounds per 100 square feet of roof area.

    A. 30   B. 60   C. 100   D. 125

23. A material used over a rough subfloor that will provide a smooth surface for the finish floor is termed a(n)

    A. soffit
    B. underlayment
    C. vapor barrier
    D. molding

24. Approximately how many square feet of wood strip flooring can be installed in one hour?

    A. 50   B. 125   C. 225   D. 300

25. The scale of a typical site plans uses 1/4" to represent

    A. 1 inch   B. 1 foot   C. 25 feet   D. 100 feet

KEY (CORRECT ANSWERS)

1. C		11. C	
2. D		12. B	
3. D		13. D	
4. B		14. D	
5. C		15. B	
6. B		16. C	
7. A		17. C	
8. B		18. B	
9. D		19. A	
10. D		20. C	

21. C
22. A
23. B
24. D
25. D

EXAMINATION SECTION
TEST 1

DIRECTIONS: Each question or incomplete statement is followed by several suggested answers or completions. Select the one that BEST answers the question or completes the statement. *PRINT THE LETTER OF THE CORRECT ANSWER IN THE SPACE AT THE RIGHT.*

1. To frame out a stair well, you need headers, 1.____

    A. trimmers, tail beams, and bridal irons
    B. trimmers, tail beams, and jacks
    C. trimmers, jacks, and bridal irons
    D. jacks, tail beams, and bridal irons

2. If it takes about 30 lbs. of 8-penny nails to nail 1000 board feet of finish flooring, the number of pounds of nails needed for the flooring in a 12' x 14' room is MOST NEARLY 2.____

    A. 4 B. 4½ C. 5 D. 5½

3. In construction drawings, the arrangement of members in a door frame is MOST frequently shown in a(n) 3.____

    A. plan view   B. section
    C. elevation   D. front view

4. A hollow ground blade would USUALLY be used on a circular saw for 4.____

    A. smooth cutting   B. rough cross cutting
    C. cutting dados   D. cutting old flooring

5. When erecting a 2" x 4" stud partition, the size of nail that should be used to toe-nail the stud to the sole plate is a _____ -penny. 5.____

    A. six B. eight C. ten D. twelve

6. A blade for use with a diamond-shaped arbor is MOST frequently found on a _____ saw. 6.____

    A. jig   B. portable circular
    C. band   D. sabre

7. The one of the following that is NOT a common type of wood joint is a 7.____

    A. chamfer B. rabbet C. dado D. butt

8. To determine whether the edge of a board has been planed square, it is BEST to use a _____ square. 8.____

    A. parallel B. try C. rafter D. T

9. To prevent splintering of wood when planing end grain, it is BEST to plane from 9.____

    A. one edge of the wood to the opposite edge, parallel to the longer edge
    B. one edge of the wood to the opposite edge, parallel to the shorter edge
    C. opposite edges of the wood to the center
    D. the center of the wood to opposite edges

10. The number of teeth per inch on a backsaw is MOST frequently 10.___
    A. 6   B. 10   C. 14   D. 18

11. The number stamped on the shank of an auger bit refers to the size of the bit in _____ 11.___
    of an inch.
    A. 64ths   B. 32nds   C. 16ths   D. 8ths

12. A line level is MOST frequently used with a 12.___
    A. plumb bob   B. piece of string
    C. transit   D. tape

13. A gouge differs from a wood chisel PRINCIPALLY in that the blade on the gouge is 13.___
    A. curved
    B. longer
    C. shorter
    D. set at an angle to the handle

14. The FIRST operation in properly sharpening a hand saw is 14.___
    A. shaping   B. jointing   C. filing   D. setting

15. A compass saw MOST closely resembles, in appearance, a _____ saw. 15.___
    A. dovetail   B. coping   C. turning   D. keyhole

16. The size of a claw hammer refers to the _____ of the _____. 16.___
    A. length; head   B. diameter; face
    C. length; handle   D. weight; head

17. The one of the following power tools that has two tables, one lower than the other, is a 17.___
    A. radial saw   B. jointer
    C. shaper   D. router

18. The one of the following types of nails that is MOST frequently used to anchor wood to 18.___
    masonry is a
    A. cut-nail   B. brad   C. wire nail   D. spike

19. One of the distinguishing features of a carriage bolt is that 19.___
    A. the head has a slot so that it can be driven with a screwdriver
    B. part of the body of the bolt, next to the head, is of square cross-section
    C. the entire body of the bolt from tip to head is threaded
    D. the head is square so that it can be turned with a wrench

20. A dog on a woodworking vise is used in conjunction with a 20.___
    A. bar clamp   B. brace
    C. bench stop   D. back bar

21. The type of wood used for finish flooring in apartments is MOST frequently 21.___
    A. pine   B. fir   C. walnut   D. oak

22. Interior trim is MOST frequently made of   22.____

    A. cedar   B. pine   C. hemlock   D. cypress

23. A *check* in lumber is caused by   23.____

    A. improper drying   B. exposure to rain
    C. too great a stress   D. a fungus

24. A *kerf* is made by a   24.____

    A. hammer   B. saw   C. chisel   D. plane

25. The term *dressed and matched* means the same as   25.____

    A. mortise and tenon   B. miter and spline
    C. dado and rabbet   D. tongue and groove

26. When framing a door opening, the wedging allowance between the trimmer stud and the side jamb is MOST frequently   26.____

    A. 1/8"   B. 1/2"   C. 1"   D. 1¼"

27. The purpose of bridging is to distribute the load   27.____

    A. over a window   B. to adjoining rafters
    C. over a door   D. to adjoining joists

28. A bird's mouth cut is USUALLY found on a   28.____

    A. joist   B. stud   C. lintel   D. rafter

29. The BEST tool to use in laying out the cuts on a rafter is a _____ square.   29.____

    A. T   B. try
    C. combination   D. framing

30. The MAIN purpose of flashing is to   30.____

    A. reflect the sun's rays   B. prevent leakage
    C. insulate walls   D. strengthen sheathing

31. The type of glue that MUST be heated before using is _____ glue.   31.____

    A. animal   B. casein   C. resin   D. contact

32. A *parting stop* is usually found   32.____

    A. between the ceiling of one story and the floor directly above
    B. between sash in a double hung window
    C. as part of a door jamb in a swinging door
    D. along the ridge in a hip roof

33. As applied to stair construction, a *carriage* is the same as a   33.____

    A. riser   B. tread   C. stringer   D. cleat

34. When laying out stairs, the product of the number of inches in the tread, exclusive of nosing, and the number of inches in the riser should be less than

    A. 60   B. 65   C. 70   D. 75

35. Both doors and windows have

    A. lock rails   B. mullions
    C. stiles   D. meeting rails

36. The chiseled out portion of a door to which the butt of a hinge is fitted is called a

    A. rabbet   B. gain   C. mortise   D. set-back

37. The one of the following tools that should be used to cut a rabbet on a curved piece of wood is a

    A. shaper   B. jointer
    C. circular saw   D. lathe

38. Assume that the rise between two floor levels is 9'0". It is required to construct a stair between these two floors with risers that have a maximum height of 7 ½".
    The SMALLEST number of risers that will satisfy this requirement is

    A. 12   B. 13   C. 14   D. 15

39. Zinc coated nails are often used in preference to ordinary nails MAINLY because they are

    A. easier to drive   B. harder to pull out
    C. stronger   D. more weather resistant

40. Of the following, the quality of white ash that is MOST important is its

    A. light weight
    B. high resistance to shock
    C. curly grain
    D. strength when wet

41. The thickness of finished maple flooring is MOST frequently

    A. 3/8"   B. 1/2"   C. 25/32"   D. 15/16"

42. Nails driven into 3/4" plywood, as compared to similar nails driven into 3/4" solid lumber made of the same grade of wood, are

    A. harder to pull out
    B. easier to pull out
    C. just as difficult to pull out
    D. harder or easier to pull out, depending on the number of plies in the plywood

43. The term *plain sawed* refers to the _____ board.

    A. direction of the grain with respect to the face of a
    B. machine that is used to cut the
    C. shape of the edge of a
    D. thickness of a

44. The one of the following that is a standard grade for a douglas fir plywood panel is

    A. #1 common   B. select
    C. A & C   D. construction

45. A gutter on a frame house is MOST frequently attached to a

    A. fascia   B. drip   C. flashing   D. header

46. When it is necessary to match the cut in a plywood or sheetrock wall panel to an existing irregular wall, the method that is MOST commonly used is called

    A. matching   B. equalling
    C. lining   D. scribing

47. The one of the following that is part of a door casing is a

    A. head frame   B. back band
    C. sill plate   D. stud

48. A ground

    A. is used as a guide for plastering
    B. supports the studs in a partition
    C. is the lowest piece of trim on a wall
    D. prevents the lowest riser in a stair from moving out

49. The one of the following wood screws that is MOST frequently countersunk is a _____ head.

    A. flat   B. round   C. binding   D. pan

50. Commercial standards distinguish a softwood from a hardwood according to

    A. the ease with which the wood can be carved
    B. the weight of the wood
    C. whether the wood can be bent in a short arc
    D. the type of tree from which the wood comes

KEY (CORRECT ANSWERS)

1. A	11. C	21. D	31. A	41. C
2. C	12. B	22. B	32. B	42. B
3. B	13. A	23. A	33. C	43. A
4. A	14. B	24. B	34. D	44. C
5. C	15. D	25. D	35. C	45. A
6. B	16. D	26. B	36. B	46. D
7. A	17. B	27. D	37. A	47. B
8. B	18. A	28. D	38. D	48. A
9. C	19. B	29. D	39. D	49. A
10. C	20. C	30. B	40. B	50. D

TEST 2

DIRECTIONS: Each question or incomplete statement is followed by several suggested answers or completions. Select the one that BEST answers the question or completes the statement. *PRINT THE LETTER OF THE CORRECT ANSWER IN THE SPACE AT THE RIGHT.*

1. Where floor joists rest on a masonry wall, they should have a minimum bearing of _____ inches.

    A. 3 B. 4 C. 5 D. 6

2. Expansion shields would be used to

    A. protect exterior corners of walls
    B. provide a base for plaster
    C. protect a ceiling over a boiler
    D. anchor an object to a brick wall

3. When framing a window for use with a spring balance such as a *unique balance*, the allowance for pulley pockets is USUALLY

    A. smaller than when a sash weight is used
    B. the same as when a sash weight is used
    C. greater than when a sash weight is used
    D. completely eliminated

4. Plywood used for sheathing is MOST frequently _____ thick.

    A. 1/4" B. 5/16" C. 3/8" D. 1/2"

5. The BEST size hinge to use for an exterior door measuring 1 3/8" thick and 36" wide is

    A. 3' x 3" B. 3" x 3½" C. 3½" x 4" D. 4" x 4"

6. The MOST frequent method of framing a 2" x 4" partition over a small window is to _____ over the window.

    A. add a steel lintel   B. truss the wall
    C. double the headers   D. use hangers

7. Batter boards are MOST frequently used to

    A. establish corners for new construction
    B. determine the pitch of rafters
    C. support concrete forms
    D. brace stud partitions

8. A steel square would MOST frequently be used to lay out

    A. stud lengths in a partition
    B. casings for a door
    C. treads and risers for a staircase
    D. cuts for a mortise and tenon joint

9. Pumice stone is VERY often used in

   A. finishing furniture
   B. honing tools
   C. setting bolts
   D. smoothing concrete

10. Hand screws are USUALLY used when

    A. hanging shelves from a hollow partition
    B. glueing two pieces of wood together
    C. connecting sheet metal to wood
    D. erecting plywood walls

11. The MAIN reason for *setting* the teeth on a saw is to

    A. prevent the saw from binding
    B. permit the saw to make an even cut
    C. allow the saw to cut across the grain as well as with the grain
    D. eliminate the possibility of the *saw jumping* out of the cut

12. Assume that a peaked roof, with a 1/4 pitch, has a run of 12 ft. The rise is

    A. 3'   B. 4'   C. 5'   D. 6'

13. A dovetail saw MOST closely resembles a _____ saw.

    A. keyhole   B. compass   C. back   D. rip

14. The one of the following that is part of a window trim is a(n)

    A. astragal   B. apron   C. panel   D. butt

15. Ship lap boards are USUALLY used as

    A. sills   B. plates   C. fascia   D. shingles

16. A plow MOST NEARLY resembles a

    A. mortise   B. dado   C. miter   D. spline

17. The one of the following types of wood that has the MOST open grain is

    A. pine   B. maple   C. oak   D. birch

18. Wood is usually treated in a kiln for the purpose of

    A. fireproofing it
    B. seasoning it
    C. preserving the wood against dampness
    D. termite-proofing it

19. The wood MOST commonly used for shingles in the East is

    A. cypress   B. birch   C. cedar   D. spruce

20. Lag screws are USUALLY driven by using a

    A. wrench
    B. screwdriver
    C. hammer
    D. brace

21. The one of the following that should be used for the final smoothing of wood before applying lacquer is   21.____

    A. #1/2 garnet paper B. a fine wood rasp
    C. 000 steel wool   D. 80 grit emery cloth

22. The total number of board feet in 18 2x4's, each measuring 8 ft. long, is MOST NEARLY   22.____

    A. 90   B. 92   C. 96   D. 100

23. A *fire cut* is NORMALLY made on   23.____

    A. studs   B. joists   C. rafters   D. plates

24. A *nail set* is a   24.____

    A. group of the same type of nails in different sizes
    B. group of different types of nails in the same size
    C. tool used to pull nails
    D. tool used to countersink nails

25. Auger bits are BEST sharpened by using a   25.____

    A. grinding wheel   B. file
    C. slip stone   D. whetstone

26. Casing nails are MOST similar in appearance to _____ nails.   26.____

    A. roofing   B. common
    C. finishing D. cut

27. A water level can be made by using   27.____

    A. two glass tubes and a rubber hose
    B. a mason's level and two eye sights
    C. a pitch board and a mason's level
    D. a pitch board and a rubber hose

28. The purpose of a vapor barrier is to   28.____

    A. prevent rain from entering a building through the wall
    B. protect the exterior wall of a building from moisture already inside the building
    C. prevent condensation of water in a cellar
    D. protect a building from ground water

29. Narrow boards are better for floor boards than wide boards of the same grade of lumber PRINCIPALLY because the narrow boards   29.____

    A. cost less
    B. are easier to lay
    C. are stronger
    D. have less tendency to warp

30. 1" x 6" subflooring is USUALLY applied diagonally to the joists rather than perpendicular to the joists PRINCIPALLY because subflooring applied diagonally   30.____

    A. costs less   B. is easier to lay
    C. is stronger   D. warps less

31. A purlin USUALLY supports

    A. rafters B. sheathing C. joists D. studs

32. Insulation board is MOST frequently used as

    A. sheathing
    B. subflooring
    C. siding
    D. scantling

33. The one of the following that is NOT a type of rafter is a

    A. hip B. valley C. jack D. tail

34. Lath is USUALLY used as a base for

    A. roofing
    B. plaster
    C. waterproofing
    D. insulation

35. A cricket is USUALLY located

    A. at the base of a parapet wall
    B. over an exterior door
    C. between the sill and the foundation
    D. in a non-bearing partition

36. The term *gambrel* refers to a type of

    A. window B. roof C. door D. floor

37. Wainscoting is part of the finish of

    A. floors B. ceiling C. walls D. doors

38. *Construction Grade* lumber is LEAST frequently used for

    A. joists B. rafters C. studs D. girders

39. A strip of board that is used to fasten several pieces of lumber together is called a

    A. band B. bracket C. girt D. cleat

40. Building paper is MOST often used to

    A. waterproof foundations
    B. insulate walls
    C. deaden sound
    D. protect floors during painting

41. One of the MAIN reasons for using furring strips is to

    A. fire retard a stairwell
    B. support floor joists
    C. provide clearance around a chimney
    D. permit building a straight ceiling

42. A *built up* girder USUALLY refers to a girder that is   42._____

   A. supported on posts
   B. cut to size at the building
   C. braced in position to prevent twisting
   D. made up of several pieces of wood fastened together

Questions 43-45.

DIRECTIONS: Questions 43 through 45, inclusive, are to be answered in accordance with the following paragraph.

Wherever a soil pipe has to be provided for in a partition, special care must be taken that the hubs do not project beyond the finish face of the plaster. Before framing a building, it is desirable to ascertain where the stacks are and to provide for them. Building regulations require the stacks to be of 4-inch cast-iron even in small dwellings. With a 4-inch stack, the hub is 6 1/8 inches in diameter and, therefore, 2 by 6 studs must be used. Special care should be taken that no plaster comes in contact with a soil pipe, for subsequent settlement may cause cracking.

43. As used in the paragraph above, *subsequent* means MOST NEARLY   43._____

   A. heavy   B. sudden   C. later   D. soon

44. According to the above paragraph, 4" cast-iron soil pipes are used because   44._____

   A. they will not project beyond the face of the plaster
   B. it is easier to plaster over 4" pipe
   C. they can be located easier
   D. they are required by law

45. According to the above paragraph, the reason plaster should NOT be in direct contact with soil pipe is because   45._____

   A. the plaster will be damaged by moisture
   B. rust will bleed through the plaster
   C. of the possibility of cracks due to settlement
   D. it is harder to plaster over 4" pipe

Questions 46-50.

DIRECTIONS: Questions 46 through 50, inclusive, refer to the floor plan of the building shown on the following page.

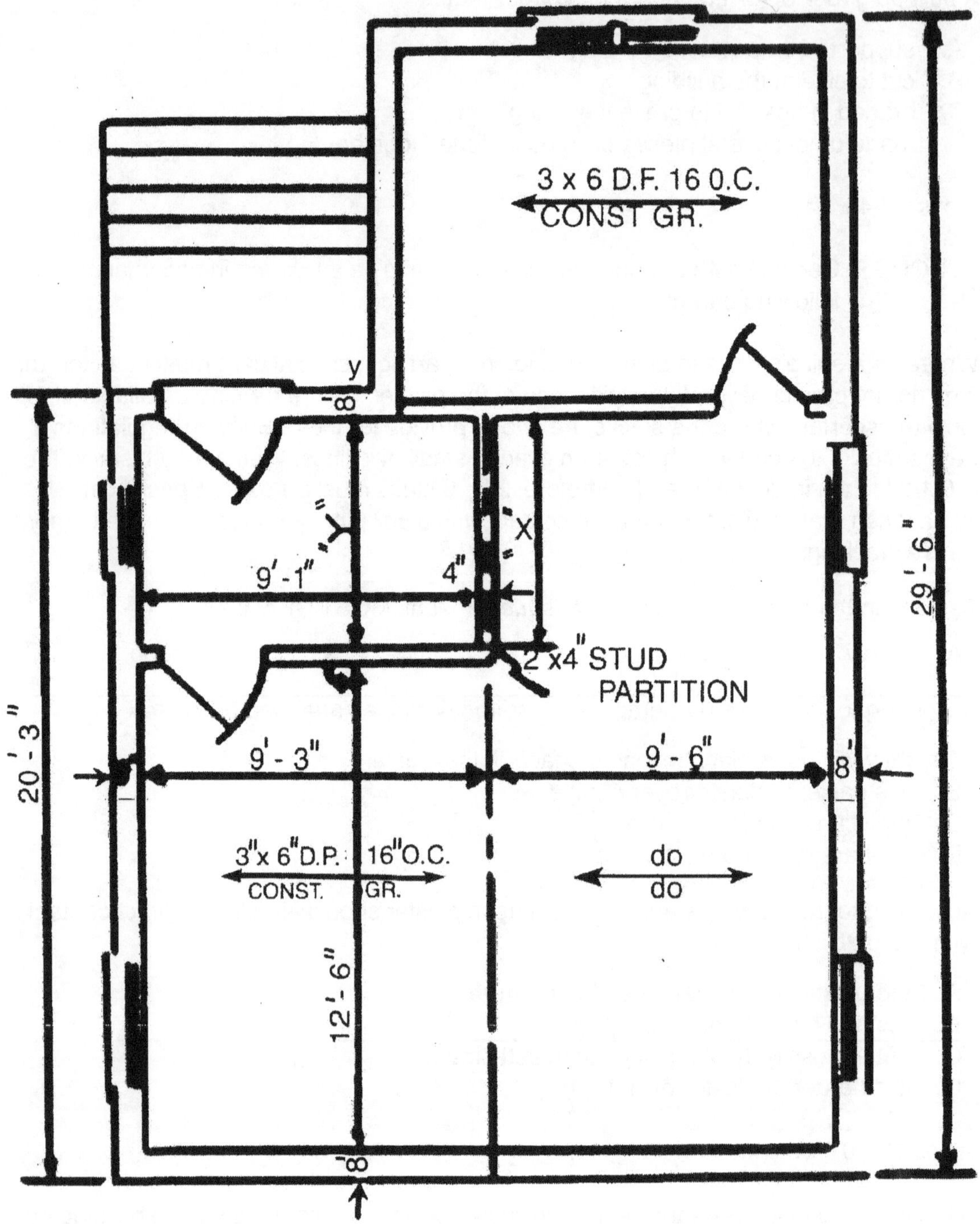

6 (#2)

46. The dimension of the vestibule indicated by y is   46.____

    A. 6'0"   B. 6'1"   C. 6'2"   D. 6'3"

47. The number of risers indicated in the steps is   47.____

    A. 2   B. 3   C. 4   D. 5

48. The area of the large room, in square feet, is MOST NEARLY 48._____

   A. 292 B. 294 C. 296 D. 298

49. The letters D.F. over the arrow mean 49._____

   A. Douglas fir
   B. diagonal subflooring
   C. doubled joists
   D. deafening finish

50. If studs are placed a maximum of 16" on centers, the minimum number of studs required in the section of wall marked X is 50._____

   A. 4 B. 5 C. 6 D. 7

KEY (CORRECT ANSWERS)

1. B	11. A	21. C	31. B	41. D
2. D	12. D	22. C	32. A	42. D
3. D	13. C	23. B	33. D	43. C
4. B	14. B	24. D	34. B	44. D
5. D	15. D	25. B	35. A	45. C
6. C	16. B	26. C	36. B	46. B
7. A	17. C	27. A	37. C	47. D
8. C	18. B	28. B	38. C	48. B
9. A	19. C	29. D	39. D	49. A
10. B	20. A	30. C	40. B	50. C

94

EXAMINATION SECTION
TEST 1

DIRECTIONS: Each question or incomplete statement is followed by several suggested answers or completions. Select the one that BEST answers the question or completes the statement. *PRINT THE LETTER OF THE CORRECT ANSWER IN THE SPACE AT THE RIGHT.*

1. The tool MOST frequently used to lay out a 45° angle on a piece of lumber is a   1.____
   - A. combination square
   - B. try square
   - C. marking gauge
   - D. divider

2. Beeswax would be MOST FREQUENTLY used on a(n)   2.____
   - A. auger bit
   - B. scraper
   - C. hand saw
   - D. draw knife

3. A tool used to plane concave edges of furniture is a   3.____
   - A. rabbet plane
   - B. wood scraper
   - C. utility knife
   - D. spoke saw

4. A cap is found on a   4.____
   - A. hammer
   - B. plane
   - C. power saw
   - D. lathe

5. The one of the following types of saw blades that is NOT commonly used on a circular saw is a   5.____
   - A. dado
   - B. ply-tooth
   - C. novelty
   - D. tyler

6. The diameter of the arbor of a 12" circular saw is MOST LIKELY to be   6.____
   - A. 3/8"
   - B. 1/2"
   - C. 5/8"
   - D. 3/4"

7. The one of the following woodworking operations that is NOT easily done on a drill press is   7.____
   - A. routing
   - B. turning
   - C. shaping
   - D. mortising

8. A jointer may ALSO be used for   8.____
   - A. mortising
   - B. routing
   - C. planing
   - D. shaping

9. The one of the following power tools that is NOT frequently built with a slot for a miter guage is a   9.____
   - A. shaper
   - B. band saw
   - C. disc sander
   - D. radial saw

10. The abrasive grit on *sandpaper* is USUALLY   10.____
    - A. pumice
    - B. boron
    - C. flint
    - D. talc

11. The abrasive grit on *open coat* paper for use on a power sander for woodwork is USUALLY   11.____
    - A. tripoli
    - B. emery
    - C. aluminum oxide
    - D. carborundum

12. The one of the following used in finishing furniture that has the FINEST grit is

   A. garnet
   B. carborundum
   C. pumice
   D. rottenstone

13. An expansive bit should be sharpened with a(n)

   A. auger bit file
   B. mill file
   C. half round file
   D. grinding wheel

14. The one of the following planes that is USUALLY used with one hand is the

   A. smoothing   B. block   C. jack   D. fore

15. When sharpening a hand saw, the FIRST operation is to file the teeth so that they are all the same height.
    This is known as

   A. shaping   B. setting   C. jointing   D. leveling

16. The tool that would be used to cut out a circular disc is a

   A. circular saw
   B. shaper
   C. planer
   D. band saw

17. A scale on which the inch graduations are divided into 12 subdivisions, each 1/12 of an inch in length, is USUALLY found on a _____ square.

   A. try
   B. combination
   C. rafter
   D. T

18. The one of the following oils that is COMMONLY used for oilstones is

   A. penetrating
   B. SAE #5
   C. vinsol
   D. pike

19. A tool used in hanging doors is a

   A. butt gauge   B. reamer   C. C-clamp   D. trammel

20. A spur center is used on a

   A. jigsaw
   B. drill press
   C. lathe
   D. disc sander

21. The length of a certain screw is measured from the top of the head to the point.
    The type of screw that this is MOST LIKELY to be is a

   A. round head   B. flat head   C. oval head   D. lag

22. The size of the drill that would be used to drill a body hole for a #7 wood screw is

   A. 3/32"   B. 5/32"   C. 7/32"   D. 9/32"

23. The one of the following types of bolts that would be used to anchor a shelf bracket to a plywood partition is a

   A. carriage   B. expansion   C. drift   D. toggle

24. For ease in driving, screws are FREQUENTLY coated with 24.____
    A. casco   B. oil   C. soap   D. urea resins

25. The length of a 10-penny nail is 25.____
    A. 3"   B. 3 1/4"   C. 3 1/2"   D. 3 3/4"

26. To increase the holding power of nails, the nails are FREQUENTLY coated with 26.____
    A. alundum   B. aluminum   C. zinc   D. cement

27. Galvanized nails would MOST PROBABLY be used in nailing 27.____
    A. shingles
    B. finished flooring
    C. joists
    D. interior trim

28. Splitting of wood can be reduced by using nails with points that are 28.____
    A. long and sharp
    B. blunt
    C. spirally grooved
    D. common

29. The standard size of a 2" X 6" S4S is 29.____
    A. 1 5/8" X 5 5/8"
    B. 1 5/8" X 5 3/4"
    C. 1 1/2" X 5 1/2"
    D. 1 1/2" X 5 5/8"

30. The West Coast Lumber Inspection Bureau has recently changed the names of the grades of lumber for Douglas Fir and Hemlock. 30.____
    The grade that was PREVIOUSLY called No. 1 common is NOW called
    A. construction
    B. utility
    C. select
    D. structural

31. The strength of lumber is affected by 31.____
    A. whether it is cut from a live tree or a dead tree
    B. the time of the year in which the lumber is cut
    C. whether the tree is virgin growth or second growth
    D. the moisture content of the lumber

32. The one of the following woods that is classed as *open grained* is 32.____
    A. douglas fir
    B. long leaf yellow pine
    C. spruce
    D. oak

33. The one of the following woods that is classed as a hardwood is 33.____
    A. cedar
    B. poplar
    C. douglas fir
    D. hemlock

34. The one of the following woods that is MOST difficult to work with hand tools is 34.____
    A. cedar, northern white
    B. pine, southern yellow
    C. hemlock, western
    D. cypress, southern

35. The one of the following heartwoods that has the GREATEST resistance to decay is 35.____
    A. douglas fir   B. spruce   C. oak   D. birch

36. The one of the following woods that is EASIEST to glue is 36.____
    A. beech   B. birch   C. cedar   D. walnut

37. Flooring, for surfaces that will have very heavy wear, such as gymnasiums, is USUALLY 37.____
    made of
    A. oak   B. maple
    C. long leaf yellow pine   D. larch

38. The BEST grades of finished flooring are _____ sawed. 38.____
    A. quarter   B. flat   C. end   D. plain

39. Lumber used for floor joists in the East is USUALLY 39.____
    A. oak   B. gum   C. hemlock   D. pine

40. The wood MOST COMMONLY used for shingles is 40.____
    A. alder   B. larch   C. cedar   D. spruce

41. Millwork is USUALLY made of 41.____
    A. ash   B. chestnut   C. hemlock   D. pine

42. The wood MOST FREQUENTLY used for the rungs of the BEST quality ladders is 42.____
    A. locust   B. hickory   C. oak   D. balsam

43. Dressed and matched lumber would MOST LIKELY be 43.____
    A. dove-tailed   B. bevel siding
    C. crown molding   D. tongue and groove

44. Creosote is used to 44.____
    A. intensify the grain of wood prior to finishing
    B. preserve wood from rot
    C. glue wood in laminated girders
    D. prevent checking

45. The one of the following that is COMMONLY used as a vapor barrier is 45.____
    A. asphalt roll roofing   B. Kraft paper
    C. plywood   D. gypsum board

46. Corners of a building are USUALLY located by means of 46.____
    A. batter boards   B. framing squares
    C. line levels   D. base plates

47. Horizontal beams used to reinforce concrete forms and sheet piling are known as 47.____
    A. stirrups   B. walers   C. sheathing   D. braces

48. When using a post to shore a form for a reinforced concrete girder, the BEST practice is to cut the post

    A. to exact length, so that no driving will be required
    B. slightly larger than required, so that the post must be driven into place
    C. with a slight bevel, so that the post can be wedged into place
    D. several inches too short, so that wedges will be needed

49. Corner posts of a frame building in the East MUST be at least the equivalent of three _____ inch timbers.

    A. 2X4   B. 2X6   C. 3X6   D. 4X4

50. The size of cross bridging between joists is MOST FREQUENTLY

    A. 1" X 2"   B. 1" X 3"   C. 2" X 4"   D. 2" X 6"

KEY (CORRECT ANSWERS)

1. A	11. C	21. B	31. D	41. D
2. C	12. D	22. B	32. D	42. B
3. D	13. A	23. D	33. B	43. D
4. B	14. B	24. C	34. B	44. B
5. D	15. C	25. A	35. A	45. A
6. D	16. D	26. D	36. C	46. A
7. B	17. C	27. A	37. B	47. B
8. C	18. D	28. B	38. A	48. D
9. D	19. A	29. A	39. C	49. A
10. C	20. C	30. A	40. C	50. B

TEST 2

DIRECTIONS: Each question or incomplete statement is followed by several suggested answers or completions. Select the one that BEST answers the question or completes the statement. *PRINT THE LETTER OF THE CORRECT ANSWER IN THE SPACE AT THE RIGHT.*

1. The MAXIMUM spacing between bridging should be

    A. 6 ft. B. 8 ft. C. 10 ft. D. 12 ft.

2. The one of the following methods of nailing cross bridging that is the MOST ACCEPTABLE is

    A. the tops and bottoms should be nailed before the subflooring is in place
    B. the tops and bottoms should be nailed after the subflooring is in place
    C. *only* the bottoms should be nailed. The tops should be nailed after the subflooring is in place
    D. *only* the tops should be nailed. The bottoms should be nailed after the subflooring is in place

3. The one of the following that may be used as a shim to raise the end of a joist resting on a concrete wall is

    A. gypsum block B. wood
    C. sheet rock   D. slate

4. When framing joists around a chimney, the MINIMUM clear distance from wood to the chimney permitted in the East is

    A. 4" B. 6" C. 8" D. 10"

5. The ends of joists are FREQUENTLY supported on

    A. hanger bolts B. tie plates
    C. bridle irons D. gusset plates

6. When there is a tight knot in a joist, the joist should

    A. be placed with the knot up
    B. be placed with the knot down
    C. be reinforced
    D. not be used

7.

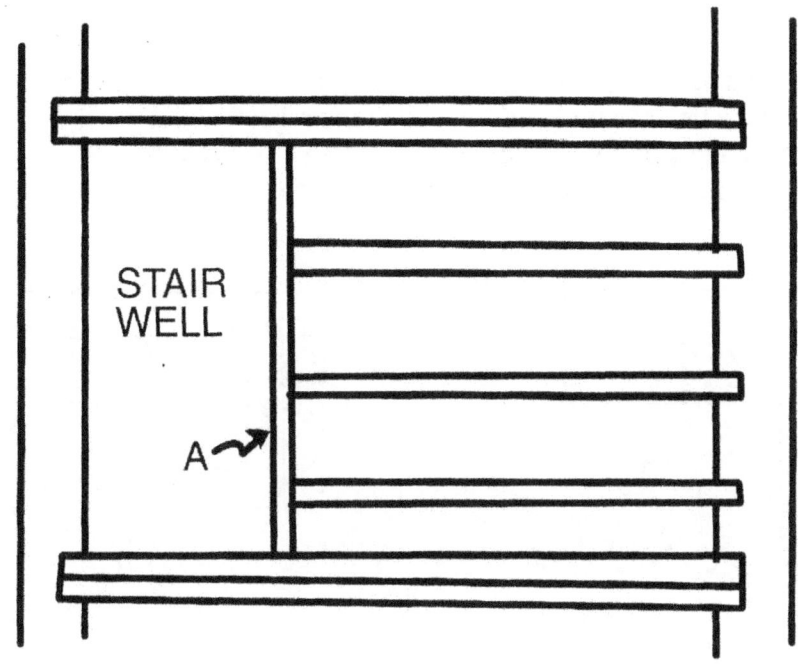

The short joist indicated by the letter A above is known as

A. trimmer   B. tail beam   C. header   D. lattice

8.

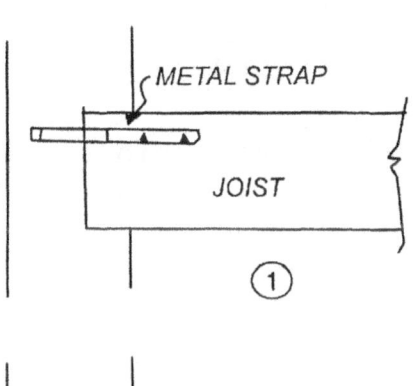
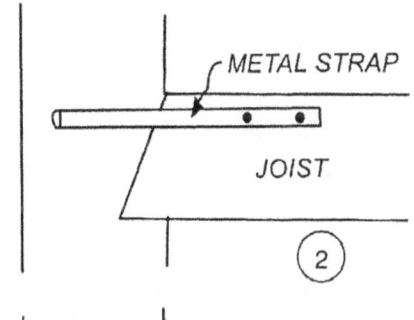
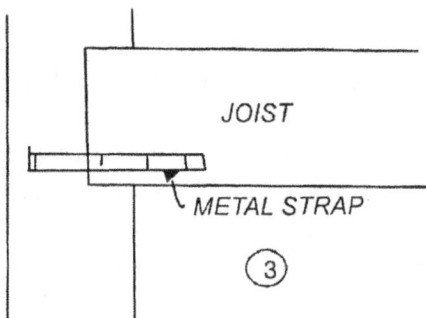
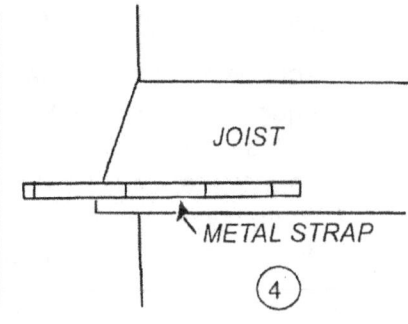

The diagram above that shows the BEST method of anchoring a wood joist to a brick is numbered

A. 1   B. 2   C. 3   D. 4

9. Where a non bearing partition runs over and is parallel to the joists, standard practice requires that

   A. a post be placed midway under the joist supporting the partition
   B. sag rods be used to transfer the load to the adjoining joists
   C. the joist directly under the partition be increased in depth
   D. the joist directly under the partition be doubled

10.

The diagram above that shows the BEST method of supporting a joist on a girder is numbered

   A. 1   B. 2   C. 3   D. 4

11. The one of the following statements that is CORRECT when *roofers* are used for sub-flooring is diagonal subflooring

   A. requires less lumber than subflooring applied at right angles to the joists
   B. requires approximately the same amount of lumber as subflooring applied at right angles to the joists
   C. requires more lumber than subflooring applied at right angles to the joists
   D. may require more or less lumber than subflooring applied at right angles to the joists, depending on the dimensions of the building

12. A timber laid directly on the ground or on a concrete base to support a floor is called a

   A. sleeper   B. sizing   C. rail   D. ledger board

13. Diagonal subflooring is preferred to subflooring laid square across the joists because the diagonal subflooring

    A. stiffens the building
    B. is easier to lay
    C. is more economical to lay
    D. does not require as much nailing

14. A meeting rail is usually found on a

    A. stair   B. door   C. roof   D. window

15. The size of a sill plate, for a frame building, laid on a continuous concrete wall in the East is USUALLY

    A. 4" X 6"   B. 4" X 10"   C. 2" X 10"   D. 2" X 8"

16. A valley is made watertight by means of a

    A. cornice   B. flashing   C. drip sill   D. furring

17. A strip of wood whose purpose is to assist the plasterers to make a straight wall is called a

    A. casing   B. ground
    C. belt course   D. gauge

18. A hip rafter is framed between

    A. plate and ridge   B. plate and valley
    C. valley and ridge   D. valley and overhang

19. 2" X 8" rafters are being used on a roof with a pitch of one quarter. The size of ridge board that would MOST PROBABLY be used is

    A. 2" X 8"   B. 3" X 8"   C. 2" X 10"   D. 2" X 12"

20. When planks intended to be used for roof rafters are not straight, the one of the following statements that is CORRECT is

    A. all rafters should be erected with the cambers (crown) up
    B. all rafters should be erected with the cambers (crown) down
    C. the rafters should be erected with the cambers (crown) alternately up and down
    D. the plank should not be used for rafters

21.

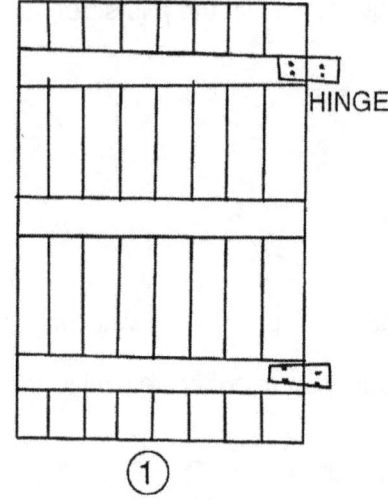

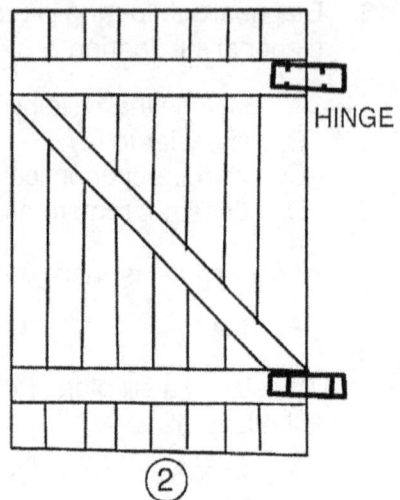

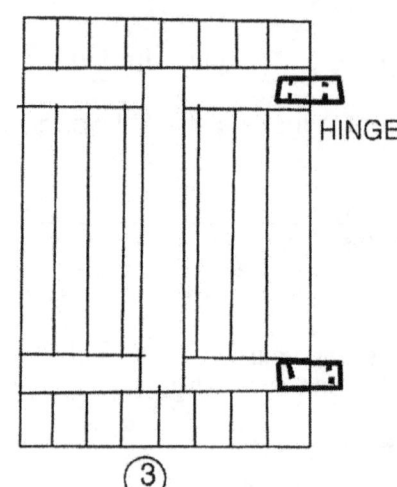

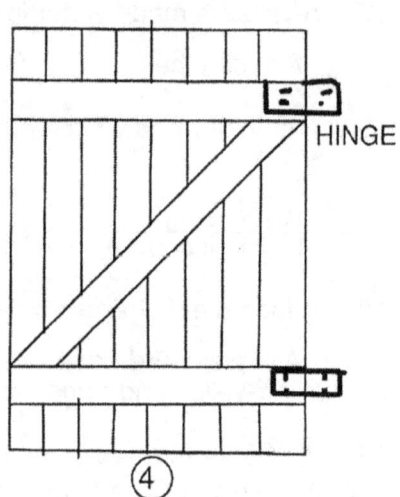

The diagram above that shows the BEST method of building a door for a shed is numbered

A. 1 B. 2 C. 3 D. 4

22. A vertical member separating two windows is called a

A. muntin B. mullion C. stile D. casing

23. Wood girders framing on a masonry wall in the East should have a MINIMUM bearing of

A. 2" B. 4" C. 6" D. 8"

24. A collar beam is used to tie

A. floor joists B. laminated girders
C. roof rafters D. columns

25. Nosing would MOST probably be found in

A. window frames B. stairs
C. saddles D. scarfs

26. To help prevent plaster cracks when a 2" X 4" stud partition is cut for a doorway, it is USUAL to

   A. provide a steel lintel B. use joint   B. hangers
   C. double the header   D. corbel the studs

27. The side support for steps or stairs is called a

   A. ledger board   B. pitch board
   C. riser   D. stringer

28. The type of joint MOST FREQUENTLY used where baseboards meet at the corner of a room is a

   A. miter   B. mortise and tenon
   C. spline   D. butt

29. The purpose of a water table is to

   A. prevent water from entering at the top of a foundation wall
   B. distribute water from a downspout directly on the ground
   C. prevent water from entering a cellar through the cellar floor
   D. prevent water from leaking through a roof at the chimney

30. The one of the following materials that will produce the MOST rigid wall is _____ sheathing.

   A. 1" X 8" horizontal
   B. 1" X 8" diagonal
   C. 29/32" fiberboard
   D. 1/4" plywood

31. Split ring connectors are COMMONLY used to

   A. anchor joists to girders
   B. join members of a truss
   C. anchor veneer to framework
   D. connect wood girder to steel column

32. A strike plate would be attached to a

   A. sill   B. fascia   C. jamb   D. saddle

33. Blanket insulation is USUALLY placed between

   A. siding and sheathing
   B. sheathing and vapor barrier
   C. vapor barrier and rock lath
   D. rock lath and finished plaster

34. A pipe column filled with concrete is called a

   A. pintle   B. buttress   C. pilaster   D. lally

35. If you were required to build forms for spandrels, the location of these forms would be at

   A. footing level between piers
   B. roof level between girders
   C. floor level between columns
   D. footing level over the grillage

36. Where a 2-inch horizontal hole must be made in a 3" X 12" floor joist supporting a uniform live load, the BEST place to make this hole is in the _____ of the joist at the _____ of the span.

   A. center; end
   B. bottom; end
   C. center; center
   D. bottom; center

37. To strengthen box corners in new furniture, common practice is to use

   A. tie rods
   B. molly bolts
   C. glue blocks
   D. webbing

38. The joint MOST frequently used for attaching the sides of drawers to the fronts is

   A. mortise and tenon
   B. doweled
   C. dovetailed
   D. splined

39. The pitch of a roof is one-sixth. If the run is 10 ft., the rise is

   A. 1'-8"   B. 3'-4"   C. 5'-0"   D. 6'-8"

40. The number of board feet in a 3" X 8", 16 ft. long, is

   A. 26   B. 28   C. 30   D. 32

41. A right triangle has sides of 5, 12, and 13 inches respectively.
    The area of the triangle, is, in square inches,

   A. 30   B. 32 1/2   C. 60   D. 78

42. The one of the following that would be the dimension used to lay out a right angle is _____ feet.

   A. 3, 4, 6   B. 4, 5, 9   C. 6, 8, 10   D. 7, 9, 13

43. A partition wall, with no openings in it, is to be 46 ft. long.
    If studs are spaced 16" o.c. maximum, the number of studs that should be used in this wall is

   A. 33   B. 34   C. 35   D. 36

44. A flight of stairs has 8 risers. The number of treads it has is

   A. 7   B. 8   C. 9   D. 10

45. A round post 4 inches in diameter and 4 feet high can carry 12,000 pounds.
    A 6-inch post of the same height, and the same grade and species of wood, can carry _____ pounds.

   A. 18,000   B. 21,000   C. 24,000   D. 27,000

8 (#2)

46. The sum of the following dimensions,
4'-3 1/4", 3'-2 15/16", 2'-3 1/2", 3'-4 3/4", 4'-7 3/16" is

   A. 17'-9 7/16"   B. 17'-9 1/2"
   C. 17'-9 9/16"   D. 17'-9 5/8"

Questions 47 - 50.

Questions 47 to 50 refer to the sketch below representing the 1st floor plan of a small tool shed.

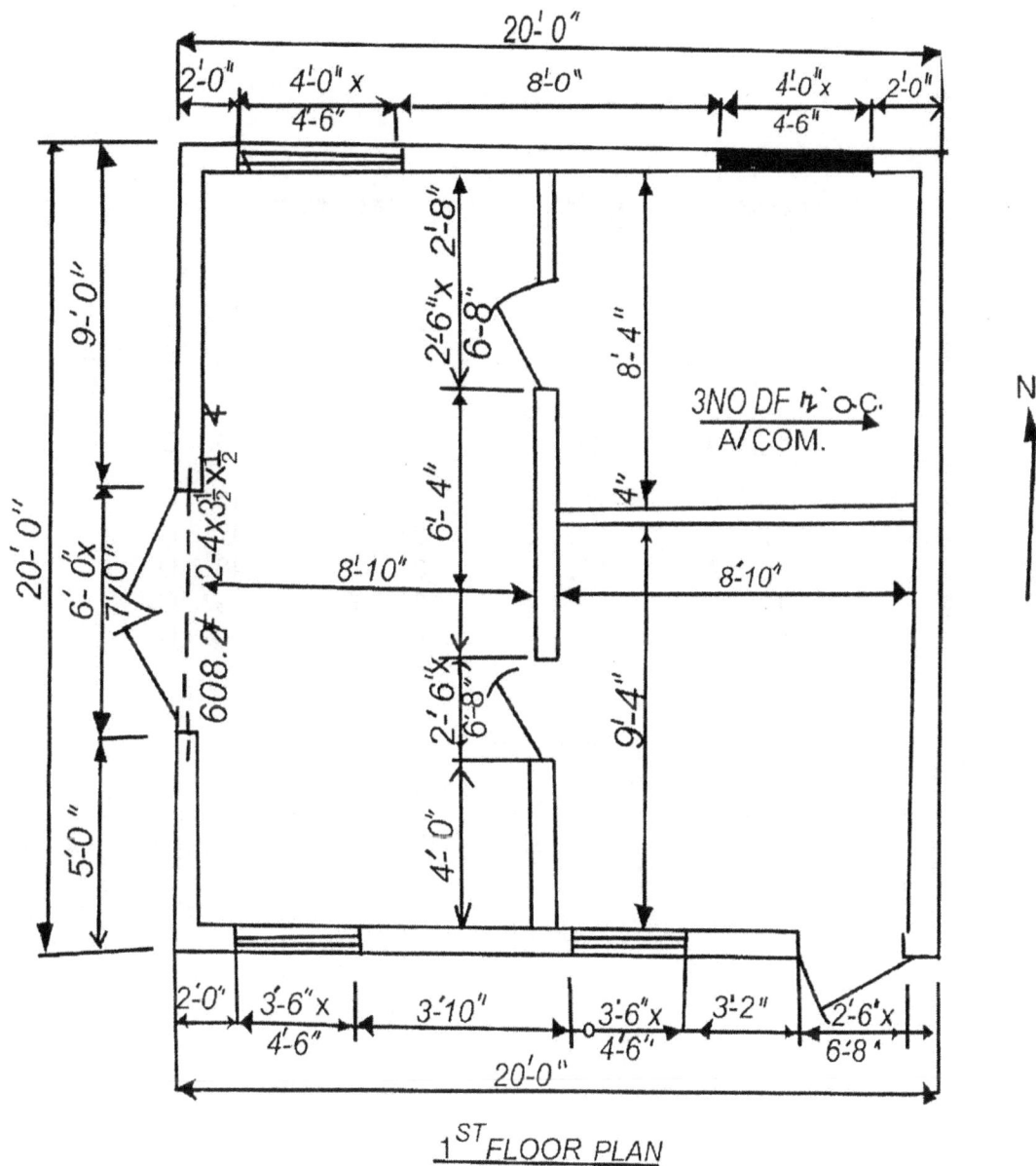

1ST FLOOR PLAN

47. The width* of the windows in the south wall of the building is

   A. 2'-6"   B. 3'-6"   C. 3'-10"   D. 4'-6"

48. The lintel over the large doorway is a

   A. single wood girder
   B. built up wood girder
   C. steel beam and plates
   D. steel channel and angles

49. The size of the LARGEST room is

   A. 8'-10" X 16'-0"
   B. 8'-10" X 17'-0"
   C. 8'-10" X 18'-0"
   D. 8'-10" X 19'-0"

50. The floor area of the SMALLEST room is, in square feet, MOST NEARLY

   A. 72
   B. 74
   C. 76
   D. 78

KEY (CORRECT ANSWERS)

1. B	11. C	21. B	31. B	41. A
2. D	12. A	22. B	32. C	42. C
3. D	13. A	23. B	33. B	43. D
4. A	14. D	24. C	34. D	44. A
5. C	15. A	25. B	35. C	45. D
6. A	16. B	26. C	36. C	46. D
7. C	17. B	27. D	37. C	47. B
8. D	18. A	28. D	38. C	48. D
9. D	19. C	29. A	39. B	49. C
10. A	20. A	30. D	40. D	50. B

EXAMINATION SECTION
TEST 1

DIRECTIONS: Each question or incomplete statement is followed by several suggested answers or completions. Select the one that BEST answers the questions or completes the statement. *PRINT THE LETTER OF THE CORRECT ANSWER IN THE SPACE AT THE RIGHT.*

1. Of the following, the FIRST operation in the demolition of a 4-story building adjacent to the property line is the 1.____

    A. erection of railings around the stairwells
    B. shoring of adjoining buildings
    C. erection of a sidewalk shed
    D. removal of windows

2. Projected sash is defined as a(n) 2.____

    A. double hung window
    B. window that opens inward or outward
    C. architectural projection from a building exterior
    D. storm window

3. Specifications for a reinforced concrete structure call for a roof fill to be placed on the concrete roof slab. Of the following, the PURPOSE of the fill is to 3.____

    A. reduce sound transmission
    B. facilitate drainage
    C. provide a smooth base for insulation
    D. protect the concrete slab

4. The Building Department requires a location survey by a licensed surveyor 4.____

    A. *only* if it is suspected that the building is not in the proper place and may impinge on adjacent property
    B. *only* of the completed foundation
    C. *only* of the completed superstructure
    D. *after* the foundation is completed and a second survey after the building is completed

5. After excavating by a contractor for a footing, the sub-grade soil appears to be below the quality shown on the borings. 5.____
   Of the following types of footings, the one that would be LEAST affected by this condition is a

    A. spread footing   B. combined footing
    C. footing on piles   D. footing and pier

6. Of the following, the information of GREATEST significance to be recorded for each pile during pile driving is the 6.____

    A. steam pressure and the temperature
    B. condition of the ground at the pile location

109

C. number of hammer blows at the last inch
D. total number of hammer blows

7. One method of dewatering an excavation for a foundation is by the use of

   A. inverted siphons
   B. well points
   C. line holes
   D. suction heads

8. An excavation for a concrete footing to support a structural steel column was dug 4" too deep.
   Of the following, the BEST construction practice would be to

   A. backfill the 4" with stone
   B. backfill the 4" with sand
   C. lower the entire footing 4"
   D. make the footing 4" thicker

9. Spudding, in a pile driving operation, is used PRIMARILY to

   A. remove a broken pile
   B. pass an obstruction
   C. compact the soil in the area
   D. splice piles

10. Where walers and form ties are used in wood formwork for tall vertical concrete walls, the walers are

    A. more closely spaced at the top of the wall than at the bottom
    B. evenly spaced at the top to the bottom of the wall
    C. more closely spaced at the bottom of the wall than at the top
    D. more closely spaced at the middle of the wall than at either the top or the bottom

11. A non-bearing wall unit between columns enclosing a structure is known as a _____ wall.

    A. panel
    B. curtain
    C. apron
    D. spandrel

12. In a multi-story building, standpipes are installed FIRST by the plumber for

    A. water supply
    B. sanitary facilities
    C. fire protection
    D. steam supply

13. It is necessary to burn reinforcing steel while they are in the wood forms in order to change their lengths.
    The STANDARD safety precaution to observe during this process is to

    A. fireproof the wood forms
    B. use a low heat flame
    C. have a man stand by with a fire extinguisher
    D. soak a 20-foot radius around the area with water

14. Specifications for a building require that the first floor beams must be in place before backfilling against the foundation walls.
    Of the following, the BEST reason for this requirement is that

    A. the utilities up to the first floor level should be in place before backfilling
    B. without the first floor beams in place, the wall may become overstressed
    C. it facilitates the inspection of the first floor construction
    D. it facilitates the inspection of the backfilling operation

15. The utility line that USUALLY enters the building at the *lowest* elevation is the

    A. electric cable   B. gas lines
    C. water lines   D. plumbing drain

16. Specifications for a building require that machine excavation for foundation footings be within a foot of final subgrade and the remaining excavation be done by hand. Of the following, the BEST reasons for this requirement is to

    A. prevent cave-ins around the excavation
    B. save the amount of fill needed
    C. prevent disturbing the surrounding excavation
    D. prevent excavation below the subgrade

17. Of the following outside lines entering a building, the one for which grades must be MOST carefully controlled is the

    A. sewer line   B. water line
    C. gas line   D. electric cable

18. On a plan, the grades for a building are as follows:
    Datum ± 0 (Elev. 24.08')
    First floor El + 1' - 0" (Elev. 25.08').
    The elevation of a ledge 6'3" below the finished first floor level with respect to datum is

    A. El. - 6.25   B. El. - 5.25
    C. El. + 18.83   D. El. + 17.83

19. Specifications for a building call for *defective material to be removed from the job site immediately.* The MAIN reason for this is to

    A. prevent accidents
    B. prevent accidental use of the defective material in the construction
    C. insure that the contractor does not make the same mistake again
    D. minimize claims against the department

20. *Drywall* is installed by

    A. carpenters   B. lathers
    C. plasterers   D. masons

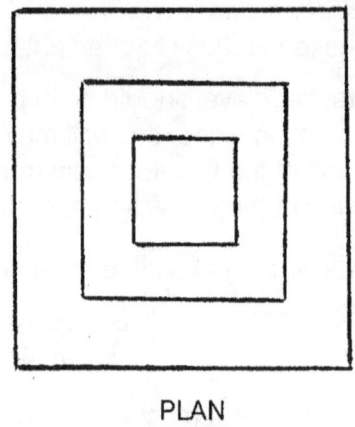

PLAN

21. The Plan of a footing and concrete column is shown above. An elevation of the footing would be shown as: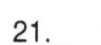

A. 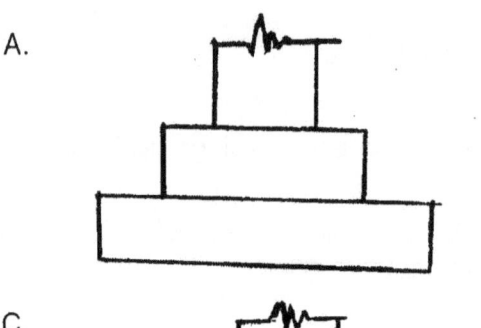 B.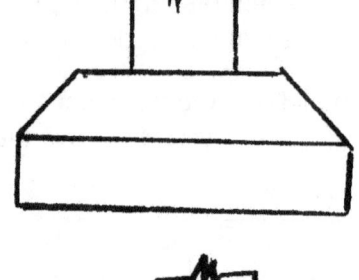

C. 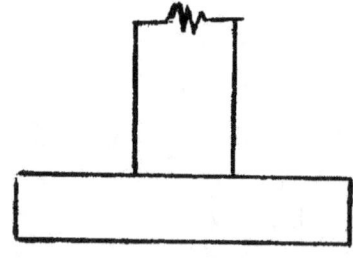 D.

22. Of the following, the BEST sequence to follow in pouring the interior footing, concrete column and basement floor as shown below is pour the footing,

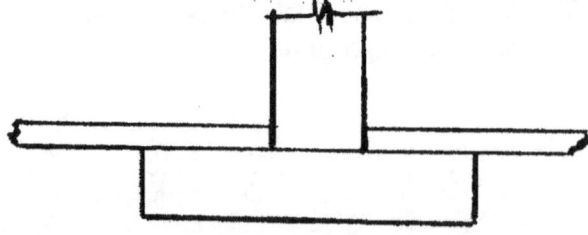

A. and floor in one pour. Pour the column
B. and column in one pour. Pour the floor
C. pour the floor above the footing, pour the column above the floor
D. box out for the floor, pour the column. Pour the floor

23. The PURPOSE of curing concrete is so that the

    A. forms for the concrete can be stripped quickly
    B. water content will not evaporate too quickly
    C. concrete will harden faster
    D. reinforcing rods will not rust

24. Air-entraining cement may be required so that the resulting concrete will resist

    A. freezing and thawing
    B. hot weather
    C. dampness
    D. heavy loads

25. Concrete test cylinders are required to

    A. provide an indication of the strength of the concrete poured in a specific location
    B. provide a basis of payment
    C. check on the inspector
    D. check the source of material

26. Concrete test cylinders are stored and cured on the job

    A. so that the contractor can then control the curing
    B. so that the inspector can then control the curing
    C. because the laboratory has no facilities for curing concrete cylinders
    D. because conditions of curing on the job are the same as at the location poured

27. The *water-cement ratio* refers to the quantity of water in a concrete mix as

    A. cubic feet of water per cubic foot of cement
    B. gallons of water per pound of cement
    C. gallons of water per sack of cement
    D. bags of cement per gallon of water

28. *Slump* of concrete refers to the

    A. shrinkage of concrete while setting
    B. drop in height relative to a standard testing cone
    C. amount of water introduced into the concrete
    D. cracking or crazing of the surface of concrete

29. Concrete mixes made with lightweight aggregate USUALLY require the addition of an air-entraining agent in order to

    A. increase the strength of the concrete
    B. reduce the weight of the concrete
    C. obtain the necessary plasticity without added water
    D. save aggregate material

30. Concrete in some instances requires integral waterproofing. This can BEST be achieved by

    A. addition of more cement in the mix
    B. longer vibration
    C. addition of a waterproofing agent to the mix
    D. longer curing period

31. In placing concrete where the vertical drop is greater than 5 feet, the use of an elephant trunk is necessary.
    The BEST reason for using an elephant trunk is to

    A. prevent segregation of the aggregate
    B. prevent waste of material
    C. safeguard health and property
    D. save time and labor

32. According to the Building Code, the maximum size of coarse aggregate for reinforced concrete shall be one-fifth of the narrowest dimension between forms or three-quarters of the clear spacing between reinforcing bars. Of the following, the MAXIMUM sized aggregate permitted for a 12" wall with #6 bars spaced at 3" center to center is

    A. 1 3/4"   B. 1 1/2"   C. 1 1/4"   D. 1"

33. Of the following, the one that is NOT a name for a lightweight aggregate is

    A. Solite   B. Vitralite
    C. Lelite   D. Nitralite

34. High early strength cement is designated as

    A. Type I   B. Type II   C. Type III   D. Type IV

35. The average weight of stone concrete is, MOST NEARLY, _____ lb./cu. ft.

    A. 125   B. 150
    C. 175   D. 200

KEY (CORRECT ANSWERS)

1. C
2. B
3. B
4. D
5. C

6. C
7. B
8. D
9. B
10. C

11. B
12. C
13. C
14. B
15. D

16. D
17. A
18. B
19. B
20. A

21. A
22. D
23. B
24. A
25. A

26. D
27. C
28. B
29. C
30. C

31. A
32. B
33. B
34. C
35. B

TEST 2

DIRECTIONS: Each question or incomplete statement is followed by several suggested answers or completions. Select the one that BEST answers the question or completes the statement. *PRINT THE LETTER OF THE CORRECT ANSWER IN THE SPACE AT THE RIGHT.*

1. The Building Code requires that concrete shall be kept in a moist condition, after placing, for at least the FIRST _____ days.

    A. 3 B. 7 C. 14 D. 28

2. In concrete work, a dummy joint is SIMILAR in purpose to a(n) _____ joint.

    A. expansion
    B. construction
    C. contraction
    D. shear

3. Specifications for concrete usually contain a statement disallowing the *retampering* of concrete. *Retampering* means

    A. adding more water to the drum after ingredients are mixed
    B. vibrating of concrete in the forms
    C. mixing of the remaining concrete after some concrete is taken from the truck
    D. mixing of concrete in the truck after it has partially set and adding water

4. Chamfers are placed on a concrete beam PRIMARILY to

    A. save weight
    B. eliminate honeycomb
    C. eliminate sharp corners
    D. save construction costs

5. Of the following, the BEST reason for using vibrators in concrete construction is to

    A. increase the workability of the concrete
    B. consolidate the concrete
    C. slow up the setting
    D. speed up the setting

6. The concrete test that will BEST determine the consistency of a concrete mix is the

    A. sieve analysis
    B. water-cement ratio test
    C. calorimetric test
    D. slump test

7. Specifications for the concrete floor treatment of a building require *dustproofing*. This process consists of

    A. scraping the floor surface to remove loose concrete material that will dust
    B. mopping the floor with a chemical solution that will harden the concrete surface
    C. adding a chemical compound to the concrete mix that will harden the surface of the concrete
    D. grinding the concrete floor with a terrazzo machine that will case harden the surface of the concrete

8. In checking the placement of reinforcing steel, it is discovered that reinforcing steel called for on the design drawings is not shown on the reinforcing steel shop drawings. Of the following, the BEST procedure to follow is to

A. check the design drawings for the errors
B. check the shop drawings for the errors
C. subtract the missing steel in the field
D. stop all work

9. While a large spread footing of about 50 cubic yards is being poured, the supply plant breaks down. Concrete is available from another supplier.
   The use of the other supplier should

   A. not be approved because the supplier may not be approved
   B. be approved since additional test cylinders can be taken
   C. not be approved since construction joints can be installed where the pour has ended
   D. be approved as the concrete in footings is relatively unimportant

10. Of the following species of lumber, the one MOST likely to be used for concrete formwork is

    A. oak   B. pine   C. maple   D. birch

11. A contractor proposes to install the roofing two days after the concrete roof slab is poured.
    This proposal should

    A. *be recommended* as it will speed the construction
    B. *be recommended* as it will cure the concrete better
    C. *not be recommended* as excess water may bulge the roofing
    D. *not be recommended* in cold weather but would be recommended in warm weather

12. For the construction of concrete floors resting on earth, the item that should be MOST carefully checked is that

    A. the earth is dry before pouring
    B. the earth is wet before pouring
    C. all backfill is properly compacted
    D. all backfill is porous soil

13. Cracks in concrete are not necessarily caused by settlement of a structure.
    Sometimes they are caused by

    A. shrinkage   B. plastic flow
    C. hydration   D. curing

14. Specifications for a building state that reinforcing bars must lap 40 diameters in the concrete.
    The length of lap for a number 6 bar should be, MOST NEARLY, _____ inches.

    A. 12   B. 20   C. 30   D. 40

15. Cement stored on the job site that has become caked and lumpy may

    A. be used only for foundations
    B. be used only for slabs on ground
    C. be used anywhere if the lumps are broken up
    D. not be used

16. Of the following statements relating to the plies in plywood, the one that is CORRECT is:

    A. The primary difference between exterior and interior plywood is the quality of the exterior plies.
    B. Exterior plywood has more plies than interior plywood.
    C. Exterior plywood has no surface defects on the outer plies while interior plywood permits surface defects on the outer plies.
    D. Plywood has an odd number of plies.

17. Of the following, the one that is NOT a principal classification of lumber according to the American Lumber Standards is

    A. building   B. structural
    C. yard   D. shop

18. Of the following types of lumber, the one that is classified as a hardwood is

    A. cedar   B. fir   C. pine   D. maple

19. When building the formwork for a 12" doubly reinforced concrete wall, the USUAL order of conctruction is to place the

    A. formwork for both faces of the wall; then place the steel
    B. formwork for one face of the wall, place all reinforcing steel, then place the formwork for the other face of the wall
    C. reinforcing steel, then place the formwork for both faces of the wall
    D. formwork for one face of the wall, place the reinforcing steel for one face, place the form-work for the other face of the wall, then place the reinforcing steel for the second face

20. To obtain information concerning the product of a particular major manufacturer of flooring, the BEST of the following sources of information is the

    A. Architectural Standards   B. ASTM
    C. Sweet's Catalogue   D. Flooring Institute

21. Of the following, loose lintels would MOST likely be found in the specifications under the item entitled

    A. Ornamental Iron   B. Miscellaneous Iron
    C. Structural Steel   D. Hollow Metal Work

22. Galvanized metal lath is metal lath coated with

    A. tin   B. copper   C. zinc   D. nickel

23. In the welding symbol the 2 represents the
    A. spacing between welds in inches
    B. length of the weld in inches
    C. number of sides to be welded
    D. thickness of the throat of the weld in inches

24. The specification for a building states that rib lath should be 3.4 pounds. This MEANS 3.4 pounds per

   A. square foot
   B. linear foot of a 3 foot roll
   C. square yard
   D. 10 square feet

24.____

25. Terrazzo floors are laid with brass dividing strips PRIMARILY for the purpose of

   A. preventing slipping
   B. appearance
   C. preventing irregular cracking
   D. easy screeding

25.____

26. The PURPOSE of a chase is to

   A. support stair stringers
   B. accomodate pipes in a wall
   C. accomodate flashing in a parapet
   D. provide venting

26.____

27. In masonry work, a bull nose brick would be located at

   A. an inside corner   B. an outside corner
   C. the key of an arch   D. the roof of a boiler setting

27.____

28. The addition of lime to cement mortar improves the workability of mortar and

   A. increases the strength
   B. decreases the shrinkage
   C. decreases the weight
   D. increases the watertightness

28.____

29. Brickwork must be cleaned after completion of setting by

   A. scrubbing with soap solution and water
   B. wire brushing
   C. washing with muriatic solution
   D. sand blasting

29.____

30. In a multi-story building, weep holes in cavity wall brick construction are USUALLY placed in the brickwork

   A. above all masonry openings
   B. at foundation level only
   C. at the parapet only
   D. at every floor

30.____

31. A brick wall which consists of all stretcher courses is said to be built with a _____ Bond.

   A. Flemish   B. Running
   C. English   D. Common

31.____

32. The whitish deposit frequently seen on brick walls can USUALLY be avoided by   32.____

    A. using brick that contains more soluable salts
    B. keeping the water-mortar ratio high
    C. adding muriatic acid to the mortar
    D. constructing properly filled weathertight joints

33. Specifications for a building require brick to be wet before using.   33.____
    Of the following, the BEST reason for this requirement is that wetting

    A. makes it easier to place brick
    B. cleans the brick
    C. prevents absorption of moisture from the mortar
    D. shows up flaws in the brick that would otherwise be hidden

34. In checking the ingredients that are to go into the concrete for a footing that is being   34.____
    poured, you notice that there is 5% too much cement.
    Of the following, the BEST action to take in this situation is to

    A. do nothing
    B. condemn the footing
    C. increase the amount of sand in the mix
    D. order core borings taken of the finished footing

35. The soil conditions for a new building are MOST frequently checked by   35.____

    A. augering   B. soundings
    C. rodding   D. borings

KEY (CORRECT ANSWERS)

1.	B	16.	D
2.	C	17.	A
3.	D	18.	D
4.	C	19.	B
5.	B	20.	C
6.	D	21.	B
7.	B	22.	C
8.	B	23.	B
9.	B	24.	C
10.	B	25.	C
11.	C	26.	B
12.	C	27.	B
13.	A	28.	B
14.	C	29.	C
15.	D	30.	D

31. B
32. D
33. C
34. A
35. D

EXAMINATION SECTION
TEST 1

DIRECTIONS: Each question or incomplete statement is followed by several suggested answers or completions. Select the one that BEST answers the question or completes the statement. *PRINT THE LETTER OF THE CORRECT ANSWER IN THE SPACE AT THE RIGHT.*

1. Of the following, the BEST reason for using vibrators in concrete construction is to   1.____

   A. remove excess water
   B. consolidate the concrete
   C. increase the slump of the concrete
   D. retard the setting of the concrete

2. When a contractor fails to adhere to an approved progress schedule, he should   2.____

   A. revise the schedule without delay
   B. ask for an extension of time on account of delays
   C. adopt such additional means and methods of construction as will make up for the time lost
   D. take no immediate action with the hope that sufficient time will be available later on that will assure the completion in accordance with the schedule

3. The usual contract for work includes a section entitled *Instructions to Bidders* which states that the   3.____

   A. contractor agrees that he has made his own examination and will make no claim for damages on account of errors or omissions
   B. contractor shall not make claims for damages of any discrepancy, error, or omission in any plans
   C. estimates of quantities and calculations are guaranteed by the board to be correct and are deemed to be a representation of the conditions affecting the work
   D. plans, measurements, dimensions, and conditions under which the work is to be performed are guaranteed by the board

4. Specifications covering brickwork usually require special precautions and protection for work in cold weather.   4.____
   The HIGHEST temperature below which these measures are required is *most nearly*

   A. 50° F   B. 40° F   C. 30° F   D. 20° F

5. Controlled concrete is required for the reinforced concrete frame of a large school building. The ultimate strength of this concrete will be *most nearly* _____ pounds per square inch.   5.____

   A. 1000   B. 3000   C. 5000   D. 7000

6. A lump sum type of contract may require the contractor to submit a schedule of unit prices.   6.____
   The BEST reason for this is that it

   A. prevents the lump sum from being too high
   B. simplifies the selection of the lowest bidder

C. enables the estimators to check the total cost
D. provides a means of making equitable partial payments

7. The concrete test that will BEST determine the consistency of a concrete mix is the

    A. slump test
    B. sieve analysis
    C. calorimetric test
    D. water-cement ratio test

8. The BEST way to evaluate the overall state of completion of a construction project is to check the progress estimate against the

    A. inspection work sheet
    B. construction schedule
    C. inspector's checklist
    D. equipment maintenance schedule

Questions 9-15.

DIRECTIONS: Questions 9 through 15 refer to the sketch below.

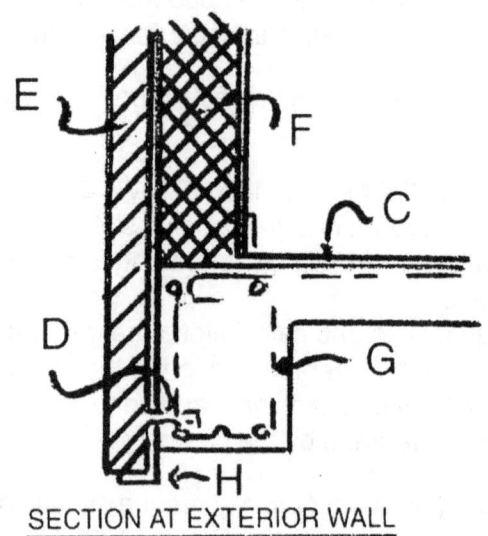

SECTION AT EXTERIOR WALL

9. The floor is made of

    A. air-entrained concrete
    B. reinforced concrete
    C. lightweight concrete
    D. concrete-encased structural steel

10. The exterior wall is a _____ wall.

    A. concrete block
    B. cavity construction
    C. veneer
    D. solid brick

11. Member C is a

    A. deformed bar
    B. hooked bar
    C. plain bar
    D. shear connector

12. Member E is made of

    A. steel   B. wood   C. brick   D. concrete

13. Member F is

    A. concrete block   B. facing brick
    C. glazed tile   D. sheetrock

14. Member G is a

    A. longitudinal bar   B. splice
    C. stirrup   D. tie wire

15. Member H is a

    A. purlin   B. brace   C. guy   D. lintel

16. A projected sash is a(n)

    A. architectural projection from a building exterior which breaks up a smooth pattern of the wall
    B. double-hung window
    C. window that opens inward or outward
    D. window that has a screen attachment

17. In the construction of cellar concrete floors resting on earth, the item that should be checked MOST carefully is that

    A. the earth is wet before pouring
    B. all backfill is granular soil
    C. the earth is dry before pouring
    D. all backfill is properly compacted

18. Specifications state that column dowels are embedded 24 diameters in the footing. The length of embedment for a number 6 bar is _____ inches.

    A. 6   B. 12   C. 18   D. 24

19. After excavating to the subgrade of a footing, an examination of the soil reveals that it is of a poorer quality than the soil in that area and at that elevation shown on the soil borings.
    Of the following types of footings, the one that would be LEAST affected by this condition is a

    A. footing on piles   B. plain concrete footing
    C. combined footing   D. spread footing

20. The MAIN reason for requiring written job reports is to

    A. avoid the necessity of oral orders
    B. develop better methods of doing the work
    C. provide a permanent record of what was done
    D. increase the amount of work that can be done

21. Of the following items, the one which should NOT be included in a proposed work schedule is 21.___

    A. a schedule of hourly wage rates and supplementary benefits
    B. an estimated time required for delivery of materials and equipment
    C. the anticipated commencement and completion of the various operations
    D. the sequence and inter-relationship of various operations with those of related contracts

22. A specification requires that brick be laid with *shoved* joints. The BEST reason for this requirement is that it helps the bricklayer to obtain _____ joint(s). 22.___

    A. full
    B. plumb vertical
    C. level horizontal
    D. the required thickness of

23. A specification states that access panels to suspended ceilings will be of metal. The MAIN reason for providing access panels is to 23.___

    A. improve the insulation of the ceiling
    B. improve the appearance of the ceiling
    C. make it easier to construct the building
    D. make it easier to maintain the building

24. A three-coat plaster job is to be 7/8 inches thick. Of the following, the thickness of the individual coats, in inches, would be *most nearly* scratch 24.___

    A. 1/8, brown 1/2, finish 1/4
    B. 3/8, brown 3/8, finish 1/8
    C. 11/16, brown 1/8, finish 1/16
    D. 5/16, brown 1/4, finish 5/16

25. You are assigned to keep a record of the number and volume of all boulders excavated that exceed one cubic yard in volume. 25.___
    The MOST probable reason for this order is:

    A. Any delays in excavating due to the boulders may result in a claim
    B. The contractor may receive additional payment for rock excavation
    C. There may be an extra charge for hauling boulders from the jobsite
    D. Excavation where there are large boulders involved is dangerous, and in the event of an accident, you will have appropriate records

KEY (CORRECT ANSWERS)

1.	B	11.	B
2.	C	12.	C
3.	A	13.	A
4.	B	14.	C
5.	B	15.	D
6.	D	16.	C
7.	A	17.	D
8.	B	18.	C
9.	B	19.	A
10.	C	20.	C

21. A
22. A
23. D
24. B
25. C

TEST 2

DIRECTIONS: Each question or incomplete statement is followed by several suggested answers or completions. Select the one that BEST answers the question or completes the statement. *PRINT THE LETTER OF THE CORRECT ANSWER IN THE SPACE AT THE RIGHT.*

1. Which one of the following is the PRIMARY object in drawing up a set of specifications for materials to be purchased?

    A. Control of quality
    B. Outline of intended use
    C. Establishment of standard sizes
    D. Location and method of inspection

2. In order to avoid disputes over payments for extra work in a contract for construction, the BEST procedure to follow would be to

    A. have contractor submit work progress reports daily
    B. insert a special clause in the contract specifications
    C. have a representative on the job at all times to verify conditions
    D. allocate a certain percentage of the cost of the job to cover such expenses

3. If there is a small amount of water on the surface of a newly-laid concrete sidewalk, the recommended procedure *before* finishing is to

    A. allow it to evaporate
    B. remove it with a broom
    C. sprinkle some dry cement on top
    D. remove it with a float

4. Prior to the installation of equipment called for in the specifications, the contractor is *usually* required to submit for approval

    A. sets of shop drawings
    B. a set of revised specifications
    C. a detailed description of the methods of work to be used
    D. a complete list of skilled and unskilled tradesmen he proposes to use

5. A specification on piles states that plumbness must be within 2% of the pile length. If the pile length is 30 feet, the MAXIMUM amount that the pile may be out of plumb is, in inches, *most nearly*

    A. 5   B. 6   C. 7   D. 8

6. The number of days that it will take high early strength concrete to equal the 28-day strength of normal portland cement concrete is *most nearly*

    A. 1   B. 3   C. 7   D. 12

7. Specifications may state that a standpipe system will be provided in each building. The MAIN purpose of a standpipe system is to

    A. supply the roof water tank
    B. provide water for firefighting

C. circulate water for the heating system
D. provide adequate pressure for the water supply

8. The drawing which should be used as a legal reference when checking completed construction work is the _____ drawing.

   A. contract
   B. assembly
   C. working or shop
   D. preliminary

9. Efflorescence may BEST be removed from brickwork by washing with a solution of _____ acid.

   A. muriatic   B. citric   C. carbonic   D. nitric

10. The MAIN difference between sheet glass and plate glass is

    A. the surface finish of the two types of glass
    B. the heat absorbing qualities of the two types of glass
    C. plate glass is thinner than sheet glass
    D. plate glass is tempered while sheet glass is not tempered

11. Construction joints in the concrete columns of a multistory building are *usually* located

    A. at floor level
    B. 1 foot above floor level
    C. at the underside of floor slab
    D. at the underside of deepest beam framing into the column

12. A contractor on a large construction project *usually* receives partial payments based on

    A. estimates of completed work
    B. actual cost of materials delivered and work completed
    C. estimates of material delivered and not paid for by the contractor
    D. the breakdown estimate submitted after the contract was signed and prorated over the estimated duration of the contract

13. According to the building code, masonry footings shall extend at least 4' below finished grade.
    The PRIMARY reason for this is to

    A. get below the frost line
    B. make the foundation stronger
    C. keep water out of the basement
    D. reach a lower soil strata where better bearing material can be found

14. Good inspection methods require that the inspector

    A. be observant and check all details
    B. constantly check with the engineer who designed the school
    C. apply specifications according to his interpretation
    D. permit slight job variation to establish good public relations

Questions 15-19.

DIRECTIONS: Questions 15 through 19 refer to the following specification for wood flooring. In answering these questions, refer to this specification.

2" x 4" wood sleepers laid flat @ 16" o.c.
1" x 6" sub flooring, laid diagonally; cut at butt joints with parallel cuts; joints at center of sleepers, well staggered, no two joints side by side. Not less than 1/8" space between boards.
One layer of 15# asphalt felt on top of sub-floor.
Finish floor - North Rock Maple, T & G, laid perpendicular to sleepers; 8d nails not more than 12" apart; end joints well scattered with at least 2 flooring strips between joints.
Flooring 25/32" x 2 1/4" face - 1st quality.

15. It is *most likely* that the floor referred to in the specification is to be laid

    A. directly on the ground   B. on a concrete base
    C. on wood joists   D. on steel beams

16. The BEST reason for specifying that the sub-flooring be parallel cut at butt joints is that this

    A. requires less material
    B. provides staggered joints
    C. provides more nailing surface
    D. allows the joint to fall between sleepers

17. The BEST reason for specifying a minimum space between the sub-floor boards is that it

    A. saves on material   B. reduces creaking
    C. allows for expansion   D. prevents dry rot

18. The BEST reason for specifying at least 2 flooring strips between joints in the finish flooring is that

    A. it looks better
    B. it is more economical
    C. each board is supported by two adjoining boards
    D. each finish board is supported by at least two sub-floor boards

19. The BEST reason for placing asphalt felt on top of the sub-floor is to

    A. deaden noise   B. preserve the wood
    C. reduce dampness   D. permit movement

20. Assume you are recommending in a report to your superior that a radical change in a standard maintenance procedure should be adopted.
Of the following, the MOST important information to be included in this report is

    A. a list of the reasons for making this change
    B. the names of the other GSSM who favor the change
    C. a complete description of the present procedure
    D. amount of training time needed for the new procedure

21. Specifications require that the first floor beams of a building must be in place before backfill is placed against the foundation walls.
The BEST reason for this requirement is that

    A. without the first floor beams in place, the wall may become overstressed
    B. it is easier to inspect the first floor construction when the backfill is not in place
    C. the utilities up to the first floor level should be in place before backfill is placed
    D. the boiler setting hung from the first floor must be in place before backfill is placed

22. The frequency with which job reports are submitted should depend MAINLY on

    A. how comprehensive the report has to be
    B. the amount of information in the report
    C. the availability of an experienced man to write the report
    D. the importance of changes in the information included in the report

23. Assume that a contractor proposed to start the roofing three days after pouring the concrete roof slab.
This proposal is

    A. *good,* mainly since it will speed the construction
    B. *good,* mainly since it will assist in curing the concrete
    C. *poor* in cold weather but is all right in warm weather
    D. *poor,* mainly since excess water in the concrete may bulge the roofing

24. In performing field inspectional work, an inspector is the contact man between the public and the board, and it is his job to secure compliance through the maximum utilization of persuasion and education and the minimum application of coercion.
According to the above statement, an inspector performing inspectional duties should

    A. seek to obtain voluntary compliance and use coercion only as a last resort
    B. be conciliatory on all issues of non-compliance and not take an attitude of firmness and authority
    C. maintain a strictly impersonal attitude in the exercise of his duties at all times
    D. use the threat of legal action to secure conformance with specified requirements

25. A specification requires that brick should be thoroughly wet before using.
Of the following, the BEST reason for this requirement is that

    A. wetting the brick uncovers hidden flaws
    B. it is easier to shove wet brick into place
    C. wetting cleans the pores of the brick ensuring a stronger bond
    D. wetting decreases absorption of water from the mortar

5 (#2)

KEY (CORRECT ANSWERS)

1.	A	11.	A
2.	C	12.	A
3.	A	13.	A
4.	A	14.	A
5.	C	15.	B
6.	C	16.	C
7.	B	17.	C
8.	A	18.	C
9.	A	19.	C
10.	A	20.	A

21. A
22. D
23. D
24. A
25. D

TEST 3

DIRECTIONS: Each question or incomplete statement is followed by several suggested answers or completions. Select the one that BEST answers the question or completes the statement. *PRINT THE LETTER OF THE CORRECT ANSWER IN THE SPACE AT THE RIGHT.*

Questions 1-4.

DIRECTIONS: Questions 1 to 4 refer to the sketch below.

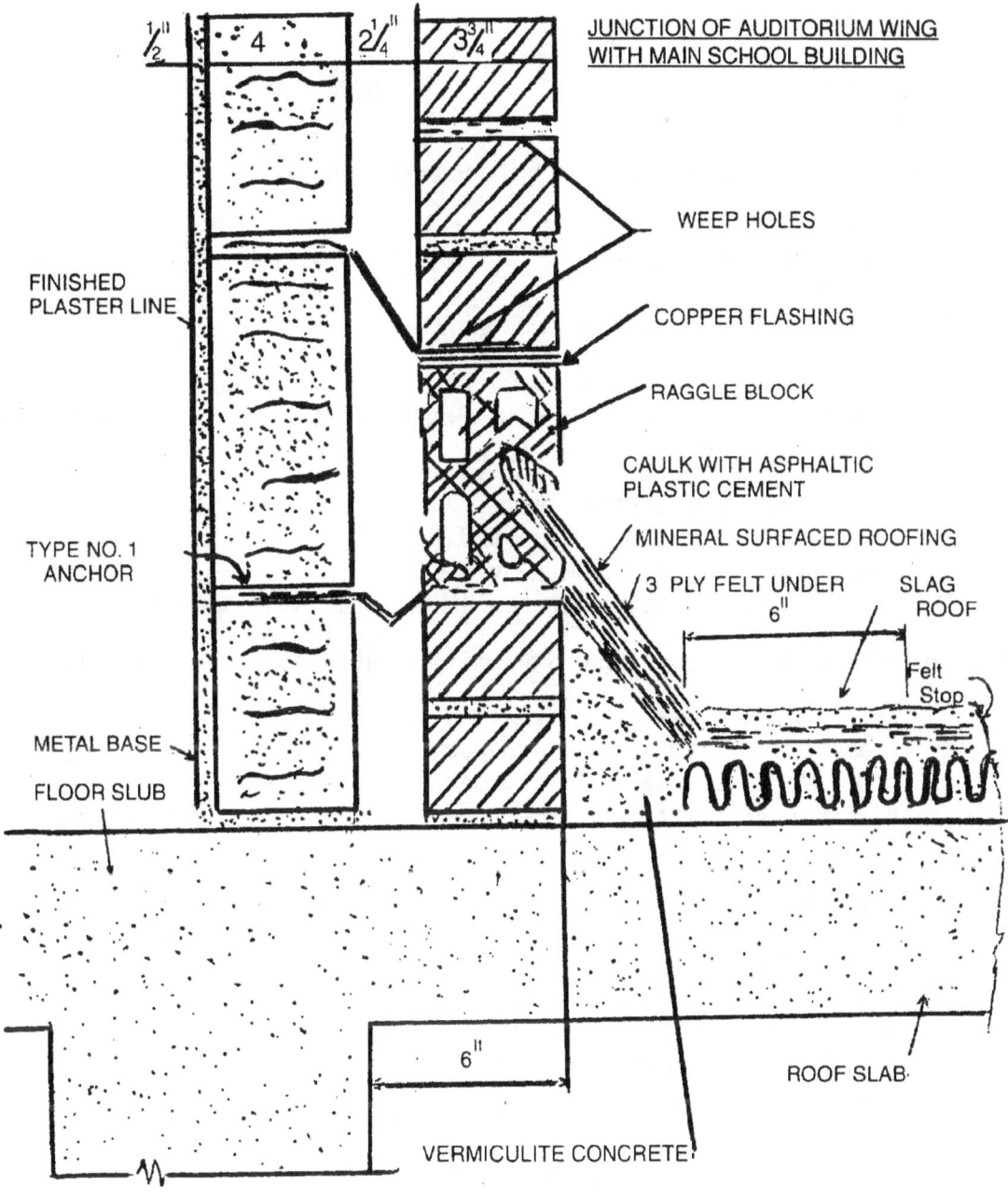

1. The 1/2" of plaster would *most likely* be applied in _____ coats. 1.____
   A. one   B. two   C. three   D. four

2. Vermiculite concrete is PRIMARILY _____ concrete.

   A. low-slump
   B. water-resistant
   C. an air-entrained
   D. a lightweight

3. Which of the following statements relating to copper flashing is CORRECT? It

   A. is perforated in the air space
   B. consists of one solid continuous sheet
   C. consists of 2-inch strips spaced every foot
   D. is provided to prevent the fall of mortar into the air space

4. The 4-inch thick material is *most likely*

   A. cinder block
   B. gypsum block
   C. brick
   D. terra cotta

5. A rowlock course of brick is one in which the bricks are laid

   A. on their 2 1/4" x 8" surface
   B. in an interlocking fashion
   C. with dowels at set intervals
   D. in a one-header followed by a one-stretcher course

6. Specifications for excavation for spread footings require that machine excavation be to within a foot of the final subgrade and the remainder of the excavation shall be by hand. The BEST reason for this requirement is to

   A. prevent cave-ins near the excavation
   B. cut down on the amount of fill needed
   C. prevent excavation below the subgrade
   D. insure that the area in the vicinity of the footing not be excessively disturbed

7. The CHIEF purpose in preparing an outline for a report is *usually* to insure that

   A. the report will be grammatically correct
   B. every point will be given equal emphasis
   C. principal and secondary points will be properly integrated
   D. the language of the report will be of the same level and include the same technical terms

8. One of the properties of tempered plate glass which affects installation is that it

   A. has a blue tinge
   B. cannot be cut after the glass is tempered
   C. does not bond with putty or glazing compound
   D. cracks more easily than ordinary plate glass

9. In assigning the men to various jobs, the BEST principle for a supervisor to follow is to

   A. study the men's abilities and assign them accordingly
   B. rotate a man from job to job until you find one which he can do well
   C. assign each of them to a job and let them adjust to it in their own way
   D. assume that men appointed to the position can do all parts of the work equally well

10. With respect to waterproofing existing basements, the MOST effective and lasting repairs are those made

   A. on the earth side of a basement wall
   B. on the inside basement wall surface
   C. on the floor
   D. in the mortar joints

11. During the actual construction work, the CHIEF value of a construction schedule is to

   A. insure that the work will be done on time
   B. reveal when production is behind schedule
   C. show how much equipment and material is required for the project
   D. furnish data as to the methods and techniques of construction operations

12. When building the formwork for a 12" doubly reinforced concrete wall, the USUAL order of construction is place the

   A. formwork for both faces of the wall; then place the reinforcing steel
   B. reinforcing steel and then place the formwork for both faces of the wall
   C. formwork for one face of the wall, place the reinforcing steel, and then place the formwork for the other face of the wall
   D. formwork for one face of the wall, place the reinforcing steel for one face, place the formwork for the other face of the wall, and then place the reinforcement for the second face

13. The GREATEST period of time must elapse between

   A. pouring and stripping concrete formwork
   B. placing reinforcing steel and pouring concrete
   C. applying the finish plaster coat and painting a plastered wall
   D. applying the first and second coats of a 3-coat plaster job for a wall

14. A fixed amount of money is generally withheld from the contractor for a definite period after the completion of construction.
    The BEST reason for this is

   A. that the money will be available for taxes due
   B. to penalize the contractor for poor work
   C. that it is a security for the repair of any defective work
   D. that the money will be available for modifications in the design of the structure

15. The practice of applying the brown coat to a wall on the day after the scratch coat of gypsum plaster was applied is GENERALLY considered

   A. satisfactory
   B. satisfactory only if the temperature is between 50° and 70° F
   C. unsatisfactory because 7 days must elapse between the application of the scratch and brown coats
   D. unsatisfactory because at least 3 days must elapse between the application of the scratch and brown coats

16. Fiberboard material 2 inches thick is placed on a flat reinforced concrete roof. 16.___
    The PRIMARY function of this 2 inch thick material is to

    A. act as a vapor barrier
    B. soundproof the rooms below
    C. prevent loss of heat from the building
    D. keep water from penetrating the ceiling below

17. The PRIMARY purpose of adding lime to a mortar mix is to 17.___

    A. improve the appearance of the mortar
    B. increase the workability of the mortar
    C. increase the strength of the mortar
    D. improve the bearing capacity of the wall

18. Assume that excavation is taking place adjacent to a building on a spread footing and a 18.___
    building on pile foundations.
    Extreme care must be exercised in excavating

    A. near the pile-supported building because the soil in the area is of poor quality
    B. near a building on spread footings because the concrete footings may crack
    C. for a pile-supported foundation because heavy loads are involved
    D. near a building on spread footings because of the danger of undermining the foundations

19. An inspector inspecting a large building under construction inspected brickwork at 9 M., 19.___
    formwork at 10 A.M., and concrete at 11 A.M. and did his office work in the afternoon. He
    followed the same pattern daily for months.
    This procedure is

    A. *bad* because not enough time is devoted to concrete work
    B. *bad* because the tradesmen know when the inspections will occur
    C. *good* because it is methodical and he does not miss any of the trades
    D. *good* because it gives equal amount of time to the important trades

20. If a supervisor finds a discrepancy between the plans and specifications, he should 20.___

    A. always follow the plans
    B. ask for an interpretation
    C. always follow the specifications
    D. follow the plans if the difference is in dimensions

KEY (CORRECT ANSWERS)

1.	B	11.	B
2.	D	12.	C
3.	B	13.	C
4.	A	14.	C
5.	A	15.	A
6.	D	16.	C
7.	C	17.	B
8.	B	18.	D
9.	A	19.	B
10.	A	20.	B

EXAMINATION SECTION
TEST 1

DIRECTIONS: Each question or incomplete statement is followed by several suggested answers or completions. Select the one that BEST answers the question or completes the statement. *PRINT THE LETTER OF THE CORRECT ANSWER IN THE SPACE AT THE RIGHT.*

Questions 1-16.

DIRECTIONS: Questions 1 through 16 deal with graphical symbols of electrical items as recommended by the ANSI (ex-ASA). For each item, select the proper graphical symbol and print the letter corresponding to it.

1. Telephone switchboard

   A. 6   B. 16   C. 17   D. 18

2. Exit light wall outlet

   A. 5   B. 12   C. 15   D. 16

3. City fire alarm station

   A. 19   B. 21   C. 22   D. 23

4. Electric door opener

   A. 9   B. 10   C. 11   D. 15

5. Duplex convenience outlet

   A. 9   B. 10   C. 15   D. 24

6. Range outlet

   A. 3   B. 6   C. 13   D. 14

7. Push button

   A. 5   B. 8   C. 11   D. 12

8. Power panel

   A. 1   B. 2   C. 3   D. 4

1. ▭
2. ▨
3. ⊡⊣
4. ⊠
5. ▱
6. Ⓣ
7. Ⓑ
8. ⊡
9. Ⓓ
10. ⊡
11. ⊗
12. -⊗
13. ≡◯R
14. ◯ⓇR
15. Ⓔ
16. S₄
17. ◁

1.____

2.____

3.____

4.____

5.____

6.____

7.____

8.____

139

2 (#1)

9. Four-way switch

   A. 4   B. 13   C. 14   D. 16

10. Controller

    A. 3   B. 4   C. 5   D. 9

11. Lighting panel

    A. 1   B. 2   C. 3   D. 4

12. Buzzer

    A. 3   B. 5   C. 8   D. 11

13. Isolating switch

    A. 3   B. 5   C. 9   D. 10

14. Interconnecting telephone

    A. 13   B. 14   C. 17   D. 18

15. Fire alarm central station

    A. 21   B. 22   C. 23   D. 26

16. Clock outlet

    A. 9   B. 10   C. 15   D. 26

18. ◁
19. S_F
20. S_{MC}
21. [FA]
22. [F]
23. ⊠
24. ─◯
25. ≡◯ 3
26. ⓒ

9. ____
10. ____
11. ____
12. ____
13. ____
14. ____
15. ____
16. ____

140

17. A riser diagram is an electrical drawing which would give information about the

    A. voltage drop in feeders
    B. size of feeders and panel loads
    C. external connections to equipment
    D. sequence of operation of devices and equipment

17._____

18. When a contractor fails to adhere to an approved progress schedule, he should

    A. revise the schedule without delay
    B. ask for an extension of time on account of delays
    C. adopt such additional means and methods of construction as will make up for the time lost
    D. take no immediate action with the hope that sufficient time will be available later on that will assure the completion in accordance with the schedule

18._____

19. The usual contract for work includes a section entitled, *Instructions to Bidders,* which states that the

    A. contractor agrees that he has made his own examination and will make no claims for damages on account of errors or omissions
    B. contractor shall not make claims for damages of any discrepancy, error or omission in any plans
    C. estimates of quantities and calculations are guaranteed by the Board to be correct and are deemed to be a representation of the conditions affecting the work
    D. plans, measurements, dimensions, and conditions under which the work is to be performed are guaranteed by the Board

19._____

20. The purpose of performing a dielectric test on a sample of oil taken from the casing of an oil-filled power transformer is to determine the

    A. viscosity   B. insulating quality
    C. flashpoint   D. extent of contamination

20._____

21. A neon test lamp can be used to test

    A. the field intensity of a relay magnet
    B. the phase rotation of a source of supply
    C. whether a supply source is A.C. or D.C.
    D. the power factor of a source of supply

21._____

22. The size, in circular mils, of a wire whose diameter is known can be calculated by

    A. multiplying the diameter in mils by $\pi/4$
    B. squaring the diameter in mils
    C. squaring the diameter in mils and multiplying the product by $\pi/4$
    D. squaring the diameter in inches

22._____

23. The short time rating and the continuous rating of a given piece of electrical machinery differ, but both are based on the

    A. cost of energy
    B. line potential

23._____

C. power factor of the machine
D. temperature rise of the machine

24. A lump sum type of contract may require the contractor to submit a schedule of unit prices.
The BEST reason for this is that it

   A. prevents the lump sum from being too high
   B. simplifies the selection of the lowest bidder
   C. enables the estimators to check the total cost
   D. provides a means of making equitable partial payments

25. In assigning his men to various jobs, the BEST principle for a supervisor to follow is to

   A. study the men's abilities and assign them accordingly
   B. rotate a man from job to job until you find one which he can do well
   C. assign each of them a job and let them adjust to it in their own way
   D. assume that men appointed to the position can do all parts of the work equally wel

---

KEY (CORRECT ANSWERS)

1.	D	11.	A
2.	B	12.	B
3.	D	13.	A
4.	B	14.	C
5.	D	15.	A
6.	C	16.	D
7.	B	17.	B
8.	B	18.	C
9.	D	19.	A
10.	B	20.	C

21. C
22. B
23. D
24. D
25. A

TEST 2

DIRECTIONS: Each question or incomplete statement is followed by several suggested answers or completions. Select the one that BEST answers the question or completes the statement. *PRINT THE LETTER OF THE CORRECT ANSWER IN THE SPACE AT THE RIGHT.*

Questions 1-8.

DIRECTIONS: Questions 1 through 8 are to be answered in accordance with the requirements of the electrical code, assuming normal procedures. Do NOT consider exceptions which are granted by special permission.

1. The MINIMUM size of A.W.G. wire which may be used on a 15-ampere branch circuit is

    A. 10 B. 12 C. 14 D. 16

2. Conductors supplying an individual motor whose full-load current is 100 amperes should have a MINIMUM carrying capacity of _____ amperes.

    A. 100 B. 115 C. 125 D. 150

3. The MINIMUM rating of a service switch is _____ amperes.

    A. 30 B. 60 C. 100 D. 200

4. In the installation of fluorescent fixtures, the MAXIMUM number of single or two-lamp type auxiliaries which can be placed on any single fifteen-ampere branch circuit is

    A. 10 B. 12 C. 15 D. 18

5. Where rubber-covered conductors are used in a conduit, the MINIMUM radius of the curve of the inner edge of any field bend, in terms of the internal diameter of the conduit, shall not be less than _____ times.

    A. 4 B. 6 C. 8 D. 10

6. Except for fixture wire of MI cable, single conductors of No. 6 A.W.G. or smaller intended for use as identified conductors of circuits shall have an outer identification of

    A. green
    B. black
    C. white or natural gray
    D. gray with a yellow marker throughout its length

7. Motor running protective devices, other than fuses, should have a continuous current-carrying capacity, in terms of the full load current rating of the motor, of AT LEAST

    A. 100% B. 115% C. 120% D. 125%

8. The one of the following which should ALWAYS be used as the grounding electrode, where available, is a

    A. driven non-ferrous metallic rod
    B. buried plate with an area of 2 sq.ft.
    C. driven iron rod with a resistance of 25 ohms
    D. continuous metallic underground water piping system

9. The MAIN reason for requiring written job reports is to

   A. avoid the necessity of oral orders
   B. develop better methods of doing the work
   C. provide a permanent record of what was done
   D. increase the amount of work that can be done

10. Of the following items, the one which should NOT be included in a proposed work schedule is

    A. a schedule of hourly wage rates and supplementary benefits
    B. an estimated time required for delivery of materials and equipment
    C. the anticipated commencement and completion of the various operations
    D. the sequence and inter-relationship of various operations with those of related contracts

11. The closed circuit is used primarily in communication and fire alarm systems to indicate, by various or audible means, which of the following abnormal circuit conditions?

    A. Open
    B. Ground
    C. Overload
    D. Direct short

12. A Board specification states that access panels to suspended ceiling will be of metal. The MAIN reason for providing access panels is to

    A. improve the insulation of the ceiling
    B. improve the appearance of the building
    C. make it easier to construct the building
    D. make it easier to maintain the building

13. The one of the following which is a successful means of decreasing electrolysis in underground metal pipes is to

    A. use galvanized pipe
    B. insert occasional insulating joints in the pipes
    C. keep the voltage drop in the ground return circuit over 15 volts
    D. coat the pipe with tar for 6 inches above and 6 inches below the point where it enters the ground

14. The abbreviation *MCM* placed next to a feeder cable in a wiring diagram would indicate the

    A. microamperes per circular mil
    B. area of the cable in millions of circular mils
    C. area of the cable in thousands of circular mils
    D. resistance of the cable in microhms per circular-mil-ft.

15. Which one of the following is the PRIMARY object in drawing up a set of specifications for materials to be purchased?

    A. Control of quality
    B. Outline of intended use
    C. Establishment of standard sizes
    D. Location and method of inspection

16. The marking or lettering that indicates a conductor having moisture-and-heat resistance thermoplastic covering and which may be used in both dry and wet locations is

    A. RHW   B. SB   C. THW   D. TW

17. In performing field inspectional work, an inspector is the contact man between the public and the authority, and it is his job to secure compliance through the maximum utilization of persuasion and education and the minimum application of coercion.
    According to the above statement, an inspector performing inspectional duties should

    A. seek to obtain voluntary compliance and use coercion only as a last resort
    B. be conciliatory on all issues of non-compliance and not take an attitude of firmness and authority
    C. maintain a strictly impersonal attitude in the exercise of his duties at all times
    D. use the threat of legal action to secure conformance with specified requirements

18. In a polarized interior lighting system, the

    A. base of the lamp sockets is connected to the identified wire
    B. branch circuit light switch is connected to the identifying wire
    C. screwshells of the lamp sockets are connected to the identified wire
    D. branch circuit light switch is connected to the screwshell of the lamp socket

19. If a supervisor finds a discrepancy between the plans and specifications, he should

    A. always follow the plans
    B. ask for an interpretation
    C. always follow the specifications
    D. follow the plans if the difference is in dimensions

20. The BEST way to evaluate the overall state of completion of a construction project is to check the progress estimate against the

    A. inspection work sheet
    B. construction schedule
    C. inspector's checklist
    D. equipment maintenance schedule

21. Two-phase power may be converted to 3-phase power, or vice versa, by using which of the following transformer connections?

    A. Scott   B. Delta-wye
    C. Open delta   D. Autotransformer

22. The CHIEF purpose in preparing an outline for a report is usually to insure that

    A. the report will be grammatically correct
    B. every point will be given equal emphasis
    C. principal and secondary points will be properly integrated
    D. the language of the report will be of the same level and include the same technical terms

23. A contractor on a large construction project USUALLY receives partial payments based on

   A. estimates of completed work
   B. actual cost of materials delivered and work completed
   C. estimates of material delivered and not paid for by the contractor
   D. the breakdown estimate submitted after the contract was signed and prorated over the estimated duration of the contract

24. In testing insulation resistance, the MAIN reason that the use of a megger is *preferable* to the use of an ordinary ohmmeter is that a megger

   A. is more rugged
   B. does not require constant care
   C. has a lower internal resistance
   D. usually operates at the proper voltage

25. In order to avoid disputes over payments for extra work in a contract for construction, the BEST procedure to follow would be to

   A. have contractor submit work progress reports daily
   B. insert a special clause in the contract specifications
   C. have a representative on the job at all times to verify conditions
   D. allocate a certain percentage of the cost of the job to cover such expenses

KEY (CORRECT ANSWERS)

1. B		11. A	
2. C		12. D	
3. C		13. B	
4. C		14. C	
5. B		15. A	
6. C		16. C	
7. B		17. A	
8. D		18. C	
9. C		19. B	
10. A		20. B	

21. A
22. C
23. A
24. D
25. C

TEST 3

DIRECTIONS: Each question or incomplete statement is followed by several suggested answers or completions. Select the one that BEST answers the question or completes the statement. *PRINT THE LETTER OF THE CORRECT ANSWER IN THE SPACE AT THE RIGHT.*

1. During the actual construction work, the CHIEF value of a construction schedule is to 1.____
    A. insure that the work will be done on time
    B. reveal whether production is falling behind
    C. show how much equipment and material is required for the project
    D. furnish data as to the methods and techniques of construction operations

2. Prior to the installation of equipment called for in the specifications, the contractor is usually required to submit for approval 2.____
    A. sets of shop drawings
    B. a set of revised specifications
    C. a detailed description of the methods of work to be used
    D. a complete list of skilled and unskilled tradesmen he proposes to use

3. An inspector inspecting a large building under construction inspected lighting fixtures at 9 A.M. and electrical feeders at 10 A.M., machine connections at 11 A.M., and did his office work in the afternoon. He followed the same pattern daily for months.
   This procedure is 3.____
    A. *bad*, because not enough time is devoted to important electrical feeders
    B. *bad*, because the tradesmen know when the inspections occur
    C. *good*, because it is methodical and he does not miss any of the trades
    D. *good*, because it gives equal amount of time to the important trades

4. A rule of thumb for calculating the area of copper conductors in C.M. as given in the AWG tables is that for every _____ size, the wire cross section _____. 4.____
    A. second gage of larger; doubles
    B. second gage of larger; increases four times
    C. third gage of smaller; is halved
    D. third gage of smaller; is one-third

5. The drawing which should be used as a legal reference when checking completed construction work is the _____ drawing(s). 5.____
    A. contract   B. assembly
    C. working or shop   D. preliminary

6. The motor starting device commonly called a compensator is actually a(n) 6.____
    A. rheostat   B. potentiometer
    C. auto-transformer   D. capacitor

7. The BEST way for a supervisor to determine whether a new employee is learning his work properly is to 7.____

A. ask the other men how this man is making out
B. question him directly on details of the work
C. assume that if he asks no questions he knows the work
D. inspect and follow up on the work which is assigned to him

Questions 8-13.

DIRECTIONS: Questions 8 through 13 refer to the circuit drawn below.

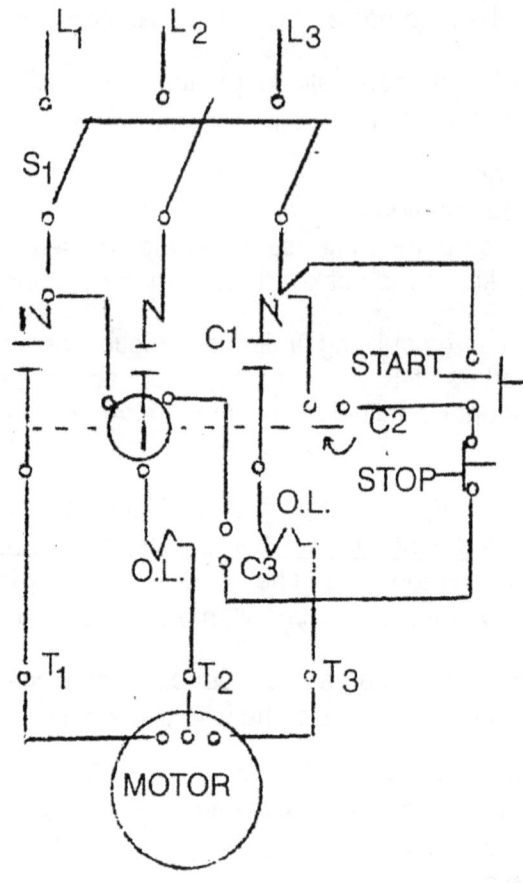

8. The circuitry shown is called a(n)

   A. D.C. motor controller
   B. reduced voltage starter
   C. two-speed motor control
   D. across-the-line starter

9. The circuit element indicated by C_1 is a

   A. capacitor
   B. circuit breaker
   C. pair of contacts which is normally open
   D. pair of start button contacts

8.____

9.____

10. If the motor is of the three-phase induction type, the incoming power is MOST likely   10._____

    A. plus and minus 115 volts D.C.
    B. 115 volts A.C. with neutral
    C. 208 volts A.C. line-to-line
    D. 230 volts D.C. with neutral

11. The PROPER designation for line switch S_1 is   11._____

    A. SPST   B. 3PDT   C. 3TSP   D. 3TDP

12. The O.L. relays are in the circuitry to   12._____

    A. protect the motor from overvoltages
    B. keep the stop button in after it has been depressed
    C. allow the motor to be operated on two lines if desired
    D. interrupt the contactor holding circuit on sustained overloads

13. The purpose of contact C_2 is to   13._____

    A. hold the start button in after it has been depressed
    B. hold the contactor in when the line voltages drop too low
    C. hold the contactor in after the start button has been depressed
    D. de-energize the contactor solenoid when the stop button is depressed

14. One ADVANTAGE of fluorescent lamps over incandescent lamps is that they   14._____

    A. are easier to handle
    B. are more efficient
    C. have simpler wiring circuits
    D. are not affected by temperature changes

15. To control a light fixture from three different locations, it is necessary to use _____ switches.   15._____

    A. one 4-way and two 3-way   B. three 3-way
    C. three 2-way   D. three single-pole

16. Good inspection methods require that the inspector   16._____

    A. be observant and check all details
    B. constantly check with the engineer who designed the school
    C. apply specifications according to his interpretations
    D. permit slight job violations to establish good public relations

17. Assume you are recommending in a report to your superior that a radical change in a standard maintenance procedure should be adopted.
Of the following, the MOST important information to be included in this report is   17._____

    A. a list of the reasons for making this change
    B. the names of the other supervisors who favor the change
    C. a complete description of the present procedure
    D. amount of training time needed for the new procedure

18. A fixed amount of money is generally withheld from the contractor for a definite period after the completion of construction.
    The BEST reason for this is

    A. that the money will be available for taxes due
    B. to penalize the contractor for poor work
    C. that it is a security for the repair of any defective work
    D. that the money will be available for modifications in the design of the structure

19. The frequency with which job reports are submitted should depend MAINLY on

    A. how comprehensive the report has to be
    B. the amount of information in the report
    C. the availability of an experienced man to write the report
    D. the importance of changes in the information included in the report

20. The use of groups of combinations of conductors in the same conduit will

    A. decrease conductor resistance
    B. be allowed for circuit voltages not exceeding 250V
    C. upgrade the current-carrying capacity of the conductors
    D. downgrade the current-carrying capacity of the conductors

KEY (CORRECT ANSWERS)

1.	B	11.	A
2.	A	12.	D
3.	B	13.	C
4.	C	14.	B
5.	A	15.	A
6.	C	16.	A
7.	B	17.	A
8.	D	18.	C
9.	C	19.	D
10.	C	20.	D

EXAMINATION SECTION
TEST 1

DIRECTIONS: Each question or incomplete statement is followed by several suggested answers or completions. Select the one that BEST answers the question or completes the statement. *PRINT THE LETTER OF THE CORRECT ANSWER IN THE SPACE AT THE RIGHT.*

1. The combustion efficiency of a boiler can be determined with a CO_2 indicator and the   1.____

    A. under fire draft
    B. boiler room humidity
    C. flue gas temperature
    D. outside air temperature

2. A quick, practical method of determining if the cast-iron waste pipe delivered to a job has been damaged in transit is to   2.____

    A. hydraulically test it
    B. "ring" each length with a hammer
    C. drop each length to see whether it breaks
    D. visually examine the pipe for cracks

3. An electrostatic precipitator is used to   3.____

    A. filter the air supply
    B. remove sludge from the fuel oil
    C. remove particles from the fuel gas
    D. supply samples for an Orsat analysis

4. The PRIMARY cause of cracking and spalling of refractory lining in the furnace of a steam generator is *most likely* due to   4.____

    A. continuous over-firing of boiler
    B. slag accumulation on furnace walls
    C. change in fuel from solid to liquid
    D. uneven heating and cooling within the refractory brick

5. The term "effective temperature" in air conditioning means   5.____

    A. the dry bulb temperature
    B. the average of the wet and dry bulb temperatures
    C. the square root of the product of wet and dry bulb temperatures
    D. an arbitrary index combining the effects of temperature, humidity, and movement

6. The piping in all buildings having dual water distribution systems should be identified by a color coding of _____ for potable water lines and _____ for non-potable water lines.   6.____

    A. green; red
    B. green; yellow
    C. yellow; green
    D. yellow; red

7. The breaking of a component of a machine subjected to excessive vibration is called   7.____

    A. tensile failure
    B. fatigue failure
    C. caustic embrittlement
    D. amplitude failure

8. The TWO MOST important factors to be considered in selecting fans for ventilating systems are

   A. noise and efficiency
   B. space available and weight
   C. first cost and dimensional bulk
   D. construction and arrangement of drive

9. In the modern power plant deaerator, air is removed from water to

   A. reduce heat losses in the heaters
   B. reduce corrosion of boiler steel due to the air
   C. reduce the load of the main condenser air pumps
   D. prevent pumps from becoming vapor bound

10. The abbreviations BOD, COD, and DO are associated with

    A. flue gas analysis
    B. air pollution control
    C. boiler water treatment
    D. water pollution control

11. The piping of a newly installed drainage system should be tested upon completion of the rough plumbing with a head of water of NOT LESS THAN _____ feet.

    A. 10   B. 15   C. 20   D. 25

12. Of the following statements concerning aquastats, the one which is CORRECT is:

    A. Aquastats may be obtained with either a narrow or wide range of settings
    B. Aquastats have a mercury tube switch which is controlled by the stack switch
    C. An aquastat is a device used to shut down the burner in the event of low water in the boiler
    D. An aquastat should be located about 4 inches above the normal water line of the boiler

13. The SAFEST way to protect the domestic water supply from contamination by sewage or non-potable water is to insert

    A. air gaps
    B. swing connections
    C. double check valves
    D. tanks with overhead discharge

14. The MAIN function of a back-pressure valve which is sometimes found in the connection between a water drain pipe and the sewer system is to

    A. equalize the pressure between the drain pipe and the sewer
    B. prevent sewer water from flowing into the drain pipe
    C. provide pressure to enable waste to reach the sewer
    D. make sure that there is not too much water pressure in the sewer line

15. Boiler water is neutral if its pH value is

    A. 0   B. 1   C. 7   D. 14

16. A domestic hot water mixing or tempering valve should be preceded in the hot water line by a

    A. strainer
    B. foot valve
    C. check valve
    D. steam trap

16.____

17. Between a steam boiler and its safety valve there should be

    A. no valve of any type
    B. a gate valve of the same size as the safety valve
    C. a swing check valve of at least the same size as the safety valve
    D. a cock having a clear opening equal in area to the pipe connecting the boiler and safety valve

17.____

18. A diagram of horizontal plumbing drainage lines should have cleanouts shown

    A. at least every 25 feet
    B. at least every 100 feet
    C. wherever a basin is located
    D. wherever a change in direction occurs

18.____

19. When a Bourdon gauge is used to measure steam pressures, some form of siphon or water seal must be maintained.
The reason for this is to

    A. obtain "absolute" pressure readings
    B. prevent steam from entering the gage
    C. prevent condensate from entering the gage
    D. obtain readings below atmospheric pressure

19.____

20. In a closed heat exchanger, oil is cooled by condensate which is to be returned to a boiler. In order to avoid the possibility of contaminating the condensate with oil should a tube fail in the oil cooler, it would be good practice to

    A. cool the oil by air instead of water
    B. treat the condensate with an oil solvent
    C. keep the oil pressure in the exchanger higher than the water pressure
    D. keep the water pressure in the exchanger higher than the oil pressure

20.____

21. A radiator thermostatic trap is used on a vacuum return type of heating system to

    A. release the pocketed air only
    B. reduce the amount of condensate
    C. maintain a predetermined radiator water level
    D. prevent the return of live steam to the return line

21.____

22. According to the color coding of piping, fire protection piping should be painted

    A. green   B. yellow   C. purple   D. red

22.____

23. The MAIN purpose of a standpipe system is to

    A. supply the roof water tank
    B. provide water for firefighting

23.____

C. circulate water for the heating system
D. provide adequate pressure for the water supply

24. The name "Saybolt" is associated with the measurement of

   A. viscosity
   B. Btu content
   C. octane rating
   D. temperature

25. Recirculation of conditioned air in an air-conditioned building is done MAINLY to

   A. reduce refrigeration tonnage required
   B. increase room entrophy
   C. increase air specific humidity
   D. reduce room temperature below the dewpoint

26. In a plumbing installation, vent pipes are GENERALLY used to

   A. prevent the loss of water seal from traps by evaporation
   B. prevent the loss of water seal due to several causes other than evaporation
   C. act as an additional path for liquids to flow through during normal use of a plumbing fixture
   D. prevent the backflow of water in a cross-connection between a drinking water line and a sewage line

27. The designation "150 W" cast on the bonnet of a gate valve is an indication of the

   A. water working temperature
   B. water working pressure
   C. area of the opening in square inches
   D. weight of the valve in pounds

28. In the city, the size soil pipe necessary in a sewage drainage system is determined by the

   A. legal occupancy of the building
   B. vertical height of the soil line
   C. number of restrooms connected to the soil line
   D. number of "fixture units" connected to the soil line

29. Fins or other extended surfaces are used on heat exchanger tubes when

   A. the exchanger is a water-to-water exchanger
   B. water is on one side of the tube and condensing steam on the other side
   C. the surface coefficient of heat transfer on both sides of the tube is high
   D. the surface coefficient of heat transfer on one side of the tube is low compared to the coefficient on the other side of the tube

30. A fusible plug may be put in a fire tube boiler as an emergency device to indicate low water level. The fusible plug is installed so that under normal operating conditions,

   A. both sides are exposed to steam
   B. one side is exposed to water and the other side to steam
   C. one side is exposed to steam and the other side to hot gases
   D. one side is exposed to the water and the other side to hot gases

31. Extra strong wrought-iron pipe, as compared to standard wrought-iron pipe of the same nominal size, has

    A. the same outside diameter but a smaller inside diameter
    B. the same inside diameter but a larger outside diameter
    C. a larger outside diameter and a smaller inside diameter
    D. larger inside and outside diameters

32. Fans may be rated on a dynamic or a static efficiency basis. The dynamic efficiency would *probably* be

    A. lower in value because of the energy absorbed by the air velocity
    B. the same as the static in the case of centrifugal blowers running at various speeds
    C. the same as the static in the case of axial flow blowers running at various speeds
    D. higher in value than the static

33. The function of the stack relay in an oil burner installation is to

    A. regulate the draft over the fire
    B. regulate the flow of fuel oil to the burner
    C. stop the motor if the oil has not ignited
    D. stop the motor if the water or steam pressure is too high

34. The type of centrifugal pump which is inherently balanced for hydraulic thrust is the

    A. double suction impeller type
    B. single suction impeller type
    C. single stage type
    D. multistage type

35. The specifications for a job using sheet lead calls for "4-lb. sheet lead." This means that each sheet should weigh

    A. 4 lbs.
    B. 4 lbs. per square
    C. 4 lbs. per square foot
    D. 4 lbs. per cubic inch

36. The total cooling load design conditions for a building are divided for convenience into two components.
    These are:

    A. infiltration and radiation
    B. sensible heat and latent heat
    C. wet and dry bulb temperatures
    D. solar heat gain and moisture transfer

37. The function of a Hartford loop used on some steam boilers is to

    A. limit boiler steam pressure
    B. limit temperature of the steam
    C. prevent high water levels in the boiler
    D. prevent back flow of water from the boiler into the return main

38. Vibration from a ventilating blower can be prevented from being transmitted to the duct work by

   A. installing straighteners in the duct
   B. throttling the air supply to the blower
   C. bolting the blower tightly to the duct
   D. installing a canvas sleeve at the blower outlet

39. A specification states that access panels to suspended ceiling will be of metal. The MAIN reason for providing access panels is to

   A. improve the insulation of the ceiling
   B. improve the appearance of the ceiling
   C. make it easier to construct the building
   D. make it easier to maintain the building

40. A plumber on a job reports that the steamfitter has installed a 3" steam line in a location at which the plans show the house trap. On inspecting the job, you should

   A. tell the steamfitter to remove the steam line
   B. study the condition to see if the house trap can be relocated
   C. tell the plumber and steamfitter to work it out between themselves and then report to you
   D. tell the plumber to find another location for the trap because the steamfitter has already completed his work

41. In the installation of any heating system, the MOST important consideration is that

   A. all elements be made of a good grade of cast iron
   B. all radiators and connectors be mounted horizontally
   C. the smallest velocity of flow of heating medium be used
   D. there be proper clearance between hot surfaces and surrounding combustible material

42. Which one of the following is the PRIMARY object in drawing up a set of specifications for materials to be purchased?

   A. Control of quality
   B. Outline of intended use
   C. Establishment of standard sizes
   D. Location and method of inspection.

43. The drawing which should be used as a LEGAL reference when checking completed construction work is the _____ drawing.

   A. contract
   B. assembly
   C. working or shop
   D. preliminary

Questions 44-50.

DIRECTIONS: Questions 44 through 50 refer to the plumbing drawing shown below.

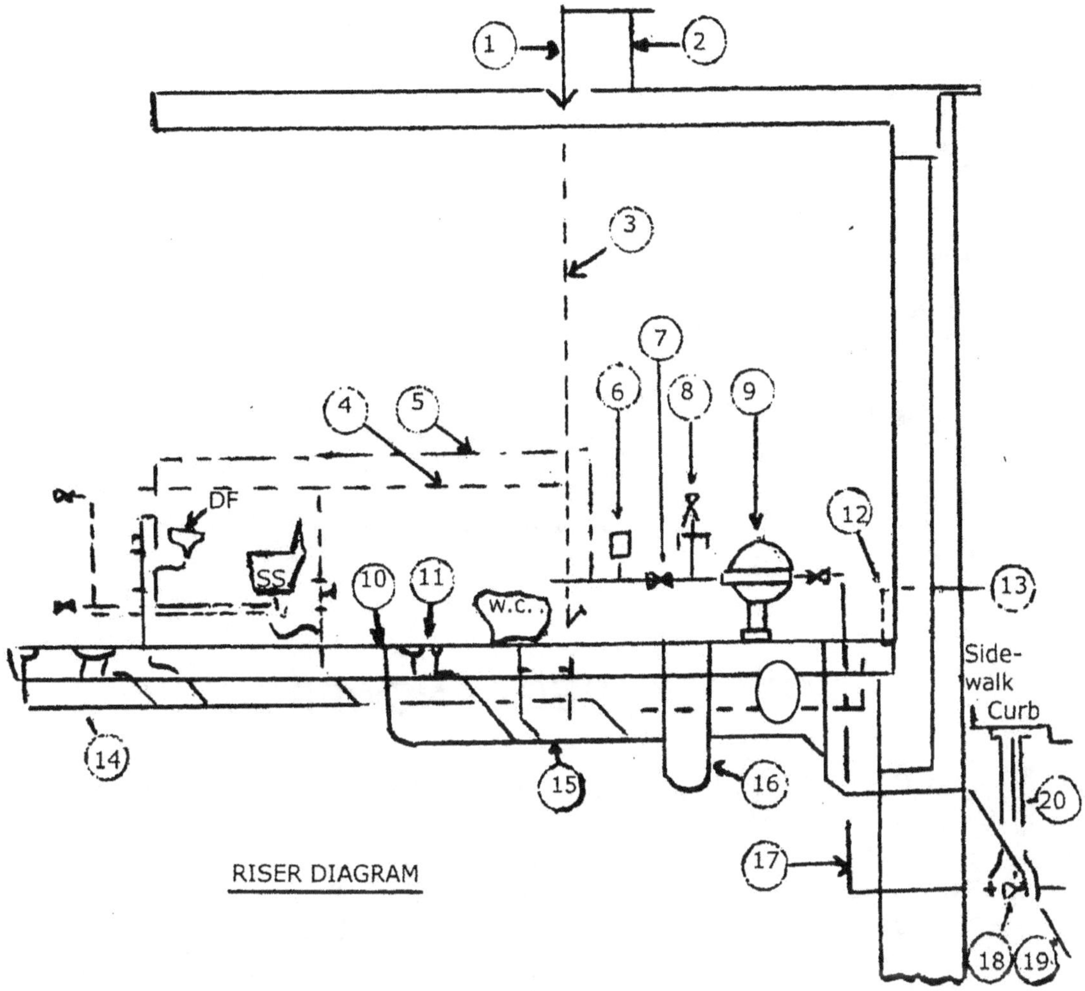

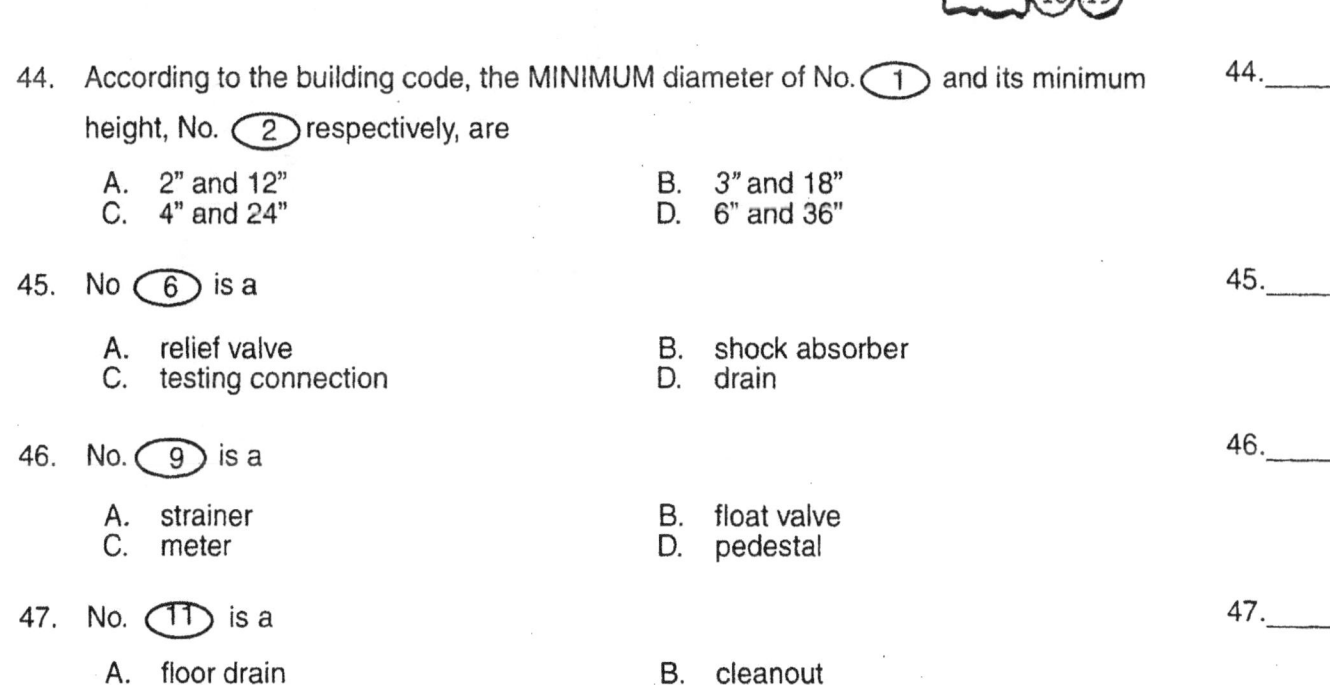

RISER DIAGRAM

44. According to the building code, the MINIMUM diameter of No. 1 and its minimum height, No. 2 respectively, are

    A. 2" and 12"
    B. 3" and 18"
    C. 4" and 24"
    D. 6" and 36"

44._____

45. No. 6 is a

    A. relief valve
    B. shock absorber
    C. testing connection
    D. drain

45._____

46. No. 9 is a

    A. strainer
    B. float valve
    C. meter
    D. pedestal

46._____

47. No. 11 is a

    A. floor drain
    B. cleanout
    C. trap
    D. vent connection

47._____

48. No. ⑬ is a

    A. standpipe
    B. air inlet
    C. sprinkler head
    D. cleanout

49. The size of No. ⑯ is

    A. 2" x 2"
    B. 2" x 3"
    C. 3" x 3"
    D. 4" x 4"

50. No. ⑱ is a

    A. pressure reducing valve
    B. butterfly valve
    C. curb cock
    D. sprinkler head

KEY (CORRECT ANSWERS)

1. C	11. A	21. D	31. A	41. D
2. B	12. C	22. D	32. D	42. A
3. C	13. A	23. B	33. C	43. A
4. D	14. B	24. A	34. A	44. C
5. D	15. C	25. A	35. C	45. B
6. B	16. A	26. B	36. B	46. C
7. B	17. A	27. B	37. D	47. A
8. A	18. D	28. D	38. D	48. B
9. B	19. B	29. D	39. D	49. D
10. D	20. D	30. D	40. B	50. C

FRAME CONSTRUCTION

Section I. FLOOR FRAMES AND FLOOR COVERINGS

1. Framing

After the foundation is built and the batterboards placed, the carpenter builds the framework. The framework includes the beams, trusses, foundation walls, outside walls, flooring, partitions, roofing, and ceiling.

a. Light Framing. Light framing is used in barracks, bathhouses, administration buildings, light shop buildings, hospitals, and similar buildings. Figure 1 shows some details for a 20-foot-wide building; the ground level; window openings, braces, and splices; and names the framing parts.

b. Light Frame Construction. Much of the framing can be done while staking out and squaring is being completed. When the skeleton is far enough along, boards can be nailed on without need for cutting if they are standard 8-, 10-, 12-, 16-, or 18-foot lengths. The better skilled men should construct the frame. With good organization, a large force of men can be kept busy during framing.

c. Expedient Framing. Expedient framing depends on the conditions. The ideas below may suggest other expedients.

(1) *Light siding.* Chicken wire and water resistant bituminous paper can be sandwiched to provide adequate temporary framing in temperate climates.

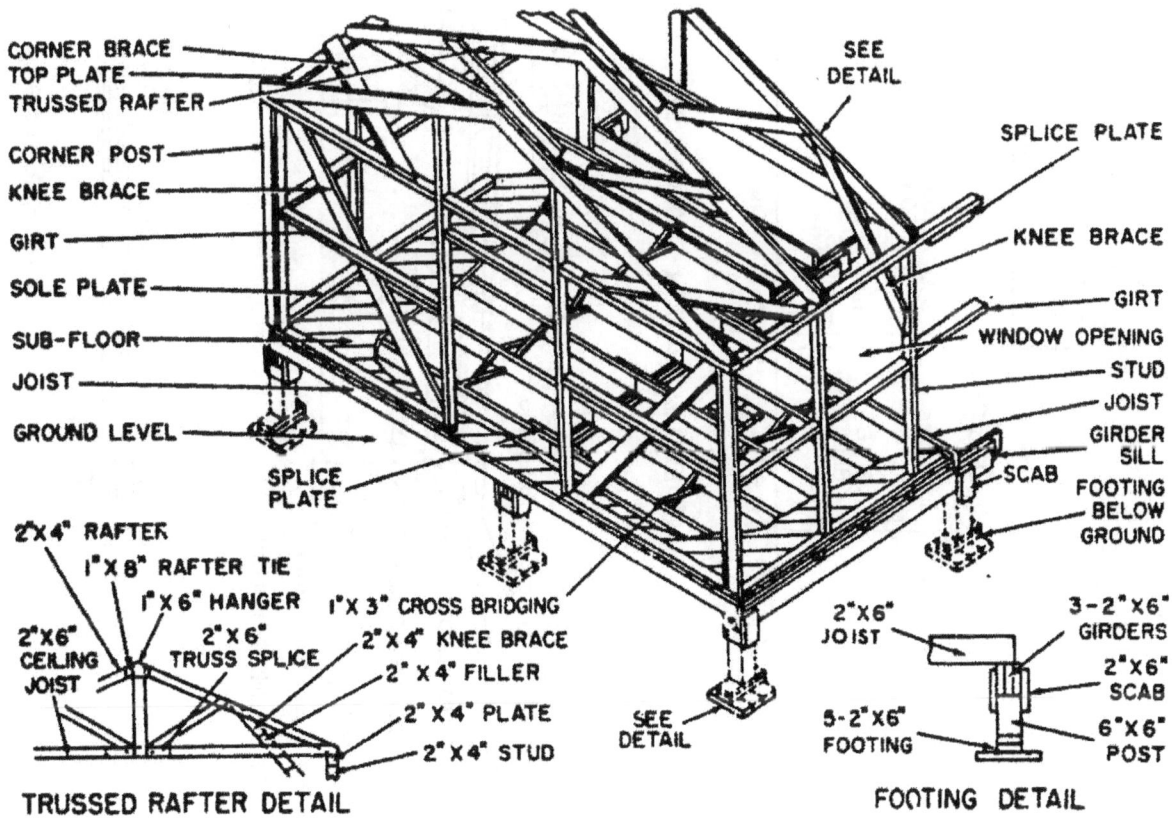

Figure 1. View of a light frame building substructure.

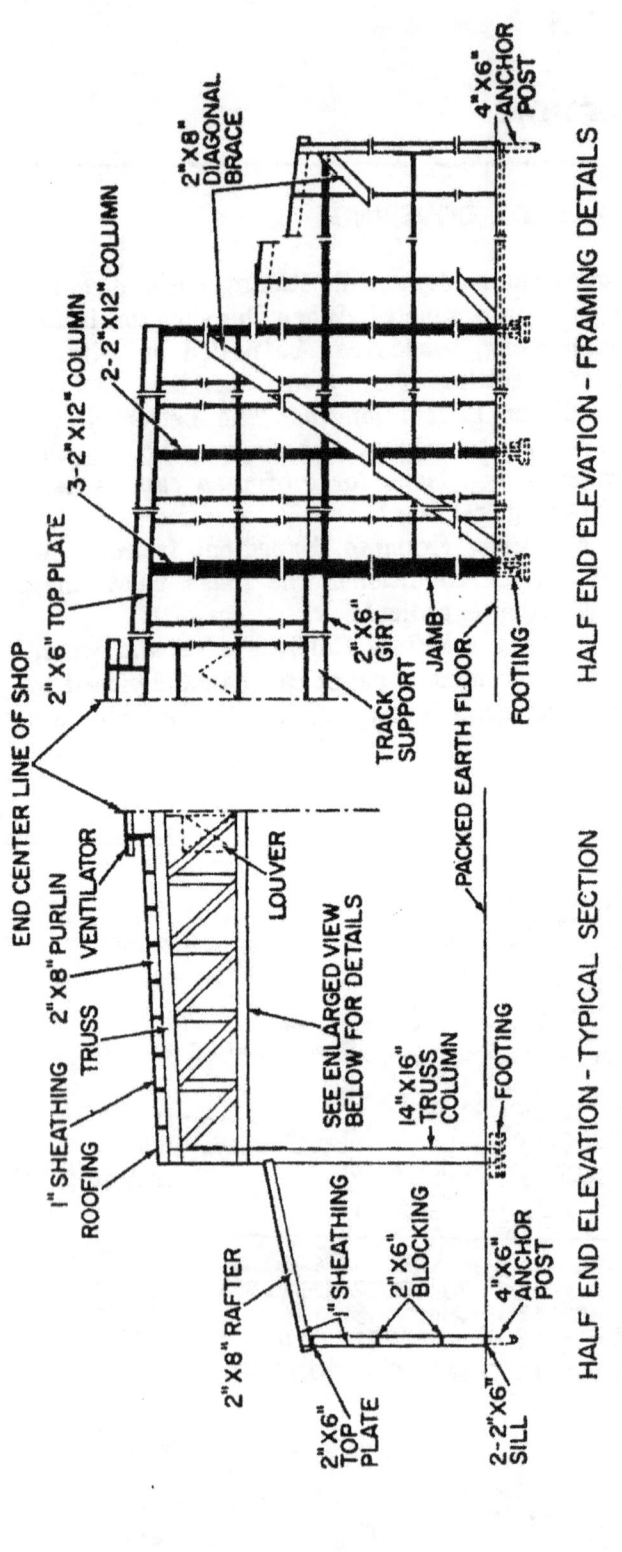
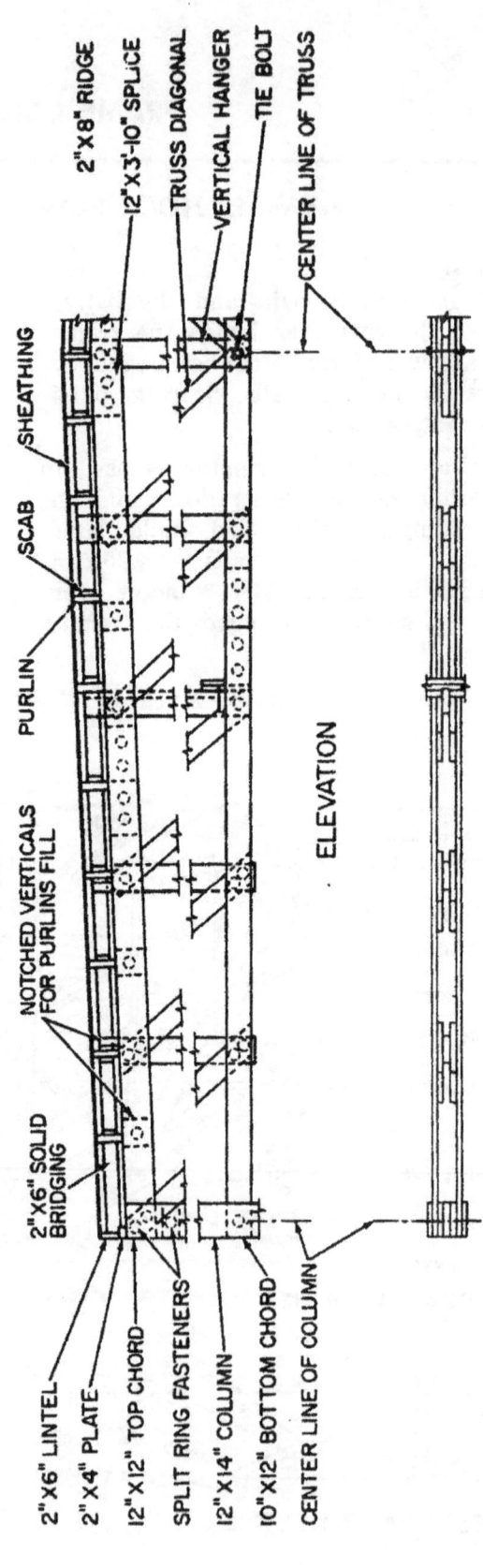

Figure 2. Sectional view of a heavy frame building.

(2) *Salvaged framing.* Salvaged sheet metal such as corrugated material or gasoline cans can be used as siding in the construction of emergency housing.

(3) *Local timber.* Poles trimmed from saplings or bamboo can be constructed into reasonably sound framing. Such materials may be secured with native vines as a further expedient.

(4) *Wood substitute framing.* Adobe soil, straw, and water puddled to proper consistency can be used for form walls, floors, and foundations. A similar mixture may be used to form sun-dried bricks for construction use.

(5) *Excavations.* Proper excavation and simple log cribbing may be covered with sod and carefully drained to provide adequate shelter.

d. *Heavy Framing.* Heavy frame buildings are more permanent, generally warehouses, depots, and shops. Figure 2 shows the details of heavy frame construction.

2. Sills

a. *Types.* The sill (fig. 1) is the foundation that supports all the building above it. It is the first part of the building to be set in place. It rests directly on the foundation piers or on the ground; it is joined at the corners and spliced when necessary. Figure 3 shows the most common sills. The type used depends on the type of construction used in the frame.

(1) *Box sills.* Box sills are used often with the very common style of platform framing, either with or without the sill plate. In this type of sill (1 and 2, fig. 3), the part that lies on the foundation wall or ground is called the sill plate. The sill is laid edgewise on the outside edge of the sill plate.

(2) *T-sills.* There are two types of T-sill construction; one commonly used in dry, warm climates (3, fig. 3), and one commonly used in less warm climates (4, fig. 3). Their construction is similar except that in the latter case the joists are nailed directly to the studs, as well as to the sills, and headers are used between the floor joists.

(3) *Braced framing sill.* The sill shown in 5, figure 3, is generally used in braced-framing construction. The floor joists are notched out and nailed directly to the sill and studs.

(4) *Built-up sills.* Where built-up sills are used, the joints are staggered (1, fig. 4). The corner joints are made as shown in 2, figure 4.

b. *Sill Requirement for Piers.* If piers are used in the foundation, heavier sills are used. They

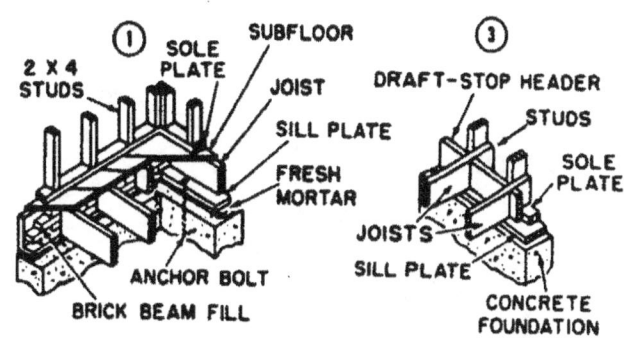

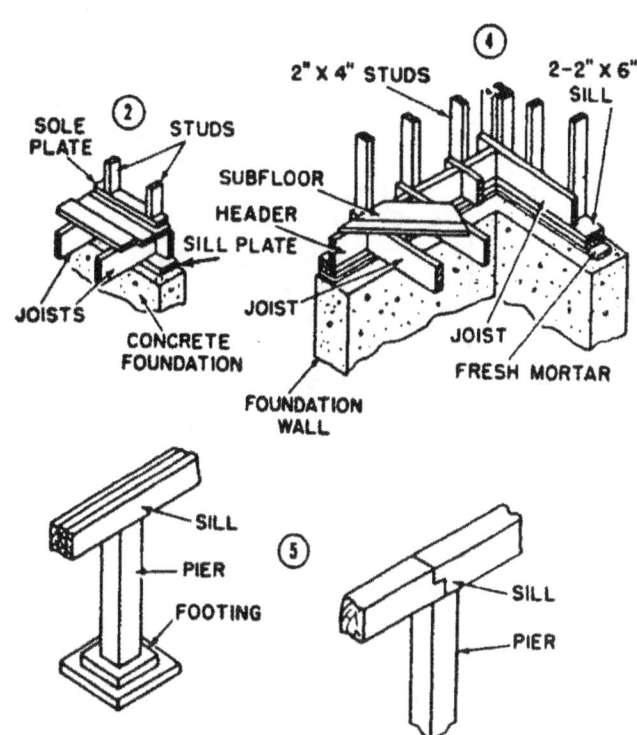

Figure 3. Types of sills.

are single heavy timbers or built up of two or more pieces of timber. Where heavy timber or built-up sills are used, the joints should occur over piers. The size of the sill depends upon the load to be carried and upon the spacing of the piers. The sill plates are laid directly on graded earth or on piers. Where earth floors are used, the studs are nailed directly to the sill plate.

3. Girders

The distance between two outside walls is often too great to be spanned by a single joist. When two or more joists are needed to cover the span, intermediate support for inboard joist-ends is provided by one or more girders. A girder is a large beam that supports other smaller beams or joists.

a. *Construction.* A girder may be made up of

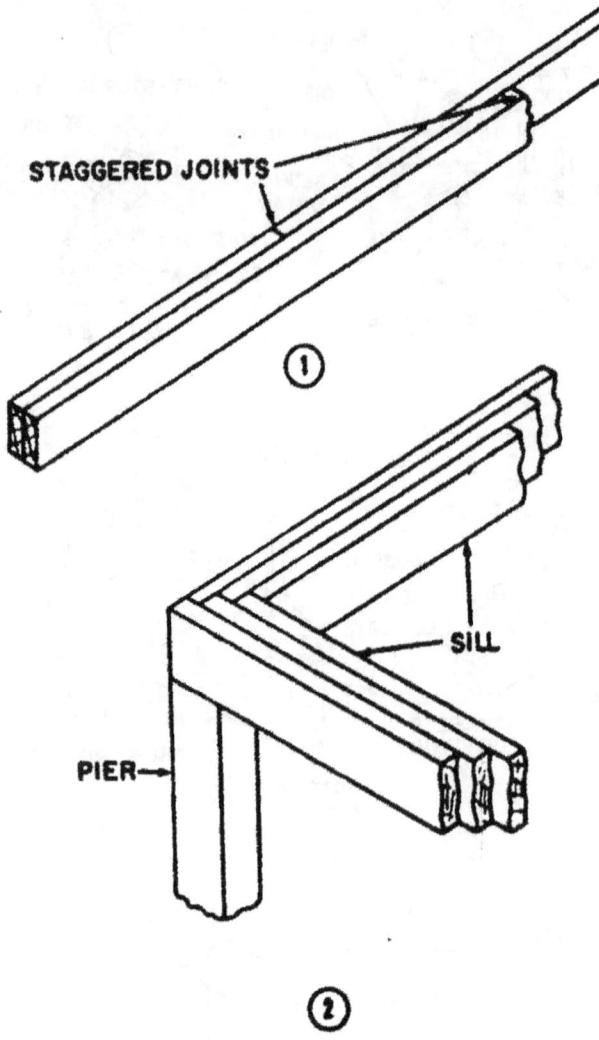

Figure 4. Sill fabrication.

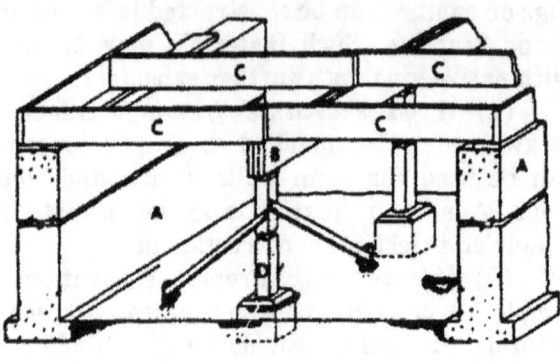

Figure 5. Built-up girder.

d. *Use of Ledger Board.* A girder with a ledge board upon which the joists rest is used where vertical space is limited. This arrangement is useful in providing more headroom in basements.

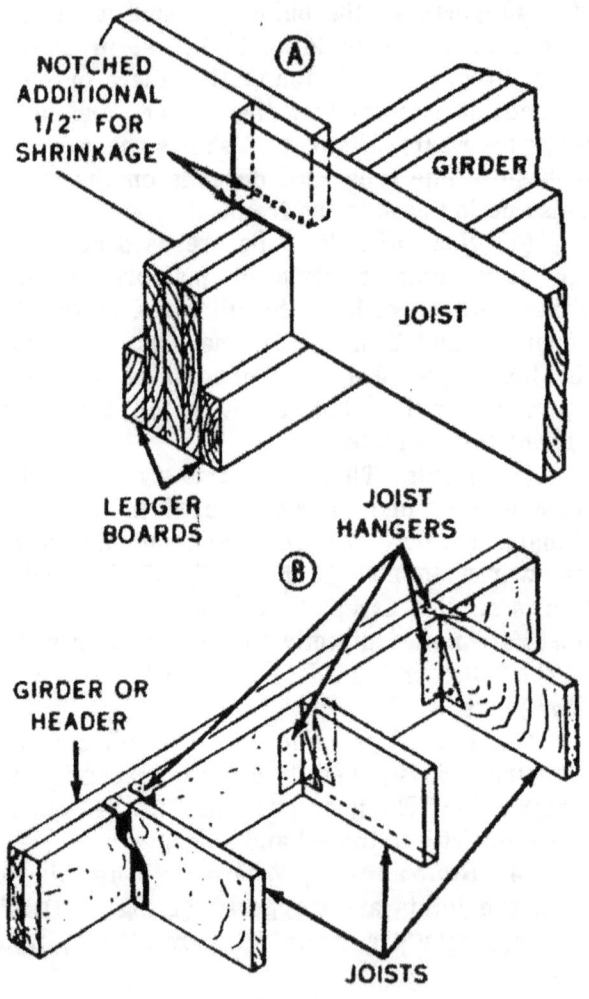

Figure 6. Joist-to-girder attachment.

several beams nailed together with 16d common nails; or it may be solid wood, steel, reinforced concrete, or a combination of these materials.

b. *Design Requirements.* Girders carry a very large proportion of the weight of a building. They must be well designed, rigid, and properly supported at the foundation walls and on the columns. Precautions must be taken to avoid or counteract any future settling or shrinking that might cause distortion of the building. The girders must also be installed so that they will properly support joists.

c. *Illustration.* Figure 5 shows a built-up girder. A shows the two outside masonry walls, B the built-up girder, C the joists, and D the support columns which support the girder B. Notice that the joists rest on top of the girder. This type of girder is commonly used in house construction. It is generally made of three planks spiked together (fig. 5) with 16d common nails.

e. Joist Hangers. A girder over which joist hangers have been placed to carry the joists is also used where there is little headroom or where the joists carry an extremely heavy load and nailing cannot be relied on. These girders are illustrated in figure 6.

f. Size Requirements. The principles which govern the size of a girder are—

(1) The distance between girder posts.
(2) The girder load area.
(3) The total floor load per square foot on the girder.
(4) The load per linear foot on the girder.
(5) The total load on the girder.
(6) The material to be used.

g. Size Determination. A girder should be large enough to support any ordinary load placed upon it; any size larger than that is wasted material. The carpenter should understand the effect of length, width, and depth on the strength of a wood girder before attempting to determine its size.

h. Depth. When the depth of a girder is doubled, the safe load is increased four times. In other words, a girder that is 3 inches wide and 12 inches deep will carry four times as much wight as a girder 3 inches wide and 6 inches deep. In order to obtain greater carrying capacity through the efficient use of material, it is better to increase the depth within limits than it is to increase the width of the girder. The sizes of built-up wood girders for various loads and spans may be determined by using table 1. (LOCATED IN BACK OF CHAPTER)

i. Load Area. The load area of a building is carried by both foundation walls and the girder. Because the ends of each joist rest on the girder, there is more weight on the girder than there is on either of the walls. Before considering the load on the girder, it may be well to consider a single joist. Suppose that a 10-foot plank weighing 5 pounds per foot is lifted by two men. If the men were at opposite ends of the plank, they would each be supporting 25 pounds.

(1) Now assume that one of these men lifts the end of another 10-foot plank with the same weight as the first one, and a third man lifts the opposite end. The two men on the outside are each supporting one-half of the weight of one plank, or 25 pounds apiece, but the man in the center is supporting one-half of each of the two planks, or a total of 50 pounds.

(2) The two men on the outside represent the foundation walls, and the center man represents the girder; therefore, the girder carries one-half of the weight, while the other half is equally divided between the outside walls. However, the girder may not always be located halfway between the outer walls. To explain this, the same three men will lift two planks which weigh 5 pounds per foot. One of the planks is 8 feet long and the other is 12 feet long. Since the total length of these two planks is the same as before and the weight per foot is the same, the total weight in both cases is 100 pounds.

(3) One of the outside men is supporting one-half of the 8-foot plank, or 20 pounds. The man on the opposite outside end is supporting one-half of the 12-foot plank, or 30 pounds. The man in the center is supporting one-half of each plank, or a total of 50 pounds. This is the same total weight he was lifting before. A general rule that can be applied when determining the girder load area is that a girder will carry the weight of the floor on each side to the midpoint of joists which rest upon it.

j. Floor Load. After the girder load area is known, the total floor load per square foot must be determined in order to select a safe girder size. Both dead and live loads must be considered in finding the total floor load.

(1) The first type of load consists of all weight of the building structure. This is called the dead load. The dead load per square foot of floor area, which is carried to the girder either directly or indirectly by way of bearing partitions, will vary according to the method of construction and building height. The structural parts included in the dead load are—

Floor joists for all floor levels.
Flooring materials, including attic if it is floored.
Bearing partitions.
Attic partitions.
Attic joists for top floor.
Ceiling lath and plaster, including basement ceiling if it is plastered.

(2) For a building of light-frame construction similar to an ordinary frame house, the dead load allowance per square foot of all the structural parts must be added together to determine the total dead load. The allowance for average subfloor, finish floor, and joists without basement plaster should be 10 pounds per square foot. If the basement ceiling is plastered, an additional 10 pounds should be allowed. When girders (or bearing partitions) support the first floor partition, a load allowance of 20 pounds must be

allowed for ceiling plaster and joists when the attic is unfloored. If the attic is floored and used for storage, an additional 10 pounds (per sq ft) should be allowed.

(3) The second type of load to be considered is the weight of furniture, persons, and other movable loads which are not actually a part of the building but are still carried by the girder. This is called the live load. Snow on the roof is considered a part of the live load. The live load per square foot will vary according to the use of the building and local weather conditions. The allowance for the live load on floors used for living purposes is usually 30 pounds per square foot. If the attic is floored and used for light storage, an additional 20 pounds per square foot should be allowed. The allowance per square foot for live loads is usually governed by specifications and regulations.

(4) When the total load per square foot of floor area is known, the load per linear foot on the girder is easily figured. Assume that the girder load area of the building shown in figure 7 is sliced into 1-foot lengths across the girder. Each slice represents the weight supported by 1 foot of the girder. If the slice is divided into 1-foot units, each unit will represent 1 square foot of the total floor area. The load per linear foot of girder is determined by multiplying the number of units by the total load per square foot. Note in figure 7 that the girder is off center. Therefore, the joist length on one side of the girder is 7 feet (one-half of 14 feet) and the other side is 5 feet (one-half of 10 feet), for a total distance of 12 feet across the load area. Since each slice is 1 foot wide, it has a total floor area of 12 square feet. Now, if we assume that the total floor load for each square foot is 70 pounds, multiply the length times the width (7' x 12') to get the total square feet supported by the girder (7' x 12' = 84 sq ft).

```
    84 sq ft
 x  70 lb per sq ft (live and dead load)
 5,880 lb total load on girder
```

k. Material. Wooden girders are more common than steel in small frame-type buildings. Solid timber may be used or they may be built up by using two or more 2-inch planks. Built-up girders have the advantage of not warping as easily as solid wooden girders and are less likely to have decayed wood in the center.

(1) When built-up girders are used, the pieces should be securely spiked together to prevent them from buckling individually. A two-

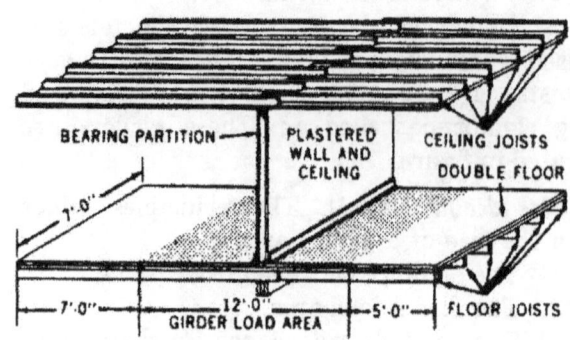

Figure 7. Girder load area.

piece girder of 2-inch planks should be spiked on both sides with 16d common nails. The nails should be located near the bottom, spaced approximately 2 feet apart near the ends and 1 foot apart in the center. A three-piece girder should be nailed in the same way as a two-piece girder.

(2) Regardless of whether the girder is built-up or solid, it should be of well-seasoned material. For a specific total girder load and span, the size of the girder will vary according to the kinds of wood used. The reason for this variation is that some kinds are stronger than others.

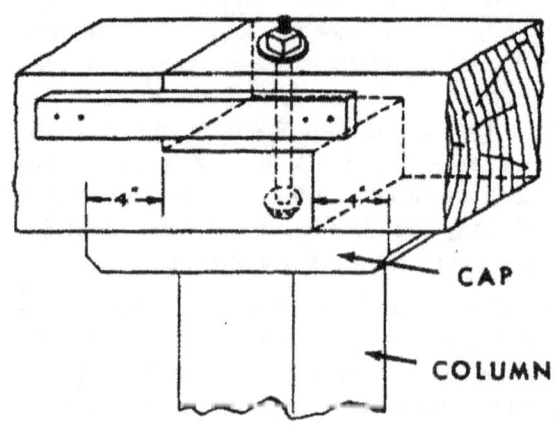

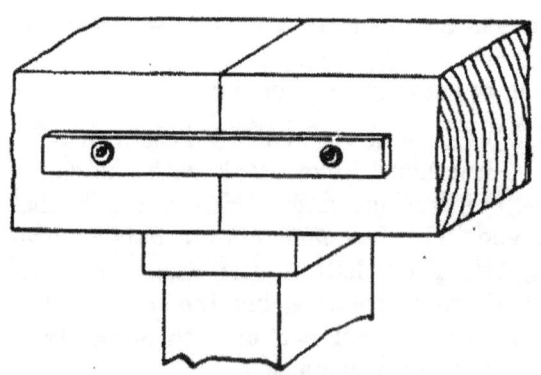

Figure 8. Half-lap and butt joints.

l. Splicing. To make a built-up girder, select straight lumber free from knots and other defects. The stock should be long enough so that no more than one joint will occur over the span between footings. The joints in the beam should be staggered, with care taken to insure that the planks are squared at each joint and butted tightly together. Sometimes a half-lap joint is used to join solid beams. In order to do this correctly, the beam should be placed on one edge so that the annual rings run from top to bottom. The lines for the half-lap joint are then laid out as illustrated in figure 8, and the cuts are made along these lines. The cuts are then checked with a steel square to assure a matching joint. To make the matching joint on the other beam, proceed in the same way and repeat the process.

(1) The next step is to tack a temporary strap across the joint to hold it tightly together. Now drill a hole through the joist with a bit about 1/16 inch larger than the bolt to be used. Fasten together with a bolt, washer, and nut.

(2) Another type of joint is called the strapped butt joint. The ends of the beam should be cut square, and the straps, which generally are 18 inches long, are bolted to each side of the beams.

m. Supports. When building small houses where the services of an architect are not available, it is important that the carpenter have some knowledge of the principles that determine the proper size of girder supports.

(1) A column or post is a vertical member designed to carry the live and dead loads imposed upon it. It may be made of wood, metal, or masonry. The wooden columns may be solid timbers or may be made up of several wooden members spiked together with 16d or 20d common nails. Metal columns are made of heavy pipe, large steel angles, or I-beams.

(2) Regardless of the material used in a column, it must have some form of bearing plate at the top and bottom. These plates distribute the load evenly over the cross sectional area of the column. Basement posts that support girders should be set on masonry footings. Columns should be securely fastened to the load-bearing member at the top and to the footing on which they rest at the bottom. Figure 9 shows a solid wooden column with a metal bearing cap drilled to provide a means of fastening it to the column and to the girder. The bottom of this type of column may be fastened to the masonry footing by a metal dowel inserted in a hole drilled in the bottom of the column and in the masonry footing. The base at this point is coated with asphalt to prevent rust or rot.

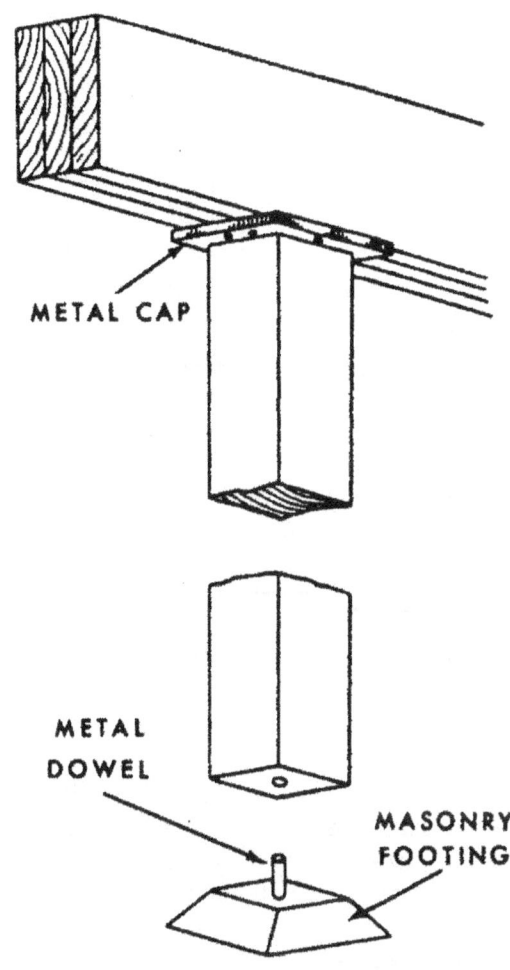

Figure 9. Solid wood column with metal bearing cap.

(3) When locating columns, it is well to avoid spans of more than 10 feet between columns that are to support the girders. The farther apart the columns are spaced, the heavier the girder must be to carry the joists over the span between the columns.

(4) A good arrangement of the girder and supporting columns for a 24- x 40-foot building is shown in figure 10. Column B will support one-half of the girder load existing in the half of the building lying between the wall A and column C. Column C will support one-half of the girder load between columns B and D. Likewise, column D will share equally the girder loads with column C and the wall E.

n. Girder Forms. Girder forms for making concrete girders and beams are constructed from 2-inch-thick material (fig. 11) dressed on all sides. The bottom piece of material should be constructed in one piece to avoid the necessity of cleats. The bottom piece of the form should never

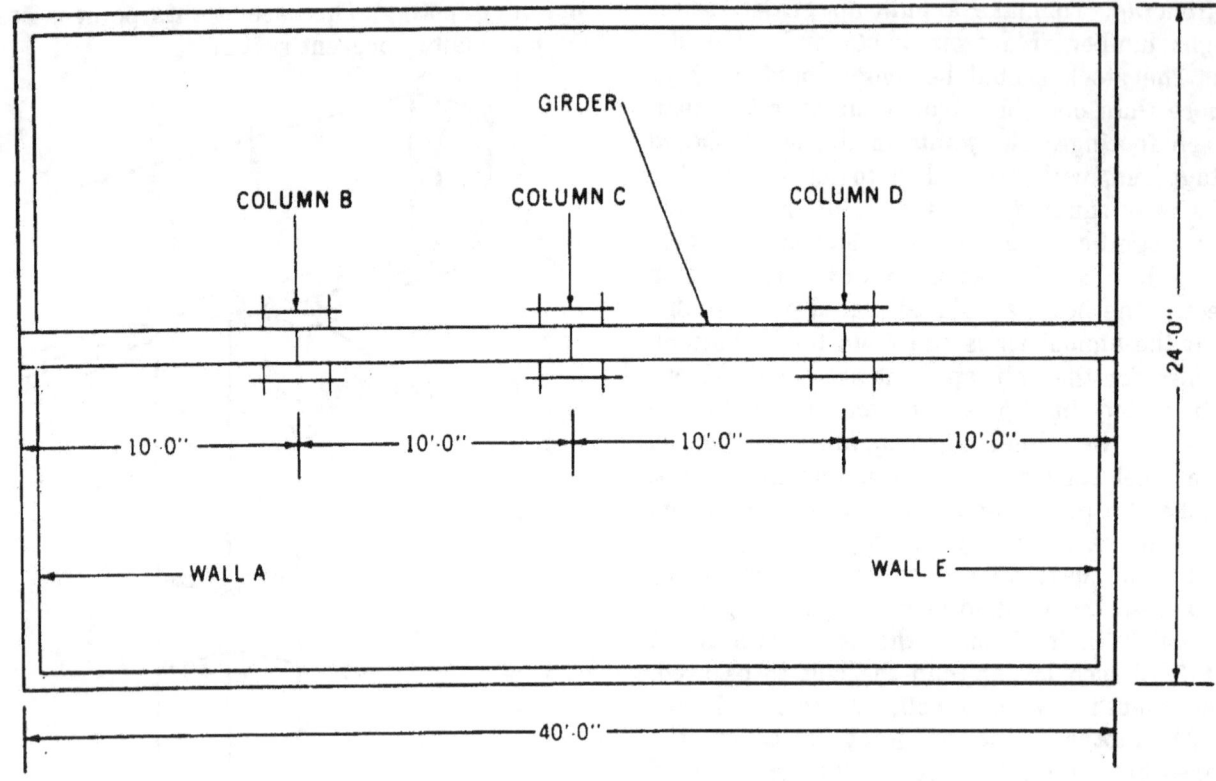

Figure 10. Column spacing.

overlap the side pieces. The side pieces must always overlap the bottom. The temporary cleats shown in figure 11 are tacked on to prevent the form from collapsing when handled.

4. Floor Joists

Joists are the wooden members that make up the body of the floor frame. The flooring or subflooring is nailed to them. They are usually 2 or 3 inches thick. Joists as small as 2 by 6 inches are sometimes used in light buildings. These are too small for floors with spans over 10 feet but are frequently used for ceiling joists. Joists usually carry a uniform load of materials and personnel. The latter loads carry a uniform

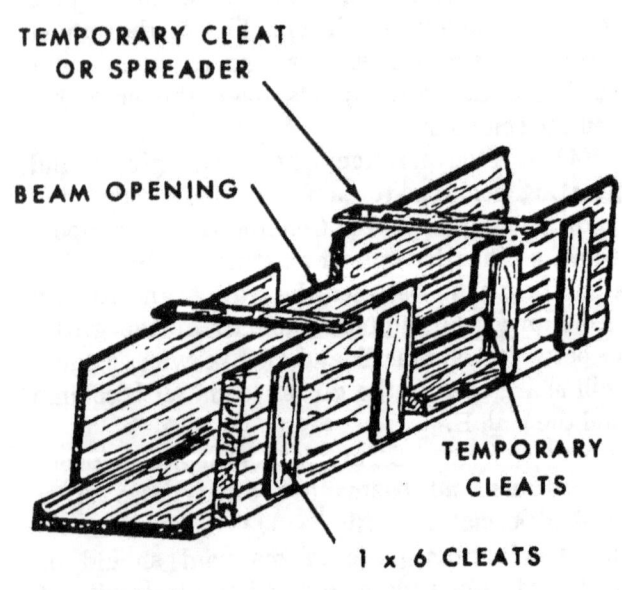

Figure 11. Girder and beam form.

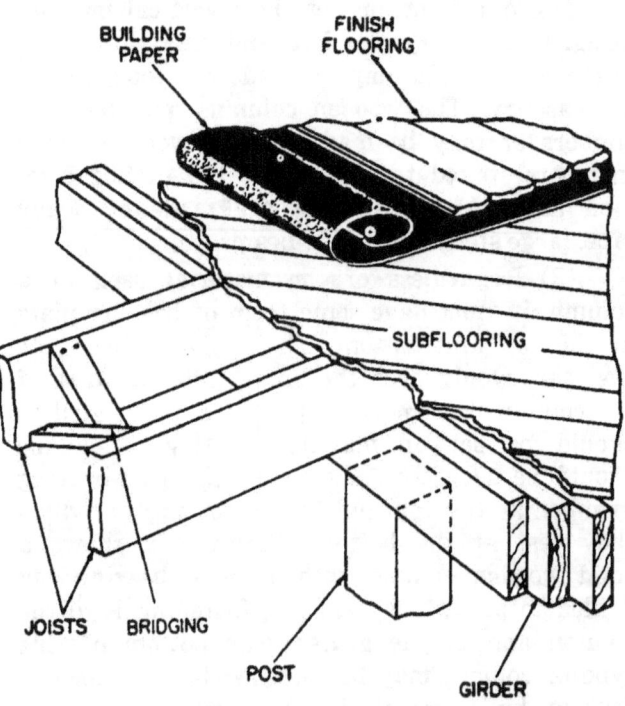

Figure 12. Floor joists.

load of materials and personnel. The latter loads are "live loads"; the weight of joists and floors is a "dead load". The joists carry the flooring directly on their upper surface and they are supported at their ends by sills, girders, bearing partitions, or bearing walls (fig. 12). They are spaced 16 or 24 inches apart, center to center; sometimes the spacing is 12 inches, but where such spacing is necessary, heavier joists should be used. Two-inch material should not be used for joists more than 12 inches apart.

5. Connecting Joists to Sills, Girders, and I-Beams

a. Joining to Sills. In joining joists to sills, be sure that the connection is able to hold the load that the joists will carry. A joist resting upon the sill is shown in 1, figure 13. This method (of several methods) is most commonly used because it provides the strongest possible joint. The methods shown in 2 and 3, figure 13, are used where it is not desirable to use joists on top of the sill. The ledger plate (*e* below) should be securely nailed and the joist should not be notched over one-third of its depth to prevent splitting (4, fig. 13).

b. Joining to Girders. In the framing of the joists to the girders, the joists must be level. Therefore, if the girder is not the same height as the sill, the joist must be notched as shown in 3, figure 13. If the girder and sill are of the same height, the joist must be connected to the sill and girder to keep the joist level. In placing joists, always have the crown up since this counteracts the weight on the joist; in most cases there will be no sag below a straight line. Overhead joists are joined to plates as shown in 1 and 2, figure 14. The inner end of the joist rests on the plates of the partition walls. When a joist is to rest on plates or girders, either the joist is cut long enough to extend the full width of the plate or girder, or it is cut so as to meet in the center of the plate or girder and is connected with a scab. Where two joist ends lie side by side on a plate, they should be nailed together. Joists may also be joined to girders by using ledger strips (3 and 4, fig. 14).

c. Iron Stirrups. One of the strongest supports for the joists is straps or hangers (iron stirrups) as shown in 5 of figure 13.

d. I-Beams. The simplest and probably the best way to carry joists on steel girders is to rest them on top, as shown in 6, figure 13, provided headroom is not too much restricted. If there is a lack of headroom, use the method shown in 5, figure 13.

e. Use of Ledger Plates (fig. 14). In connecting joists to girders and sills where piers are used, a 2 by 4 is nailed to the face of the sill or girder, flush with the bottom edge; this is called a "ledger plate" (1, fig. 14). These pieces should be nailed securely with 20-penny nails about 12 inches apart. Where 2 by 4 or 2

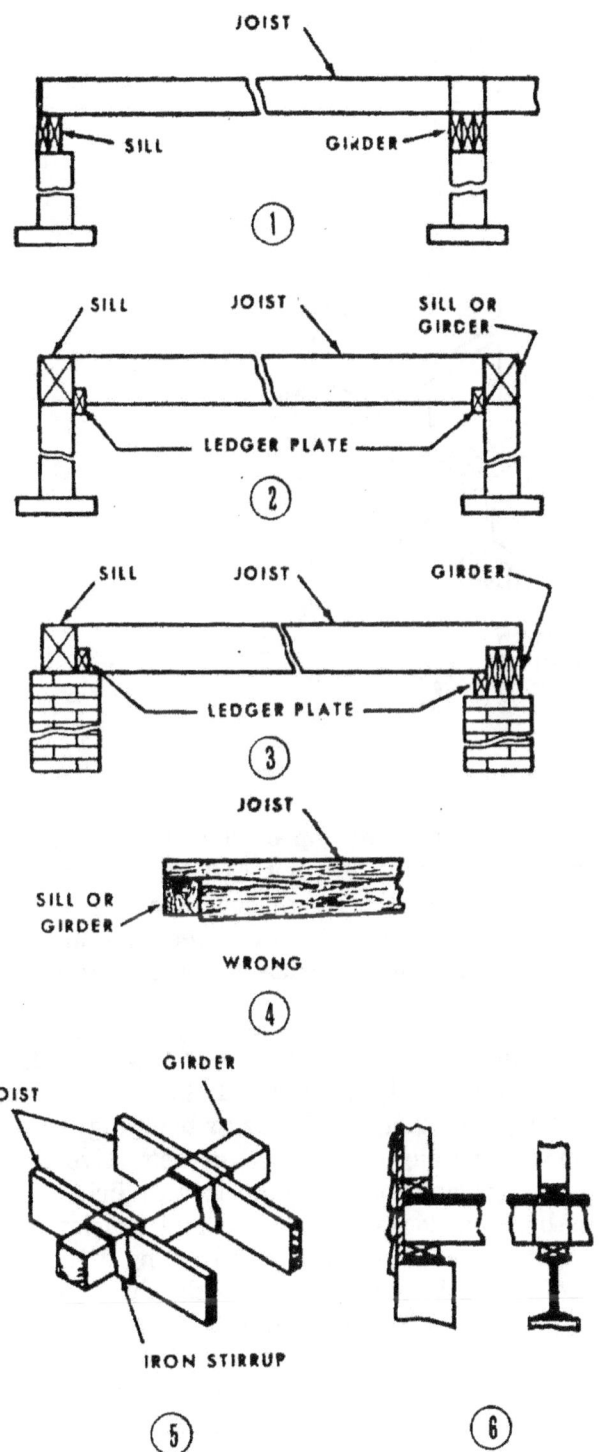

Figure 13. Sill and joist connections.

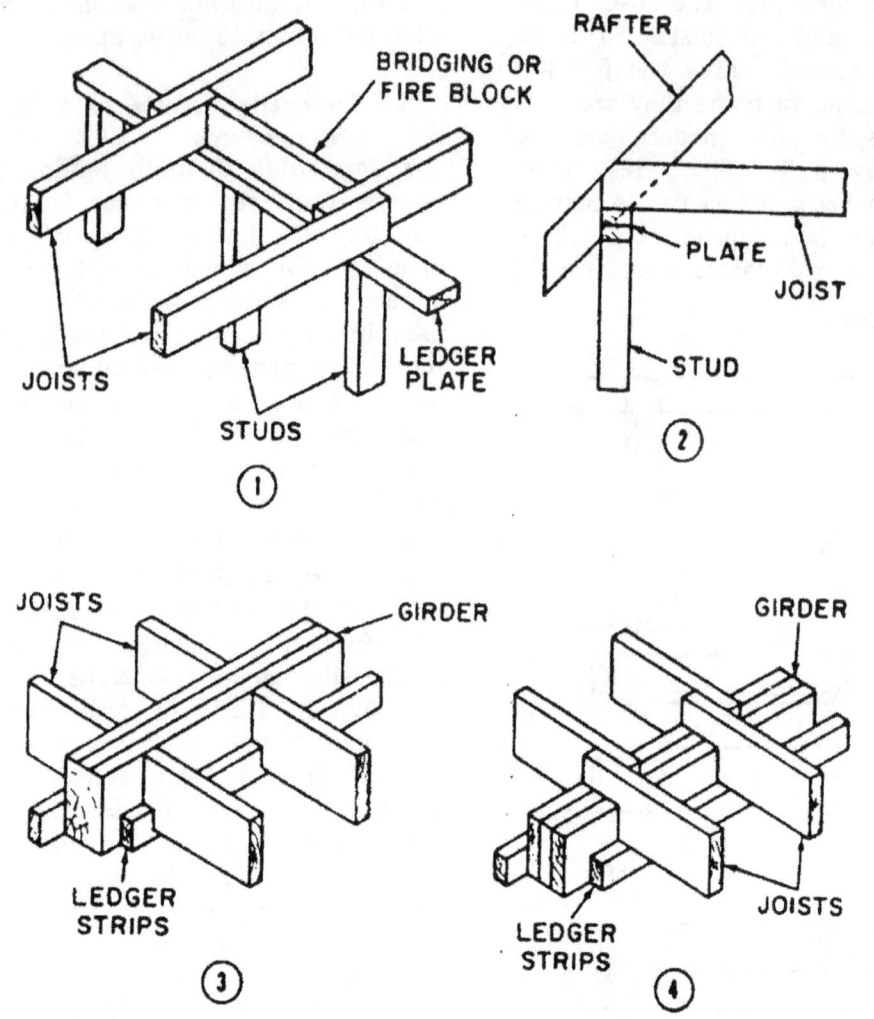

Figure 14. Ledger plates.

by 8 joists are used, it is better to use 2 by 2's to prevent the joists from splitting at the notch. When joists are 10 inches deep and deeper, 2 by 4's may be used without reducing the strength of the joists. If a notch is used, joist ties may be used to overcome this loss of strength. These ties are short 1 by 4 boards nailed across the joist; the ends of the boards are flush with the top and bottom edge of the joists.

6. Bridging

a. General. When joists are used over a long span, they have a tendency to sway from side to side. Floor frames are bridged in order to stiffen the floor frame, to prevent unequal deflection of the joists, and to enable an overload joist to receive some help from the joists on either side of it. A pattern for the bridging stock is obtained by placing a piece of material between the joists as shown in figure 15, then marking and sawing it. When sawed, the cut will form the correct angle. Always nail the top of the bridging with 8- or 10-penny nails. Do not nail the bottom of the bridging until the rough floor has been laid, in order to keep the bridging from pushing up any joist which might cause an unevenness in the floor.

b. Construction. Bridging is of two kinds: solid (or horizontal) bridging (1, fig. 15) and cross bridging (2, fig. 15). Cross bridging is the one most generally used; it is very effective and requires less material than horizontal bridging. Cross bridging looks like a cross and consists of pieces of lumber, usually 1 by 3 or 2 by 3 inches in size, cut in diagonally between the floor joists. Each piece is nailed to the top of each joist and forms a cross (x) between the joists. These pieces between joists should be placed as near to each other as possible. Bridging should be nailed and the bottoms left until the subfloor is laid. This permits the joists to adjust themselves to their final positions. The bottom ends of bridging

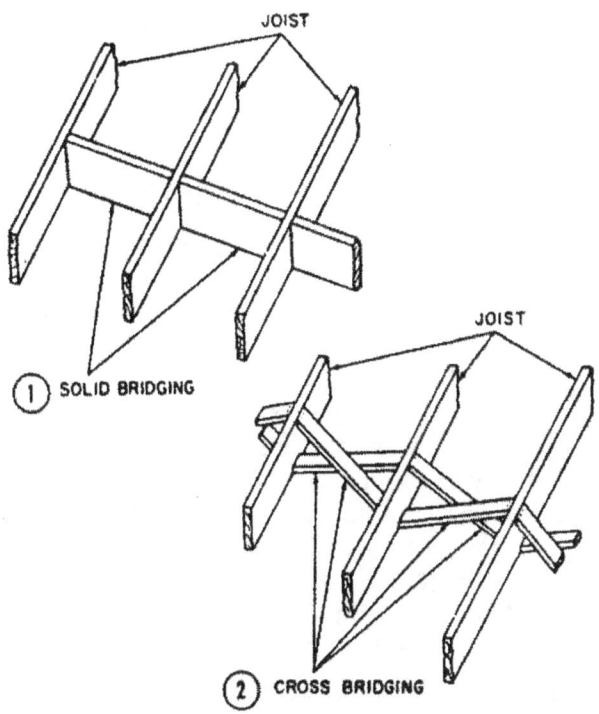

Figure 15. Types of bridging.

may then be nailed, forming a continuous truss across the whole length of the floor and preventing any overloaded joist from sagging below the others. Cutting and fitting the bridging by hand is a slow process; a power saw should be used if it is available. After joists have once been placed, a pattern may be made and used to speed up the process of cutting. On joists over 8 feet long, one line of bridging should be placed and on joists over 16 feet long, two lines.

7. Floor Openings

a. General. Floor openings for stairwells, ventilators, and chimneys are framed by a combination of headers and trimmers (fig. 16). Headers run at right angles to the direction of the joists and are doubled. Trimmers run parallel to the joists and are actually doubled joists. The joists are framed to the headers where the headers form the opening frame at right angles to the joists. These shorter joists, framed to the headers, are called tail beams, tail joists, or header joists. The number of headers and trimmers needed at any opening depends upon the shape of the opening, whether it is a simple rectangle or contains additional angles; upon the direction in which the opening runs in relation to the direction in which the joists run; and upon the position of the opening in relation to partitions or walls. Figure 16 gives examples of openings, one of which runs parallel to the

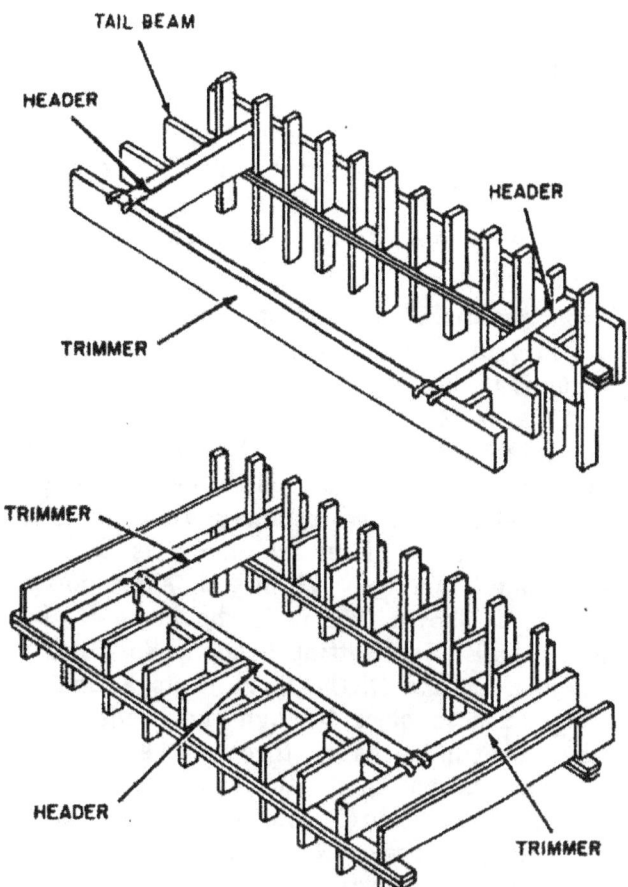

Figure 16. Floor openings.

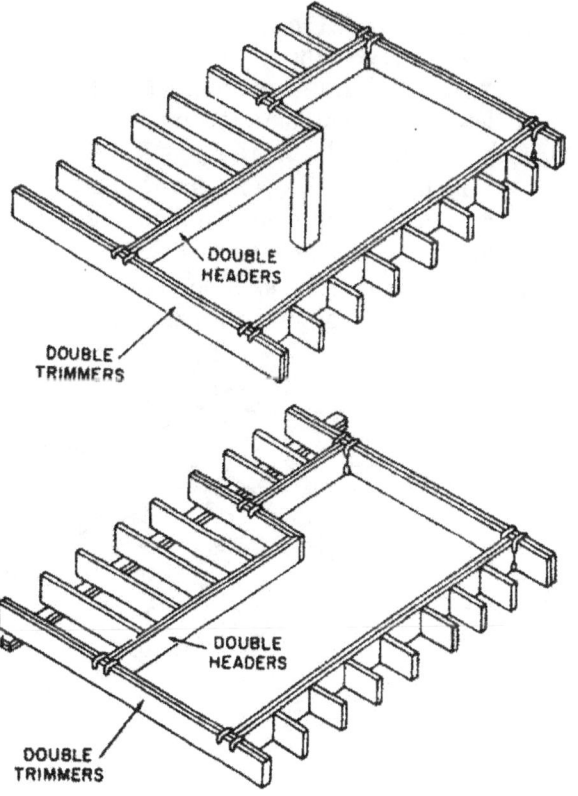

Figure 17. Double headers and double trimmers.

joist and requires two headers and one trimmer, while the other runs at right angles to the run of the joists and, therefore, requires one header and two trimmers. The openings shown in figure 17 are constructed with corner angles supported in different ways. The cantilever method requires that the angle be fairly close to a supporting partition with joists from an adjacent span that run to the header.

b. Construction. To frame openings of the type shown in figure 18, first install joists A and C, then cut four pieces of timber that are the same size as the joists with their length corresponding to the distance between the joists A and C at the outside wall. Nail two of these pieces between the joists at the desired distances from the ends of the joists; these pieces are shown as headers Nos. 1 and 2, figure 18. Install short joists X and Y, as shown. The nails should be 16- or 20-penny nails. By omitting headers Nos. 3 and 4 and joists B and D, the short joists X and Y can be nailed in place through the header and the headers can be nailed through the joists A and B into its end. After the header and short joists have been securely nailed, headers Nos. 3 and 4 are nailed beside Nos. 1 and 2. Then joist B is placed beside joists A and joist D beside C, and all are nailed securely.

8. Subfloors and Finish Floors

a. Subfloors. After the foundation and basic framework of a building are completed, the floor is constructed. The subfloor, if included in the plans, is laid diagonally on the joists and nailed with 8- to 10-penny nails. The floor joists form a framework for the subfloor. Subflooring boards 8 inches wide or over should have three or more nails per joist. Where the subfloor is over 1 inch thick, larger nails should be used. Figure 12 shows the method of laying a subfloor. Preferably it is laid before the walls are framed so that it can be used as a floor to work on while framing the walls.

b. Finish Floors.

(1) *General.* A finish floor in the theater of operations, in most cases, is of 3/4-inch material, square edged (fig. 19) or tongued and grooved (fig. 20), and varying from 3 1/4 to 7 1/4 inches wide. It is laid directly on floor joists or on a subfloor and nailed with 8-penny common nails in every joist. When laid on a subfloor, it is best to use building paper between the two floors to keep out dampness and insects. In warehouses, where heavy loads are to be carried on the floor, 2-inch material should be used. The flooring, in this case, also is face-nailed with 16- or 20-penny nails. It is not tongued and grooved and ranges in width from 4 to 12 inches. The joints are made on the center of the joist.

(2) *Wood floors.* Wood floors must be strong enough to carry the load. The type of building and the use for which it is intended determines the general arrangement of the floor system,

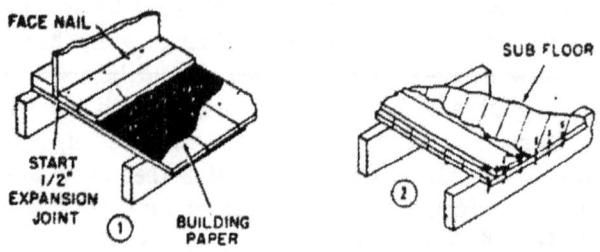

Figure 19. Methods for nailing square-edged flooring.

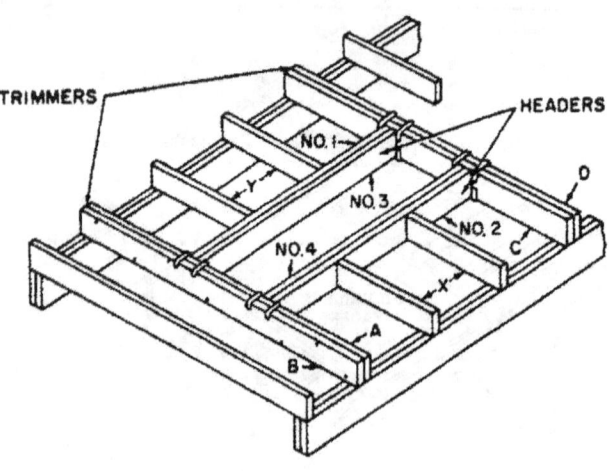

Figure 18. Floor opening construction.

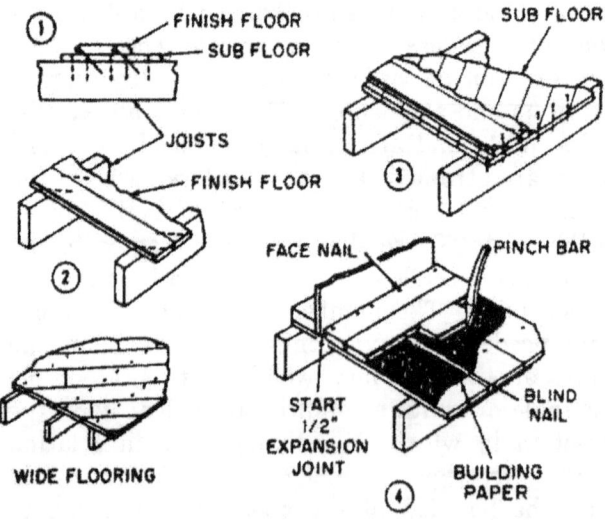

Figure 20. Methods for nailing tongued-and-grooved flooring.

thickness of the sheathing, and approximate spacing of the joists.

(3) *Concrete floors.* Concrete floors may be constructed for shops where earthen or wood floors are not suitable such as in repair and assembly shops for airplanes and heavy equipment and in certain kinds of warehouses. These floors are made by pouring concrete on the ground after the earth has been graded and tamped. This type of floor is likely to be damp unless protected. Drainage is provided, both for the floor area and for the area near the floor, to prevent flooding after heavy rains. The floor should be reinforced with steel or wire mesh. Where concrete floors are to be poured, a foundation wall may be poured first and the floor poured after the building is completed. This gives protection to the concrete floor while it sets.

(4) *Miscellaneous types of floors.* Miscellaneous floors may include earth, adobe brick, duckboard, or rushes. Use of miscellaneous flooring is usually determined by a shortage of conventional materials, the need to save time or labor, the extremely temporary nature of the facilities, or the special nature of the structure. The selection of material is usually determined by availability. Duckboard is widely used for shower flooring; earthen floors are common and conserve both materials and labor if the ground site is even without extensive grading. Rush or thatch floors are primarily an insulating measure and must be replaced frequently.

(5) *Supports.* In certain parts of the floor frame, in order to support some very heavily concentrated load or a partition wall, it may be necessary to double the joist or to place two joists together (fig. 21).

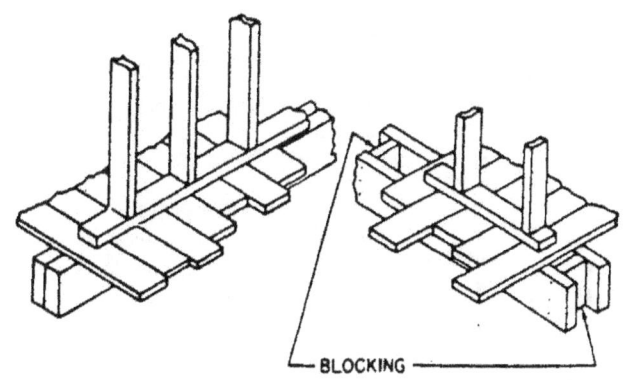

Figure 21. Reinforced joists.

Section II. WALLS AND WALL COVERINGS

9. General

Wall framing (fig. 22) is composed of regular studs, diagonal bracing, cripples, trimmers, headers, and fire blocks and is supported by the floor sole plate. The vertical members of the wall framing are the studs, which support the top plates and all of the weight of the upper part of the building or everything above the top plate line. They provide the framework to which the wall sheathing is aniled on the outside and which supports the lath, plaster, and insulation on the inside.

10. Wall Components

Walls and partitions which are classed as framed constructions (fig. 23) are composed of structural elements which are usually closely spaced, slender, vertical members called studs. These are arranged in a row with their ends bearing on a long horizontal member called a bottom plate or sole plate, and their tops capped with another plate, called a top plate. Double top plates are used in bearing walls and partitions. The bearing strength of stud walls is determined by the strength of the studs.

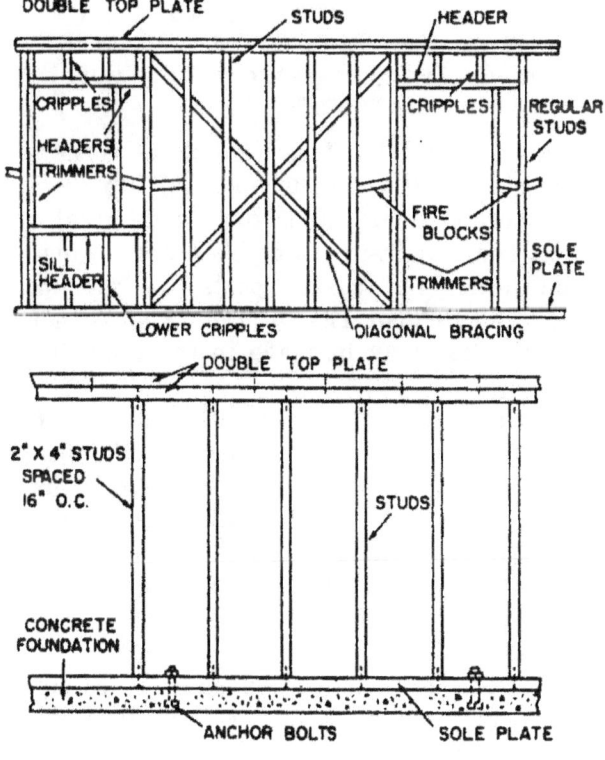

Figure 22. Typical wall frame details.

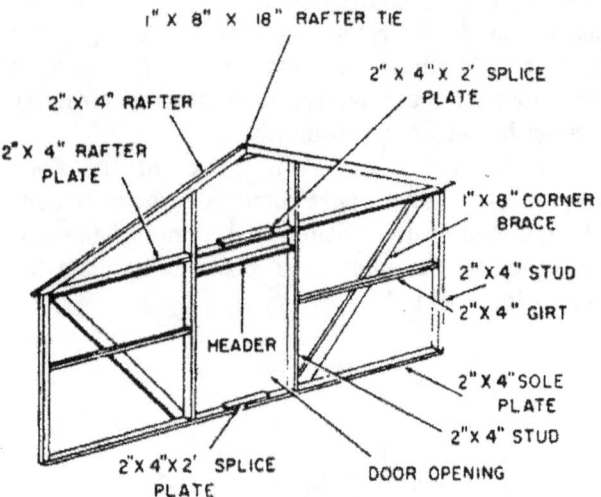

① END PANEL - FRAMING DETAILS

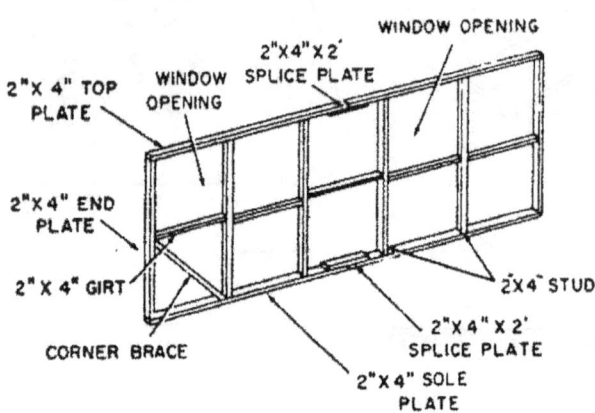

② SIDE PANEL - FRAMING DETAILS

Figure 23. Typical wall construction showing openings.

a. *Corner Posts.* The studs used at the corners of frame construction are usually built up from three or more ordinary studs to provide greater strength. These built-up assemblies are corner-partition posts. The corner posts are set up, plumbed, and temporarily braced. The corner posts (fig. 24) may be made in the following ways:

(1) A corner post may consist of a 4 by 6 with a 2 by 4 nailed on the board side, flush with one edge, as shown in figure 24. This type of corner is for a 4-inch wall. Where walls are thicker, heavier timber is used.

(2) A 4 by 4 may be used with a 2 by 4 nailed to two of the adjoining sides, shown in 2, figure 24.

(3) Two 2 by 4's may be nailed together with blocks between and a 2 by 4 flush with one edge, shown in 3, figure 24.

(4) A 2 by 4 may be nailed to the edge of another 2 by 4, the edge of one flush with the side of the other (4, fig. 24). This type is used extensively in the theater of operations where no inside finish is needed.

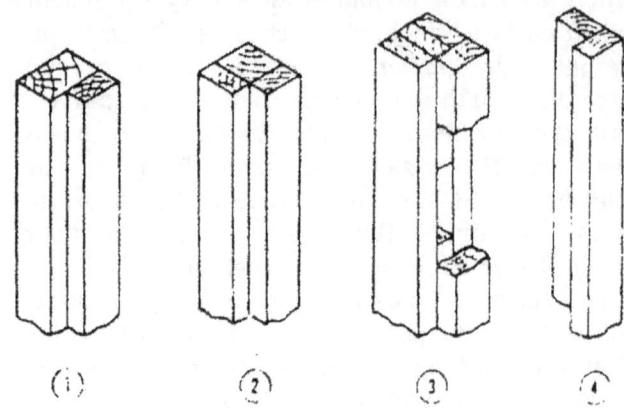

Figure 24. Corner post construction.

b. *T-Posts.* Whenever a partition meets an outside wall, a stud wide enough to extend beyond the partition on both sides is used; this provides a solid nailing base for the inside wall finish. This type of stud is called a T-post (fig. 25) and is made in the following different ways:

(1) A 2 by 4 may be nailed and centered on the face side of a 4 by 6 (1, fig. 25).

(2) A 2 by 4 may be nailed and centered on two 4 by 4's nailed together (2, fig. 25).

(3) Two 2 by 4's may be nailed together with a block between them and a 2 by 4 centered on the wide side (3, fig. 25).

(4) A 2 by 4 may be nailed and centered on the face side of a 2 by 6, with a horizontal bridging nailed behind them to give support and stiffness (4, fig. 25).

c. *Partition and Double T-Posts.* Where a partition is finished on one side only, the partition post used consists of a simple stud, set in the outside wall, in line with the side of the partition

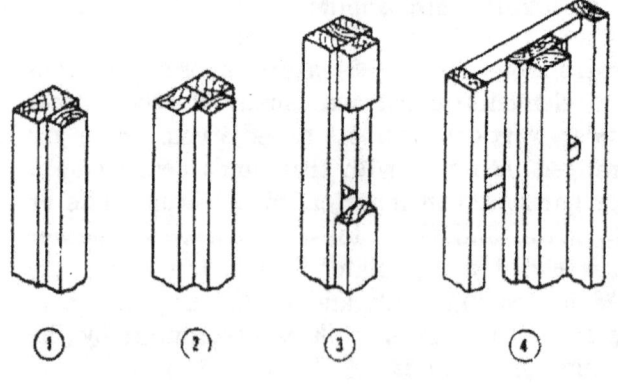

Figure 25. T-post construction.

wall, and finished as stud A in 1, figure 26. These posts are nailed in place along with the corner post. The exact position of the partition walls must be determined before the posts are placed. Where the walls are more than 4 inches thick, wider timber is used. In special cases, for example where partition walls cross, a double T-post is used. This is made by using methods in *b*(1), (2), or (3) above, and nailing another 2 by 4 to the opposite wide side, as shown in 2, 3, and 4, figure 26.

d. Studs.

(1) After the sills, plates, and braces are in place, and the window and door openings are laid out, the studs are placed and nailed with two 16- or 20-penny nails through the top plate. Then the remaining or intermediate studs are laid out on the sills or soles by measuring from one corner the distances the studs are to be set apart. Studs are normally spaced 12, 16, and 24 inches on centers, depending upon the type of outside and inside finish. Where vertical siding is used, studs are set wider apart since the horizontal girts between them provide nailing surface.

(2) When it is desirable to double the post of the door opening, first place the outside studs into position and nail them securely. Then cut short studs, or *filler studs*, the size of the opening, and nail these to the inside face of the outside studs as shown in figure 27. In making a window opening, a bottom header must be framed; this header is either single or double. When it is doubled, the bottom piece is nailed to the opening studs at the proper height and the top piece of the bottom header is nailed into place flush with the bottom section. The door header is framed as shown in figure 27. The filler stud rests on the sole at the bottom.

e. Girts. Girts are always the same width as the studs and are flush with the face of the stud, both outside and inside. Girts are used in hasty construction where the outside walls are covered with vertical siding. Studs are placed from 2 to 10 feet apart, with girts, spaced about 4 feet apart, running horizontally between them (fig. 27). The vertical siding acts in the same way as to studs and helps to carry the weight of the roof. This type of construction is used extensively in the theater of operations.

f. Top Plate and Sole Plate.

(1) *Top plate.* The top plate ties the studding together at the top and forms a finish for the walls; it furnishes a support for the lower ends of the rafters (fig. 22). The top plate serves as a connecting link between the wall and the roof, just as the sills and girders are connecting links between the floors and the walls.

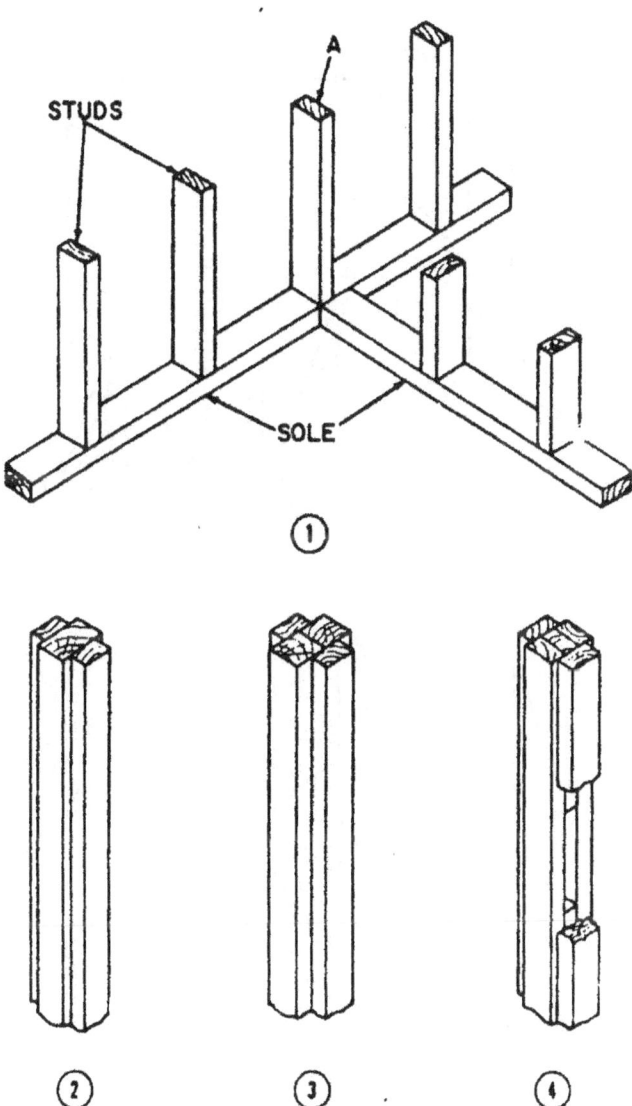

Figure 26. Partition posts.

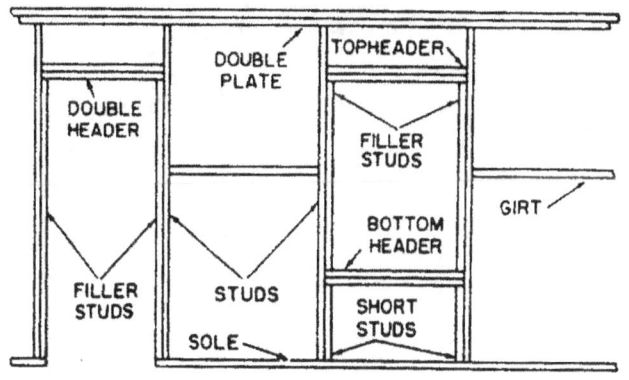

Figure 27. Door and window framing.

The plate is made up of one or two pieces of timber of the same size as the studs. In cases where the studs at the end of the building extend to the rafters, no plate is used at the end of the building. When it is used on top of partition walls, it is sometimes called the cap. Where the plate is doubled, the first plate or bottom section is nailed with 16- or 20-penny nails to the top of the corner posts and to the studs. The connection at the corner is made as shown in 1, figure 28. After the single plate is nailed securely and the corner braces are nailed into place, the top part of the plate is then nailed to the bottom section with 16- or 20-penny nails either over each stud, or spaced with two nails every 2 feet. The edges of the top section should be flush with the bottom section and the corner joints lapped as shown in 1 and 2, figure 28.

(2) *Sole plate.* All partition walls and outside walls are finished either with a 2 by 4 or with a piece of timber corresponding to the thickness of the wall; this timber is laid horizontally on the floor or joists. It carries the bottom end of the studs (fig. 22). This timber is called the "sole" or "sole plate". The sole should be nailed with two 16- or 20-penny nails at each joist that it crosses. If it is laid lengthwise on top of a girder or joist, it should be nailed with two nails every 2 feet.

g. Bridging. Frame walls are bridged, in most cases, to make them more sturdy. There are two methods of bridging:

(1) *Diagonal bridging.* Diagonal bridging is nailed between the studs at an angle (1, fig. 29). It is more effective than the horizontal type since it forms a continuous truss and tends to keep the walls from sagging. Whenever possible, both interior partitions and exterior walls should be bridged alike.

(2) *Horizontal bridging.* Horizontal bridging is nailed between the studs horizontally and halfway between the sole and the plate (2, fig. 29). This bridging is cut to lengths which correspond to the distance between the studs at the bottom. Such bridging not only stiffens the wall but also will help straighten studs.

11. Partitions

Partition walls divide the inside space of a building. These walls in most cases are framed as part of the building. Where floors are to be installed after the outside of the building is completed, the partition walls are left unframed. There are two types of partition walls: the bearing, and the non-bearing types. The bearing type supports ceiling joists. The nonbearing type supports only itself. This type may be put in at any time after

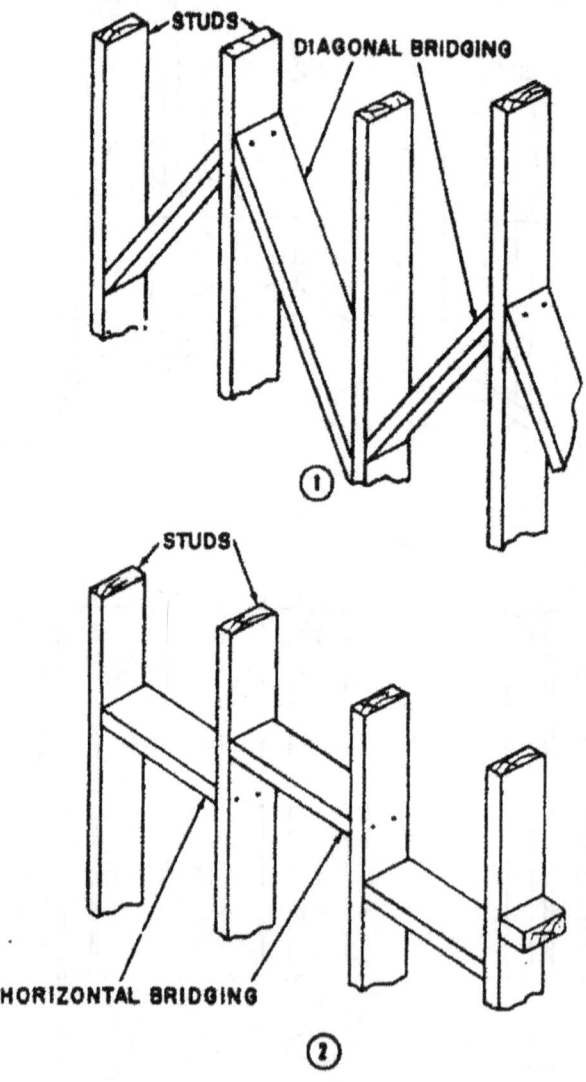

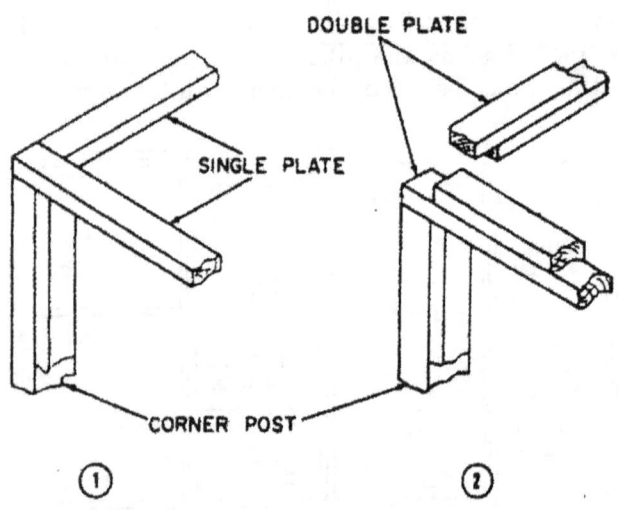

Figure 28. Plate construction.

Figure 29. Types of wall bridging.

the other framework is installed. Only one cap or plate is used. A sole plate should be used in every case, as it helps to distribute the load over a larger area. Partition walls are framed the same as outside walls, and door openings are framed as outside openings. Where there are corners or where one partition wall joins another, corner posts or T-posts are used as in the outside walls; these posts provide nailing surfaces for the inside wall finish. Partition walls in the theater of operations one-story building may or may not extend to the roof. The top of the studs has a plate when the wall does not extend to the roof; but when the wall extends to the roof, the studs are joined to the rafters.

12. Methods of Plumbing Posts and Straightening Walls

a. General. After the corner post, T-post, and intermediate wall studs have been nailed to the plates or girts, the walls must be plumbed and straightened so that the permanent braces and rafters may be installed. This is done by using a level or plumb bob and a chalkline.

b. Plumbing Posts.

(1) To plumb a corner with a plumb bob, first attach to the bob a string long enough to extend to or below the bottom of the post. Lay a rule on top of the post so that 2 inches of the rule extends over the post on the side to be plumbed; then hang the bob-line over the rule so that the line is 2 inches from the post and extends to the bottom of it, as shown in 1, figure 30. With another rule, measure the distance from the post to the center of the line at the bottom of the post; if it does not measure 2 inches, the post is not plumb. Move the post inward or outward until the distance from the post to the center of the line is exactly 2 inches. Then nail the temporary brace in place. Repeat this procedure from the other outside face of the post. The post is then plumb. This process is carried out for the remaining corner posts of the building. If a plumb bob or level is not available, a rock, a half-brick, or some small piece of metal may be used instead.

(2) An alternate method of plumbing a post is illustrated in 2, figure 30. Attach the plumb bob string securely to the top of the post to be plumbed, making sure that the string is long enough to allow the plumb bob to hang near the bottom of the post. Use two blocks of wood identical in thickness as gage blocks. Tack one block near the top of the post between the plumb bob string and the post (gage block No. 1), in-

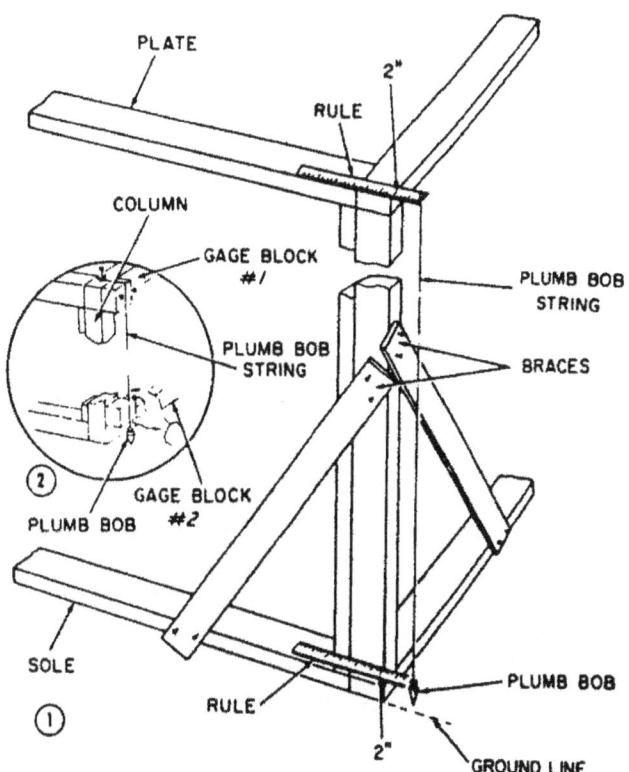

Figure 30. Plumbing a post.

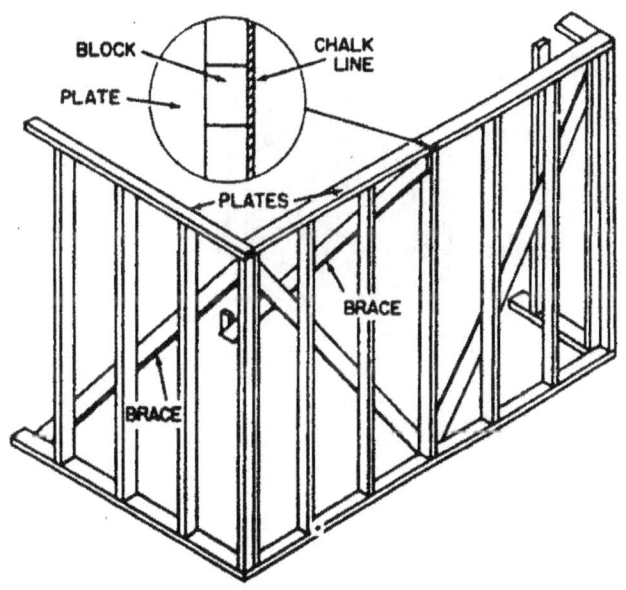

Figure 31. Straightening a wall.

serting the second block between the plumb bob string and the bottom of the post (gage block No. 2). If the entire face of the second block makes contact with the string, the post is plumb.

c. Straightening Walls (fig. 31). Plumb one corner post with the level or plumb bob and nail temporary braces to hold the post in place (*b* above). Repeat this procedure for all corner posts. Fasten a chalkline to the outside of one post at the top and stretch the line to the post the same as for the first post. Place a small 3/4-inch block under each end of the line as shown in figure 31 to give clearance. Place temporary braces at intervals small enough to hold the wall straight. When the wall is far enough away from the line to permit a 3/4-inch block to slide between the line and the plate, the brace is nailed. This procedure is carried out for the entire perimeter of the building. Inside partition walls should be straightened the same way.

13. Braces

Bracing is used to stiffen framed construction and make it rigid. The purpose of bracing may be to resist winds, storm, twist, or strain stemming from any cause. Good bracing keeps corners square and plumb and prevents warping, sagging, and shifts resulting from lateral forces that would otherwise tend to distort the frame and cause badly fitting doors and windows and the cracking of plaster. There are three commonly used methods of bracing frame structures:

a. Let-In Bracing (1, fig. 32). Let-in bracing is set into the edges of studs so as to be flush with the surface. The studs are always cut to let in the braces; the braces are never cut. Usually 1 by 4's or 1 by 6's are used, set diagonally from top plates to sole plates.

b. Cut-In Bracing (2, fig. 32). Cut-in bracing is toenailed between studs. It usually consists of 2 by 4's cut at an angle to permit toenailing, inserted in diagonal progression between studs running up and down from corner posts to sill or plates.

c. Diagonal Sheathing (3, fig. 32). The strongest type of bracing is sheathing applied diagonally. Each board acts as a brace of the wall. If plywood sheathing 5/8-inch thick or more is used, other methods of bracing may be omitted.

14. Exterior Walls

The exterior surfaces of a building usually consist of vertical, horizontal, or diagonal sheathing and composition, sheet-metal, or corrugated roofing. However, in theaters of operation the materials are not always available and substitutes must be provided. Concrete block, brick, rubble stone, metal, or earth may be substituted for wood in treeless regions. In the tropics, improvised siding and roofs can be made from bamboo and grasses. Roofing felt, sandwiched between two layers of light wire mesh, may serve for wall and roof materials where climate is suitable.

a. Sheathing. Sheathing is nailed directly onto the framework of the building. Its purpose is to strengthen the building, to provide a base wall onto which the finish siding can be nailed,

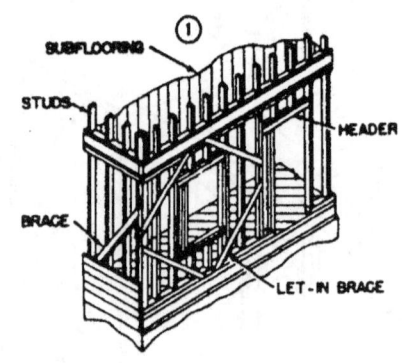
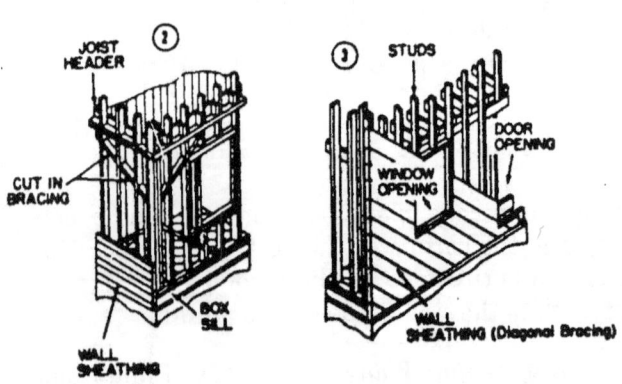

Figure 32. Common types of bracing.

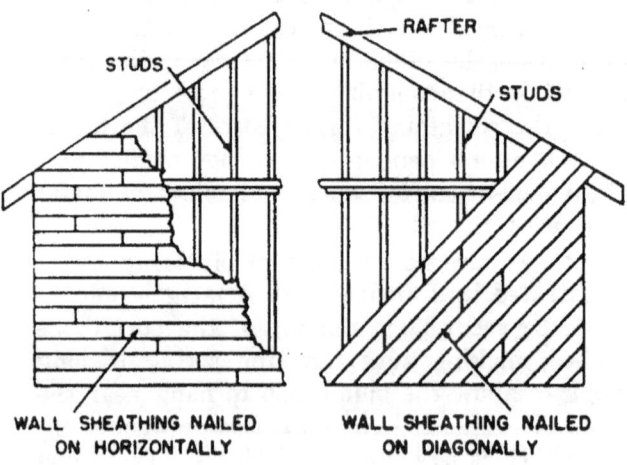

Figure 33. Diagonal and horizontal wooden sheathing.

to act as insulation, and in some cases to be a base for further insulation. Some of the common types of sheathing include—

(1) Wood, 11/16-inch thick by 6, 8, 10, or 12 inch wide of No. 1 common square or matched-edge material. It may be nailed on horizontally or diagonally (fig. 33).

(2) Gypsum board wall-sheathing, 1/2 inch thick by 24 inches wide and 8 feet long.

(3) Fiberboard, 25/32 inch thick by 24 by 48 inches wide and 8, 9, 10, and 12 feet long.

(4) Plywood, 5/16, 3/8, 1/2, 5/8 inches thick by 48 inches wide and 8, 9, 10, and 12 feet long.

b. Application.

(1) Wood wall sheathing comes in almost all widths, lengths, and grades. Generally, widths are from 6 to 12 inches, with lengths selected for economical use. Almost all solid wood wall sheathing used is 13/16 inches thick and either square or matched edge. This material may be nailed on horizontally or diagonally (fig. 33). Diagonal application adds much greater strength to the structure. Sheathing should be nailed on with three 8-penny common nails to each bearing if the pieces are over 6 inches wide. Wooden sheathing is laid on tight, with all joints made over the studs. If the sheathing is to be put on horizontally, it should be started at the foundation and worked toward the top. If it is to be put on diagonally, it should be started at the corners of the building and worked toward the center or middle of the building.

(2) Gypsum board sheathing (fig. 34) is made by casting a gypsum core within a heavy water-resistant fibrous envelope. The long edges of the 4- by 8-foot boards are tongued and grooved. Each board is a full 1/2 inch thick. Its use is mostly with wood siding that can be nailed directly through the sheathing and into the studs. Gypsum sheathing is fireproof, water resistant, and windproof; does not warp nor absorb water; and does not require the use of building papers.

(3) Plywood as a wall sheathing (fig. 34) is highly recommended by its size, weight, stability, and structural properties, plus the ease and speed of application. It adds consider-

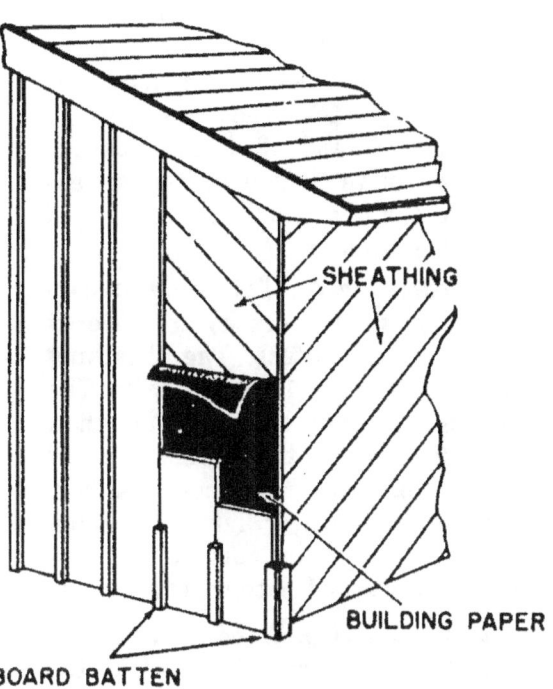

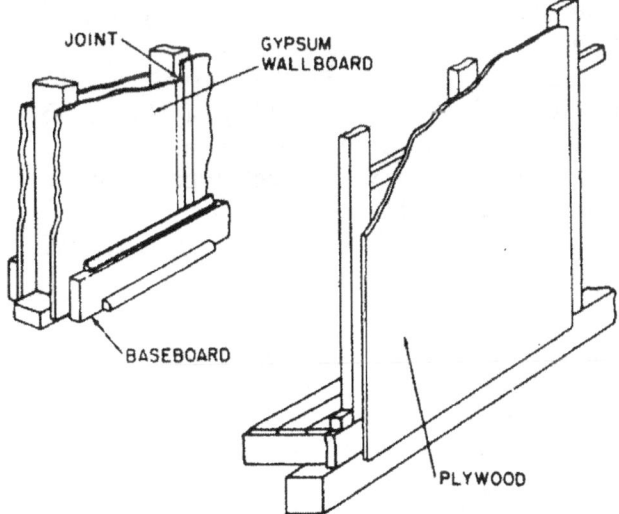

Figure 34. Gypsum and plywood sheathing.

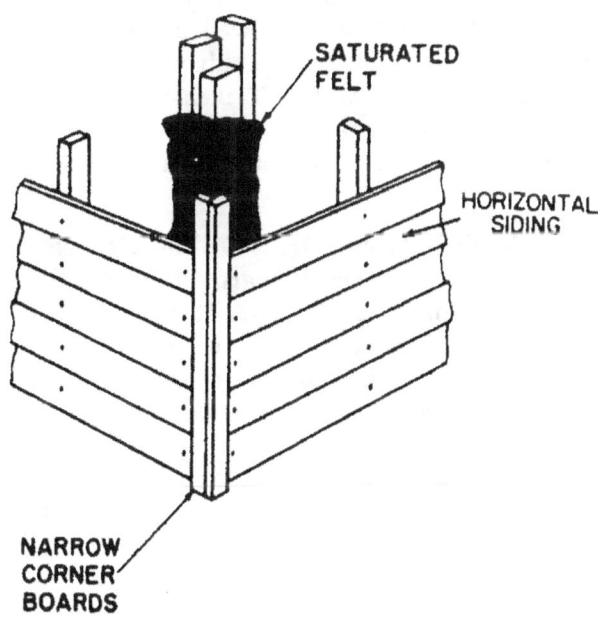

Figure 35. Vertical and horizontal wooden siding.

ably more strength to the frame than does diagonally applied wood boards. When plywood sheathing is used, corner bracing can be omitted. Large size panels save the time required for application and still provide a tight, draft-free installation of high insulation value. Minimum thicknesses of plywood wall sheathing is 5/16 inch for 16-inch stud spacing and 3/8 inch for 24-inch stud spacing. The panels should be installed with the face grain parallel to the studs. A little more stiffness can be gained by installing them across the studs, but this requires more cutting and fitting. Use 6-penny common nails for 5/16-, 3/8-, and 1/2-inch panels and 8-penny common nails for 5/8- and 13/16-inch panels. Space the nails not more than 6 inches on center at the edges of the panels and not more than 12 inches on center elsewhere.

c. Vertical Wooden Siding. This type of coverage is nailed to girts. The cracks are covered with wood strips called battens. The sheathing is nailed securely with 8- or 10-penny nails. The vertical sheathing requires less framing than siding since the sheathing acts as a support for the plate. To make this type of wall more weatherproof, some type of tar paper or light roll roofing may be applied over the entire surface and fastened with roofing nails and battens (fig. 35).

d. Horizontal Wood Siding. Wood siding is cut to various patterns and sizes to be used as the finished outside surface of a structure. The siding for outside wall coverings should be of a decay-resisting species that will hold tight at the joints and take and hold paint well. It should by all means be well seasoned lumber. Siding is made in sizes ranging from 1/2 inch to 3/4 inch by 12 inches. There are two principal types of siding (fig. 3): beveled siding and drop siding.

(1) *Beveled siding* (fig. 3). Beveled siding is made with beveled boards thin at the top edge and thick at the butt. It is the most common form of wood siding and comes in 1 inch for narrow widths, and 2 inches and over for the wide types. They are usually nailed at the butt edge and through the tip edge of the board below. Very narrow siding is quite often nailed near its thin edge like shingles. It is nailed to solid sheathing over which building paper has been attached. Window and door casings are first framed. The siding butts are put against the edges of these frames. Corners may be mitered, or the corner boards may be first nailed to the sheathing and then the siding is fitted against the edges.

(2) *Drop siding* (fig. 3). Drop siding is designed to be used as a combination of sheathing and siding, or with separate sheathing. It comes in a wide variety of face profiles and is either shiplapped or tongued and grooved. If used as a combined sheathing and siding material, tongue and grooved lumber is nailed directly to the studs with the tongue up. When sheathing is not used, the door and window casings are set after the siding is up. If sheathing is first used and then building paper is added, drop siding is applied like beveled siding, after the window and door casings are in place.

(3) *Corrugated metal sheets.* Corrugated metal is used extensively as a wall cover since little framing, time, and labor are required to install it. It is applied vertically and nailed to girts with the nails placed in the ridges. Sheathing can be used behind the iron with or without building paper. Since tar paper used behind metal will cause the metal to rust, a resin-sized paper should be used.

(4) *Building paper.*

(*a*) Building paper is of several types, the most common of which is the resin-sized. It is generally red or buff in color (sometimes black) and comes in rolls, usually 36 inches wide. Each roll contains 500 square feet and weighs from 18 to 50 pounds. Ordinarily, it is not waterproof. Another type is heavy paper saturated with a coaltar product, sometimes called sheathing paper. It is waterproof and protects against heat and cold.

(*b*) In wood-frame buildings to be covered with either siding, shingles, or iron, building paper is used to protect against heat, cold, or dampness. Building paper is applied horizontally along a wall from the bottom of the structure upward and nailed with roofing nails at the laps. Thus the overlapping of the paper helps water runoff. Care must be taken not to tear the paper. The waterproof type paper is used also in the built-up roof where the roof is nearly flat. Several layers are used with tar between each layer.

15. Interior Walls and Partitions

a. Wall and Partition Coverings. Wall and partition coverings are divided into two general types—wet wall material, generally plaster; and dry wall material including wood, plaster board, plywood, and fiberboard. Only dry wall material will be covered in this manual.

b. Dry Wall Materials. Dry wall material—

gypsumboard, fiberboard, or plywood, usually comes in sheets 1/2 inch thick and 4 x 8 feet in size, but may be obtained in other sizes. It is normally applied in either single or double thickness with panels placed as shown in figure 36. When covering both walls and ceilings, always start with the ceiling (para 17). Annular ringed nails should be used for applying finished-joint drywall to reduce nail popping.

(1) Apply dry wall as follows:

(a) Start in one corner and work around the room. Make sure that joints break at the centerline of a stud.

(b) Use 1/2-inch thick recessed-edge wallboard and span the entire height of the wall if possible.

(c) Use 13-gage nails, 1 5/8 inches long. Start nailing at the center of the board and work outward. Space the nails 3/8 inch in from the edge of the board and about 8 inches apart. Dimple nails below surface of panel with a ball-peen hammer. Be careful not to break the surface of the board by the blow of the hammer.

(d) Procedures for cutting and sealing wallboard are covered in (3) below.

(2) Fit dry wall materials to rough or uneven walls as follows:

(a) Place a piece of scrap material in the angle (fig. 37) and scribe (mark) it to indicate the surface peculiarities.

(b) Saw the scrap material along the scribed line.

(c) Place the scribed strip on the wallboard to be used. Keep the straight edge of the scrap material parallel with the edge of the wallboard. Scribe the good piece of wallboard.

(d) Saw the wallboard along the scribed line.

(3) Cut panels by sawing, or by scoring with an awl and snapping over a straight edge (fig. 38). *Cut with finish side up to avoid damaging surface.* Cut openings for pipe and electrical receptacles with a keyhole saw. Nail panels to wall studs with 13-gage nails, 8 inches on centers. *All panel end joints must center on studs.* Cover nails with cement. Joints may be left open, beveled, lapped, filled, covered with battens or moldings, or treated with cement and tape. The treatment of joints varies slightly with different materials. Generally, all cracks over 1/8 inch must be filled with special crack filler before joint cement is applied. The cement is spread over joints with a plasterer's trowel. Apply the cement evenly and thin (feather) edges on surface of wall panel. Fill channels in recessed edges with cement, carrying it 1 inch past channel edges. At corners, apply cement in a channel-wide band and feather edges. Press perforated tape into wet cement and smooth tape down with trowel. Clean off excess cement. At corners, fold tape down center before applying, and smooth each side of corner separately when applied. When cement is dry, apply a second coat of thinned cement to hide tape.

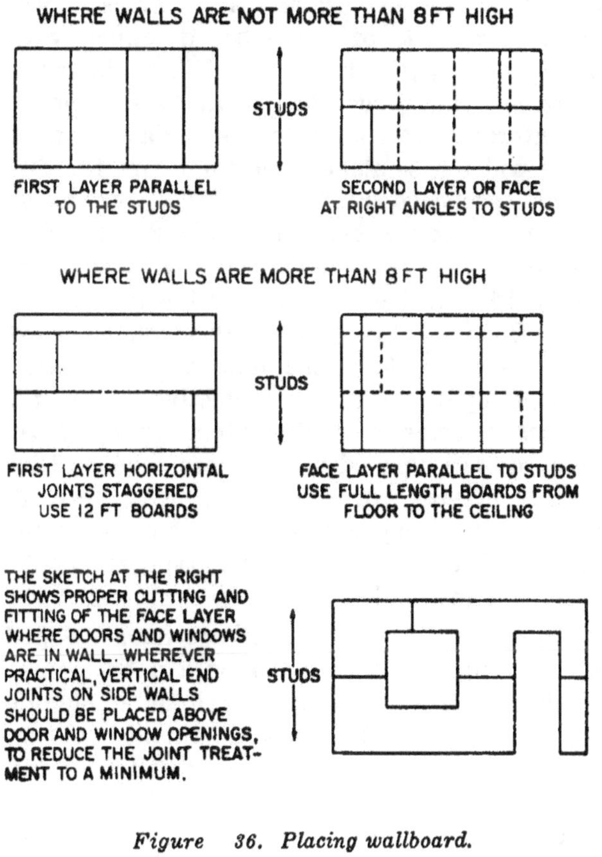

Figure 36. Placing wallboard.

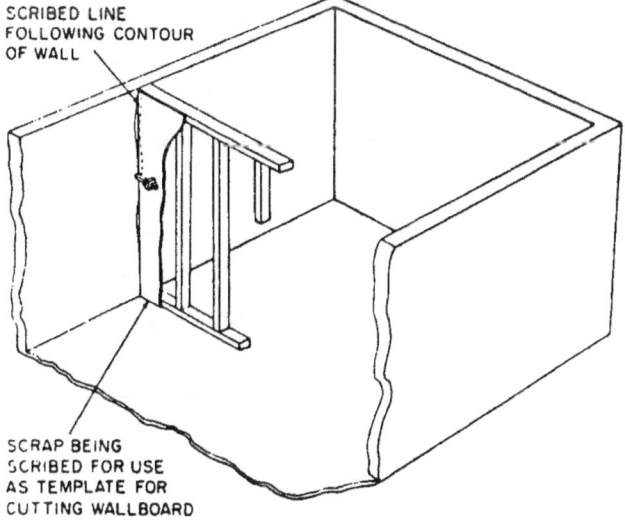

Figure 37. Fitting single-piece wallboard to uneven walls.

179

Feather the edges carefully to preserve flat appearance of wall. When the final coat is dry, smooth the joint with sandpaper.

c. Sheetrock. Sheetrock sheets are very brittle and require careful handling to prevent breakage. Approximately 1 1/4 inches of a sheet's edge is made 1/16 inch thinner than the body of the sheet. When two sheets are placed side by side, their edges form a recess to receive perforated paper tape and gypsum cement which conceals the joints between the sheets. A 1/8-inch space between the edges of the sheets helps to hold the filler cement in place. The sheets are usually fastened in place with blued nails which have an oversize head and are 1 1/2 inches long. The nails along the edges are covered with perforated tape and cement. Nails are spaced about 5 inches apart and 3/8 inch from the edge. Those in the middle of the sheets are spaced 8 or 9 inches apart and are set below the surface to receive the filler cement. It is common practice to strike the nailheads one extra blow for setting. This makes a slight depression (hammer mark) which holds the cement around the nailhead.

d. Wood Paneling. Plywood panels are used extensively as interior wall covering and can be obtained on the market in sizes from 1/4 to 3/4 inch thick; 36 to 48 inches wide; and 60, 72, 84, or 96 inches long. Plywood gives a wall a wood finish surface. If desired, the less expensive plywoods can be used and covered with paint or wallpaper or can be decorated in the same way as plastered surfaces. These panels are usually applied vertically from floor to ceiling and fastened with 4d finishing nails. Special strips or battens of either wood or metal may be used to conceal the joints when flush joints are used. Joints can also be treated with moldings, either in the form of battens fastened over the joints or applied as splines between the panels.

16. Moldings

The various interior trims of a building should have a definite architectural relationship in the design to that of the doors, windows, and the general architecture of the building.

a. Base Molding. Base molding serves as a finish between the finished wall and floor. It is available in several widths and forms. Two-piece base consists of a baseboard topped with a small base cap (A, fig. 39). When plaster is not straight and true, the small base molding will conform more closely to the variations than will the wider base alone. A common size for this type of baseboard is 5/8 by 3 1/4 inches or wider. One-piece baseboard is 5/8 by 3 1/4 inches or wider. One-piece base varies in size from 7/16 by 2 1/4 inches to 1/2 by 3 1/4 inches and wider (Band C, fig. 39). Although a wood member is desirable at the junction of the wall and carpeting to serve as a protective "bumper", wood trim is sometimes eliminated entirely. Most baseboards are finished with a base shoe, 1/2 by 3/4 inch in size (A, B, and C, fig. 39). A single-base molding without the shoe is sometimes placed at the wall-floor junction, especially where carpeting might be used.

b. Installation of Base Molding. Square-edged baseboard should be installed with a butt joint at inside corners and a mitered joint at outside corners (D, fig. 39). It should be nailed to each stud with two eightpenny finishing nails. Molded single-piece base, base moldings, and base shoe should have a coped joint at inside corners and

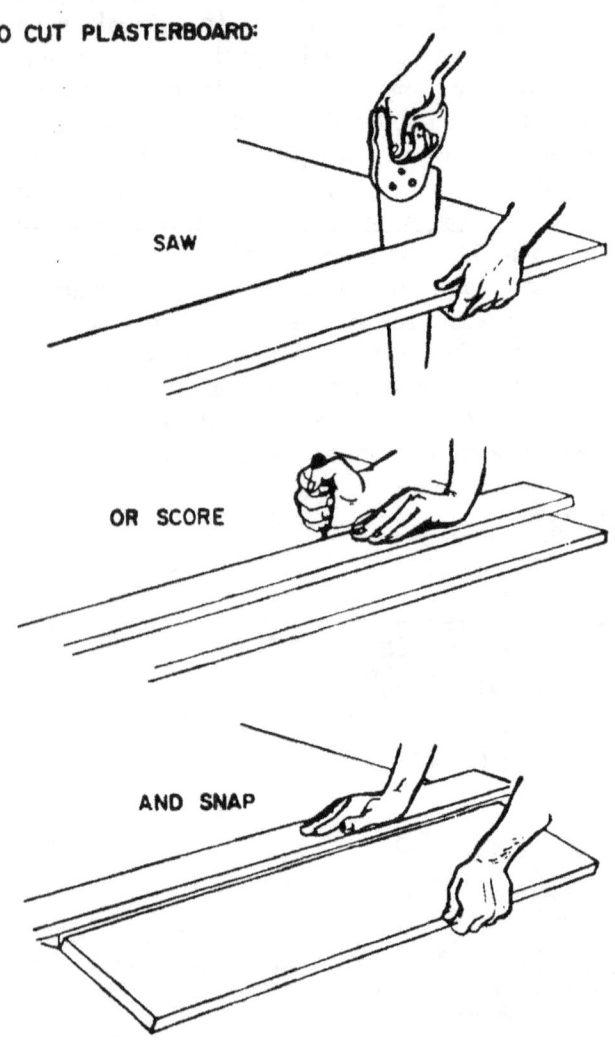

Figure 38. Cutting wallboard.

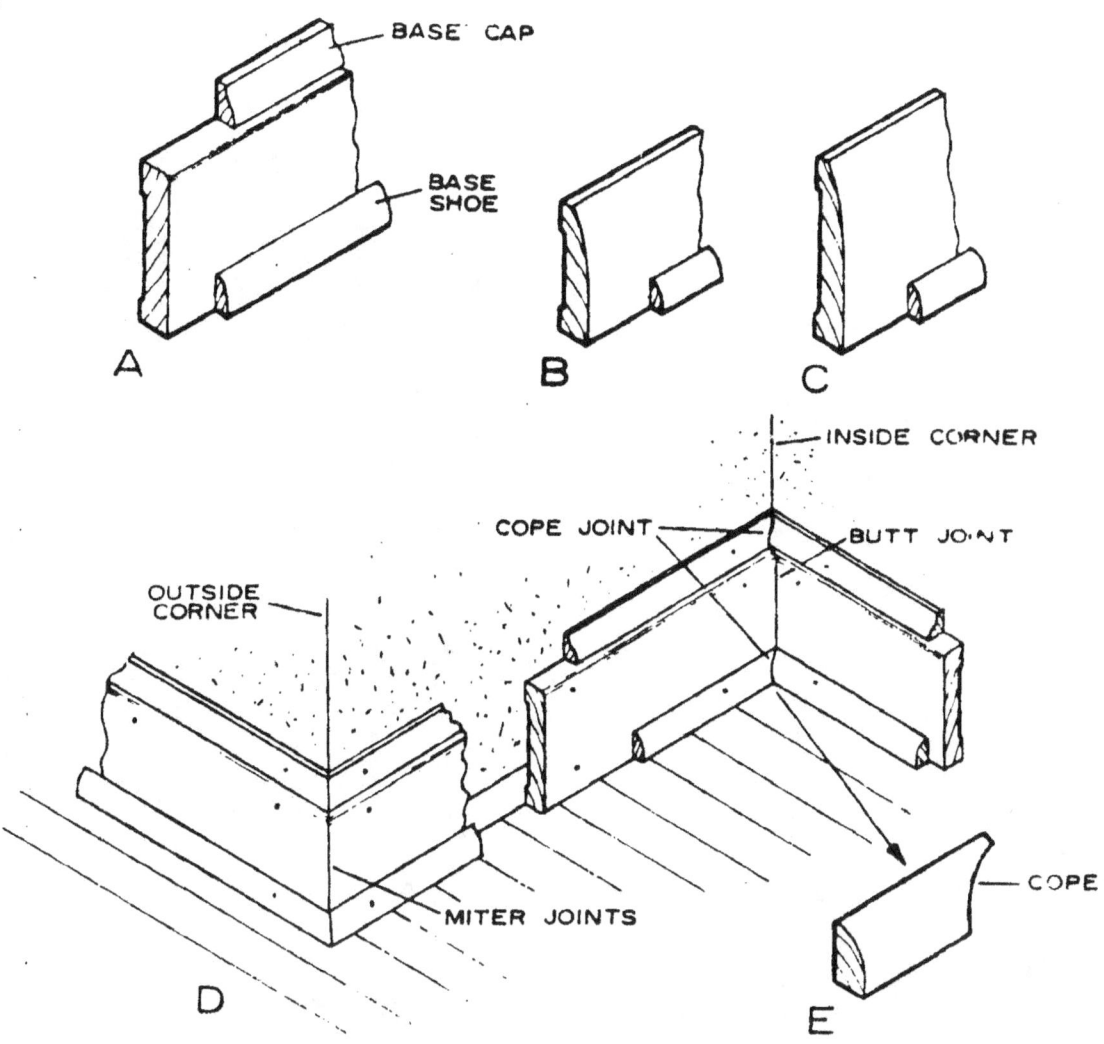

A, Square-edge base; B, narrow ranch base; C, wide ranch base; D, installation; E, cope.

Figure 39. Base molding.

a mitered joint at outside corners. A coped joint is one in which the first piece is square-cut against the plaster or base and the second molding coped. This is done by sawing a 45° miter cut and with a coping saw trimming the molding along the inner line of the miter (E, fig. 39). The base shoe should be nailed into the subfloor with long slender nails and not into the baseboard itself. Thus, if there is a small amount of shrinkage of the joists, no opening will occur under the shoe.

17. Ceiling Covering

In present-day construction, dry, rigid wallboards are used instead of laths and plaster to cover ceilings, as well as walls (para 15). The most common drywall finishes are gypsumboard, fiberboard, and plywood. Sheets of gypsumboard and fiberboard are attached directly to the joists. Smaller pieces of fiberboard (tiles) require furring strips (wooden strips nailed across joints) to which they are attached.

a. Gypsumboard.

(1) *Nailing to ceiling.* The 4-foot by 8-foot boards are nailed to the ceiling with 5-penny nails through 1/2-inch thick gypsum or 4-penny nails through 3/8-inch gypsum. The nails are spaced 5 to 7 inches apart, off center, and driven about 1/16 inch below the surface of the board.

(2) *Cutting panels and treatment of joints.* The cutting of the panels and the treatment of joints are the same as those of walls and partitions (para 15b(3).

(3) *Brace for paneling ceiling.* A brace is constructed and used (fig. 40) to raise and hold a panel in place to aid in fitting and nailing

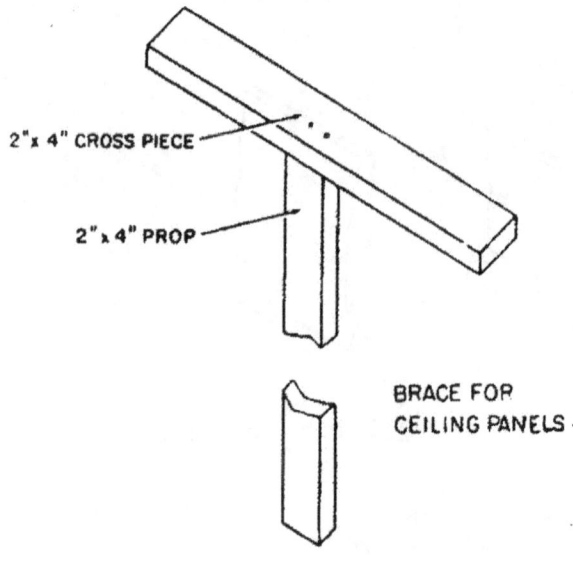

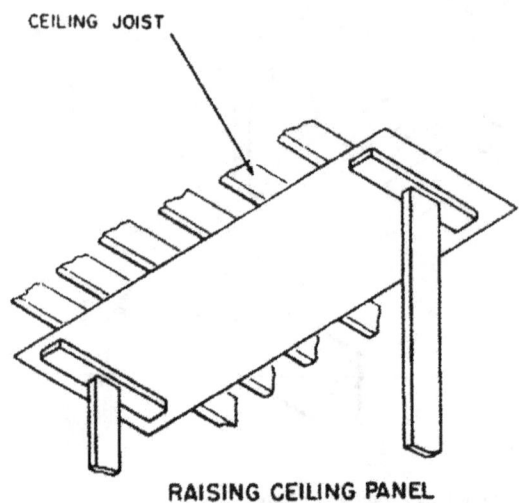

Figure 40. Brace for raising and holding ceiling panels.

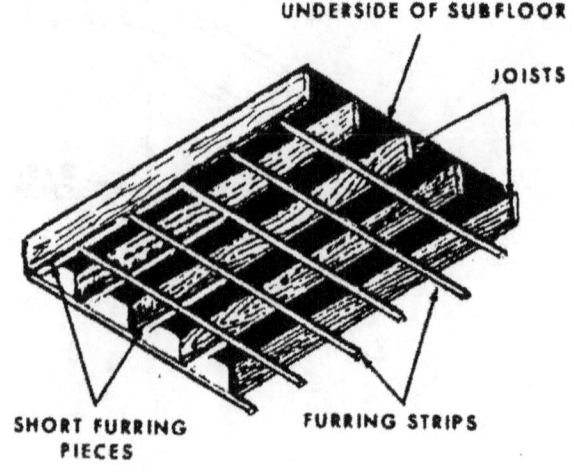

Figure 41. Furring strips on ceiling joists.

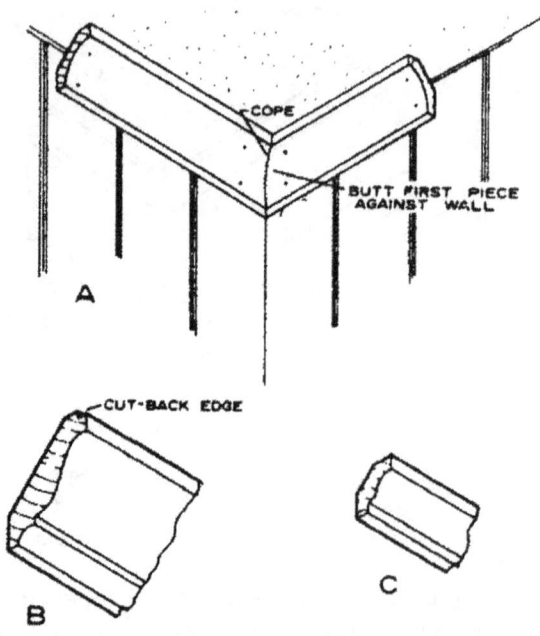

Ceiling moldings; A, Installation (inside corner); B, crown molding; C, small crown molding.

Figure 42. Ceiling molding.

the wallboard to the ceiling. Eight inch nail spacing is used in nailing the panels to the joists.

b. Fiberboard. Fiberboard sheets are obtained in thicknesses from 1/2 to 2 inches. The joints between the sheets may be covered with batten strips of either wood or fiberboard to further improve its appearance. When fiberboard sheets must be cut, a special fiberboard knife is recommended to obtain a smooth cut.

(1) *Tiles.* Fiberboard sheets are also made in small pieces called tiles which are often used for covering ceilings. These tiles may be square or rectangular to fit standard joist spacing. They may be made with a lap joint which permits blind nailing or stapling through the edge. They may also be of tongue-and-groove construction fastened in place with 2-penny box nails driven through special metal clips.

(2) *Furring strips.* For fiberboard tiles that need solid backing, furring strips are placed at right angles across the bottom of the joists and short furring pieces are placed along the joists between the furring strips, as shown in figure 41.

(3) *Tile installed in metal channels.* Metal channels are nailed to furring strips and the tiles are slid into them horizontally. In lowering ceilings, usually in older buildings, metal channels are suspended on wire to "drop" a ceiling below the original ceiling. Some large (2 x 4-ft) panels are installed in individual frames.

18. Ceiling Molding

Ceiling moldings are sometimes used at the junction of wall and ceiling for an architectural effect or to terminate dry-wall paneling of gypsumboard or wood (A, fig. 42). As in the base moldings, inside corners should also be copejointed. This insures a tight joint and retains a good fit if there are minor moisture changes. A cutback edge at the outside of the molding will partially conceal any unevenness of the plaster and make painting easier where there are color changes (B, fig. 42). For gypsum dry-wall construction, a small simple molding might be desirable (C, fig. 42). Finish nails should be driven into the upper wallplates and also into the ceiling joists for large moldings when possible.

Section III. DOOR FRAMES, WINDOW FRAMES, AND OTHER WALL OPENINGS

19. Doors

Door and window openings in exterior walls generally require headers. Regular studs are normally placed 16 inches on center apart. Extra studs are added at the sides of all such openings. Openings should allow 1/2 inch between the back at jambs and framing member for the plumbing and leveling of jambs.

a. Door Frames.

(1) Before the exterior covering is placed on the outside walls, the door openings are prepared for the frames. To prepare the openings, square off any uneven pieces of sheathing and wrap heavy building paper around the sides and top. Since the sill must be worked into a portion of the rough flooring, no paper is put on the floor. Position the paper from a point even with the inside portion of the stud to a point about 6 inches on the sheathed walls and tack it down with small nails.

(2) Outside door frames are constructed in several ways. In most hasty construction, the frames will be as shown in figure 43. This type requires no construction of frame because the studs on each side of the opening act as a frame. The outside finish is applied to the wall before the door is hung. The casing is then nailed to the sides of the opening which is set back the width of the stud. A 3/4- by 3/4-inch piece is nailed over the door to act as a support for the drip cap and is also set back the width of the stud. Hinge blocks are nailed to the casing where the hinges are to be placed. The door frame is now complete and ready for the door to be hung. Figure 43 shows the elevation of a single outside door.

(3) Inside door frames, like outside frames, are constructed in several ways. In most hasty construction, the type shown in figure 44 is used. The interior type is constructed like the outside type, except that no casing is used on inside door frames. Hinge blocks are nailed to the inside wall finish, where the hinges are to be placed, to provide a nailing surface for the hinge flush with the door. Figure 44 shows the elevation of a single inside door. Both the outside and inside door frames may be modified to suit climatic conditions.

b. Door Jambs. Door jambs (fig. 45) are the linings of the framing of door openings.

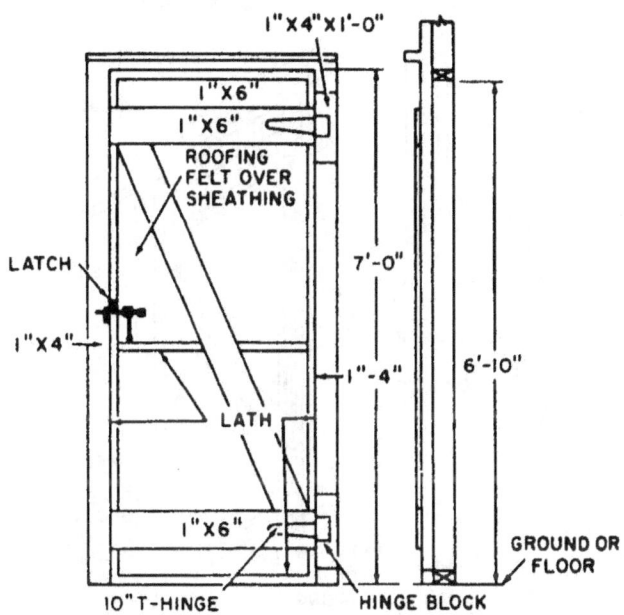

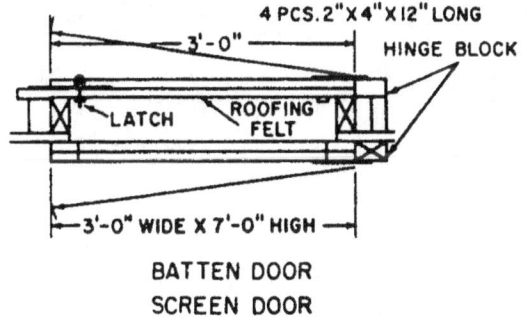

Figure 43. Single outside door.

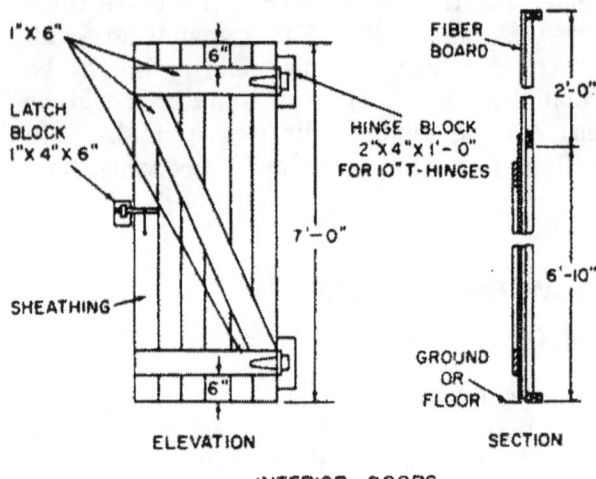

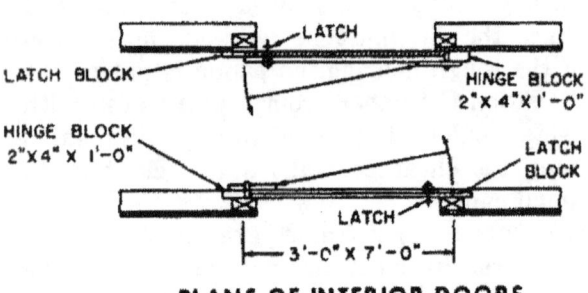

Figure 44. Single inside door.

Casings and stops are nailed to the door jambs and the door is hung from them. Inside jambs are made of 3/4-inch stock and outside jambs of 1 3/8-inch stock. The width of the stock will vary with the thickness to the walls. Inside jambs are built up with 3/8- by 1 3/8-inch stops nailed to the jamb, while outside jambs are usually rabbeted out to receive the door. Jambs are made and set as follows:

(1) Regardless of how carefully rough openings are made, be sure to plumb the jambs and level the heads, when jambs are set.

(2) Rough openings are usually made 2 1/2 inches larger each way than the size of the door to be hung. For example, a 2-foot 8-inch by 6-foot 8-inch door would need a rough opening of 2 feet 10 1/2 inches by 6 feet 10 1/2 inches. This extra space allows for the jambs, the wedging, and the clearance space for the door to swing.

(3) Level the floor across the opening to determine any variation in floor heights at the point where the jambs rest on the floor.

(4) Now cut the head jamb with both ends square, having allowed width of the door plus the depth of both dadoes and a full 3/16 inch for door clearance.

(5) From the lower edge of the dado, measure a distance equal to the height of the door plus the clearance wanted under it. Mark and cut square.

(6) On the oposite jamb do the same, only make additions or subtractions for the variation in the floor, if any.

(7) Now nail the jambs and jamb heads together with 8-penny common nails through the dado into the head jamb.

(8) Set the jambs into the opening and place small blocks under each jamb on the subfloor just as thick as the finish floor will be. This is to allow the finish floor to go under.

(9) Plumb the jambs and level the jamb head.

(10) Wedge the sides with shingles between the jambs and the studs, to aline, and then nail securely in place.

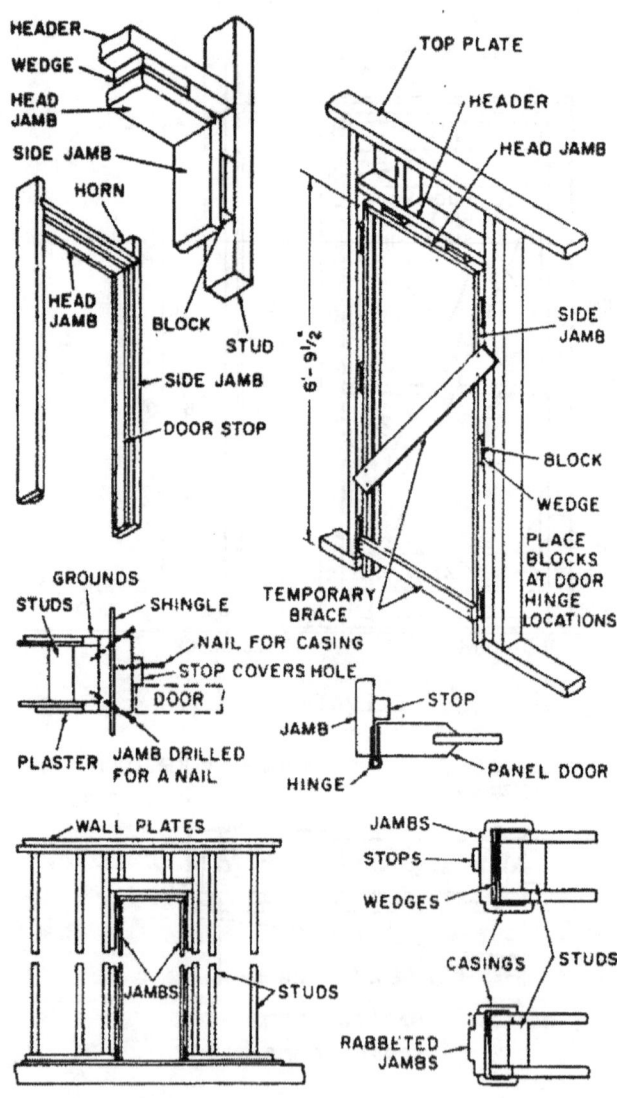

Figure 45. Door jamb and door trim.

(11) Take care not to wedge the jamb unevenly.

(12) Use a straightedge 5 or 6 feet long inside the jambs to help prevent uneven wedging.

(13) Check jambs and head carefully, because jambs placed out of plumb will have a tendency to swing the door open or shut, depending on the direction in which the jamb is out of plumb.

c. Door Trim. Door trim material is nailed onto the jambs to provide a finish between the jambs and the wall. It is frequently called "casing" (fig. 45). Sizes vary from 1/2 to 3/4 inch in thickness, and from 2 1/2 to 6 inches in width. Most trim has a concave back, to fit over uneven plaster. In mitered work, care must be taken to make all joints clean, square, neat, and well fitted. (If the trim is to be mitered at the top corners, a miter box, miter square, hammer nail set, and block plane will be needed.) Door openings are cased up as follows:

(1) Leave a margin of 1/4-inch from the edge of the jamb to the casing all around.

(2) Cut one of the side casings square and even at the bottom, with the bottom of the jamb.

(3) Cut the top or mitered end next, allowing 1/4-inch extra length for the margin at the top.

(4) Nail the casing onto the jamb and even with the 1/4-inch margin line, starting at the top and working toward the bottom.

(5) Use 4-penny finishing nails along the jamb side and 6-penny or 8-penny case nails along the outer edge of the casings.

(6) The nails along the outer edge will need to be long enough to go through the casing and into the studs.

(7) Set all nailheads about 1/8 inch below the surface of the wood with a nail set.

(8) Now apply the casing for the other side and then the head casing.

20. Windows

Windows are generally classified as sliding, double hung, and casement (fig. 46). All windows, whatever the type, consist essentially of two parts, the frame and the sash. The frame is made up of four basic parts: the head, the jambs (two), and the sill. The sash is the framework which holds the glass in the window. Where the openings are provided, studding must be cut away and its equivalent strength replaced by doubling the studs on each side of the opening to form trimmers and inserting a header at the top. If the opening is wide, the header should be doubled and trussed. At the bottom of the opening, the bottom header or rough sill is inserted.

a. Window Frames. These are the frames into which the window sashes are fitted and hung. They are set into the rough opening in the wall framing and are intended to hold the sashes in place. The rough window opening is made at least 10 inches larger each way (width and height) than the window glass (pane) size to be used. If the sash to be used is, for instance, a two-light window, 24 by 26 inches, add 10 inches to the width (24 inches) to obtain the total width of 34 inches for the rough opening. Add the upper and lower glasses (26 inches each) and an additional 10 inches for the total height of the rough opening, 62 inches. These allowances are standard and provide for weights, springs, balances, room for plumbing and squaring, and for regular adjustments.

b. Double-Hung Window. The double-hung window (fig. 47) is made up of two parts: an upper and a lower sash, which slide vertically past one another. Screens can be located on the outside of a double-hung window without interfering with its operation, and ventilators and window air conditioners can be placed with the window mostly closed. However, for full ventilation of a room, only one-half of the area of the window can be used, and any current of air

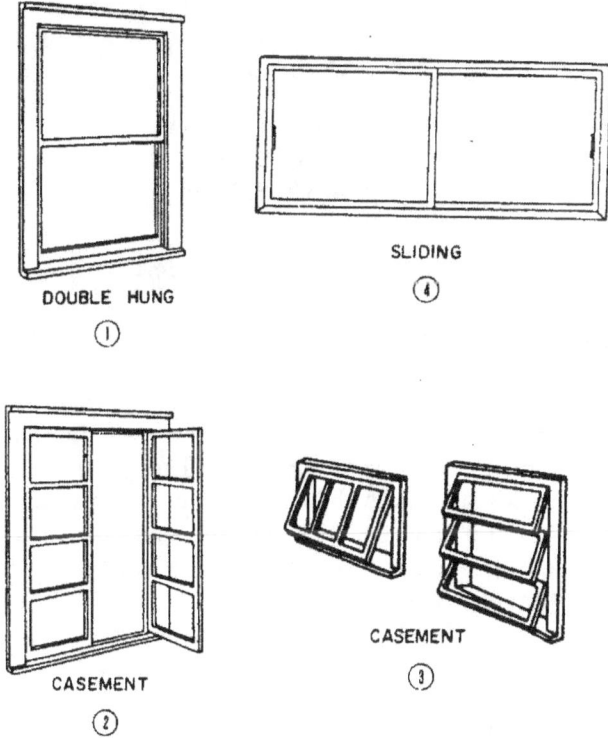

Figure 46. Types of windows.

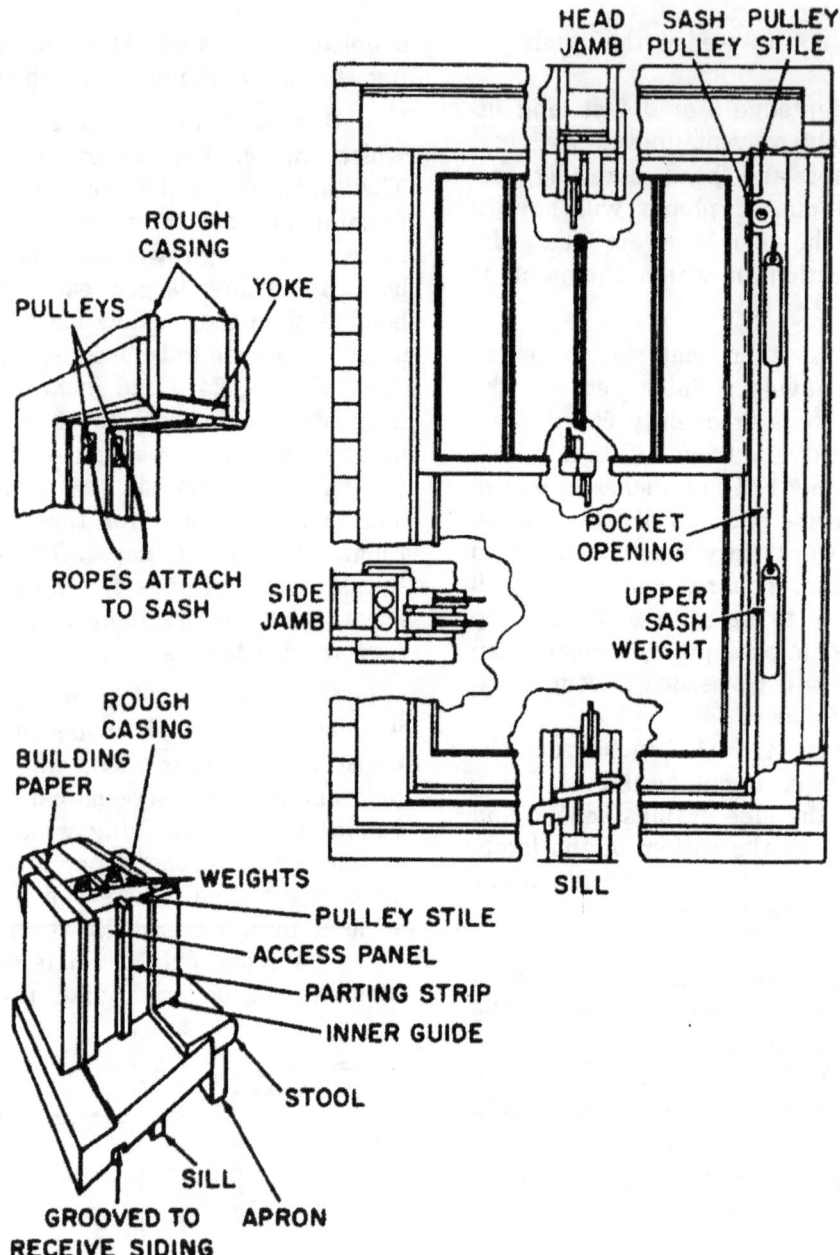

Figure 47. Double-hung window.

passing across its face is to some extent lost to the room.

(1) The box frame (fig. 47) consists of a top piece or yoke, two side pieces or jambs called pulley stiles, and the sill. The yoke and pulley stiles are dadoed into the inner and outer pieces (rough casing), forming an open box with the opening toward the studs and headers. The rough casing provides nailing surface to the studs and headers forming the plaster stop. The outside rough casing is also a blind stop for sheathing which should fit snugly against it, with building paper lapping the joint.

(2) The 2-inch space between the framing studs and the pulley stile forms the box for counterweights which balance the window sash. The weight box is divided by a thin strip known as the pendulum, which separates the weights for the two sash units. In the stiles near the sill is an opening for easy access to the weights. This opening has a removable strip which is part of the stile and channel for the lower sash (fig. 47).

(3) Yoke and stile faces are divided by a parting strip which is dadoed into them, but removable so that the upper sash can be taken out. The strip forms the center guide for the upper and lower sash, while the outerrough casing.

projecting slightly beyond the stiles and yoke, forms the outer guide. The inner guide for the sash is formed by a strip or stop, usually with a molding form on the inner edge. This stop is removable to permit the removal of the lower sash.

(4) At the upper parts of the stiles, two pulleys on each side (one for each sash) are mortised flush with the stile faces for the weight cord or chain.

(5) The sill is part of the box frame and slants downward and outward. It usually has one or two 1/4-inch brakes, one occurring at the point where the lower sash rests on the sill, and another near the outer edge to form a seat for window screens or storm sash. These brakes prevent water, dripping on the sill, from being blown under the sash. The underside of the sill, near its outer edge, is grooved to receive the edge of siding material to form a watertight seal.

(6) On the room side of the sill is another piece, the stool, which has a rabbet on its underside into which the sill fits. The stool edge projects from the will, forming a horizontal stop for the lower sash. The stool is part of the interior trim of the window, made up of side and top casings and an apron under the stool. The framed finished side and top casings are on the weather face. A drip cap rests on top of the outside head casing and is covered with metal flashing to form a watertight juncture with the siding material.

c. *Hinged or Casement Windows.* There are basically two types of casement windows, the outswinging and the inswinging types, and these may be hinged at the sides, top, or bottom. The casement window which opens out requires the window screen to be located on the inside with some device cut into its frame to operate the casement. Inswinging casements, like double-hung windows, are clear of screens, but they are extremely difficult to make watertight, particularly against a driving rainstorm. Casements have the advantage of their entire area being opened to air currents, with the added advantage of catching a parallel breeze and slanting it into a room.

(1) Casement windows are considerably less complicated in their construction, being simple frames and sash. The frames are usually made of planks 1 3/4 inch thick with rabbets cut in them to receive the sash. Usually there is an additional rabbet for screens or storm sash. The frames are rabbeted 1/2 inch deep and 1 1/2 or 1 7/8 inches wide for sash 1 3/8 or 1 3/4 inches thick. The additional rabbet is usually 15/16 or 1 3/16 inches wide, depending on whether the screen or storm sash is 7/8 or 1 1/8-inch thick.

(2) Outswinging casement windows have the rabbet for the sash on the outer edges of the frame, the inner edge being rabbeted for the screen. Sill construction is like that for a double-hung window, with the stool much wider and forming a stop for the bottom rail. Casement-window frames are of a width to extend to the sheathing face on the weather side and to the plaster face on the room side (fig. 48).

(3) When there are two casement windows in a row in one frame, they may be separated by a vertical double jamb called a mullion, or the stiles may come together in pairs like a french door. The edges of the stiles may be a reverse rabbet; a beveled reverse rabbet with battens, one attached to each stile; or beveled astragals (T-shaped molding), one attached to each stile. The battens and astragals insure better weathertightness. The latter are more resistant to loosening through use. Two pairs of casement sash in one frame are hinged to a mullion in the center (fig. 48).

(4) Inswinging casement-window frames are like the outswinging type with the sash rabbet cut in the inner edge of the frame (fig. 48). The sill construction is slightly different, being of one piece (similar to that of a door sill) with

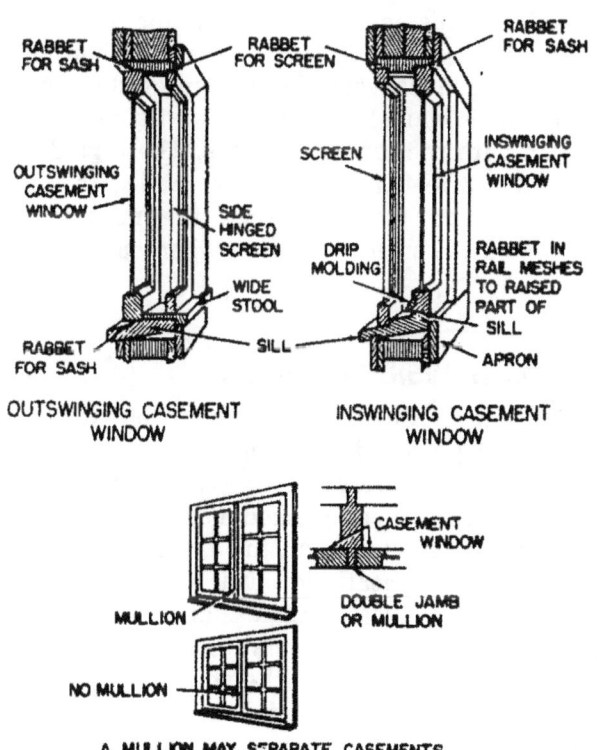

Figure 48. Casement windows.

a rabbet cut for a screen or storm sash toward the front edge, and the back raised where the sash rail seats. This surface is rabbeted at its back edge to form a stop for the rail which is also rabbeted to mesh.

(5) Sills in general have a usual slope of about 1 in 5 inches so that they shed water quickly. They are wider than the frames, extending usually about 1½ inches beyond the sheathing. They also form a base for the outside finished casing.

(6) The bottom sash rail of an inswinging casement window is constructed differently from the outswinging type. The bottom edge is rabbeted to mesh with the rabbet on the sill, and a drip molding is set in the weather face to prevent rain from being blown under the sash.

d. Window Frames In hasty construction, millwork window frames are seldom used. The window frames are mere openings left in the walls with the stops all nailed to the stud. The sash may be hinged to the inside or the outside of the wall or constructed so as to slide. The latter type of sash is most common in Army construction because it requires little time to install. Figure 49 shows the section and plan of a window and window frame of the type used in the field. After the outside walls have been finished, a 1 by 3 is nailed on top of the girt at the bottom of the window opening to form a sill. A 1 by 2 is nailed to the bottom of the plate and on the side studs which acts as a top for the window sash. One guide is nailed at the bottom of the opening flush with the bottom of the girt, and another is nailed to the plate with the top edge flush with the top of the plate. These guides are 1 by 3's, 8 feet long. Stops are nailed to the bottom girt and plate, between the next two studs, to hold the sash in position when open (fig. 49).

21. Other Wall Openings

a. Stovepipes. Stovepipes carried outside a building through a side wall eliminate the need for flashing and waterproofing around the pipe (fig. 50). The opening should be cut in an area selected to avoid cutting studs, braces, plates, and so on. Sheathing must be cut back in a radius 6 inches greater than that of the pipe. Safety thimbles or other insulation must be used on the inside and outside of the sheathing. Sheet metal insulation may be constructed and used as a single insulator on the outside. Make openings as follows:

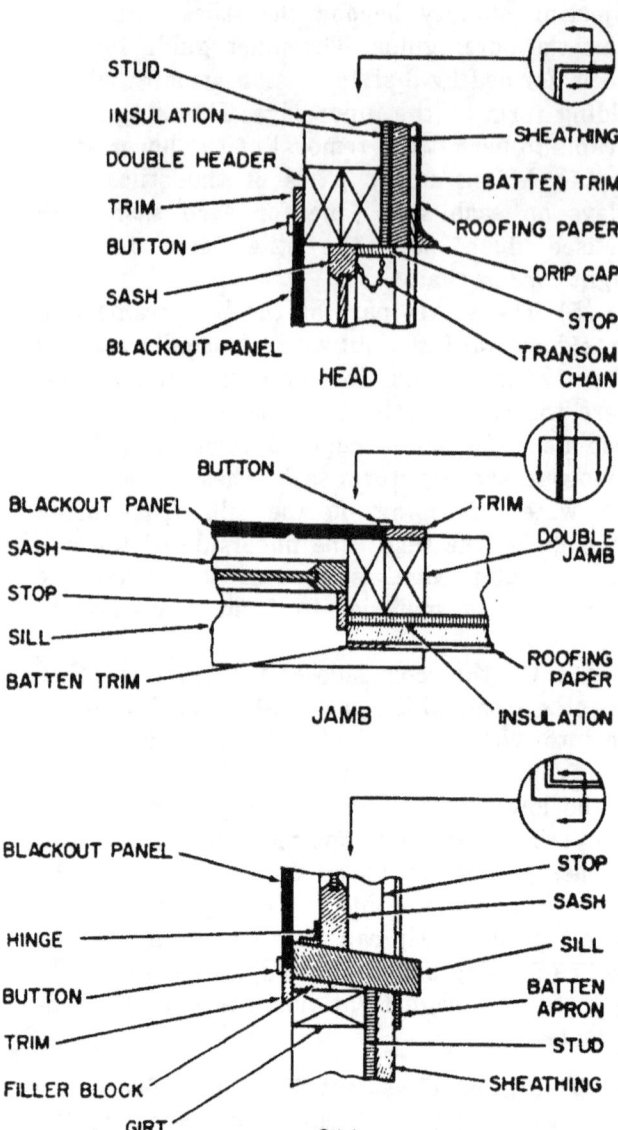

Figure 49. Detail of wall section with window frame and sash.

(1) Cut a hole through the sheet metal where the stovepipe is to penetrate.

(2) Mark a circle on the metal 1/2-inch larger in diameter than the pipe and then make another circle within this circle with a diameter 2 inches less than the diameter of the first.

(3) With a straightedge, draw lines through the center of the circle from the circumference. These marks should be from 1/2 to 3/4 inch apart along the outer circumference.

(4) Cut out the center circle, then cut to the outside of the circle along the lines drawn. After the lines have been cut, bend the metal strips outward at a 45° angle and force the pipe through the hole to the desired position. Very little water will leak around this joint.

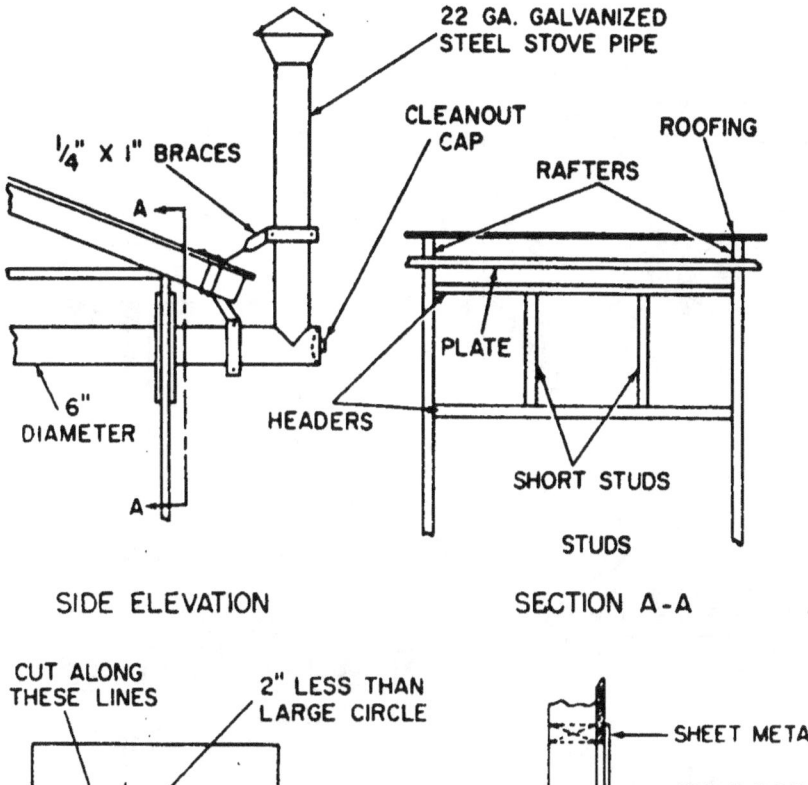

Figure 50. Preparation of wall opening for stovepipe.

b. *Ventilators.* Adequate ventilation is necessary to prevent condensation in buildings. Condensation may occur in the walls, in the crawl space under the structure, in basements, on windows, and so on. Condensation is most likely to occur in structures during the first 6 to 8 months after a building is built and in extreme cold weather when interior humidity is high. Proper ventilation under the roof allows moisture-laden air to escape during the winter heating season and also allows the hot dry air of the summer season to escape. The upper areas of a structure are usually ventilated by the use of louvers or ventilators.

(1) *Types of ventilators* (fig. 51). Types of ventilators used are as follows:

(a) Roof louvers (1).

(b) Cornice ventilators (2).

(c) Gable louvers (3).

(d) Flat-roof ventilators (4).

(e) Crawl-space ventilation (5).

(f) Ridge ventilators (6).

(2) *Upper structure ventilation.* One of the most common methods of ventilating is by the use of wood or metal louver frames. There are many types, sizes, and shapes of louvers. The following are facts to consider when building or installing the various kinds of ventilation:

(a) The size and number of ventilators are determined by the size of the area to be ventilated.

(b) The minimum net open area should be 1/4 square inch per square foot of ceiling area.

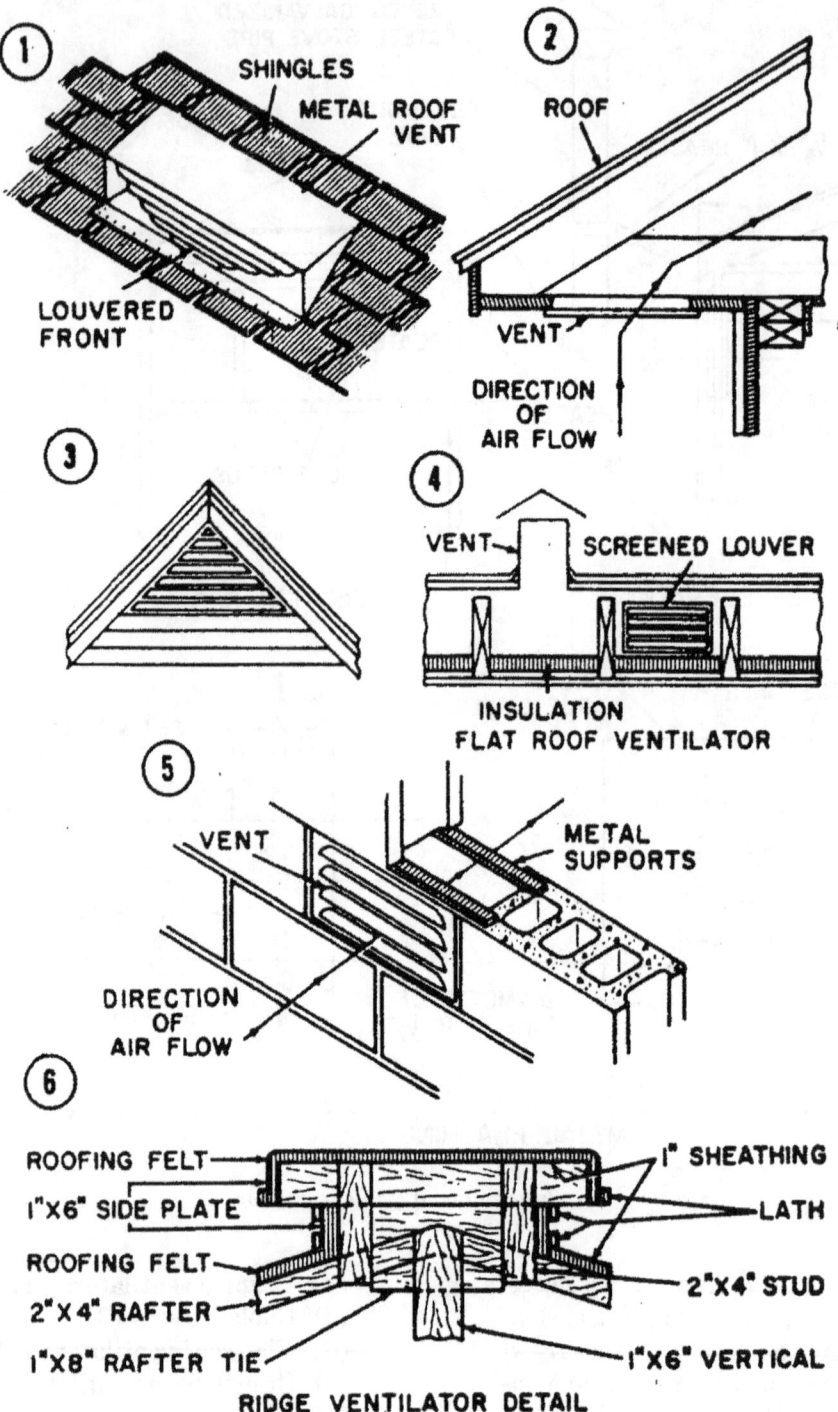

Figure 51. Types of ventilators.

(c) Most louver frames are usually 5 inches wide.

(d) Back edge should be rabbeted out for a screen or door, or both.

(e) Three-quarter-inch slats are used and spaced about 1 3/4 inches apart.

(f) Sufficient slant or slope to the slats should be provided to prevent rain from driving in.

(g) For best results, upper structure louvers should be placed as near the top of the gable as possible.

(3) *Crawl-space ventilation.* Crawl spaces under foundations of basementless structures should be well ventilated. Air circulation under the floors prevents excessive condensation that causes warping, swelling, twisting, and rotting of the lumber. These crawl-space ventilators are usually called "foundation louvers" (5, fig. 51). They are set into the foundation at the time it is

being built. A good foundation vent should be equipped with a copper or bronze screen and adjustable shutters for opening and closing the louver. The sizes for the louvers should be figured on the same basis as that used for upper structure louvers—1/4-inch for each square foot of underfloor space.

Section IV. STAIRWAYS

22. Steps and Stairs

Stairwork is made up of the framing on the sides, known as stringers or carriages, and the steps, known as treads. Sometimes pieces are framed into the stairs at the back of the treads; these pieces are known as risers. The stringers or carriages may consist of materials 2 or 3 inches thick and 4 or more inches wide which are cut to form the step of the stairs. Blocks (fig. 52) may also be nailed on to form the steps. There are usually three stringers to a stair, one at each of the two outer edges and one at the center. The floor joists must be properly framed around the stair well, or wellhole, in order to have enough space for the erection of the stair framing and the finished trim of the entire staircase.

a. The step or stair stringer may be made of 2 by 4's, with triangular blocks nailed to one edge to form the stringer. The blocks are cut from 2 by 6's and nailed to the 2 by 4, as shown in 1, figure 52. The step stringers are fastened at the top and bottom as shown in 2, figure 52. Figures 52 and 53 show the foundation and give the details of the sizes of the step treads, handrails, the methods of installing them, and the post construction. This type of step is most common in field construction.

b. When timbers heavier than 2 by 4's are used for stringers, they are laid out and cut as shown in figure 54.

23. Stairway Framing

a. To frame simple, straight string stairs, take a narrow piece of straight stock, called a story pole, and mark on it the distance from the lower

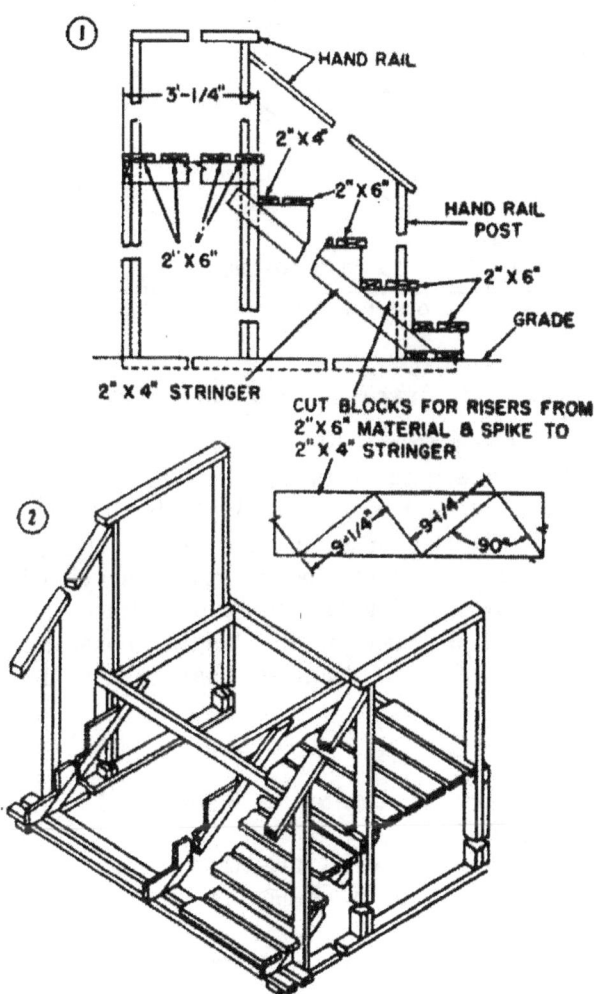

Figure 52. Step construction.

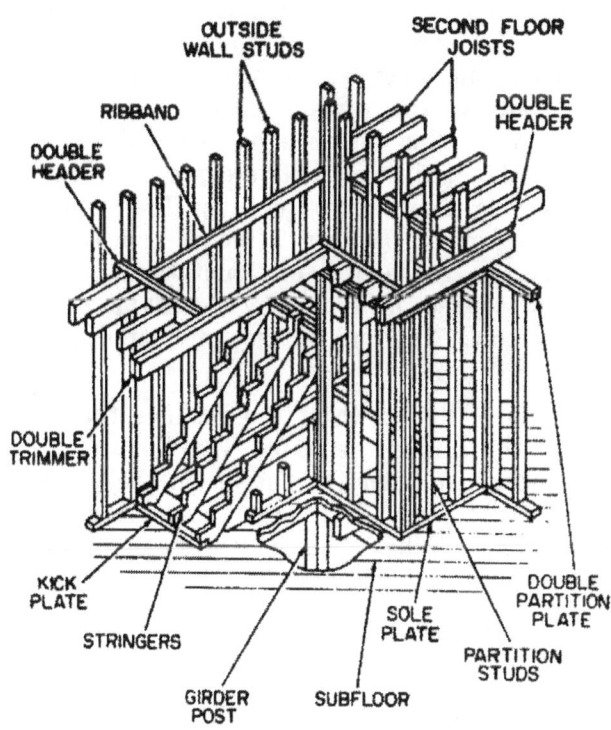

Figure 53. Details of complete stair construction.

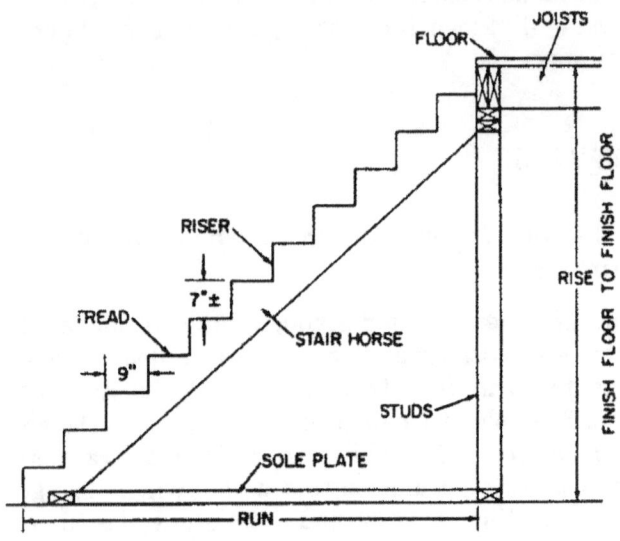

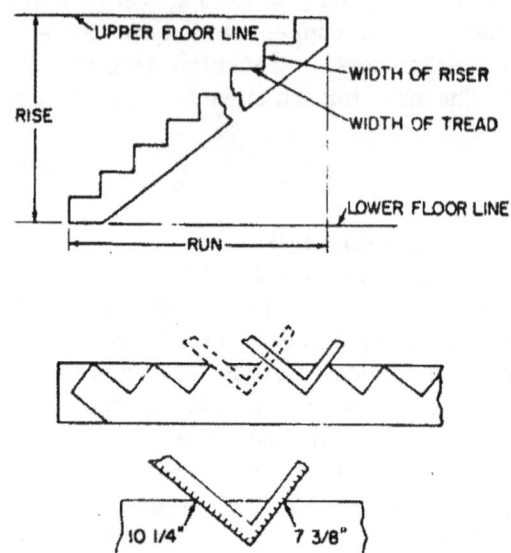

Figure 54. Method of laying out stair stringers.

floor to the upper floor level. This is the lower room height, plus the thickness of the floor joists, and the rough and finished flooring. It is also the total rise of the stairs. If it is kept in mind that a flight of stairs forms a right angled triangle (fig. 55), with the rise being the height of the triangle, the run being the base of the triangle, and the length of the stringers being the hypotenuse of the triangle, it will help in laying out the stair distances. Set dividers at 7 inches, the average distance from one step to another, and step off this distance on the story pole. If this distance will not divide into the length of the story pole evenly, adjust the divider span slightly and again step off this distance on the story pole. Continue this adjusting and stepping off until the story pole is marked off evenly. The span of the dividers must be near 7 inches and represents the rise of each step. Count the number of spaces stepped off evenly by the dividers, on the story pole. This will be the total number of risers in the stairs.

b. Measure the length of the wellhole for the length of the run of the stairs. This length may also be obtained from the details on the plans. The stair well length forms the base of a right-angled triangle. The height of the triangle and the base of the triangle have now been obtained.

c. To obtain the width of each tread, divide the number of risers, less one—since there is always one more riser than tread—into the run of the stairs. The numbers thus obtained are to be used on the steel square in laying off the run and rise of each tread and riser on the

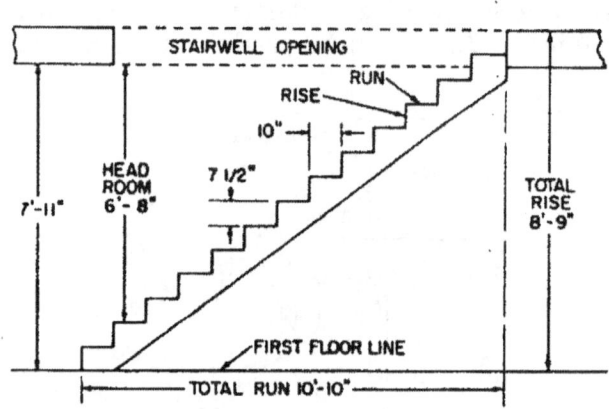

Figure 55. Principal parts of stair construction.

stringer stock (fig. 54). These figures will be about 7 inches and 10 inches, respectively, since the ideal run and rise totals 17 inches. Lay off the run and rise of each step on the stringer stock equal to the number of risers previously obtained by dividing the story pole into equal spaces. The distance of the height, base, and hypotenuse of a right-angled triangle are thus obtained.

24. Check on Design of Risers and Treads

a. Rules. The following are two rules of thumb that may be used to check the dimensions of risers and treads:

(1) Riser + tread = between 17 and 19 inches.

(2) Riser x tread = between 70 and 75 inches.

b. Check. If the sum of the height of the riser and the width of the tread ((1) above) falls between 17 and 19 inches, and the product of the height of the riser and the width of the tread equals between 70 and 75 inches, the design is satisfactory.

TABLE 1

SIZES OF BUILT—UP WOOD GIRDERS FOR VARIOUS LOADS AND SPANS

Based on Douglas Fir 4—SQUARE Guide—Line FRAMINIG

Deflection Not Over 1/360 Of Span—Allowable Fiber Stress 1600 lbs. per sq. in.

LOAD PER LINEAR FOOT OF GIRDER	LENGTH OF SPAN				
	6'-0"	7'-0"	8'-0"	9'-0"	10'-0"
	NOMINAL SIZE OF GIRDER REQUIRED				
750	6x8 in.	6x8 in.	6x8 in.	6x10 in.	6x10 in.
900	6x8	6x8	6x10	6x10	8x10
1050	6x8	6x10	8x10	8x10	8x12
1200	6x10	8x10	8x10	8x10	8x12
1350	6x10	8x10	8x10	8x12	10x12
1500	8x10	8x10	8x12	10x12	10x12
1650	8x10	8x12	10x12	10x12	10x14
1800	8x10	8x12	10x12	10x12	10x14
1950	8x12	10x12	10x12	10x14	12x14
2100	8x12	10x12	10x14	12x14	12x14
2250	10x12	10x12	10x14	12x14	12x14
2400	10x12	10x14	10x14	12x14	
2550	10x12	10x14	12x14	12x14	
2700	10x12	10x14	12x14		
2850	10x14	12x14	12x14		
3000	10x14	12x14			
3150	10x14	12x14			
3300	12x14	12x14			

The 6-in. girder is figured as being made with three pieces 2 in. dressed to 1-5/8 in. thickness.

The 8-in. girder is figured as being made with four pieces 2 in. dressed to 1-5/8 in. thickness.

The 10-in. girder is figured as being made with five pieces 2-in. dressed to 1-5/8 in. thickness.

The 12-in. girder is figured as being made with six pieces 2 in. dressed to 1-5/8 in. thickness.

Note—For solid girders multiply above loads by 1.130 when 6-inch girder is used; 1.150 when 8-in. girder is used; 1.170 when 10-in. girder is used and 1.180 when 12-in. girder is used.

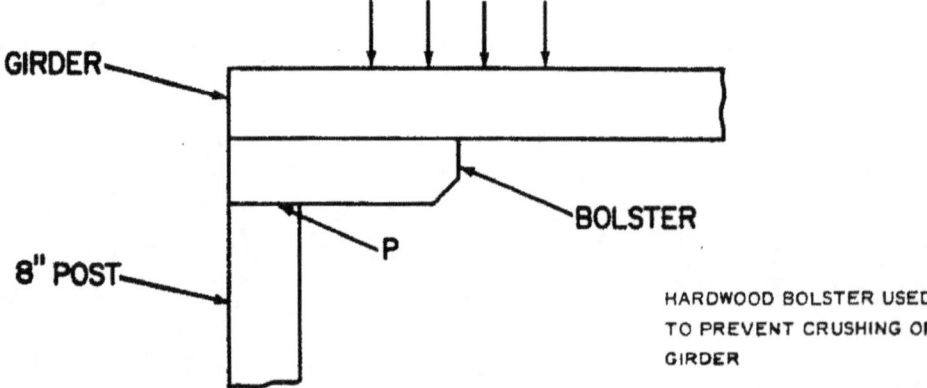

HARDWOOD BOLSTER USED TO PREVENT CRUSHING OF GIRDER

BUILDING ACCESSORIES

Section I. DOORS

1. Job-Built Doors

a. Types. Doors, both exterior and interior, are classified as batten, panel, and flush (fig.1). The batten door is the most commonly used and most easily constructed type of job-built door. It can be made in several ways, one of the simplest consisting of diagonal boards nailed together as two layers, each layer at right angles to the other. This type of door frequently is used as the core for metal-sheathed fire doors. Another type of batten door is made up of vertical boards tongued and grooved or shiplapped and held rigid by two to four crosspieces, ledgers, which may or may not be diagonally braced. If two additional pieces forming the sides of the door and corresponding to the ledgers are used, these are known as the frames.

b. Construction. In hasty construction, the carpenter makes a batten door from several 2 by 6 boards with ledgers and braces as shown in 1, figure 1. The ledgers are nailed with their edge 6 inches from the ends of the door boards. A diagonal is placed between the ledgers, beginning at the top ledger end opposite the hinge side of the door and running to the lower ledger diagonally across the door. If it is an outside door, roofing felt is used to cover the boards on the weather side. The ledgers are nailed over the felt. Wooden laths are nailed around the edges and across the middle of the door to hold the roofing felt in place. In hanging these doors, one-quarter of an inch clearance should be left around the door to take care of expansion. T-strap hinges are fastened to the ledgers of the door and to the hinge blocks on the door casing or post (1, fig.1).

2. Mill-Built Doors

a. Exterior Doors. The usual exterior door is the panel type (1, fig. 2). It consists of stiles (solid vertical members), rails (solid cross members), and filler panels.

b. Interior Doors. The two general interior types are the panel and the flush doors (fig.3). The louvered doors (fig. 3) are also popular and are used as hinged or as sliding doors. Any hinged interior door should not open or swing in the direction of a natural entry, or swing into hallways, against a blank wall, or be obstructed by other swinging doors.

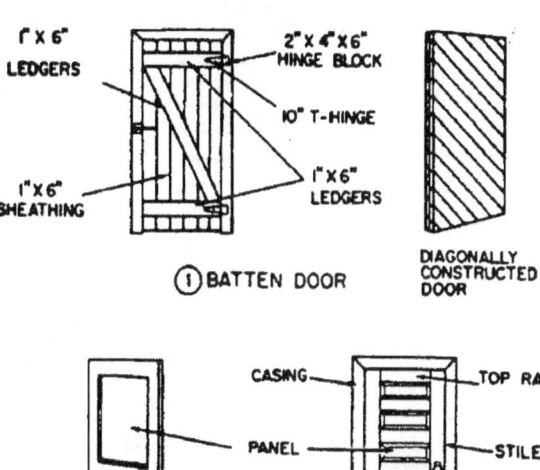

① BATTEN DOOR — DIAGONALLY CONSTRUCTED DOOR

② PANEL DOOR

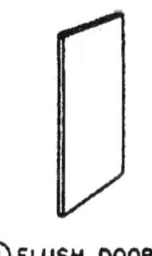

③ FLUSH DOOR

Figure 1. Types of doors.

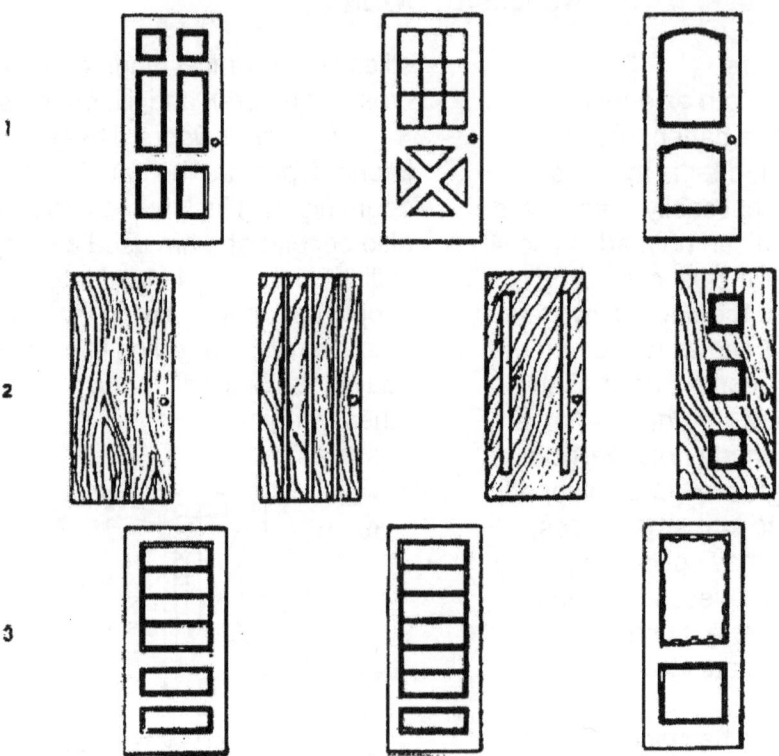

1 TRADITIONAL PANEL
2 FLUSH
3 COMBINATION

Figure 2. Exterior doors.

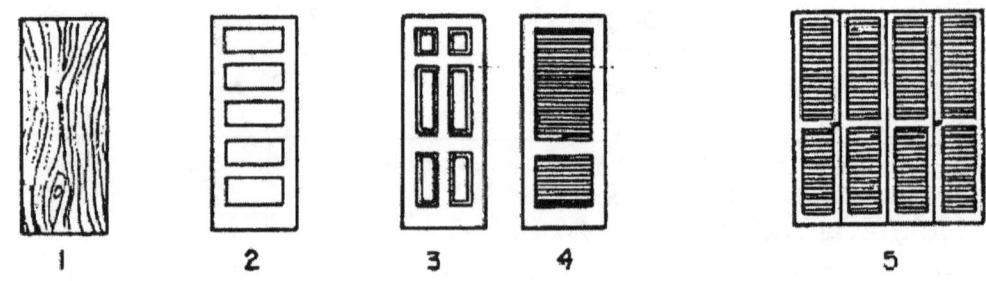

1, FLUSH; 2, PANEL (FIVE CROSS); 3, PANEL (COLONIAL); 4, LOUVERED; 5, FOLDING (LOUVERED).

Figure 3. Interior doors.

3. Exterior Door Frames

a. Before the exterior covering is placed on the outside walls, the door openings are prepared for the frames. To prepare the openings, square off any uneven pieces of sheathing and wrap heavy building paper around the sides and top. Since the sill must be worked into a portion of the rough flooring, no paper is put on the floor. Position the paper from a point even with the inside portion of the stud to a point about 6 inches on the sheathed walls and tack it down with small nails.

b. In most hasty construction, the outside doors will be as shown in figure 4. This type requires no frame, since the studs on each side of the opening act as a frame. The outside finish is applied to the wall before the door is hung. The casing is then nailed to the sides of the opening, set back the width of the stud. A 3/4-by 3/4-inch piece is nailed over the door to support the drip cap and is also set back the width of the stud. Hinge blocks are nailed to the casing where the hinges are to be placed. The door frame is now complete and ready for the door to be hung.

c. The principal parts of a door frame are shown in figure 5. On an outside door, the outside casings and the sill are also considered as parts of the door frame. A prefabricated outside door frame, delivered to the site assembled, looks like the right-hand view in figure 5.

d. The starting point for door frame layout calculations is the size of the door (height, width, and thickness) as given on the door schedule. Construction information on door frames is usually given in detail drawings like those shown in figure 6 and the left-hand view of figure

7. In the type of frame shown in figure 6 the door jambs (linings of the framing of door openings) are rabbeted to a depth of 1/2 inches. The rabbet prevents the door from swinging through the frame when it is closed. Other types of frames instead of a rabbet use a strip of wood, nailed to the inner faces of the jamb and called a stop. The stop also serves as a basis for weatherproofing the door. Most project drawings call for exterior door jambs to be of the rabbeted type.

e. The side jambs of an entrance door are cut to the height of the door, less the depth of the head jamb rabbet (if any), plus the following:

(1) The diagonal thickness of the sill, plus the sill bevel allowance (the sill bevel allowance is shown in figure 5).

(2) The thickness of the threshold, if any (the distinction between the sill and the thres-

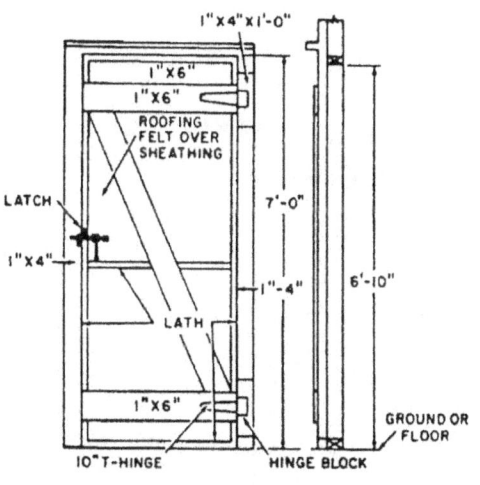

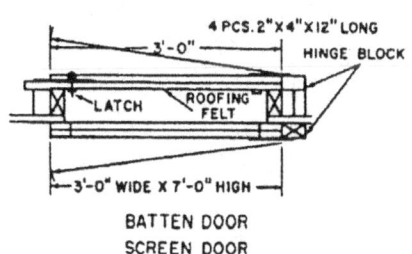

Figure 4. Single outside door.

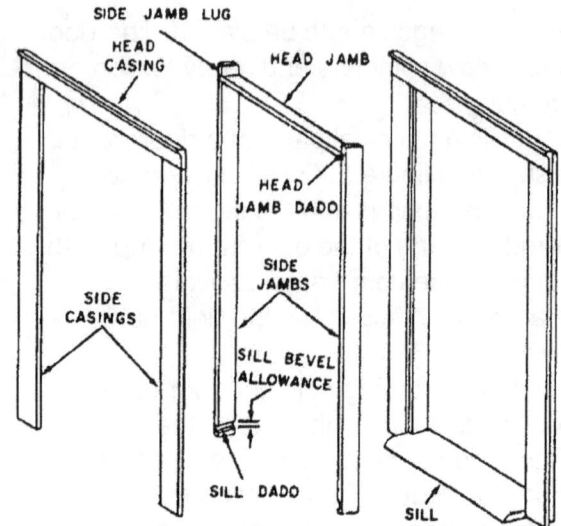

Figure 5. Principal parts of a door frame.

g. The casing layout depends on the way the side and head casings are to be joined at the corners. The casings are usually set back about 3/8 inch from the faces of the jambs.

4. Interior Door Frames

Inside door frames, like outside frames, are constructed in several ways. In most hasty construction, the type shown in figure 8 is used. The interior type is constructed like the outside type except that no casing is used on inside door frames. Hinge blocks are nailed to the inside wall finish, where the hinges are to be placed, to provide a nailing surface for the hinge flush with the door. Figure 8 shows the elevation of a single inside door. Both the outside and inside door frames may be modified to suit a climatic condition.

hold is shown in the left-hand view of figure 7).

(3) The thickness of the head jamb.

(4) The height of the side jamb lugs.

f. The head jamb is cut to the width of the door, less the combined depths of the side jamb rabbets (if any), plus the combined depths of the head jamb dadoes (grooves).

5. Door Jambs

Casings and stops are nailed to the door jambs (fig. 9) and the door is hung from them. Inside jambs are made of 3/4-inch stock and outside jambs of 1 3/8-inch stock. The width of the stock will vary with the thickness of the walls. Inside jambs are built up with 3/8- by 1 3/8-inch stops nailed to the jamb, while outside

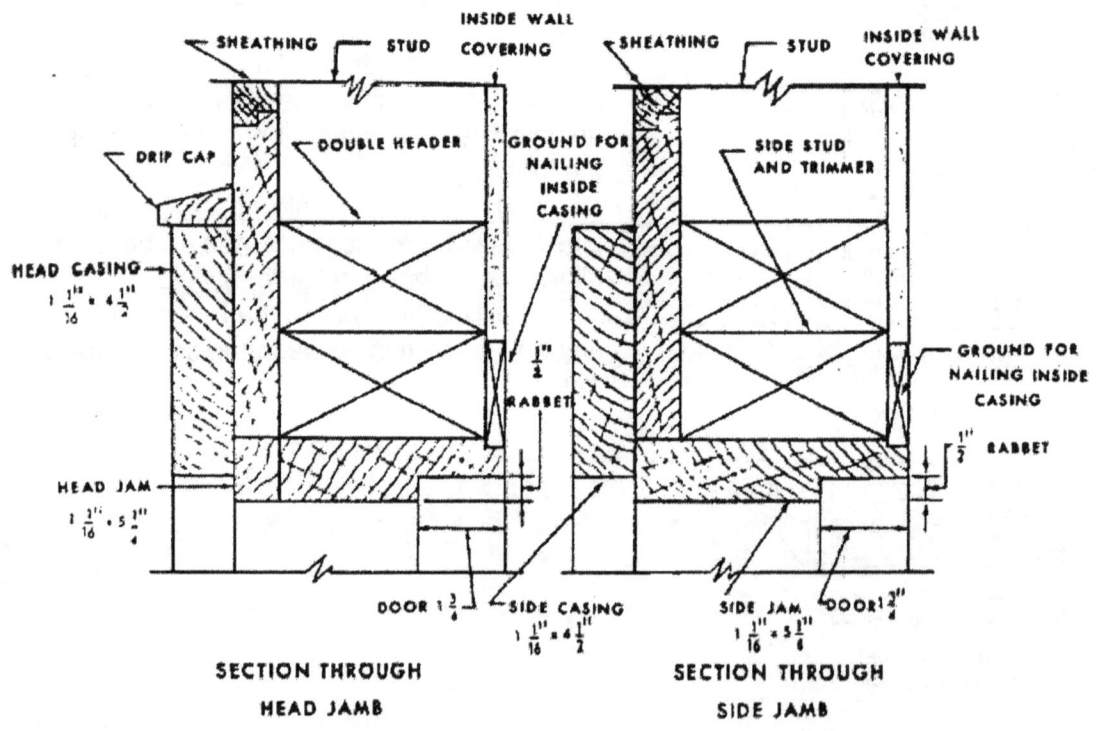

Figure 6. Typical door frame detail drawings.

jambs are usually rabbeted out to receive the door. Jambs are made and set as follows:

a. Regardless of how carefully rough openings are made, be sure to plumb the jambs and level the heads, when jambs are set.

b. Rough openings are usually made 21/2 inches larger each way than the size of the door to be hung. For example, a 2-foot 8-inch by 6-foot 8-inch door would need a rough opening of 2 feet 10 1/2 inches by 6 feet 10 1/2 inches. This extra space allows for the jambs, the wedging, and the clearance space for the door to swing.

c. Level the floor across the opening to determine any variation in floor heights at the point where the jambs rest on the floor.

d. Now cut the head jamb with both ends square, having allowed width of the door plus the depth of both dadoes and a full 3/16 inch for door clearance.

e. From the lower edge of the dado, measure a distance equal to the height of the door plus the clearance wanted under it. Mark and cut square.

f. On the opposite jamb do the same, only make additions or subtractions for the variation in the floor, if any.

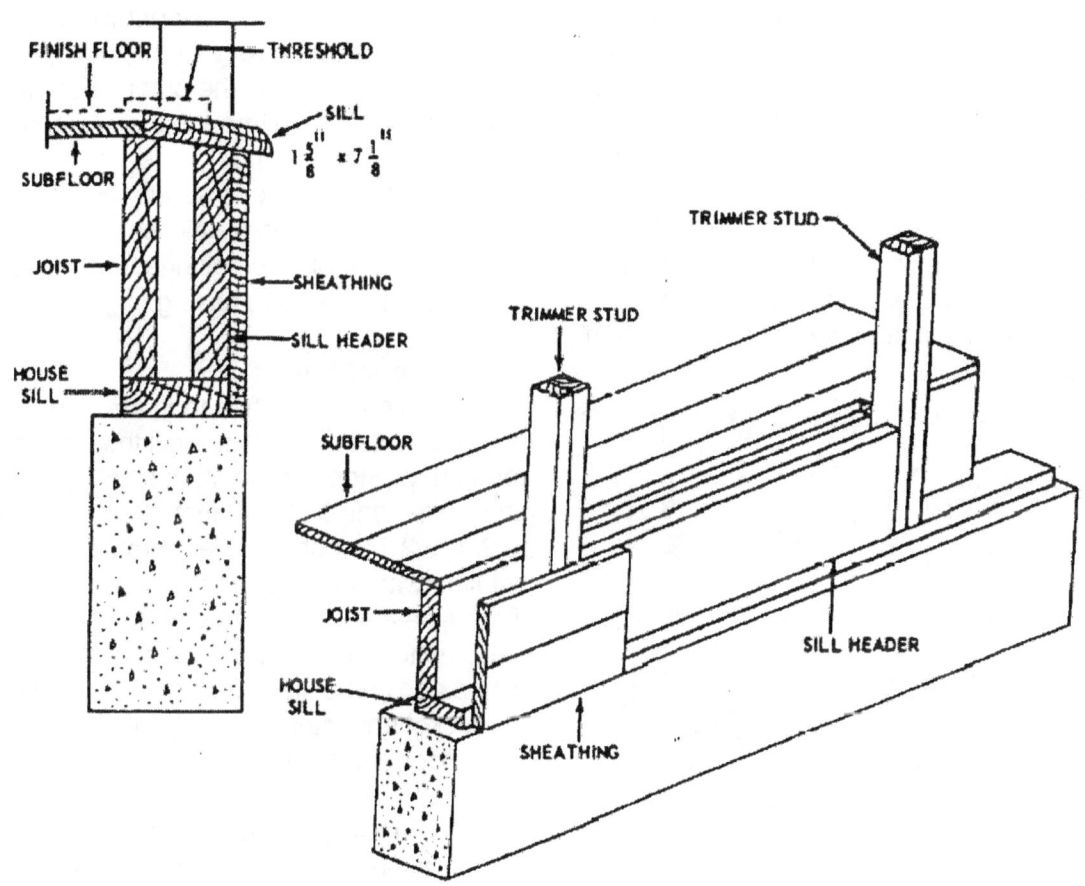

Figure 7. Sill installation.

g. Now nail the jambs and jamb heads together with 8-penny common nails through the dado into the head jamb.

h. Set the jambs into the opening and place small blocks under each jamb on the subfloor just as thick as the finish floor will be. This is to allow the finish floor to go under.

i. Plumb the jambs and level the jamb head.

j. Wedge the sides with shingles between the jambs and the studs, to aline, and then nail securely in place.

k. Take care not to wedge the jamb unevenly.

l. Use a straightedge 5 or 6 feet long inside the jambs to help prevent uneven wedging.

m. Check jambs and head carefully, because jambs placed out of plumb tend to swing the door open or shut, depending on the direction in which the jamb is out of plumb.

6. Door Trim

Door trim material is nailed onto the jambs to provide a finish between the jambs and the plastered wall. It is the edge trim around interior door openings and the interior side of exterior doors and windows, frequently called "casing" (fig. 9). Sizes vary from 1/2 to 3/4 inch in thickness, and from 2 1/2 to 6 inches in width. Most trim has a concave back, to fit over uneven plaster. In mitered (beveled edges) work, care must be taken to make all joints clean, square, neat, and well fitted. (If the trim is to be mitered at the top corners, a miter box, miter square, hammer, nail set, and block plane will be needed.) Door openings are cased up as follows:

a. Leave a margin of 1/2 inch from the edge of the jamb to the casing all around.

b. Cut one of the side casings square and even at the bottom with the bottom of the jamb.

c. Cut the top or mitered end next, allowing 1/4-inch extra length for the margin at the top.

d. Nail the casing onto the jamb and even with the 1/4-inch margin line, starting at the top and working toward the bottom.

e. Use 4-penny finish nails along the jamb side and 6-penny or 8-penny case nails along the outer edge of the casings.

f. The nails along the outer edge must be long enough to go through the casing and plaster and into the studs.

g. Set all nailheads about 1/8 inch below the surface with a nail set.

h. Now apply the casing for the other side and then the head casing.

7. Door Stops

In fitting doors, the stops are usually temporarily nailed in place until the door has been hung. Stops for doors in single-piece jambs are generally 7/16 inch thick and may be 3/4 to 2 1/2 inches wide. They are installed with a mitered joint at the junction of the side and head jambs. A 45 bevel cut at the bottom of the stop, about 1 to 1 1/2 inches above the finish floor, will eliminate a dirt pocket and make cleaning or re-finishing of the floor easier (fig. 9).

8. Hanging Mill-Built Doors

If mill-built doors are used, install them in the finished door frames as described below.

a. Cut off the stile extensions, if any, and place the door in the frame. Plane the edges of the stiles until the door fits tightly against the hinge side and clears the lock side of the jamb about 1/16 inch. Be certain the top fits squarely into the rabbeted recess and that the bottom swings free of the fin-

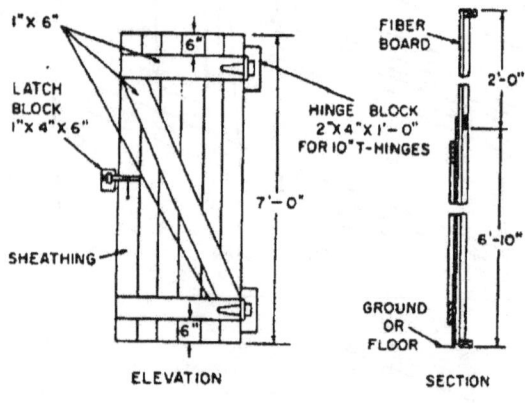

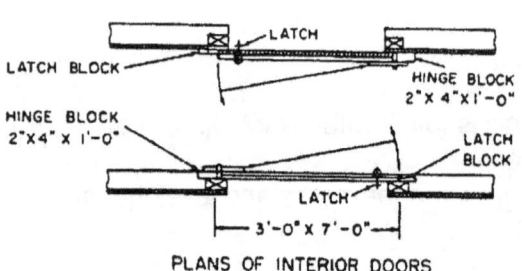

Figure 8. Single inside door.

ished floor about 1/2 inch. The lock stile of the door must be beveled slightly so that the edge of the stile will not strike the edge of the door jamb.

b. After proper clearances have been made, tack the door in position in the frame and wedge at the bottom (fig. 10). Mark positions of hinges with a sharp pointed knife on the stile and on the jamb. The lower hinge must be placed slightly above the lower rail of the door and the upper hinge slightly below the top rail of the door in order to avoid cutting out part of the tenons of the door rails which are housed in the stile. Three measurements are to be marked the location of the butt on the jamb; the location of the butt on the door; and the thickness of the butt on both jamb and door.

c. Door butts or hinges are mortised into door and frame as shown in figure 11. Butt sizes indicate the height of each leaf and the width of the pair when open. Use three butt hinges on all full length doors, to prevent warping and sagging. Place butts and mortise them with the utmost accuracy so the door will open and close properly and so the door, when open, will not strike the casing. The butt pin must project more than half its thickness from the casing.

d. Using the butt as a pattern, mark the dimensions of butts on the door edge and the face of the jamb.

e. Cut the marked areas, called gains, on the door jambs and door to fit the butts. Use a 1-inch chisel and mallet.

f. Test the gains. The butts must fit snugly and exactly flush with the edge of the door and the face of the jamb.

g. Screw three halves of the butt joints on the door and the other three halves on

the jamb. Place butts so that pins are inserted from the top when the door is hung.

h. Set the door against the frame so the two halves of the top butt engage. Insert the top pin. Engage and insert pins in bottom and center butts.

9. Lock Installation

Since types of door locks differ, follow the installation instructions that come with lock sets. After placing hinges in position, mark off the position of the lock (fig. 12) on the lock stile, about 36 inches from the floor level. Hold the case of the mortise lock on the face of the lock stile and mark off, with a sharp knife, the area to be removed from the edge of the stile which is to house the entire case. Next, mark off the position of the door knob hub and the position of the key. Then mark off the position of strike place on the jamb. Bore out the wood to house the lock and strike chisel and mortises, clean, and then install the lock set. The strike plate should be flush or slightly below the face of the door jamb (fig. 13).

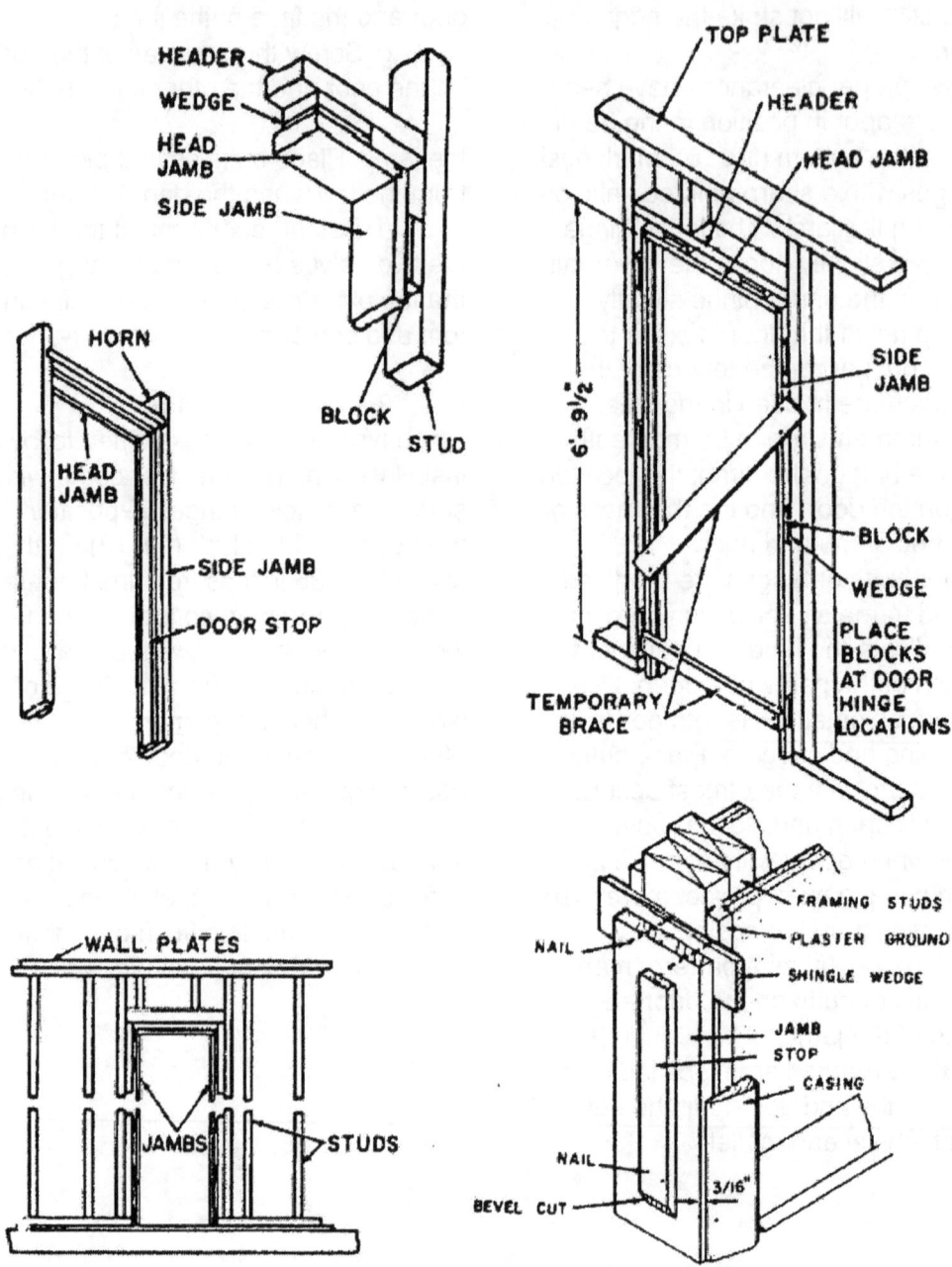

Figure 9. Door jamb and door trim.

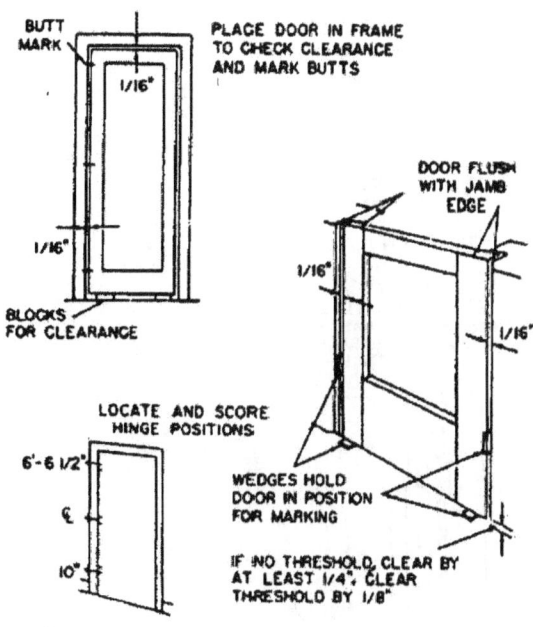
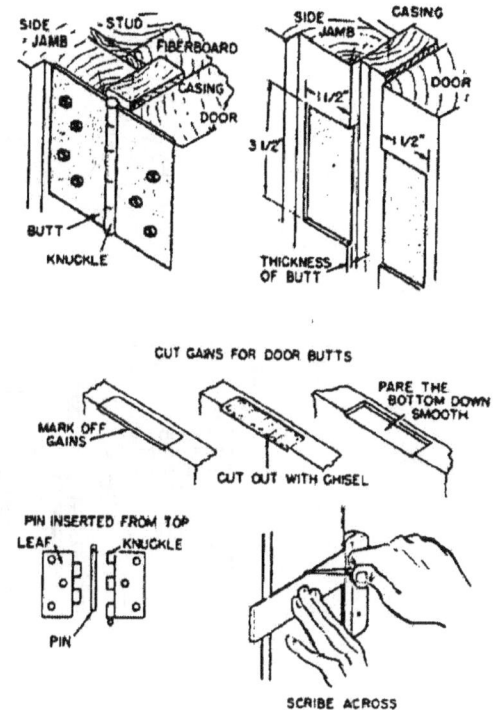

Figure 10. *Wedging door, locating and scribing hinge positions.*

10

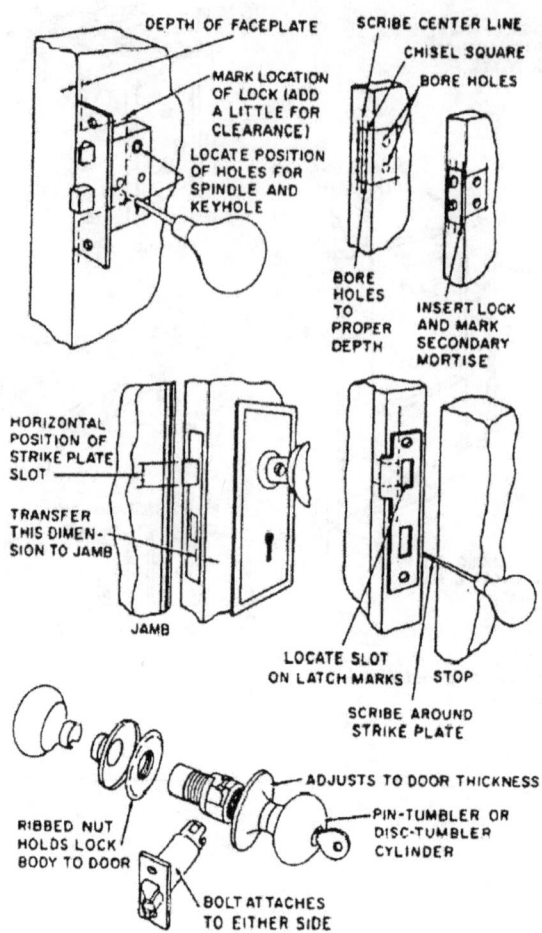

Figure 12. Installation of lock.

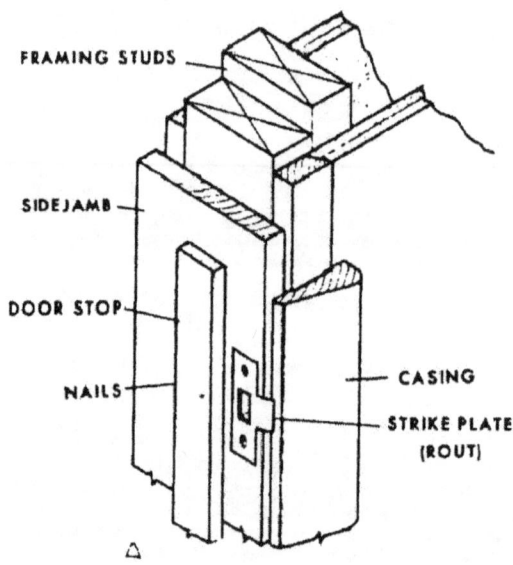

Figure 13. Installation of strike plate.

Section II. WINDOWS

10. Types of Windows

Windows are generally of the double hung and casement type (fig. 14). All windows, whatever the type, consist essentially of two parts, the frame and the sash. The frame is made up of four basic parts: the head, the jambs (two), and the sill. Where openings (window) are desired, studding must be cut away and its equivalent strength replaced by doubling the studs on each side of the opening to form trimmers and inserting a header at the top. If the opening is wide, the header should be doubled and trussed. At the bottom of the opening, the bottom header or rough sill is inserted.

11. Window Frames

a. These are the frames into which the window sashes are fitted and hung. They are set into the rough opening in the wall framing and are intended to hold the sashes in place. The rough window opening is made at least 10 inches larger each way (width and height) than the window glass size to be used. If the sash to be used is, for instance, a two-light window, 24 by 26 inches, add 10 inches to the width (24 inches) to obtain the total width of 34 inches for the rough opening. Add the upper and lower glasses (26 inches each) and an additional 10 inches for the total weight of the rough opening, 62 inches. These allowances are standard and provide for weights, springs, balances, room for plumbing and squaring, and for regular adjustments.

b. In hasty construction, millwork window frames are seldom used. The window frames are mere openings left in the walls with the stops all nailed to the stud. The sash may be hinged to the inside or the outside of the wall or constructed so as to slide. The latter type of sash is most common in Army construction because it requires little time to install. Figure 15 shows the section and plan of a window and window frame of the type used in the field. After the outside walls have been finished, a 1 by 3 is nailed on top of the girt at the window opening to form a sill. A 1 by 2 is nailed to the bottom of the plate and on the side studs and acts as a top for the window sash. One guide is nailed at the bottom of the opening flush with the bottom of the girt, and another is nailed to the plate with the top edge flush with the top of the plate. These guides are 1 by 3"s. Stops are nailed to the bottom girt and plate, between the next two studs, to hold the sash in position when open (fig. 15).

12. Double-Hung-Windows

The double-hung window (fig. 16) is made up of an upper and a lower sash, which slide vertically past one another. Its frame construction and operation are more involved than that of casement windows. The double-hung window consists of the following:

a. The box frame consists of a top piece or yoke; two side pieces or jambs called pulley stiles, and the sill. The yoke and pulley stiles are dadoed into the inner and outer pieces (rough casing), forming an open box with the opening toward the studs and headers. The rough casing provides nailing surface to the studs and headers forming the plaster stop. The outside rough casing is also a blind stop for sheathing which should fit snugly against it, with building paper lapping the joint.

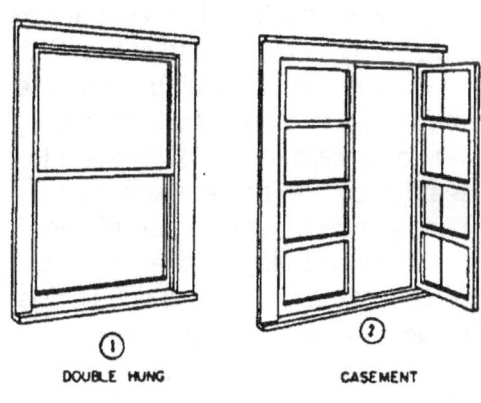
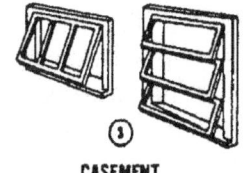

Figure 14. Double hung and casement windows.

b. The 2-inch space between the framing studs and the pulley stile forms the box for counterweights which balance the window sash. The weight box is divided by a thin strip known as the pendulum, which separates the weights for the two sash units. In the stiles near the sill is an opening for easy access to the weights. This opening has a removable strip which is part of

inner edge. This stop is removable to permit the removal of the lower sash.

d. At the upper parts of the stiles, two pulleys on each side (one for each sash) are mortised flush with the stile faces for the weight cord or chain.

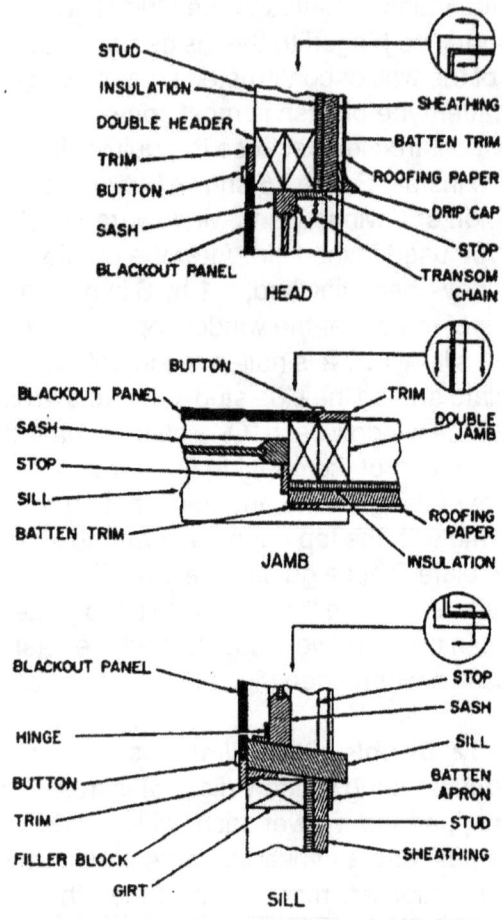

Figure 15. Detail of wall section with window frame and sash.

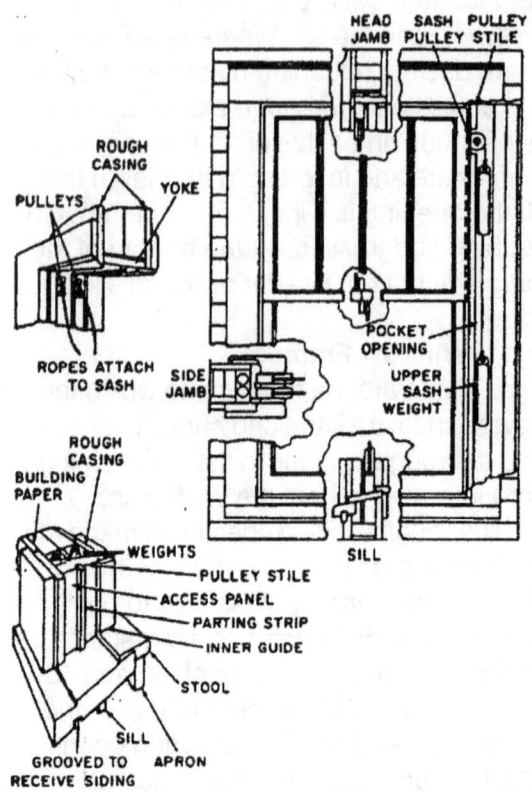

Figure 16. Double-hung windows.

the stile and channel for the lower sash (fig. 16).

c. Yoke and stile faces are divided by a parting strip which is dadoed into them, but removable so that the upper sash can be taken out. The strip forms the center guide for the upper and lower sash, while the outer rough casing, projecting slightly beyond the stiles and yoke, forms the outer guide. The inner guide for the sash is formed by a strip or stop, usually with a molding form on the

e. The sill is an integral part of the box frame and slants downward and outward. It usually has one or two 1/4-inch brakes, one at the point where the lower sash rests on the sill, and another near the outer edge to form a seat for window screens or storm sash. These brakes prevent water dripping on the sill from being blown under the sash. The underside of the sill, near its outer edge, is grooved to receive the edge of siding material to form a watertight seal.

f. On the room side of the sill is another piece, the stool, which has a rabbet on its underside into which the sill fits. The stool edge projects from the sill, forming a horizontal stop for the lower sash. The stool is part of the interior trim of the window, made up of side and top casings and an apron under the stool. The framed finished side and top casings are on the weather face. A drip cap rests on top of the outside head casing and is covered with metal flashing to form a watertight juncture with the siding material.

13. Hinged or Casement Windows
There are basically two types of casement windows, the outswinging and the inswinging types, and these may be hinged at the sides, top, or bottom. The casement window which opens out requires the window screen to be located on the inside with some device cut into its frame to operate the casement, otherwise the window screen must be hinged and swung up to operate the window. Inswinging casements, like double-hung windows, are clear of screens, but they are extremely difficult to make watertight, particularly against a driving rainstorm. This is why most casement windows are constructed to swing out. The following explains the construction of casement window frames.

a. The casement window frames (fig. 17) are usually made of planks 1 3/4 inch thick with rabbets cut in them to receive the sash. Usually there is an additional rabbet for screens or storm sash. The frames are rabbeted 1/2-inch deep and 1 1/2 or 1 7/8 inches wide for sash 1 3/8 or 1 3/4 inches thick. The additional rabbet is usually 15/16 or 13/16 inches wide, depending on whether the screen or storm sash is 7/8 or 1 1/8 inch thick.

b. Outswinging casement windows have the rabbet for the sash on the outer edges of the frame, the inner edge being rabbeted for the screen. Sill construction is very much like that for a double-hung window, with the stool much wider and forming a stop for the bottom rail. Casement-window frames are wide enough to extend to the sheathing face on the weather side and to the plaster face on the room side (fig. 17).

c. When there are two casement windows in a row in one frame, they may be separated by a vertical double jamb called a mullion, or the stiles may come together in pairs like a french door. The edges of the stiles may be a reverse rabbet; a beveled reverse rabbet with battens, one attached to each stile; or beveled astragals (T-shaped molding), one attached to each stile. The battens and astragals insure better weathertightness. The latter are more resistant to loosening through use. Two pairs of casement sash in one frame are hinged to a mullion in the center (fig. 17).

d. Inswinging casement-window frames are like the outswinging type with the sash rabbet cut in the inner edge of the frame. The sill construction is slightly different, being of one piece (similar to that of a door sill) with a rabbet cut for a screen or storm sash toward the front edge,

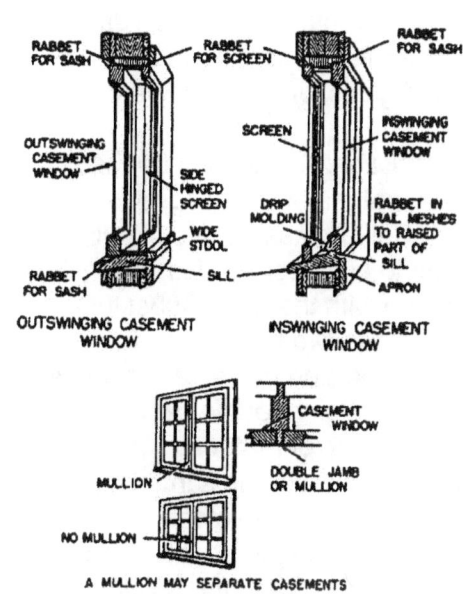

Figure 17. Casement windows.

and the back raised where the sash rail seats. This surface is rabbeted at its back edge to form a stop for the rail which is also rabbeted to mesh.

e. Sills in general have a usual slope of about 1 in 5 inches so that they shed water quickly. They are wider than the frames, extending usually to the plaster line and about 1 1/2 inches beyond the sheathing. They also form a base for the outside finishing casing.

f. The bottom sash rail of an inswinging casement window is constructed differently than the outswinging type. The bottom edge is rabbeted to mesh with the rabbet on the sill, and a drip molding is set in the weather face to prevent rain from being blown under the sash.

14. Window Sashes

a. Types of Job-Built Sashes. A window normally is composed of an upper and a lower sash. These sashes slide up and down, swing in or out, or may be stationary. There are two general types of wood sash-fixed or permanent; and movable. Fixed sashes are removable only with the aid of a carpenter. Movable sash may slide up and down in channels in the frame (double-hung), or swing in or out and be hinged at the side (casement type). Sliding sashes are counter balanced by sash weights whose actual weight is one-half that of each sash. Sashes are classified according to the number of pieces of glass, or lights-single or divided.

b. Construction. A sash can be made of 1- by 3-inch material with Cel-O-glass or an equivalent. Cel-O-glass comes in rolls and can be cut to any desired size. Two frames are made with the glass substitute installed on one; the two frames are then nailed together. The side pieces are cut to a length equal to the height of the sash less the width of one piece of material. The top and bottom pieces are cut the same length as the window, less the width of the material. They are fastened at the joints with corrugated metal fasteners. When the two frames are nailed together, they should be turned so that the joints are not over each other. This staggers the joints and strengthens the sash. If the sash is too large for the glass substitute to cover, a muntin may be placed in the sash to hold the glass substitute and should be fastened with corrugated metal fasteners. Where long sashes are made, a muntin should be placed in the center to give added strength. Figure 18 shows the window frame and sash detail.

c. Window Sash Installation.

(1) *Double-hung windows.* Place the upper sash in position and trim off a slight portion of the top rail of the sash to insure a good fit. Then tack the upper sash in position. Fit the lower sash in position by trimming off the stiles. Place the lower sash in the opening and trim off, from the bottom rail, enough to permit the meeting rails (lower rail of supper sash and top rail of bottom sash) to meet on the level.

(2) *Sash weights.* If sash weights are used, remove each sash after it has been properly fitted and weight each one. Select sash weights equal to half the weight of each sash and place in position in the weight pocket. Measure proper length of sash cord for lower sash and attach to the stile and weight on both sides. Adjust length of cord so that sash moves up and down easily and the weight does not strike the pulley or rest on the frame. Install the cords and weights for the upper sash and adjust the cord and weight so that each cord and weight runs smoothly. Close the pockets in the frame and install the blind stop, parting stop, and bead stop (fig. 18).

(3) *Sliding windows.* Details of installation of sliding windows and the typical side wall section are shown in figure 19.

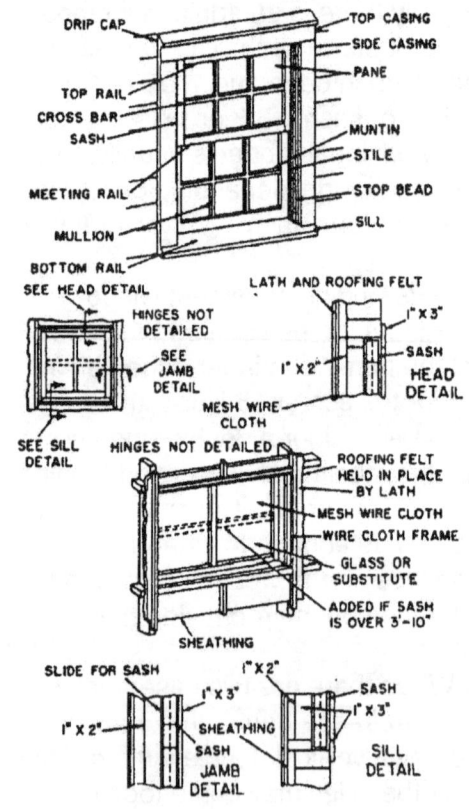

Figure 18. Window frame and sash detail.

15. Mill-Built-Sashes

a. Types. Sashes are mill built of wood or steel. They are made for fixed or movable emplacement and may be casement or doublehung as desired. The sash size is determined by the size of the glass (fig. 20). Overall dimensions are generally standard and made to fit standard construction frames. The thickness of sash is usually 11/8, 1 3/8, or 1 3/4 inches. The 1 3/8 inch sash generally is used in frame construction. In giving the size of a sash, the width of the glass is always given first, then the height, then the number of pieces of glass, or lights. Thus a sash might be spoken of as a 24 by 26 by 1 light. This means that the glass itself is 24 by 26 inches and that there is only one piece of glass. However, the sash would be larger than 24 by 26 inches because of the

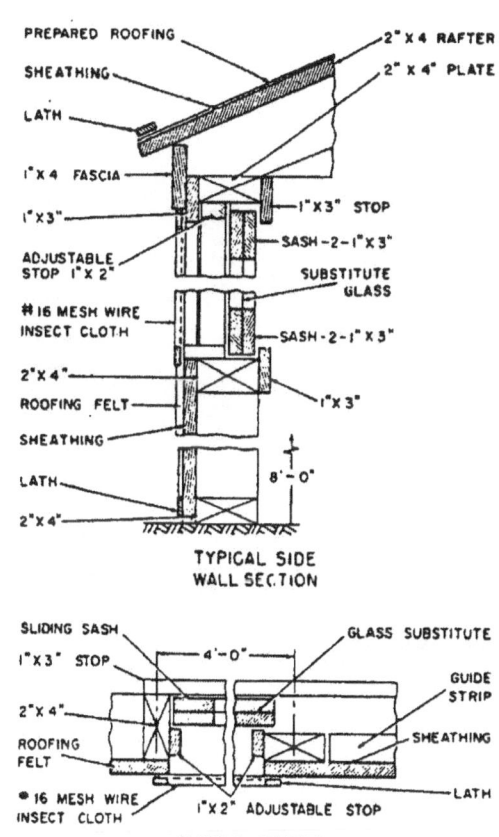

Figure 19. Window sash installation.

frame around the glass. For the frame of a two-light window with a 1 3/8-inch check rail, add 4 inches to the width and 6 inches to the length.

Example: A two-light window has a glass size of 24 by 26. Find the size of the window frame. *Solution:* 24 inches + 4 inches = 28 inches, or 2 feet 4 inches, the width. 26 inches x 2 = 52 inches, 52 inches + 6 inches = 58 inches, or 4 feet 10 inches, the length. Therefore, the window frame size for these sashes would be 2 feet 4 inches by 4 feet 10 inches.

b. Installation.

(1) Prepare the sash cords, chains, or balances that are to be used. If cords are used, tie them to the weights, run them through the pulleys at the top, and tie a knot in the end of each. This knot will be set in the side of the sash in a recess made to receive it.

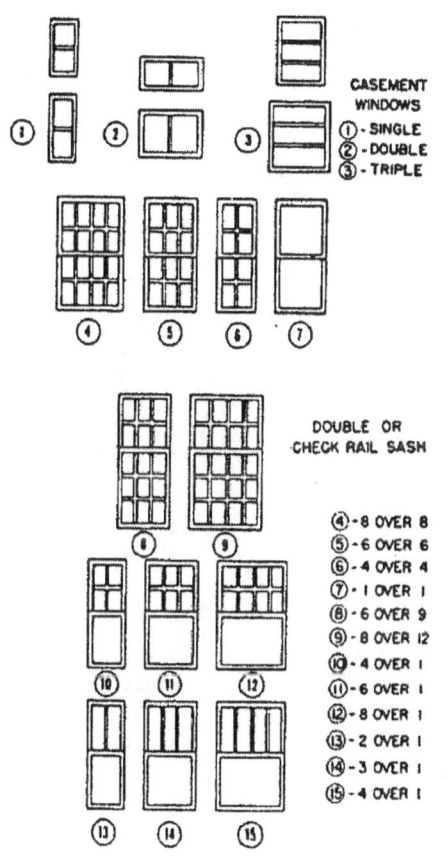

Figure 20. Types and sizes of milled sashes.

(2) Adjust the length of the cord. The length can be determined by placing the sash in its position and measuring. When the inside sash is down in place, the weight for that sash should be near the top pulley. When the outside sash is up in place, the weight for it should be down, not quite touching the bottom.

(3) Fit the outside top sash first. Do not fit it too tightly; allow for swelling. Use a sharp plane for squaring.

(4) Remove the parting bead on one side of the frame to put the sash into place. This is the strip about 1/2 by 3/4 inch which is grooved into the frame on each side separating the two sashes.

(5) Notch out each end of the check rail as far as the parting bead extends beyond the frame.

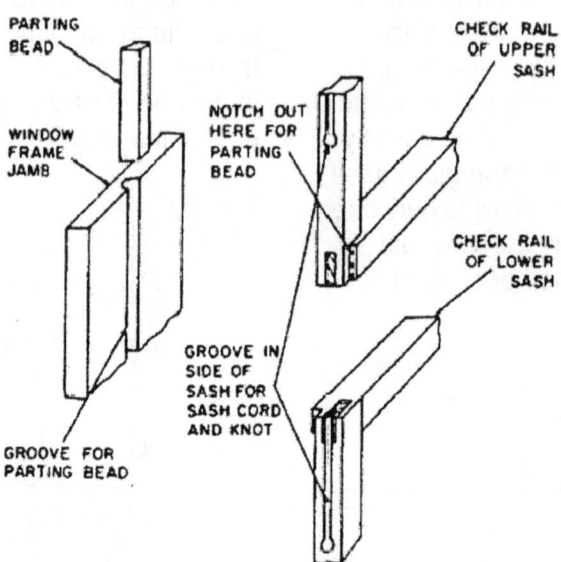

DETAIL OF JAMB AND PARTING BEAD

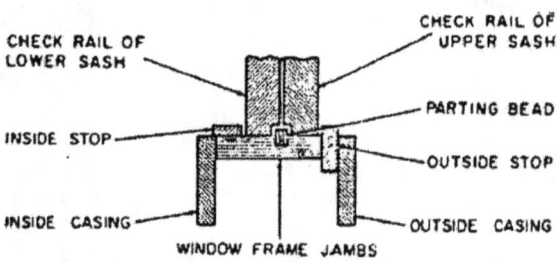

CROSS SECTION OF WINDOW SASH AND JAMB

Figure 21. Details of check rails for double-hung

This should be done accurately to prevent bad fitting, which would either let in wind and cold or, if too tight, cause the sash to slide with difficulty (fig. 21).

(6) When the sash is fitted, put it in place, replace the parting beads, and attach sash cords to the sides.

(7) Plane and fit the inside bottom sash next for easy operation. Fit the sides of it first.

(8) After the sides have been fitted, set the sash in place and determine how much, if any, need come off the bottom, other than the bevel that is always planed on to match the slant of the window sill. The two check rails must come together and be even at the middle of the window. If not, the window locks will not meet or be workable.

(9) If the rails do not match, scribe off the necessary amount at the bottom, taking care to keep the same bevel on the bottom edge of the sash.

(10) When the lower sash is fitted, put it in place, secure the sash cords, and check both sashes for each operation.

Section III. SCENES

16. Window Screens

Screen sash is usually 3/4-inch stock, but for large windows and doors 1 1/8-inch material frequently is used or 3/4-inch lumber is braced with a horizontal member.

SCREENS

a. Construction. Window-screen sash is usually 1 3/4 or 2 1/4 inches wide. Screen may be attached by stapling or tacking. Cut screen about 1 inch wider and longer than the opening; cover the edges with molding; then rabbet the inside

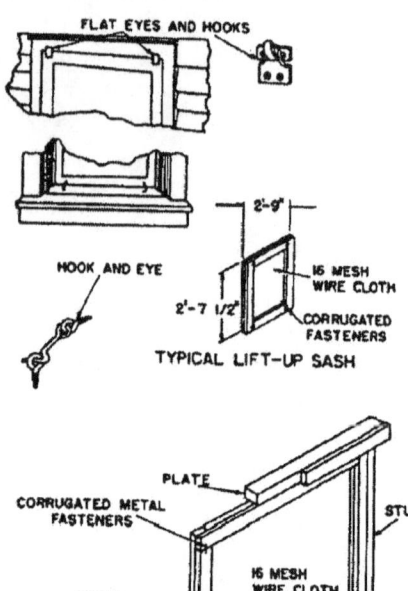

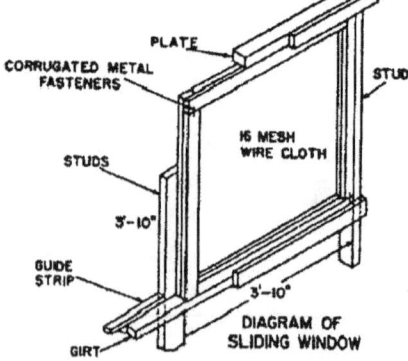

Figure 22. Window-screen sash construction.

edges about 3/8 by 1/2 inch, attach the screen in the rabbet, and nail 3/8 by 1/2 inch molding flush with face of sash. Figure 22 illustrates the construction of screen sashes using mesh wire cloth.

b. Joints. Window sashes may be made with open mortise, four tenons, with rails tenoned into stiles; with half-lap corners; or with butt joints or corrugated fasteners. In either of the first two cases, the joints may be nailed or glued.

c. Attaching Screen Material. When attaching screen material, start at one end and tack or staple it with copper staples, holding the material tightly. Then, hand-stretch the screen along the side, working toward the other end and attach, making sure that the weave is parallel to the ends and sides. Tack the sides and apply the

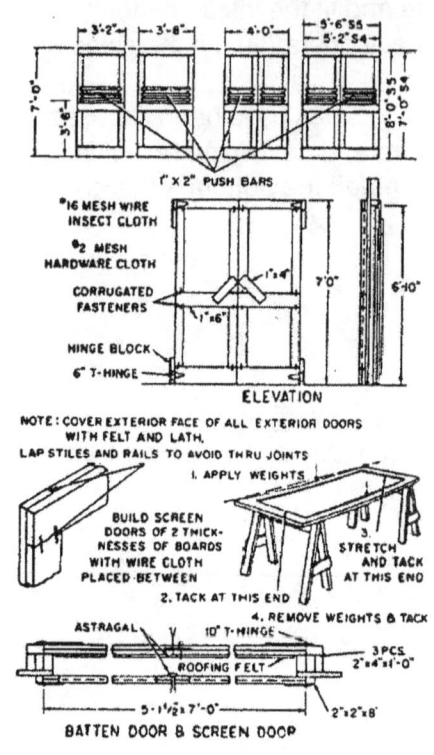

Figure 23. Door screen construction.

molding. Copper staples should be used for bronze or copper screen, and cadmium staples for aluminum screens.

17. Door Screens

Door screens are made as shown in figure 23. Two separate frames are made of 1 by 4 material for the sides and top and of 1 by 6 material for the bottom and middle pieces. The first frame is made of two side pieces the full length of the door; the crosspieces are the width of the door less the width of the two side pieces. This frame is put together with corrugated metal fasteners, then the screen wire is applied. The second frame is made with the crosspiece the full width of the door. The side pieces are cut to correspond with the distance between the crosspieces. The second frame is placed over the first frame and nailed securely. For push-and-pull plates, two short braces of 1 by 4 are nailed to the side opposite the hinge side.

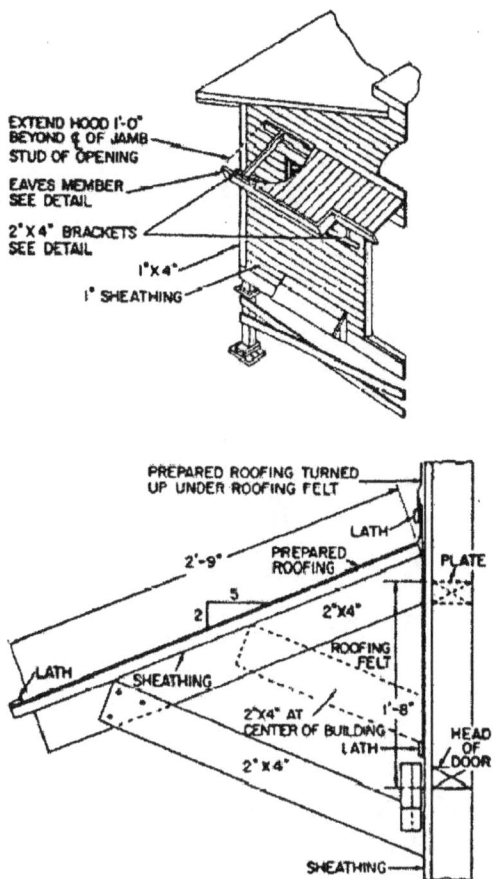

Figure 24. Hood or canopy.

BUILDING LAYOUT AND FOUNDATION

1. Introduction
Layout means the actions performed in preparing the materials and work area before beginning construction. As soon as the construction site has been selected, layout may begin.

2. Tools and Materials
Tools and materials used in layout must be carefully selected. The most commonly used are as follows: figure 1.

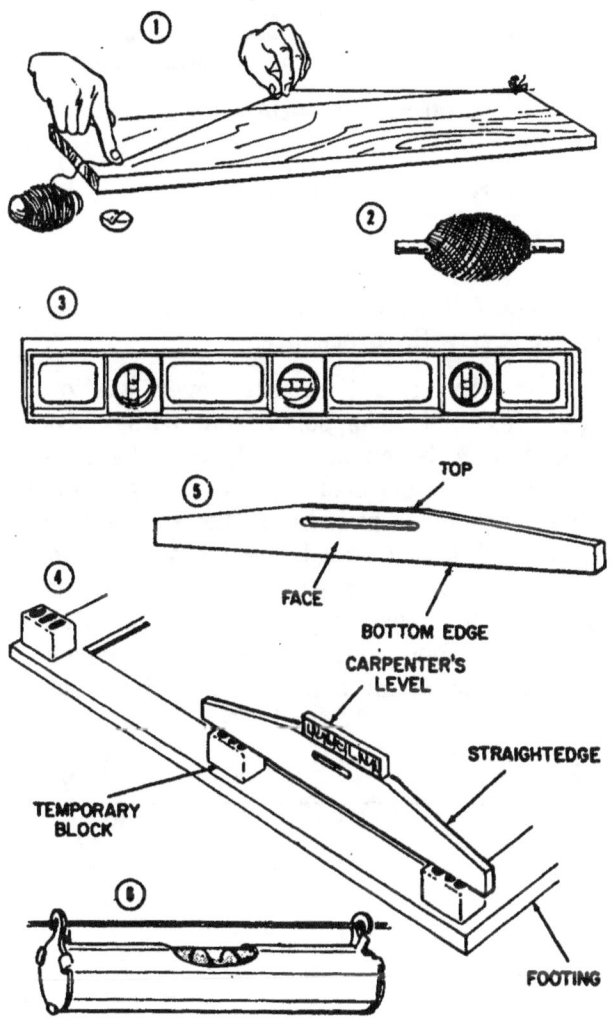

Figure 1. Layout tools.

a. Sledge Hammer or Maul. The sledge hammer or maul is used to sink corner stakes or batter board posts.

b. Post-Hole Auger. The post hole auger is used to dig the holes required to set posts properly in some soils.

c. Hand Saw. The hand saw is used to cut batter boards and posts.

d. Chalkline. A chalkline is a white, twisted mason's line consisting of a reel, line, and chalk. It is coated with chalk and stretched taut between points to be connected by a straight line, just off the surface. When snapped, the line makes a straight guideline.

e. Tracing Tape. Tracing tape is a cotton tape approximately 1 inch wide. It is generally in a 200-foot length for laying out excavation or foundation lines.

f. Ax or Hatchet. The ax or hatchet is used to sharpen batter boards and stakes.

g. Hammer. The hammer is used for building batter boards.

h. Posts and Stakes. Batter board posts are made from 2 x 4 or 4 x 4 material; corner stakes, from 4 x 4's. Batter boards are made from 1 x 4 or 1 x 6 pieces.

i. Carpenter's Level. The carpenter's level (4, fig. 1) determines levelness of surface and sights level lines. It may be used directly on the surface or used with a straightedge (fig. 1). Levelness is determined by the bubbles suspended within glass tubes parallel to one or more surfaces of the level.

j. Straightedge. The straightedge usually has a handhole, a bottom edge at least 30 inches long used as a leveling surface, and a top edge 8 to 10 inches long used as a working surface. It may be used with the level to increase the area checked (5, fig. 1). It is most often used to lay out straight lines between points close enough together to use the edge as a ruler.

k. Line Level. The line level has a spirit bubble

215

to show levelness; it can be hung from a line (6, fig. 1). Placement halfway between the points to be leveled gives the greatest accuracy.

l. Engineer's Transit or Leveling Instrument. The engineer's transit establishes reference points or grade lines which permit building up or down with accuracy as to vertical level. It locates corners and lays out lines for buildings or excavation.

(1) *Engineer's transit.* The engineer's transit has an adjustable tripod and head. It measures horizontal or vertical angles (fig. 2).

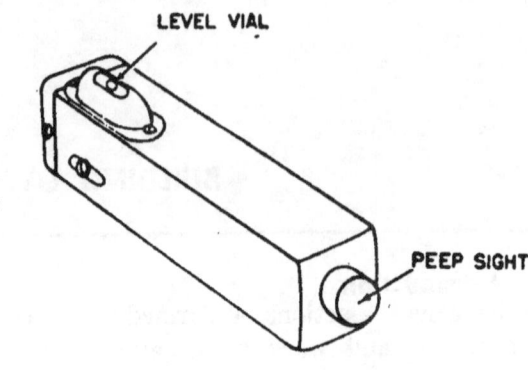

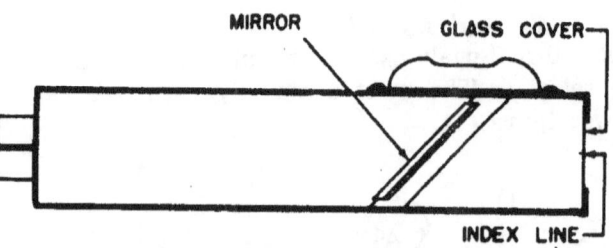

LEVELING INSTRUMENT

Figure 3. Leveling instrument.

do so on the job.

The following guidance will help those who wish to review the procedure.

a. Set up the transit directly over station mark (A) (fig 4), the point from which layout is sighted. A bench mark (B) may be provided by surveying engineers as a point of reference. The bench mark may be on the foundation of an adjacent building or a buried stone marker. If bench marks have been established in the area and the architect's drawings have been created specifically for that particular area, the bench mark will appear on the drawings and the plans

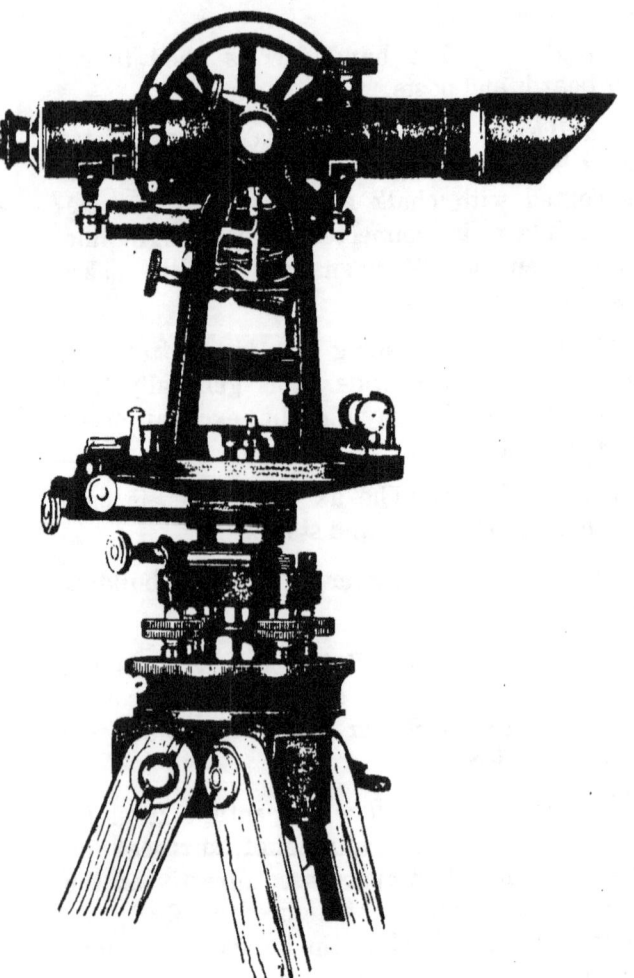

Figure 2. Engineer's transit.

(2) *Locator's hand level.* The locator's hand level measures approximately differences in elevation and can establish grades over limited distances (fig. 3). The landscape, level bubble, and index line are seen in the tube.

3. Use of the Engineer's Transit

The carpenter ordinarily does not use the engineer's transit but many of them learn how to

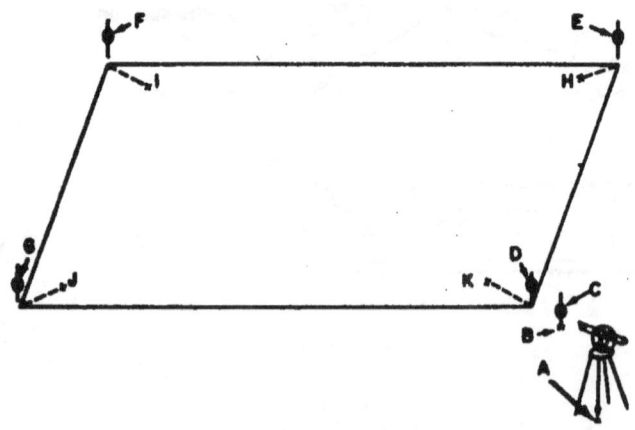

Figure 4. Layout of a plot with a transit.

will be oriented to that point. If no bench mark exists, a post may be driven into the ground to provide this reference point. This post can establish floor levels, foundation levels, or any definite point of elevation. When setting up the engineer's transit or leveling instrument, a plumb bob may be used to center the instrument directly over the selected station mark.

b. Adjust the tripod so that it rests firmly on the ground with the sighting tube at eye level. Level up the head of the instrument by turning the leveling screws, so that the sight tube and head are level when turned in any direction. Once set up, all contact with the legs of the tripod should be avoided.

c. Place a leveling rod (C) upright on any point to be checked, and sight through the sight tube of the instrument at the leveling rod. In accurate work, a spirit level may be attached to the leveling rod. An assistant should hold the leveling rod, and should move the target on the rod up or down until the crossline on the target comes in line with the crosshair sights in the sighting tube.

d. To obtain the difference in elevation between two points, such as the surveyor's bench mark (B) and the target point (D), hold the rod on the point (B) and take a rod reading. This will be the length of the bottom of the rod below the line of sight. Take a rod reading at point (D). The difference between the two rod readings is the difference.

e. To establish a level for the depth of an excavation or for the level of foundation walls, measure equal distances at all corners from these target points to the desired elevations (H, I, J, and K).

f. To lay out a right angle with an engineer's transit, set up the transit directly over the line (use plumb bob) at the point where the right angle is to occur (A, fig. 5). Sight a reference point on that line (B) to be sure the transverse axis of the engineer's transit is parallel to the line. Turn the eyepiece end of the sight tube to the left until the scale indicates that an arc of 90° has been completed. Establish a leveling rod in position along this line of sight at the desired distance. A line extended from the leveling rod (D) to the point from which the sight was taken will be perpendicular to the base line and will form a right angle at the point at which they bisect (DAB).

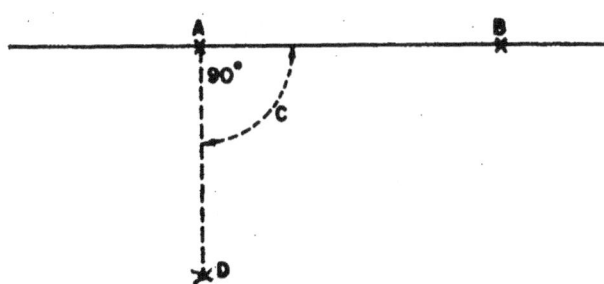

Figure 5. Laying out a right angle with an engineer's transit.

4. Staking Out

When the location and alinement of a building have been determined, a rectangle comprising the exterior dimensions of the structure is staked out. If the building is other than rectangular, a rectangle large enough to comprise the major outline of the irregular structure is staked out and the irregularities plotted and proved by smaller rectangles within or without the basic form.

5. Laying Out a Rectangle Without a Transit

If the construction is parallel to an identifiable line that may be used as a guide, staking out may be accomplished without a builder's transit. If a clearly defined line which construction is to parallel is present (AB) (fig. 6) and the maximum outer perimeter of the building area (AC, CD, DB) is known, proceed in the following manner:

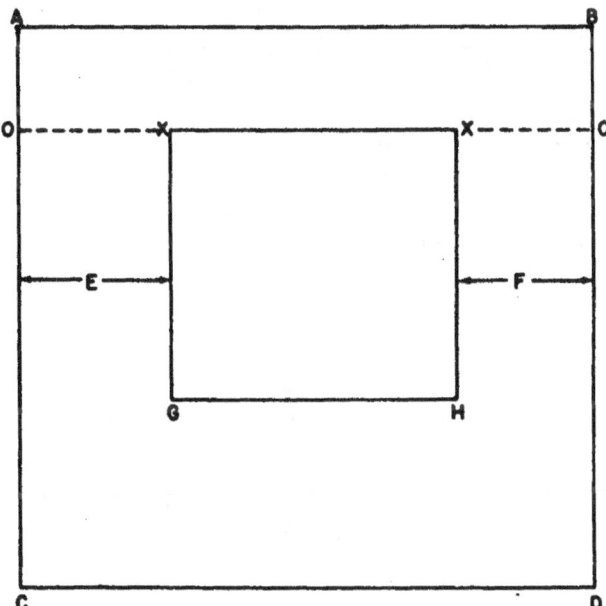

Figure 6. Laying out a rectangle without use of transit.

217

a. Measure away from the front line (AB) along the side lines (AC and BD) the distances (AO and BO) desired to the dimension of the project that is to run parallel to the front line.

b. Stretch a line tightly from point O to O. This line will mark out what will be frontage of the project.

c. Measure in from lines AC and BD along line OO, one-half the difference between the length of OO and the desired length of the project. The points (X and X) will constitute the front corners of the project.

d. The two distances, OX and XO, establish the distance E and F. Extending lines from the two front corners, X and X, parallel to AC and BD at the distances established as E and F for the required depth of the project provides the side lines of the project XG and XH.

e. Joining the extreme ends of side lines XG and XH will provide the rear line of the project.

f. After the four corners (X, X, G, and H) have been located, drive stakes at each corner. Batter boards may be erected at these points either after all the stakes have been set or while they are being set. Dimensions are determined accurately during each step.

g. If the building is not rectangular, several lines such as OO may be run and appropriate adjacent rectangles constructed from these lines in the same fashion as indicated above.

6. Laying out a Simple Rectangle With an Engineer's Transit or Leveling Instrument

a. Working from an established line AB (fig. 7) such as a road or street line, property line, or an established reference line, select a point to represent the lateral limit for a front corner of the project.

b. Set up the engineer's transit at point C and establish point D, a front corner of the project.

c. Set up the engineer's transit at a point E a greater distance along line AB from point C than the intended length of the project. Set a stake at F, the same distance from AB as D. CD and EF are equal.

d. Establish the front line of the project by marking off the length of the project DG along the established line DF. The two front corners of the project will be located at D and G.

e. With engineer's transit at point C, shoot E and then swing the transit 90 degrees and sight along this position to establish H, the rear corner of the project.

f. With the engineer's transit set up at G, sight D and swing the transit sight tube 90 degrees and shoot I, the other rear corner of the project.

g. To prove the work, set up the transit at I and take a sighting on H. If IH is equal to DG, the work is correct. If it is not, the work must be repeated until correct.

7. Laying Out an Irregularly Shaped Project

Where the outline of the building is not a rectangle, the procedure in establishing each point is the same as described above, but more points have to be located and the final proving of the work is more likely to reveal a small error. It is usually advisable with an irregularly shaped building to lay out first a large rectangle which will comprise the entire building or a greater part of it. This is shown in 2, figure 7, as the rectangle HOPQ. Having once established this accurately, the remaining portion of the layout will consist of small rectangles, each of which can be laid out and proved separately. The other rectangles as LMNP, ABCQ, DEFG, and LJKO are illustrated in 2, figure 7.

8. Batter Boards

a. *Staking Procedure.* At the points at which the various corners of the project are located, a corner stake is driven to mark the exact spot (fig. 8). If the area must be excavated for a foundation, the excavating will disturb the pegs. Batter boards are therefore set up to preserve definite and accurate building lines to work toward or from. This is done by stretching heavy cord or fine wire from one batter board to the

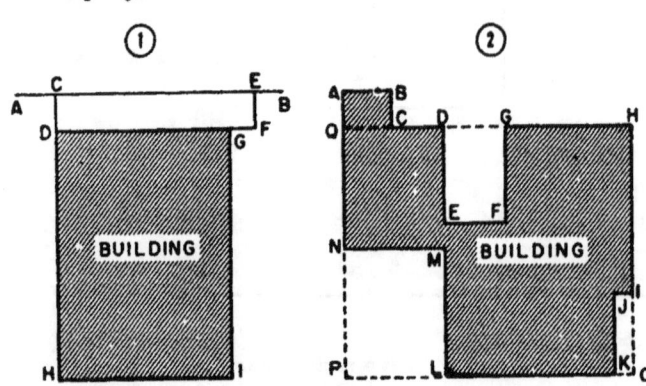

Figure 7. Laying out regular and irregular projects.

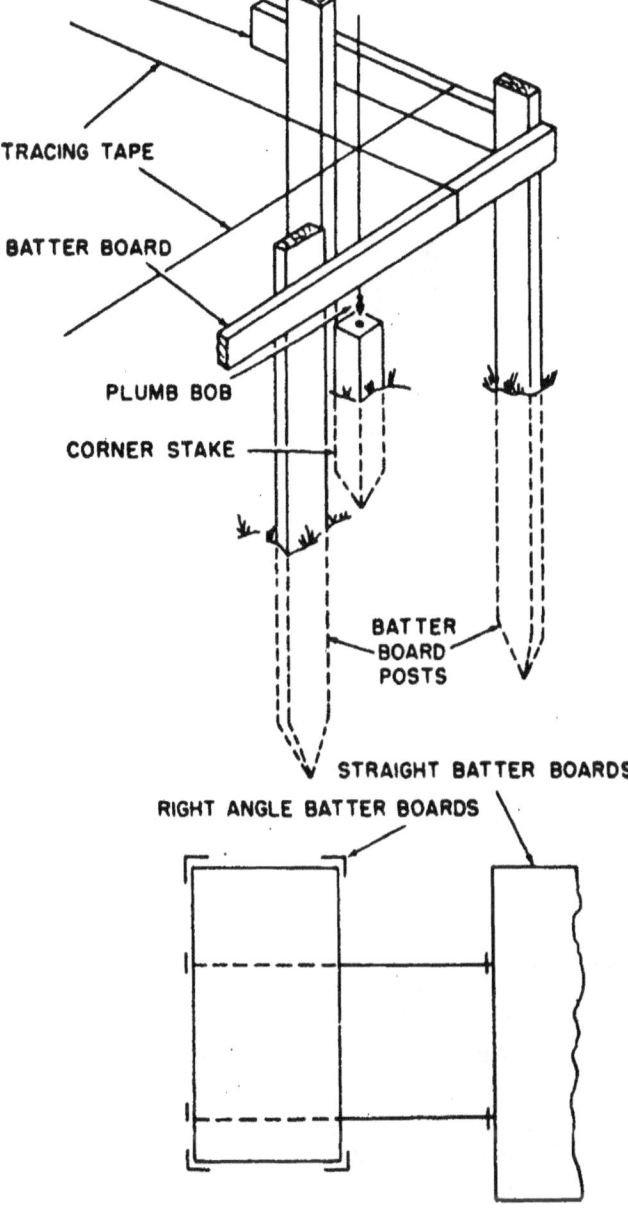

Figure 8. Batter boards.

other to define the lines of excavations.

b. Locating Batter Boards. Right-angle batter boards are erected 3 or 4 feet outside each corner stake (fig. 8). Straight batter boards are erected 3 or 4 feet outside of the line stakes set at points provided for the extension of foundation lines (fig. 8) which intercept side lines.

c. Construction of Batter Boards. Batter board stakes may be 2 x 4's, 2 x 6's, or 4 x 4's. Right-angle batter boards usually are two 1 x 6 boards and three stakes. They can be nailed or bolted to the stakes either before or after they are sunk. Batter boards are firmly anchored. Since the boards should be at the exact height of the top of the foundation, it may be desirable to adjust the height by nailing the boards to the stakes after the stakes have been sunk. Right-angle batter boards may be nailed at close to perpendicular by the use of a framing square and should be leveled by means of a carpenter's level before they are secured. When the final adjustments have been made for accuracy and squareness, saw cuts may be made or nails driven into the tops of the boards to hold the lines and keep them in place. Separate cuts or nails may be used for the building line, the foundation line, footing line, and excavation lines. These grooves permit the removal and replacement of the lines in the correct position.

9. Extending Lines

The following procedure applies to a simple layout (fig. 9) and must be amended to apply to different or more complex layout problems:

a. After locating and sinking stakes A and B, erect batter boards 1, 2, 3, and 4. Extend the chalkline X from batter board 1 over stakes A and B to batter board 3.

b. After locating and sinking stake C, erect batter boards 5 and 6. Extend the chalkline Y from batter board 2 over stakes A and C to batter board 6.

c. After locating and sinking stake D, erect batter boards 7 and 8. Extend chalkline Z from batter board 5 over stakes C and D to batter board 7.

d. Extend line O from batter board 8 over stakes D and B to batter board 4.

e. Where foundation walls are wide at the bottom and extend beyond the outside dimensions of the building, the excavation must be larger than the size laid out. To lay out dimensions for this excavation, measure out as far as required from the building line on each batter board, and stretch lines between these points and outside the first layout.

f. The lines may be brought to an approximate right angle where they cross by holding a plumb bob over the corner layout stakes and adjusting the lines until they touch the plumb bob line perfectly.

g. The lines should be checked by means of a line level, or carpenter's level.

10. Squaring Foundation Lines

There are two methods for squaring extended

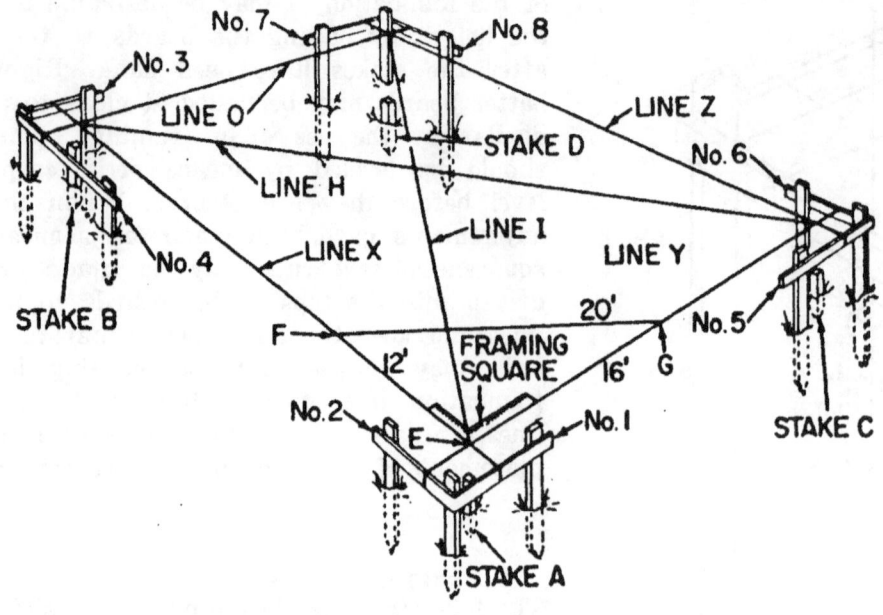

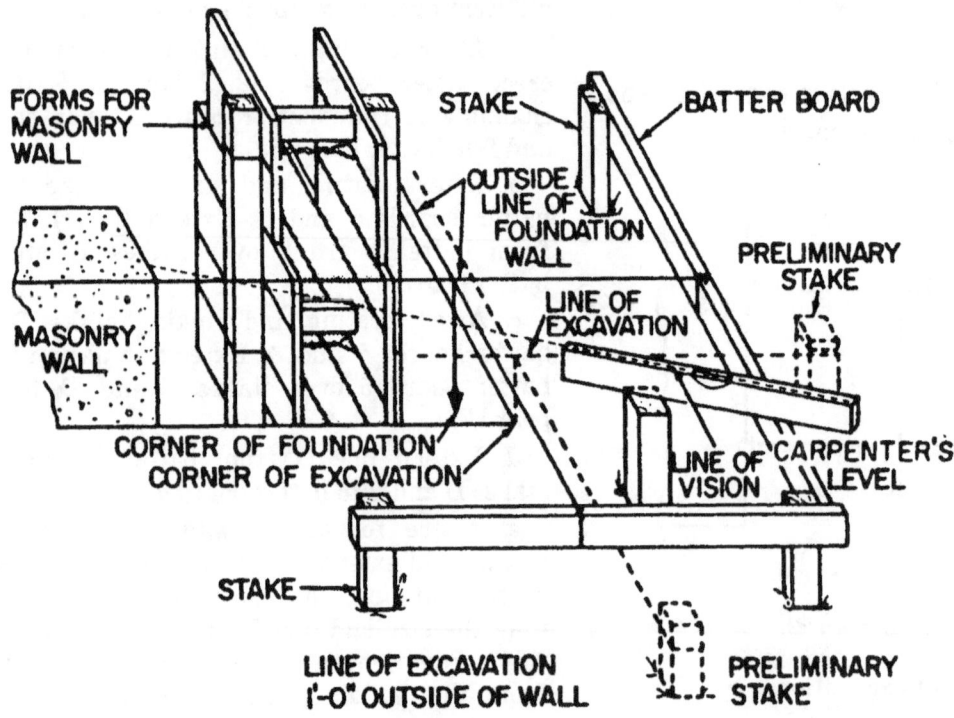

Figure 9. Laying out building lines from batter boards.

lines commonly used by the carpenter: the 6–8–10 method and the diagonal method.

a. 6–8–10 Method (fig. 9). After lines have been extended and are in place, measure the distance EF (6 feet or a multiple thereof, such as 12 feet). Measure off EF (to a distance of 8 feet if the previous figure used was 6 feet, or to a distance 16 feet if the previous figure was 12 feet). Adjust the lines until FG equals 10 feet if the other two measurements used are 6 feet and 8 feet, or 20 feet if the other two are 12 feet and 16 feet.

b. The Diagonal Method (fig. 9). If the layout is rectangular, line H and I cutting the rectangle from opposing corners will form two triangles. If the rectangle is perfect, these lines will be equal in length and the corners perfectly square. If lines H and I are not equal in length, adjust the corners by moving the lines right or left until H and I are equal.

11. Foundations

Foundations vary according to their use, the bearing capacity of the soil, and the type of material available. The material may be cut stone, rock, brick, concrete, tile, or wood, depending upon the weight which the foundation is to support. Foundations may be classified as wall or column (pier) foundations.

a. Wall Foundations. Wall foundations are built solid for their total length when heavy loads are to be carried or where the earth has low supporting strength. These walls may be made of concrete, rock, brick, or cut stone, with a footing at the bottom (fig. 10). Because of the time, labor, and material required to built it, this type of wall will be used in the theater of operations only when other types cannot be used. Steel rod reinforcements should be used in all concrete walls.

laid up with or without mortar; if strength and stability are desired, mortar must be used.

(2) *Coursed rubble.* Coursed rubble is assembled of roughly squared stones in such a manner as to produce approximately continuous horizontal bed joints.

(3) *Random rubble.* This is the crudest of all types of stonework. Little attention is paid to laying the stone in courses. Each layer must contain bonding stones that extend through the wall. This produces a wall that is well tied together.

b. Column or Pier Foundations. Column or pier foundations save time and labor. They may be constructed from masonry or wood. The piers or columns are spaced according to the weight to be carried. In most cases, the spacing is from 6 to 10 feet. Figure 11 shows the different types of piers with different types of footing. Wood piers are generally used since they are installed with the least time and labor. Where wood piers are 3 feet or more above the ground, braces are necessary (fig. 12).

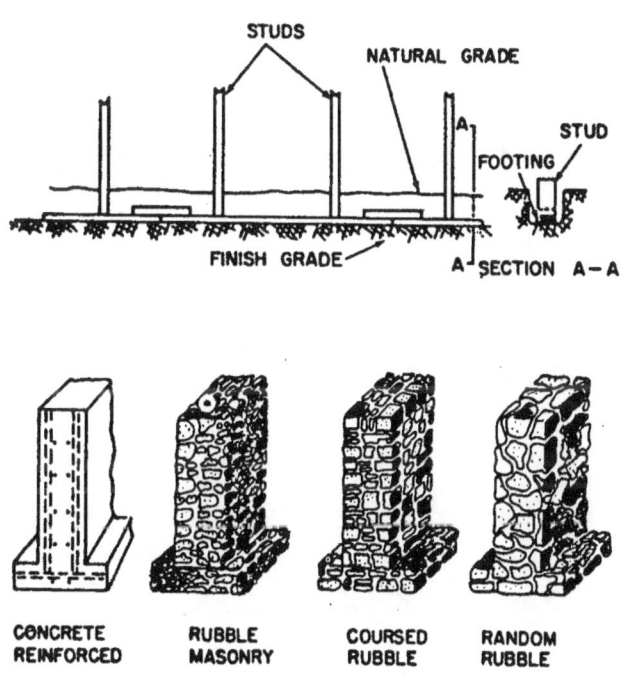

Figure 10. Foundation walls.

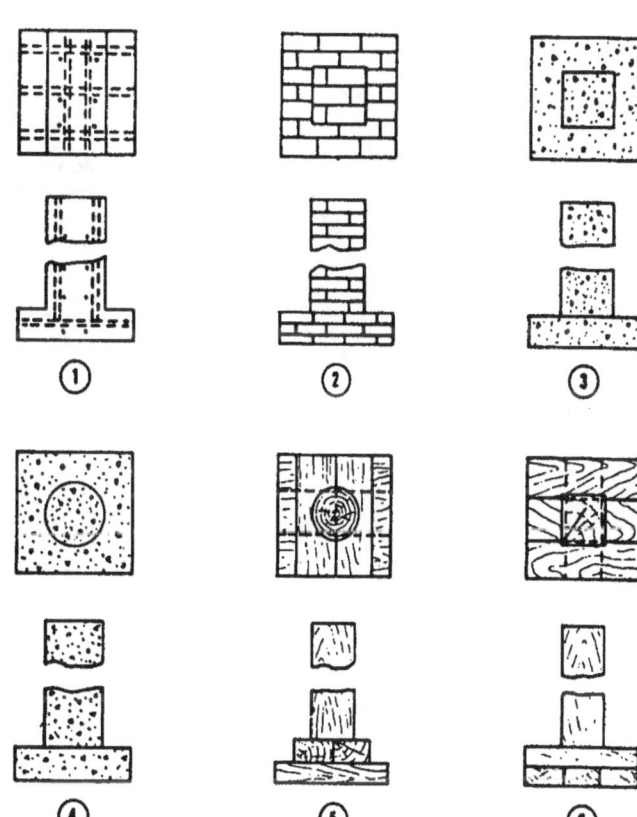

Figure 11. Column and piers.

(1) *Rubble masonry.* Rubble stone masonry is used for walls both above and below ground and for bridge abutments. In military construction, it is used when form lumber or masonry units are not available. Rubble masonry may be

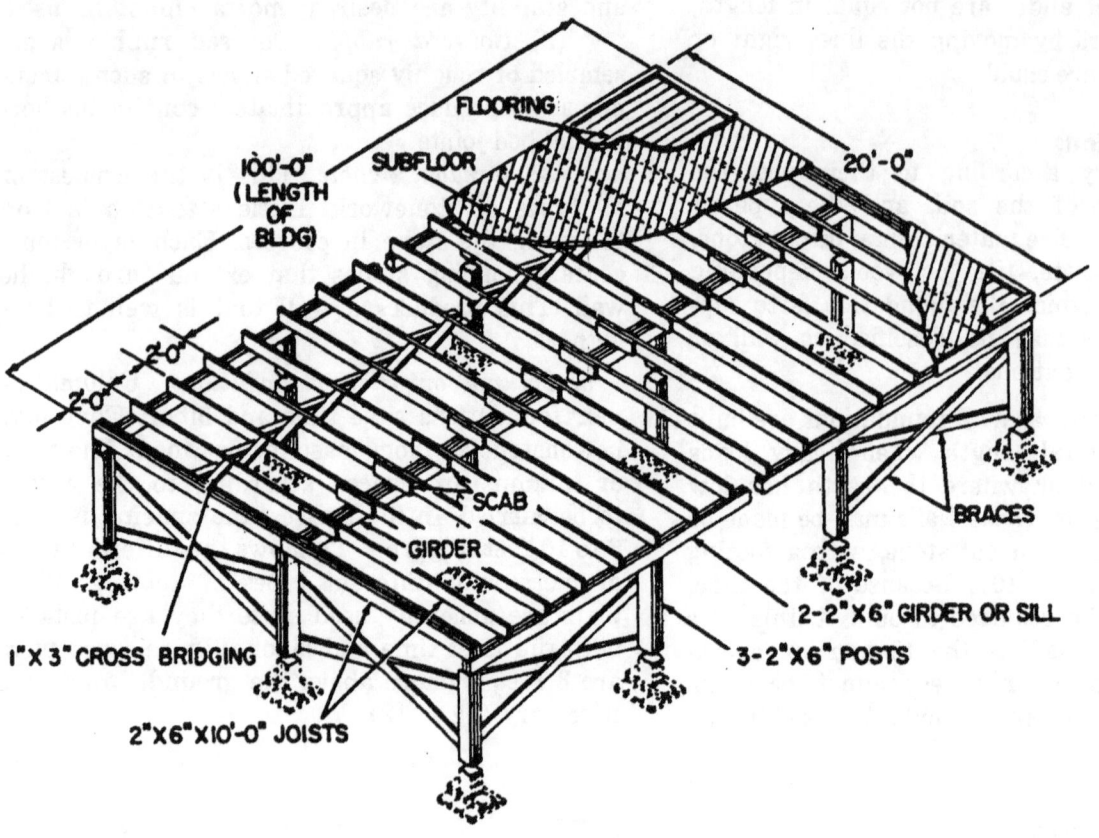

Figure 12. Braced piers, sills, girders, and joist construction.

FORMS FOR CONCRETE

1. Use

Forms are a major part of concrete construction work. They must support the plastic concrete until it hardens. Forms protect the concrete, assist in curing it, and support any reinforcing rods or conduit embedded in it.

2. Design

Forms for concrete must be tight, rigid, and strong. If not tight, loss of mortar may cause a honeycomb effect or loss of water may cause sand streaking. The forms must be braced enough to stay in alinement. Special care is needed in bracing and tying down forms, such as for retainer walls, where the mass of concrete is large at the bottom and tapers toward the top. In this type of construction and in the first pour for walls and columns, the concrete tends to lift the form above its proper elevation. Concrete and Masonry, gives formulas and tables for designing forms of proper strength.

3. Construction Materials

Forms are generally constructed from one of four different materials: earth, metal, wood, and fiber. The carpenter usually constructs wood and fiber forms.

a. Wood. Wood forms are the most common in building construction; they are economical, easy to handle, easy to produce, and adaptable to many shapes. Form lumber can be reused for roofing, bracing, or similar purposes.

(1) Lumber should be straight, strong, and only partially seasoned. Kiln-dried timber tends to swell when soaked with water. Swelling may cause bulging and distortion. If green lumber is used, allowance should be made for shrinkage or it should be kept wet until the concrete is in place. Softwoods (pine, fir, and spruce) are the most economical, light, easy to work, and generally available.

(2) Wood coming in contact with concrete should be surfaced (smooth) on the side towards the concrete and on both edges. The edges may be square, shiplap, or tongue and groove.

Tongue-and-groove lumber makes a more watertight joint, which reduces warping.

(3) Plywood can be used economically for wall and floor forms if made with waterproof glue and marked for use in concrete forms. Plywood is warp resistant and can be used more often than other lumber. It is made in thicknesses of 1/4, 3/8, 9/16, 5/8, and 3/4 of an inch and in widths up to 48 inches. The 8-foot lengths are most commonly used. The 5/8- and 3/4-inch thicknesses are most economical; thinner plywood requires solid backing to prevent deflection. The 1/4-inch thickness is useful for curved surfaces.

b. Waterproof cardboard and other fiber materials are used for round concrete columns and other preformed shapes. Forms are made by gluing layers of fiber together and molding them to the right shape. The advantage is that fabrication at the job site is not necessary.

4. Oiling

a. Oiling. Before concrete is placed, forms are treated with oil or other coating material to prevent the concrete from sticking. The oil should penetrate the wood and prevent water absorption. A light-bodied petroleum oil will do. On plywood, shellac is more effective than oil. If forms are to be reused, painting helps preserve the wood. Occasionally, lumber contains enough tannin to cause softening of the concrete surface; if so, the form surface should be treated with whitewash or limewater before the oil is used.

b. Wetting. If form oil is not available, wetting with water may be substituted to prevent sticking but only in an emergency.

5. Form Removal

Forms should be built so as to permit easy removal without danger to the concrete. When necessary to wedge against the concrete, only wood wedges should be used rather than a pinchbar or other metal tool. Forms should not be jerked off after wedging has been started at one end to avoid breaking the edges of the concrete. Forms to be reused should be cleaned and oiled immediately. Nails should be removed as forms are stripped.

6. Components of Wall Forms

Figure 1 shows the various parts of a wall form. These parts are described as follows:

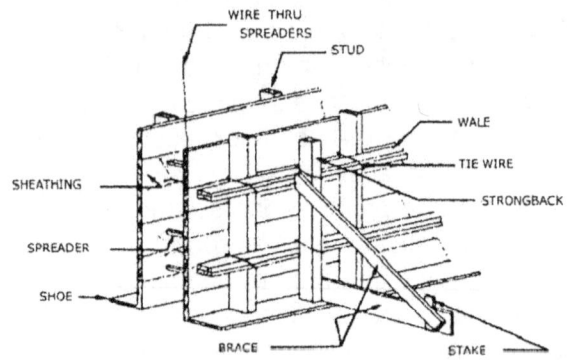

Figure 1. Form for a concrete wall.

a. Sheathing. Sheathing forms the surface of the concrete. It should be smooth, especially if the finished surface is to be exposed. Since concrete is plastic when placed in the form, sheathing should be watertight. Tongue-and-groove lumber or plywood gives a watertight surface.

b. Studs. The weight of the concrete causes the sheathing to bulge if it is not reinforced. Vertical studs make the wall form rigid. They are generally made from 2x4 or 3x6 lumber.

c. Wales (walers). Studs also require reinforcing when they extend more than 4 or 5 feet. Double wales give this reinforcing; they also tie prefabricated panels together and keep them in a straight line. They run horizontally and are lapped at the corners.

d. Braces. Many types of braces give the forms stability. The most common brace is a horizontal member and a diagonal member nailed to a stake and to a stud or wale. The diagonal member should make a 30-degree angle with the horizontal member. Additional bracing may be strongbacks (vertical members) behind the wales or in the corner formed by intersecting wales. Braces are not part of the form design and are not considered as providing additional strength.

e. Shoe Plates. The shoe plate is nailed into the foundation or footing and must be carefully placed to maintain the wall dimensions and alinement. Studs are tied into the shoe.

f. Spreaders. Spreaders are cut to the same length as the thickness of the wall and placed between the forms. They are not nailed but held in place by friction because they must be removed before the concrete hardens. A wire is attached to the spreaders to pull them out of the form after the concrete has put enough pressure on the walls to permit easy removal.

g. Tie Wires. Tie wires hold the forms secure against the lateral pressure of unhardened concrete. Double strands are always used.

7. Construction of Wall Forms

a. Wall panels should be about 10 feet long so they can be easily handled. Panels are made by nailing the sheathing to the studs. Sheathing is normally 1-inch (13/16 inches dressed) tongue and groove lumber or 3/4-inch plywood. Figure 2 shows how panels are connected: figure 3 shows details for the corner of a wall.

b. Figure 4 shows how to use a wood strip as a wedge when curtain walls and columns are placed at the same time. In removing the forms, the wedge is removed first.

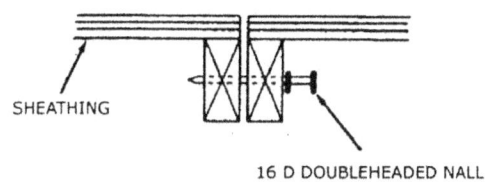

Figure 2. Method of connecting wall form panels together.

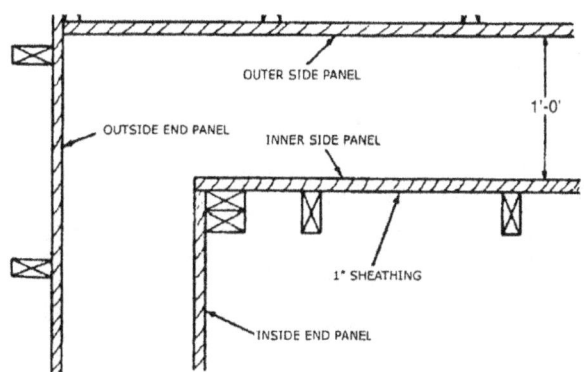

c. Ties keep wall forms together as the concrete is poured; figures 5 and 6 show two ways of doing this. Figure 5 shows how to use wire ties, which are for low walls only or when tie rods are not available. The wire should be No. 8 or No. 9 gage, soft, black, annealed iron wire, but barbed wire can be used in an emergency. Tie spacing should be the same as the stud spacing, but never more than 3 feet. Each tie is formed by looping the wire around a wale, bringing it through the form, crossing it inside the form walls, and looping it around the wale on the opposite side. The tie wire is made taut by twisting it with a wedge,

d. Spreaders keep the wall forms together as the concrete is placed. Spreaders must be placed near each tie wire; they are removed as the forms are filled so they will not become embedded in the concrete. Figure 7 shows how to remove spreaders. A wire fastened to the bottom spreader passes through a hole drilled in each spreader above it. Pulling on the wire will remove the spreaders one after another as the concrete level rises in the forms.

e. Figure 6 shows a tie rod and spreader combination. After the form is removed, each rod is broken off at the notch. If appearance is important, the holes should be filled with a mortar mix.

8. Foundation and Footing Forms

a. *Footing Forms.* When possible, earth is excavated to form a mold for concrete wall footings. If wood forms are needed, the four sides are built in panels. Panels for two opposite sides are made at exact footing width (*a,* figure 8); the other pair (*b,* figure 8) have two end cleats on the inside spaced the length of the footing *plus* twice the sheathing thickness. The 1-inch thick sheathing is nailed to vertical cleats spaced on 2-foot centers. Two-inch dressed lumber should be used for the cleats.

(1) Panels are held in place with form nails until the tie wire is installed; nails

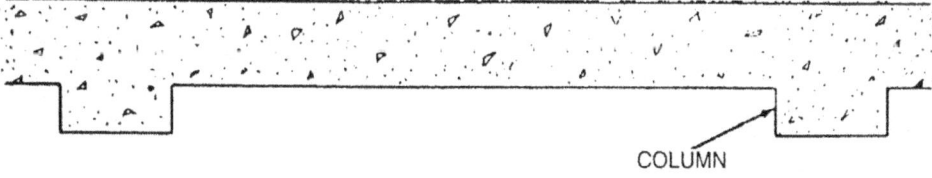

PLAN VIEW OF THE WALL

4

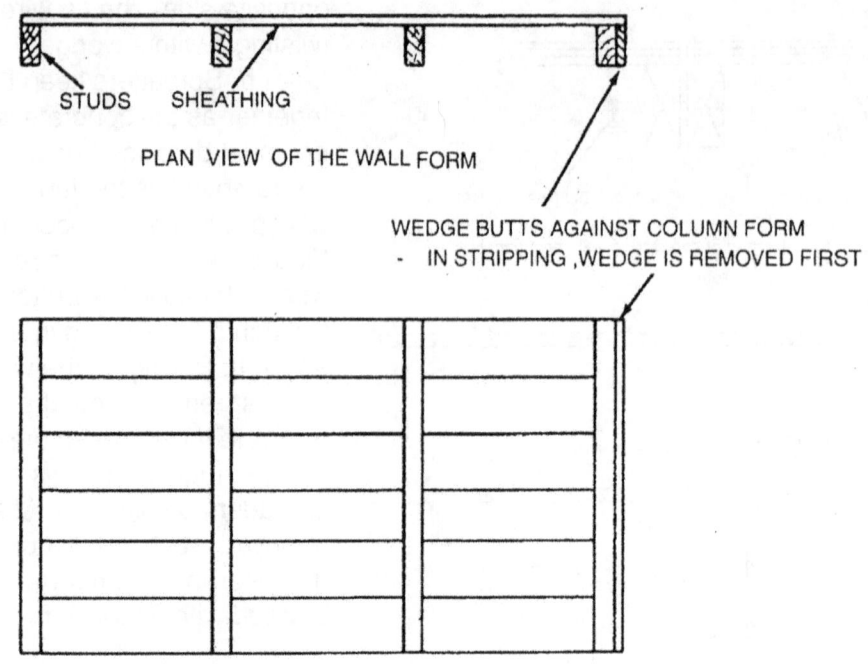

Figure 4. Wall form for curtain walls.

should be driven from the outside part way so they can be easily removed.

(2) Tie wires are wrapped around the center cleats. Wire holes on each side of the cleat should be less than 1-inch diameter to prevent leakage of mortar. All reinforcing bars must be placed before the wire is installed.

(3) For forms 4 feet square or larger, stakes are driven as shown in figure 8.

These stakes and 1x6 boards nailed across the top prevent spreading. Panels may be higher than the required depth of footing since they can be marked on the inside to show the top of the footing. If the footings are less than 1 foot deep and 2 feet square, forms can be constructed of

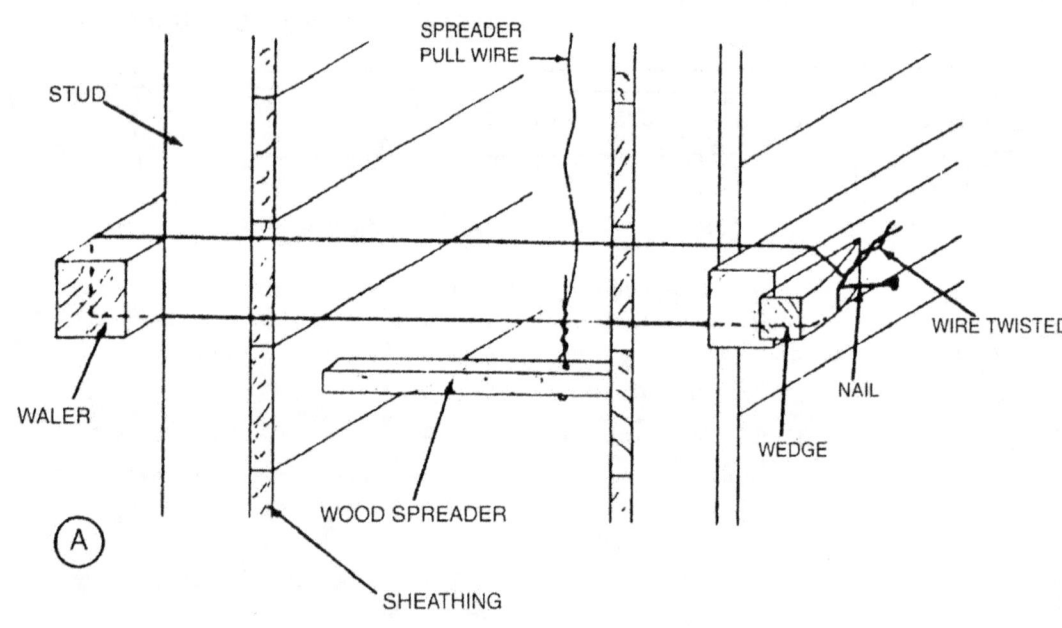

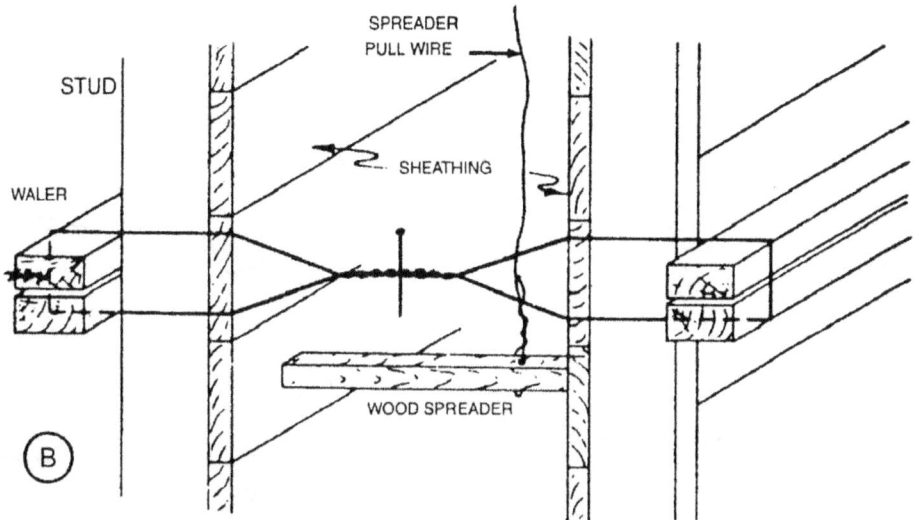

Figure 5. Wire ties for form walls.

1-inch sheathing without cleats as shown in figure 9.

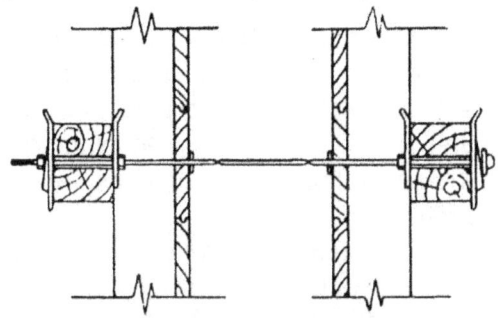

Figure 6. Tie rod and spreader for wall form.

b. Footing and Pier Forms. When placing a footing and a small pier at the same time, the form is built as shown in figure 10. Support for the upper form must not interfere with the placement of concrete in the lower form. This is done by nailing 2 x 4 or 4 x 4 pieces to the lower form as shown. The top form is then nailed to these pieces.

c. Wall Footings. Figures 11 and 12 show how to construct and brace forms for wall footings. The sides are 2-inch lumber held in place by stakes and apart by spreaders. The short brace shown at each stake holds the form in line.

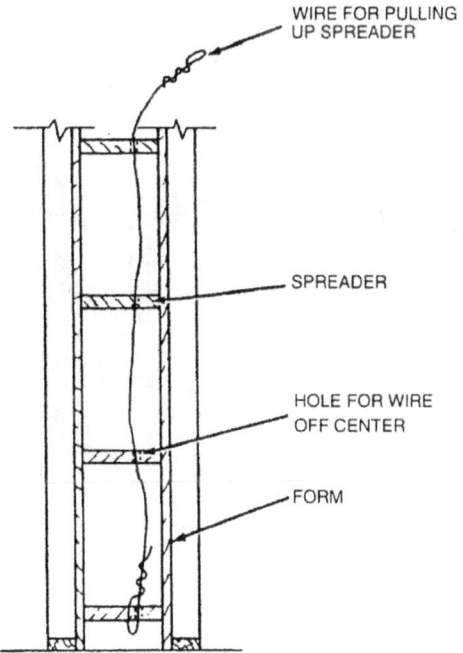

Figure 7. Removing wood spreaders.

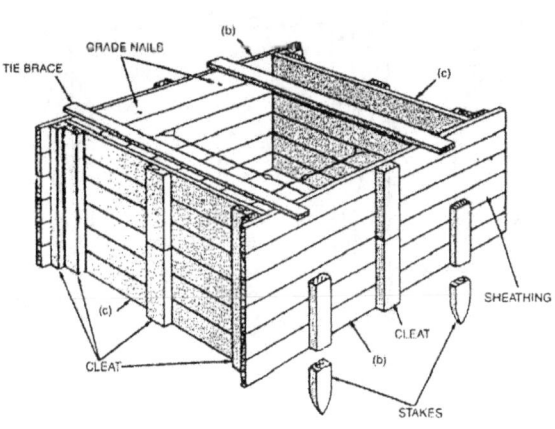

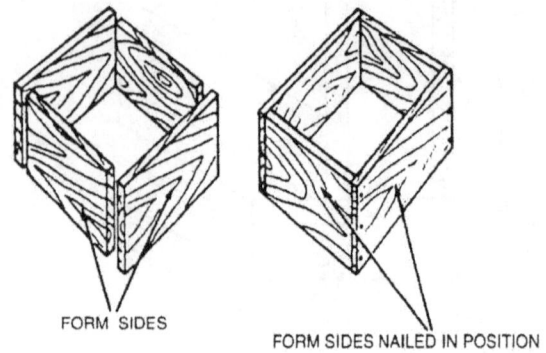

Figure 9. Small footing forms.

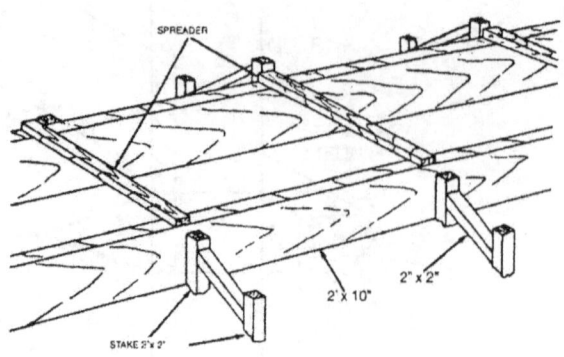

Figure 11. Wall all footing form.

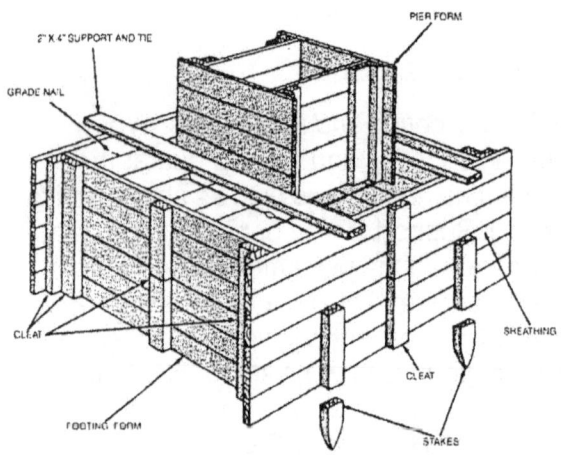

Figure 10. Footing and pier forms.

9. Column Forms

Figure 13 shows elements of column forms. holes should be nailed to the form so it can be put back in the hole before concrete is placed.

a. *Components.* Sheathing runs vertically to save the number of sawcuts; corner joints are firmly nailed to insure water-tightness. Batten are narrow strips of boards (cleats) placed directly over the joints to fasten the several pieces of vertical sheathing together.

b. *Construction.* Figure 13 shows a column and footing form. The column form is erected after the steel reinforcing is

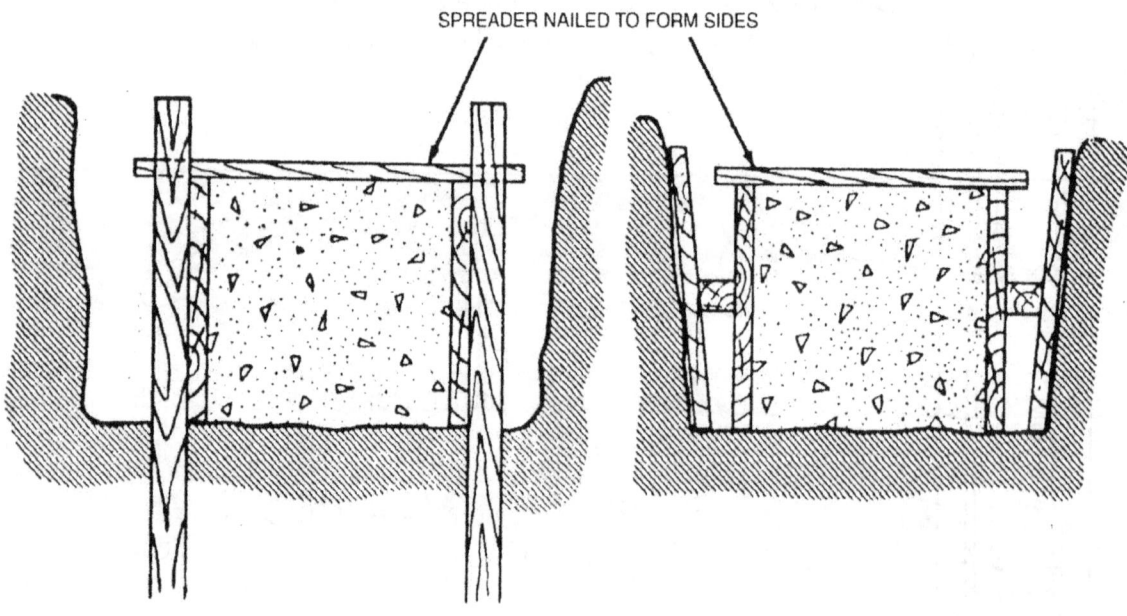

Figure 12. Bracing the wall footing form.

assembled and tied to dowels in the footing. The form should have a cleanout hole in the bottom to help remove debris. The lumber removed to make the cleanout holes should be nailed to the form so it can be put back in the hole before concrete is placed.

10. Beam and Girder Forms

Figure 14 shows a beam form. The type of construction depends on whether the form is to be removed in one piece or whether the bottom is to be left until the concrete is strong enough to remove the shoring. Beam forms receive little bursting pressure but must be shored at close intervals to prevent sagging.

a. *Construction.* The bottom has the same width as the beam and is in one piece the full width. Form sides are 1-inch tongue and groove material and lap over the bottom as shown in figure 14. The sheath is nailed to 2 x 4 struts placed on 3-foot centers. A 1 x 4 piece is nailed along the struts to support the joists for the floor panel. The sides of the form are not nailed to the bottom but held in position by continuous strips. Crosspieces nailed on top serve as spreaders. After erection, the slab panel joints hold the beam in place.

b. *Assembly.* Beam and girder assembly is shown in figure 15. The beam bottom butts up tightly against the side of the girder and rests on a 2 x 4 nailed to the girder side. Details in the figure show the clearances for stripping and allow for movement caused by the weight of the concrete. The 4x4 posts are spaced to support the concrete and are wedged at bottom or top for easy removal.

11. Floor Forms

Floor panels are built as shown in figure 16. The 1-inch tongue and groove sheathing or 3/4-inch plywood is nailed to 1 x 4 cleats on 3-foot centers. These panels are supported by 2 x 6 joists. Spacing of joists depends on the

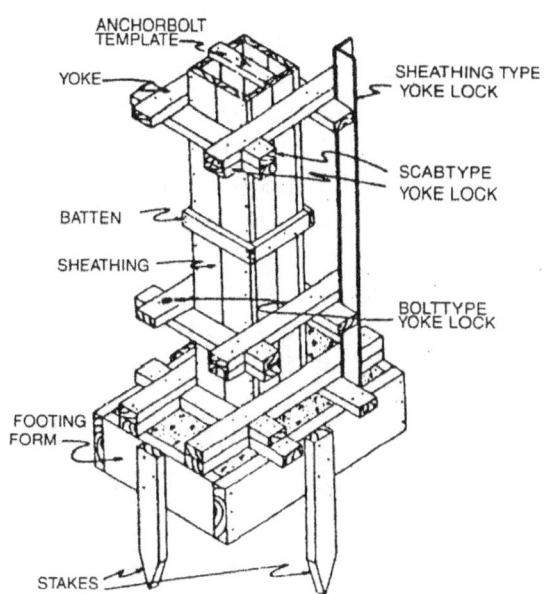

Figure 13. Form for a concrete columm.

thickness of the concrete slab and the span of the beams. If the slab spans the distance between two walls, the panels are used in the same manner as when beams support the floor slab.

12. Stair Forms

Figure 17 shows a method for building stair forms up to 3 feet in width. The sloping wood platform forming the underside of the steps should be 1-inch tongue and groove sheathing. This platform should extend 12 inches beyond each side of the stairs to support stringer bracing blocks. The back of the panel is shored with 4x4 pieces as shown. The 2x6 cleats nailed to the shoring should rest on wedges to make adjustment easy and to make removal of the posts easy. The side stringers are 2 x 12 pieces cut as required for the tread and risers. The riser should be 2-inch material beveled as shown.

13. Safety Precautions

The following safety rules apply to form construction and removal.

a. *Construction.*

(1) Consider protruding nails as the principal source of accidents on form work.

(2) Inspect tools frequently.

(3) Place mud sills under shoring that rests on the ground.

(4) On elevated forms, take care to protect men on scaffolds and on the ground.

(5) Do not raise large form panels in heavy gusts of wind.

(6) Brace all shoring securely to prevent collapse of form work.

b. *Stripping.*

(1) Permit only workmen doing the stripping in the immediate area.

(2) Do not remove forms until the concrete has set.

(3) Pile stripped forms immediately to avoid congestion, exposed nails, and other hazards.

(4) Cut wires under tension with caution to avoid backlash.

Figure 13. Form for a concrete column.

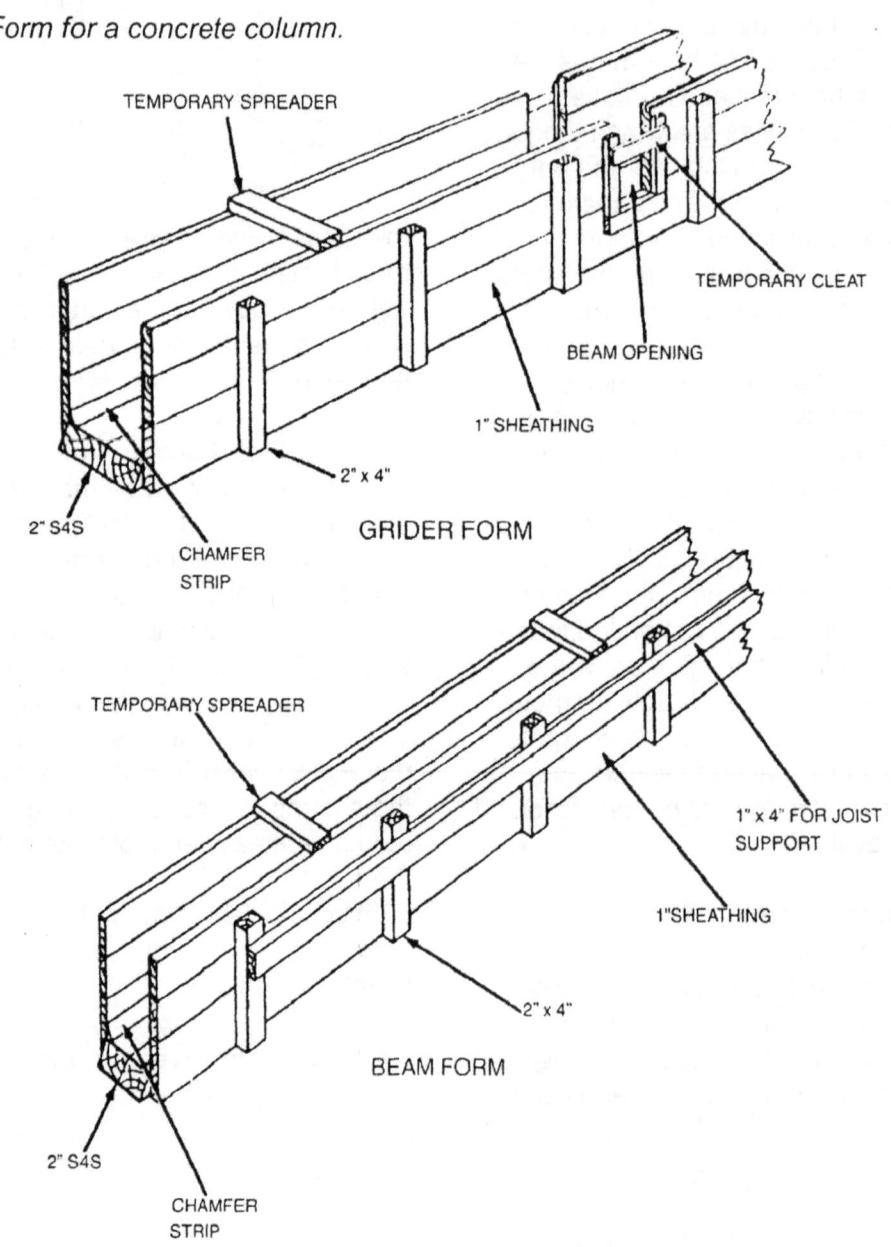

Figure 14. Beam and girder forms.

9

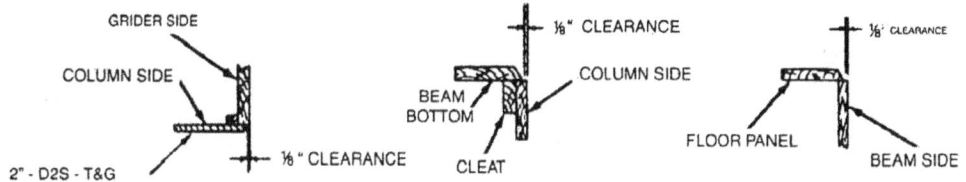

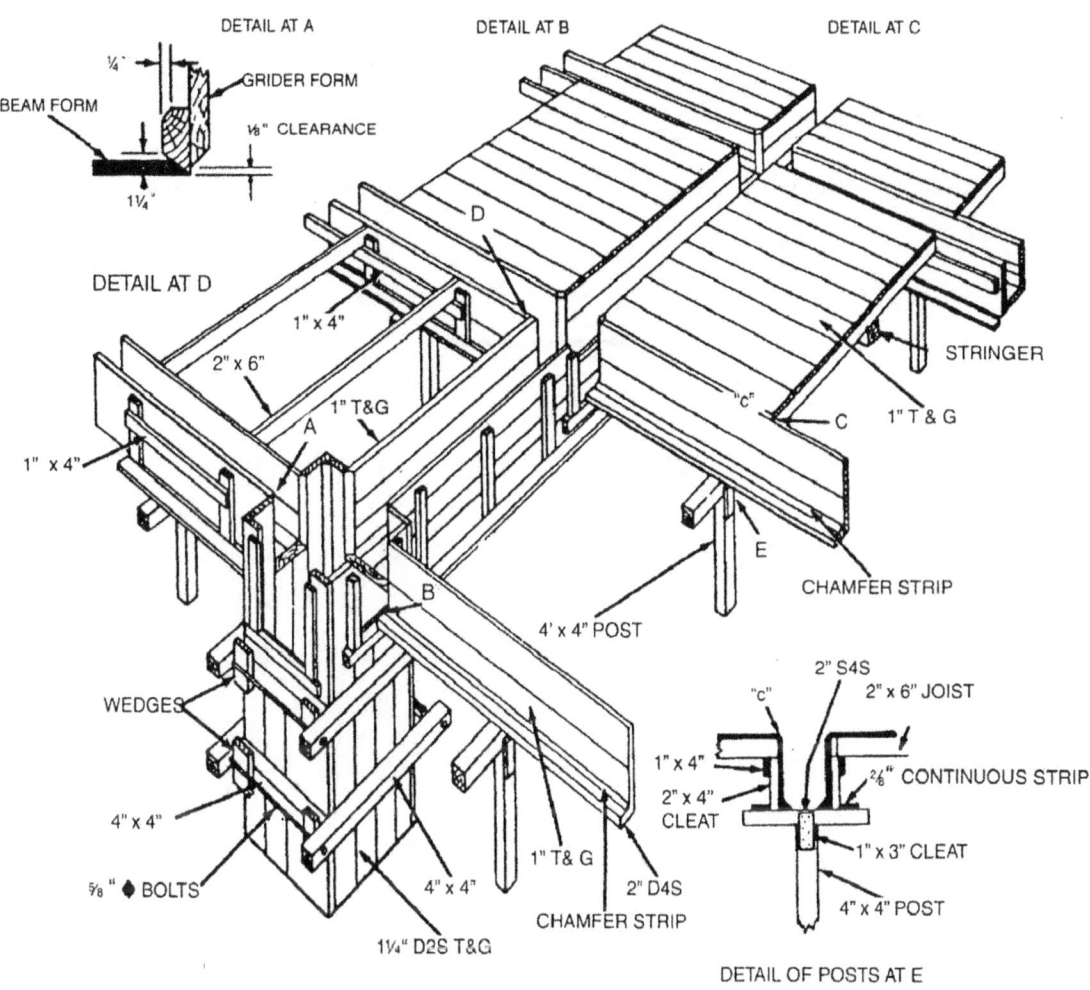

Figure 15. Assembly details, beam and floor forms.

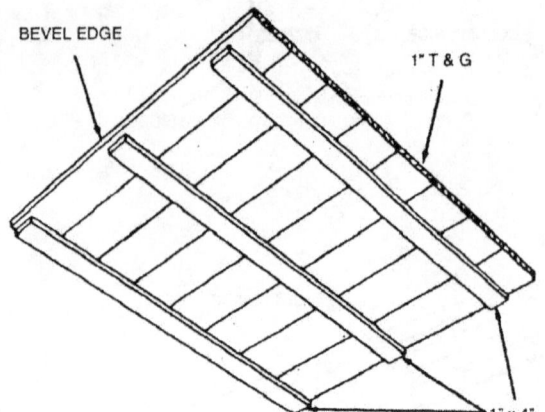

Figure 16. Form for floor slab.

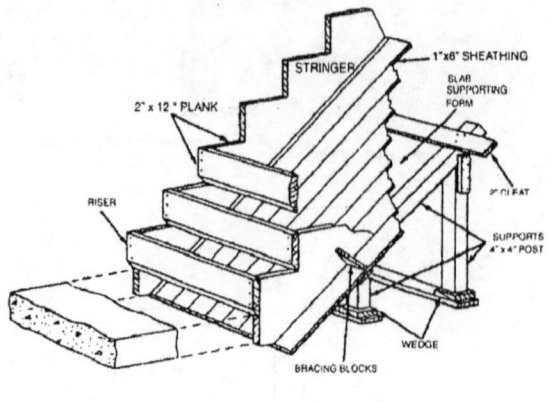

Figure 17. Stairway form.

CONSTRUCTION PRINT READING

Section I. WORKING DRAWINGS

1. Introduction

a. Working drawings plus specifications are the main sources of information for supervisors and technicians responsible for the actual work of construction. The construction working drawing gives a complete graphic description of the structure to be erected, the construction site, the materials to be used, and the construction method to be followed. Most construction drawings consist of orthographic views (right angles and perpendicular lines). A set of working drawings includes both general and detail drawings. General drawings consist of plans and elevations, while detail drawings consist of sections and detail views.

b. Site plans, elevations, floor plans, sections, and details are described in this section together with the most common architectural symbols and material conventions in military use.

2. Architectural Symbols and Material Conventions

a. Architectural Symbols. Architectural symbols on construction plans show the type and location of doors, windows, and other features. They have the same general shape as the feature itself and show any motion that is supposed to occur. Figure 1 shows several of these symbols.

b. Material Conventions. Material conventions are symbols that show the type of material used in the structure. Appendix B illustrates those for the more common types of materials. The symbol selected normally represents the material in some way where possible. For example, the symbol for wood shows the grains in the wood. It is not always possible to use a common characteristic of the material for the symbol. The carpenter should know all these symbols for materials to help him read a construction print. A symbol should always be checked if there is any doubt about its meaning.

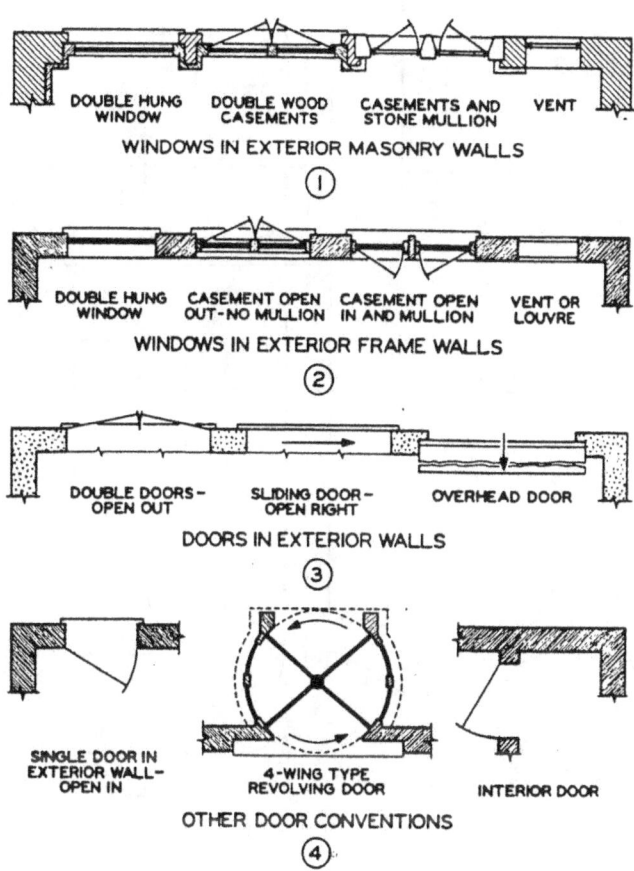

Figure 1. Window, door, and wall symbols.

3. Site Plans

a. A site plan (also called plot plan) shows all necessary property lines and locations, contours and profiles, building lines, location of structures to be constructed, existing structures, approaches, finished grades, existing and new utilities such as sewer, water, gas, and the like. Figure 2 shows a typical site plan. Appropriate outlines show the location of the new facility. The site plan has a north-pointing arrow to indicate site north (not magnetic north). Each facility has a number (or code letter) to identify it in the schedule

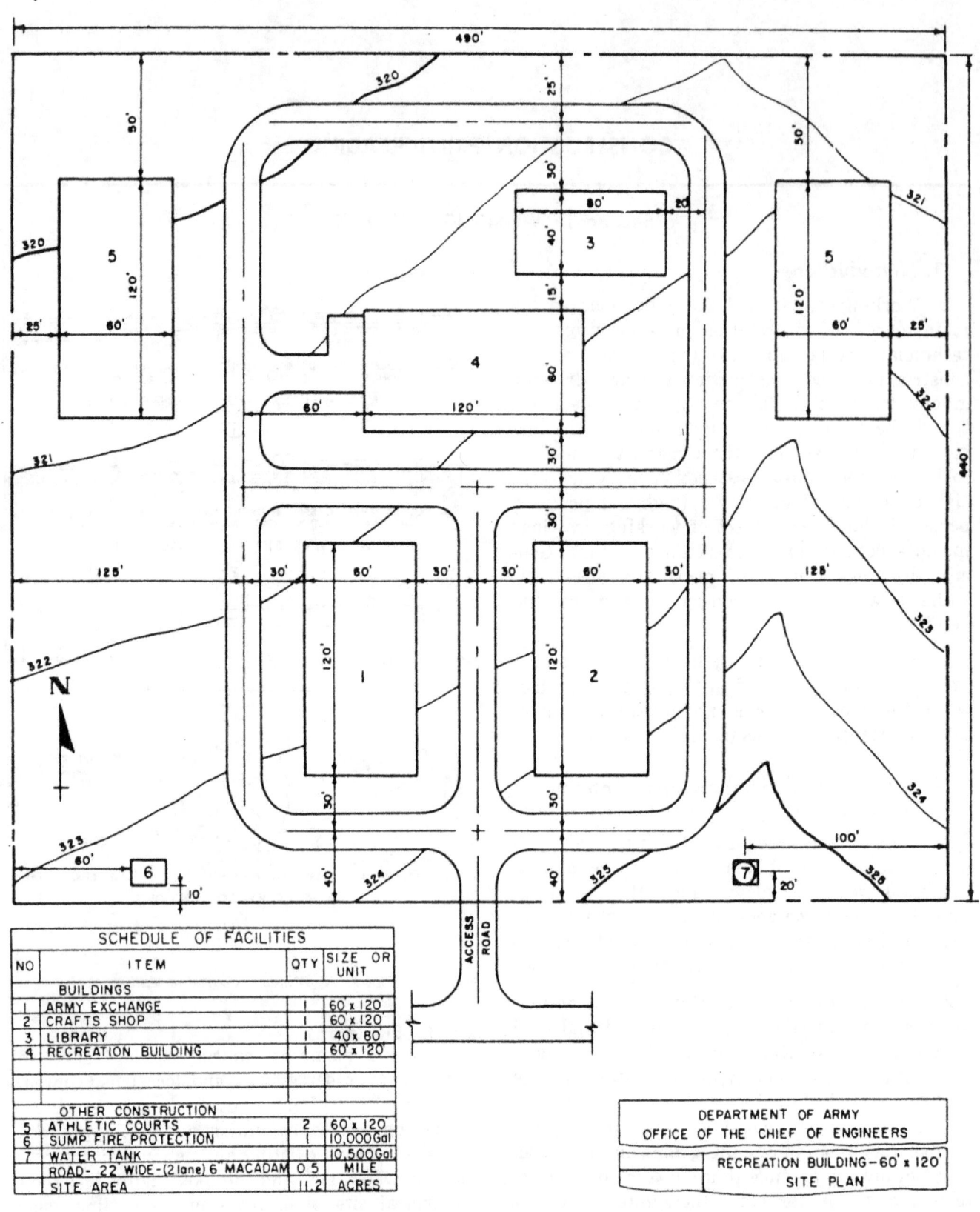

Figure 2. Typical site plan.

of facilities. The contour lines show the elevation of the earth surfaces; all points on a contour have the same elevation. Distances are given between principal details and reference lines. (The coordinate reference lines on figure 2 are centerlines of the roads surrounding the area.) All distances in a plan view simply give the horizontal measurement between two points and do not show terrain irregularities. The sizes of proposed facilities are given in the schedule of facilities.

b. Examine the site plan shown in figure 2 to see what information can be obtained from it. For example, the contour lines show that the ground surface of the site area slopes. The plan locates and identifies each facility. Most of the facilities are spaced at least 60 feet apart, while the library (facility No. 3) and the recreation building (facility No. 4) must be only 15 feet apart. Besides being the smallest of the four buildings, the library is closest to the road; that is, the east wall of the library is 20 feet from the centerline of the road, while the other buildings are 30 or 60 feet from the centerline.

4. Elevations

a. Elevations are drawings that show the front, rear, or side view of a building or structure. Sample elevation views are given in figure 3. Construction materials may be shown on the elevation. It may also show the ground level surrounding the structure, called the grade. When more than one view is shown on a drawing sheet, each view is given a title. If any view has a scale different from that shown in the title block, the scale is given beneath the title of that view.

b. The centerline symbol of alternate long and short dashes in an elevation shows finished floor lines. Foundations below the grade line are shown by the hidden line symbol of short, evenly spaced dashes. Note in figure 3 that the footings are shown below grade.

c. Elevations show the locations and kind of doors and windows. Each different type window shown in the elevations is marked (in figure 3, the three types of windows are marked W-1, W-2, and W-3). These identifying marks refer to a particular size window whose dimensions are given in a table known as the window schedule. In some cases, the rough opening dimensions of

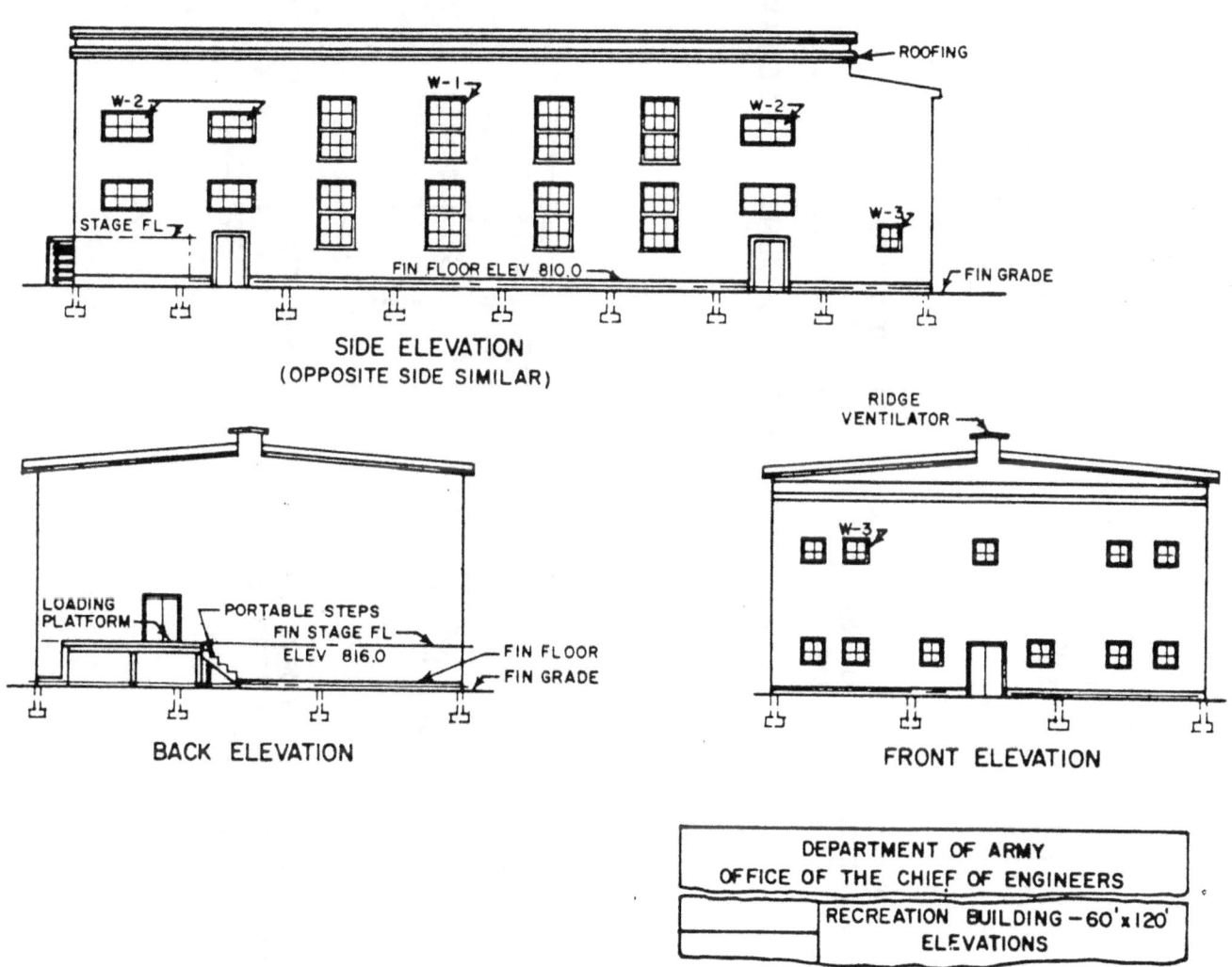

Figure 3. Elevation views.

DEVELOPED FLOOR PLAN
ABCD

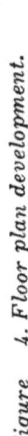

DEVELOPED FLOOR PLAN
WXYZ

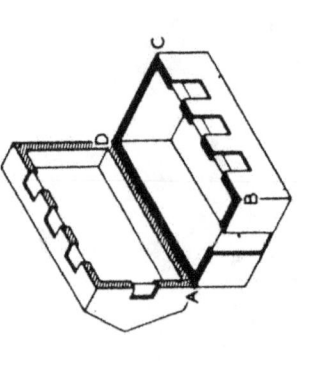

PREVIOUS PERSPECTIVE VIEW AT
CUTTING PLANE ABCD,
HINGED AND TOP LAID BACK

PLAN DEVELOPMENT – SIMPLE BUILDING

①

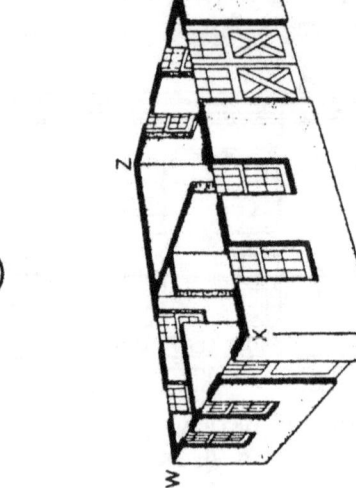

PREVIOUS PERSPECTIVE VIEW AT
CUTTING PLANE WXYZ,
TOP REMOVED

PLAN DEVELOPMENT – TYPICAL T.O. BUILDING

②

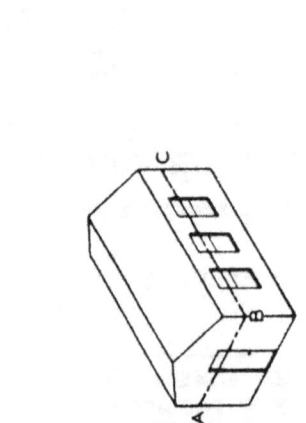

PERSPECTIVE VIEW OF A
SIMPLE BUILDING SHOWING
CUTTING PLANE ABC

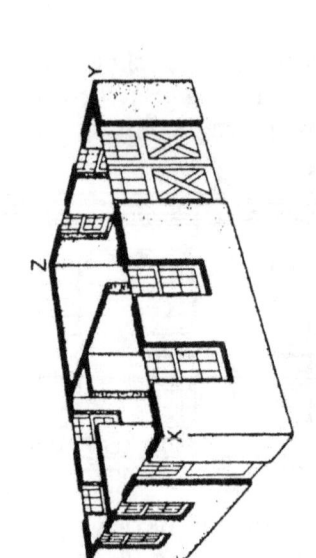

PERSPECTIVE VIEW OF A
TYPICAL T/O BUILDING SHOWING
CUTTING PLANE WXY

Figure 4. Floor plan development.

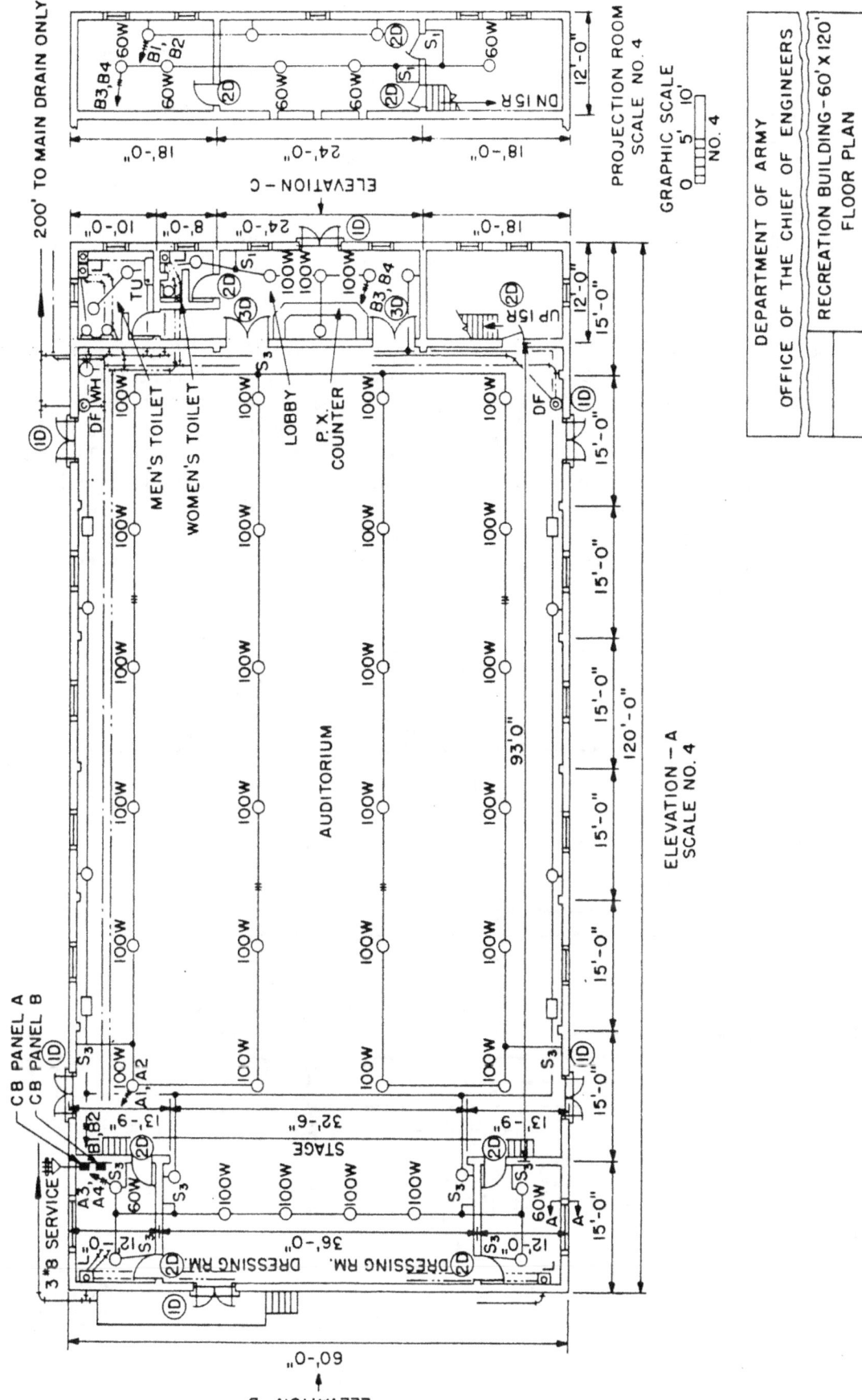

Figure 5. Typical floor plan.

windows are given on the drawing. Note that the recreation building shown in figure 3 has two double doors on each side and a double door at each end. The elevation also shows that at the end of the building with loading platform, the door is at the level of the stage floor and all the other doors are at grade level.

5. Floor Plans

a. A floor plan is a cross-sectional view of a building. The horizontal cut crosses all openings regardless of their height from the floor. The development of a floor plan is shown in figure 4. Note that a floor plan shows the outside shape of the building; the arrangement, size, and shape of the rooms; the type of materials; and the length, thickness, and character of the building walls at a particular floor. A floor plan also includes the type, width, and location of the doors and windows; the types and locations of utility installations; and the location of stairways. A typical floor plan is shown in figure 2

b. Read the floor plan shown in figure 5 and note the features of the recreation building. Basically, the lines with small circles show wiring for electrical outlets; appropriate symbols show the plumbing fixtures. These features are important to the carpenter from the standpoint of coordination. He may have to make special provisions, at various stages of construction, for the placement of electrical or plumbing fixtures. These provisions should be studied on the floor plan and coordinated with the electrician, plumber, and foreman.

c. Figure 6 shows how a stairway is drawn in a plan and how riser-tread information is given. The symbol shows the direction of the stairs from the floor shown in the plan and the amount of risers in the run. For example, 17 DN followed by an arrow means that there are 17 risers in the run of stairs going from the floor shown on the plan to the floor below in the direction indicated by the arrow. The riser-tread diagram provides height and width information. The standard for the riser, or height from step-to-step, is from 6 1/2 to 7 1/2 inches. The tread width is usually such that the sum of riser and tread is about 18 inches (a 7-inch riser and 11-

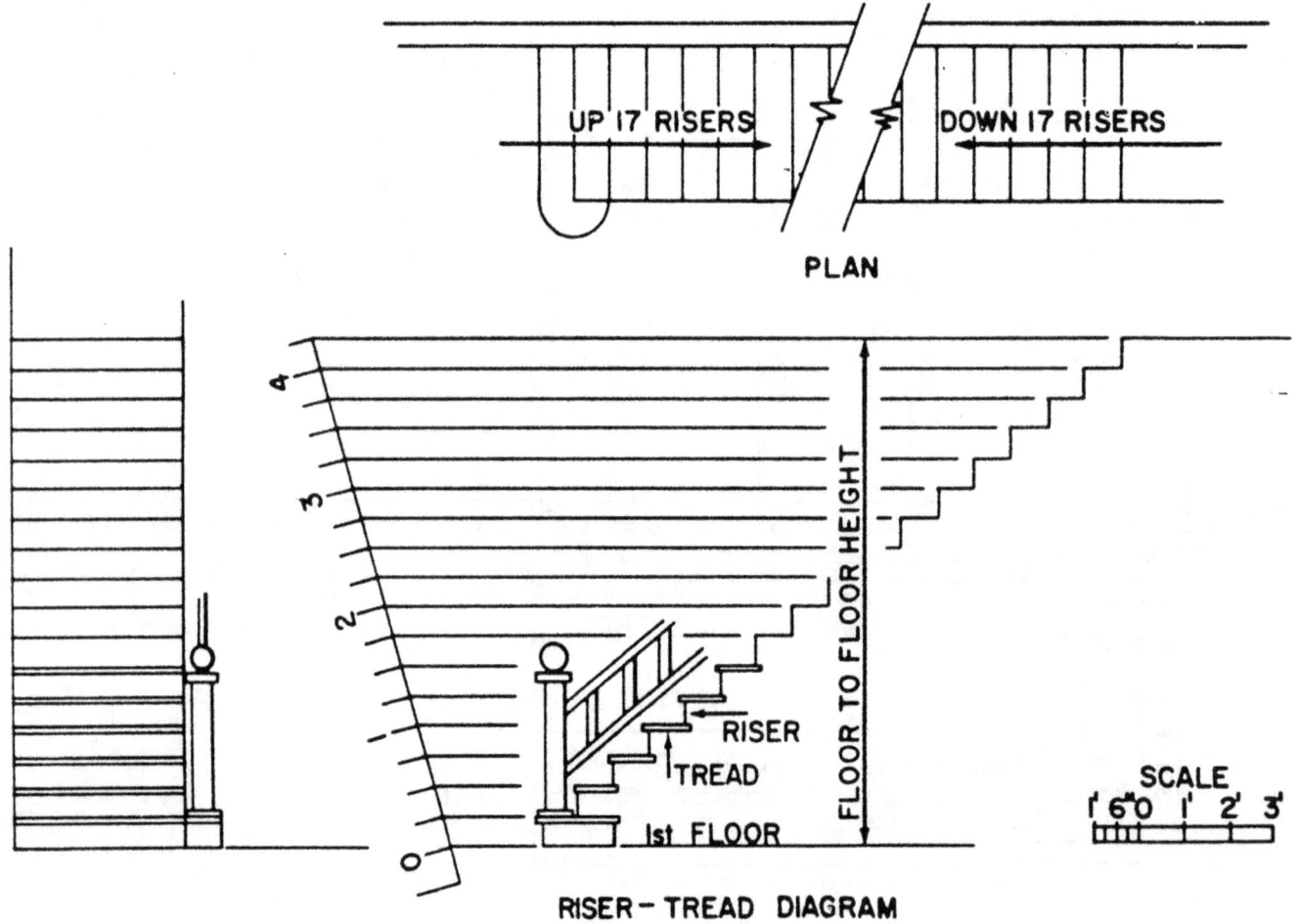

Figure 6. Stairway and steps.

inch tread is standard). On the plan, the distance between the riser lines is the width of the tread.

d. By examining the floor plan (fig. 5) it is seen that the interior of the building will consist of an auditorium, a lobby with a P.X. counter, a men's toilet, a women's toilet, a projection room on a second level above the lobby, two dressing rooms, and a stage. The stage may not be apparent but, by noting the steps adjacent to each dressing room, it can be seen that there is a change in elevation. The elevation view, as in figure 3, will show the stage and its elevation. The plan gives the dimensions of the areas specified. Note that all building entrances and/or exit doors are the same type (1D) and that all windows are the double-hung type. All interior single doors (2D) are the same and two double doors (3D) open into the lobby from the auditorium. The projection room will be reached via a 15-riser stairway located in a 12- by 18-foot room. Entrances to this room will be from the auditorium through a single door opening into the room. At the top of the stairway, a single door opens into the projection room. The wall of the projection room that faces the stage (inside wall) has three openings. Note that no windows are shown for the sides of the building where the projection room is located, but are shown at the main level.

e. The symbols shown in figure 7 are typical representations of exterior and interior walls. Note how the material conventions are used in the makeup of the symbols for masonry, brick, and concrete walls. The carpenter should become familiar with these symbols, which can be found in appendix B.

6. Sections

a. A section shows how a structure looks when

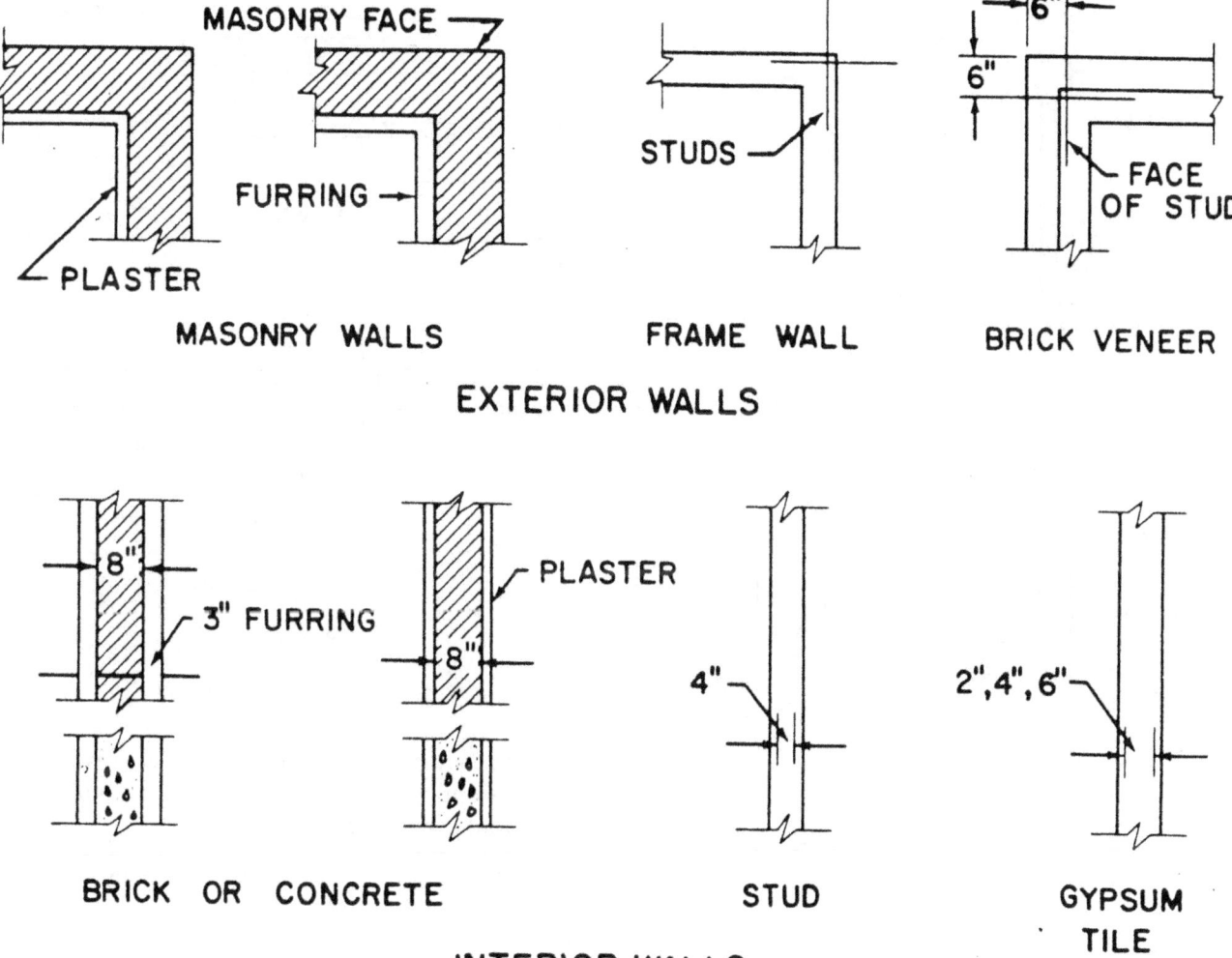

Figure 7. Typical wall symbols.

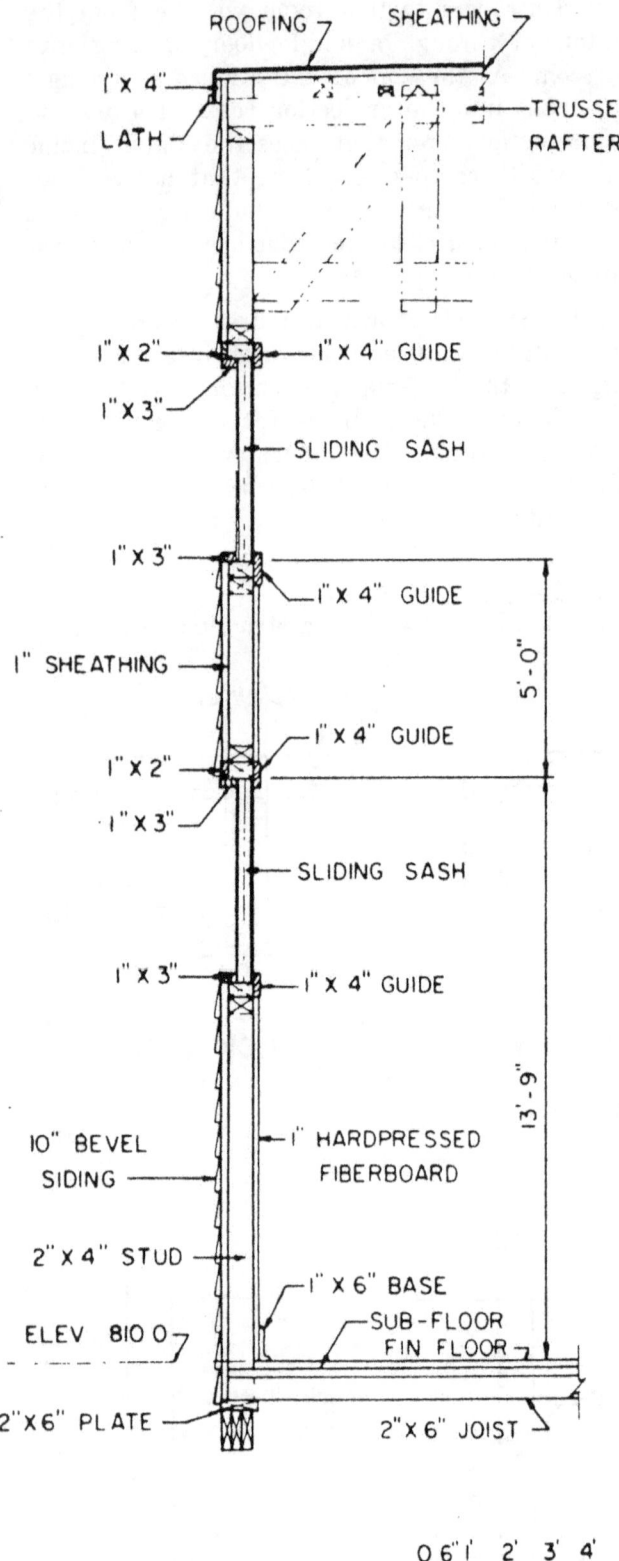

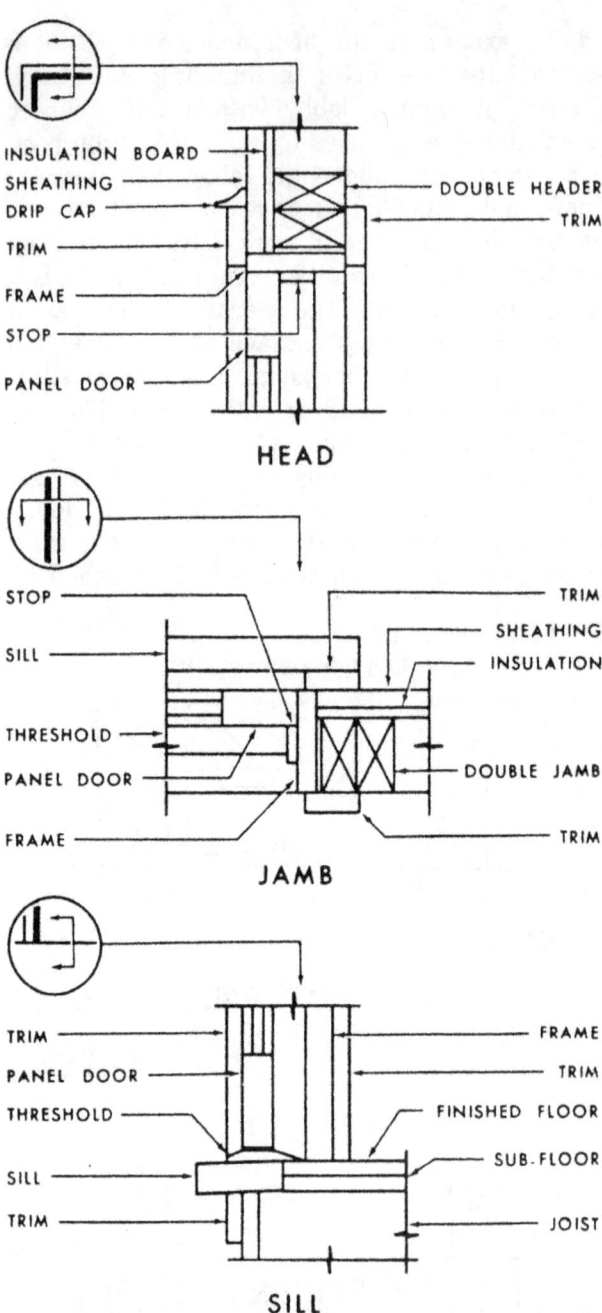

EXTERIOR DOOR DETAILS

Figure 9. Typical door details.

Figure 8. Typical wall section.

general drawing. The section provides information on height, materials, fastening and support systems, and concealed features.

b. Of primary importance to construction supervisors and to the craftsmen who do the actual building are the wall sections. These show the construction of the wall as well as the way in which structural members and other features are joined to it. Wall sections extend vertically from the foundation bed to the roof. A typical wall cut vertically by a cutting plane. It is drawn to a large scale showing details of a particular construction feature that cannot be given in the

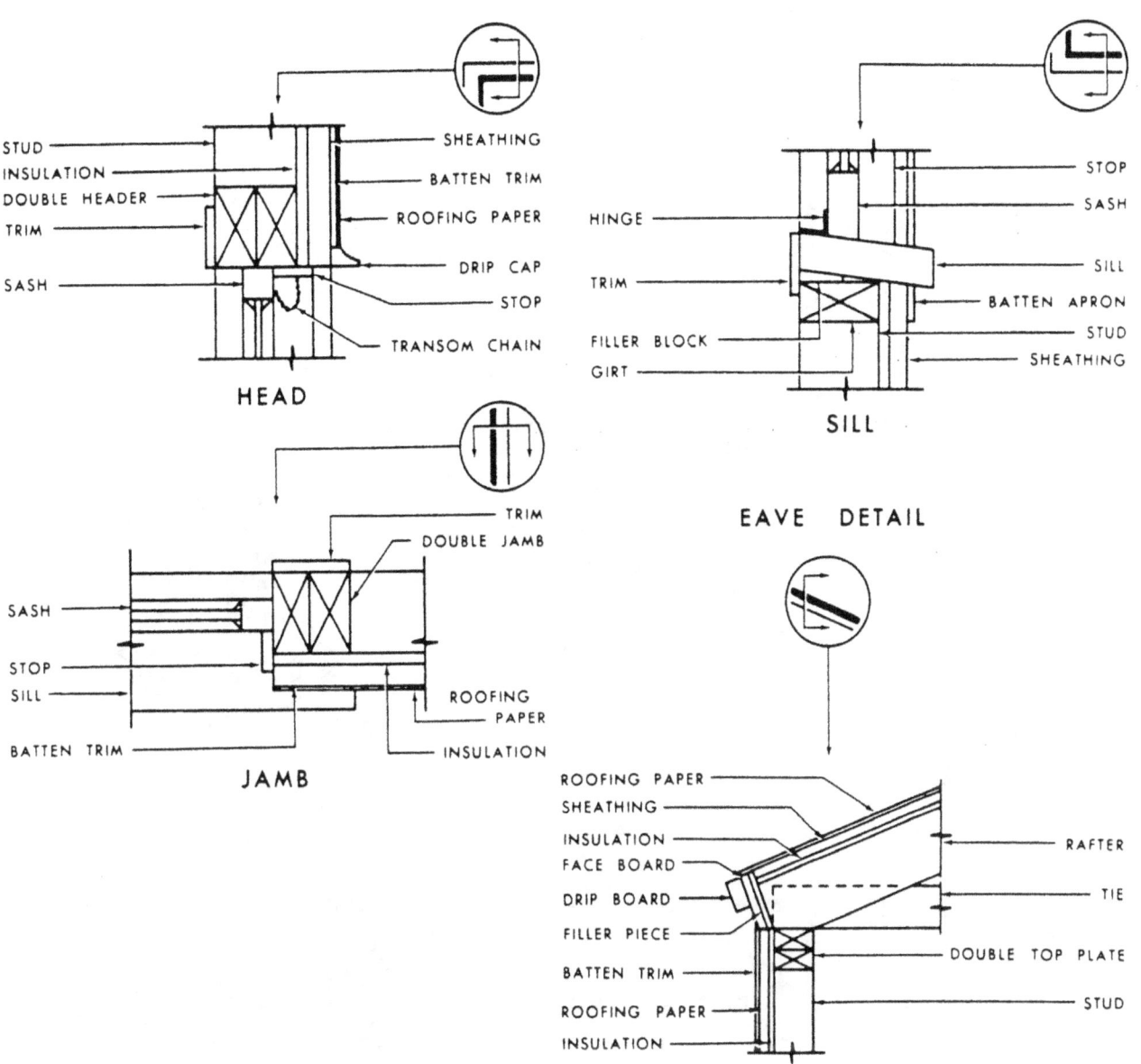

Figure 10. Typical window and eave details.

section with the parts identified by name and/or size is illustrated in figure 8.

7. Details
Details are large scale drawings which show features that do not appear (or appear on too small a scale) on the plans, elevations, and sections. Details do not have a cutting-plane indication, but are simply noted by a code. The construction of doors, windows, and eaves is usually shown in detail drawings. Figure 9 shows some typical door framing details and figure 10 shows that of window wood framing and an eave detail for a simple type of cornice. Other details which are customarily shown are sills, girder and joist connections, and stairways.

Section II. LIGHT AND HEAVY WOOD FRAMING

8. Light Wood Framing
Framing is the rough timberwork of a building. It includes exterior walls, flooring, roofing, beams, trusses, partitions, and ceilings. Working prints for theater of operations type buildings usually show details of all framing. Light framing is used in barracks, bathhouses, administration buildings, light shop buildings, hospital build-

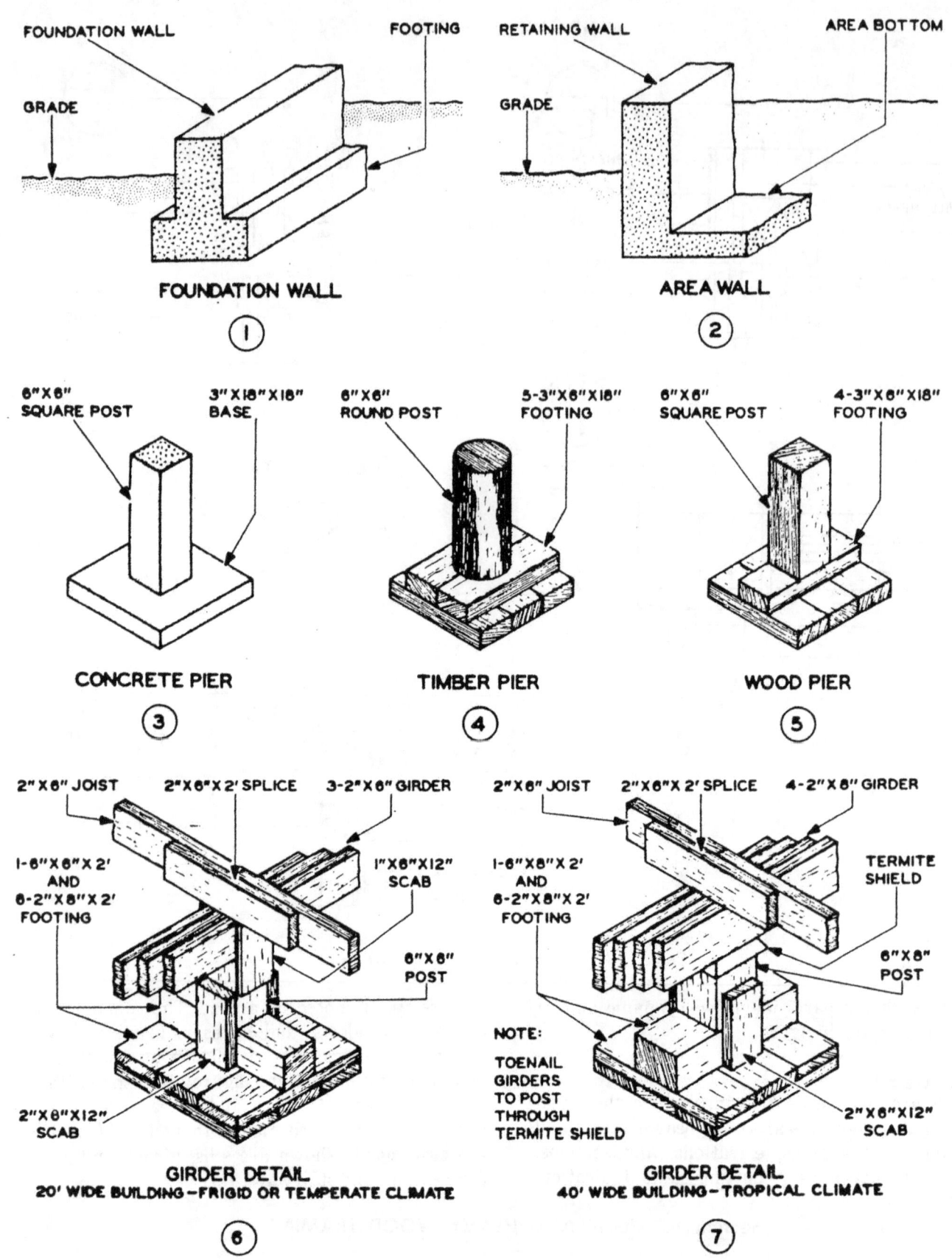

Figure 11. Typical foundation walls, piers, footings, and girder details.

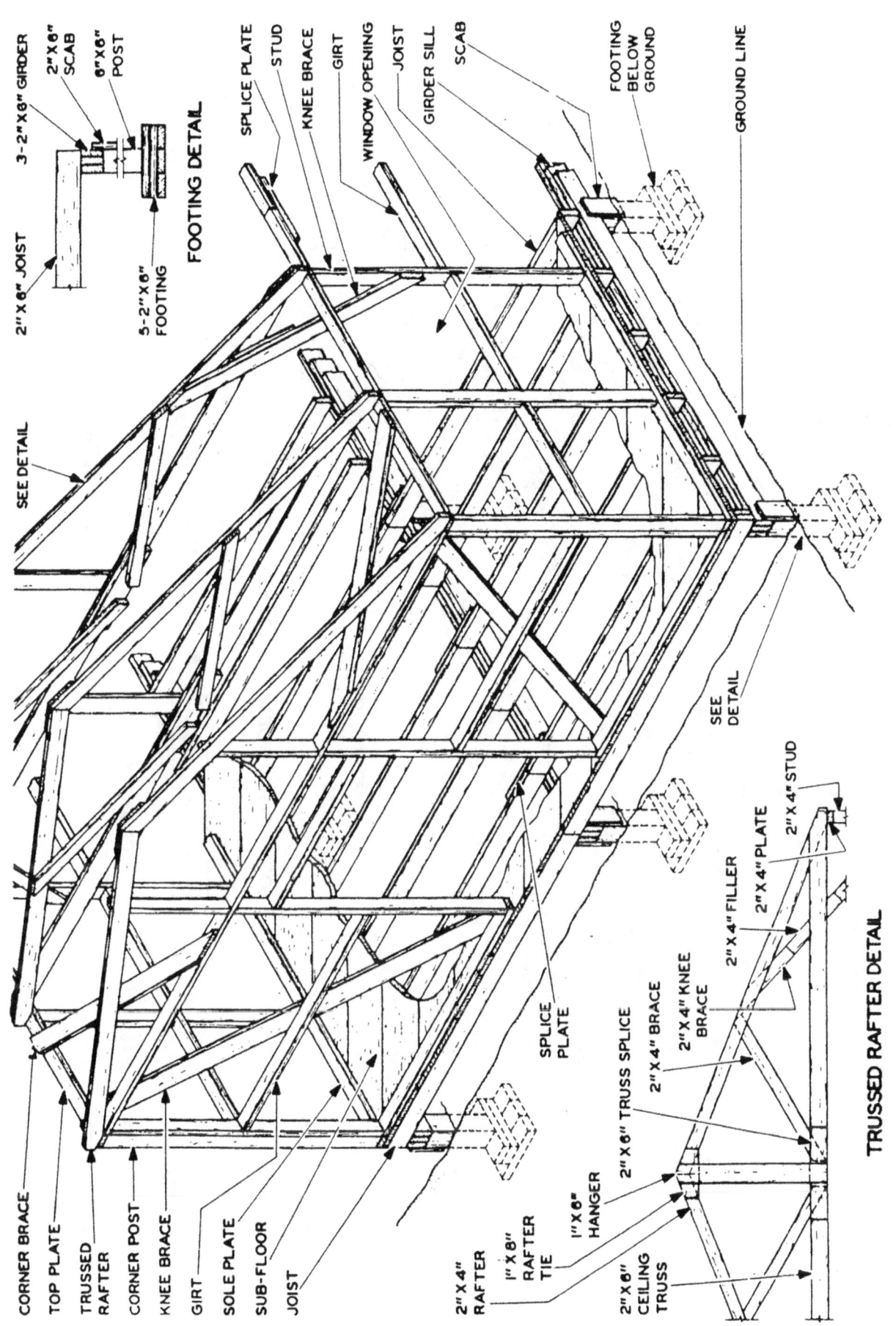

Figure 12. Light framing details (20-foot-wide building).

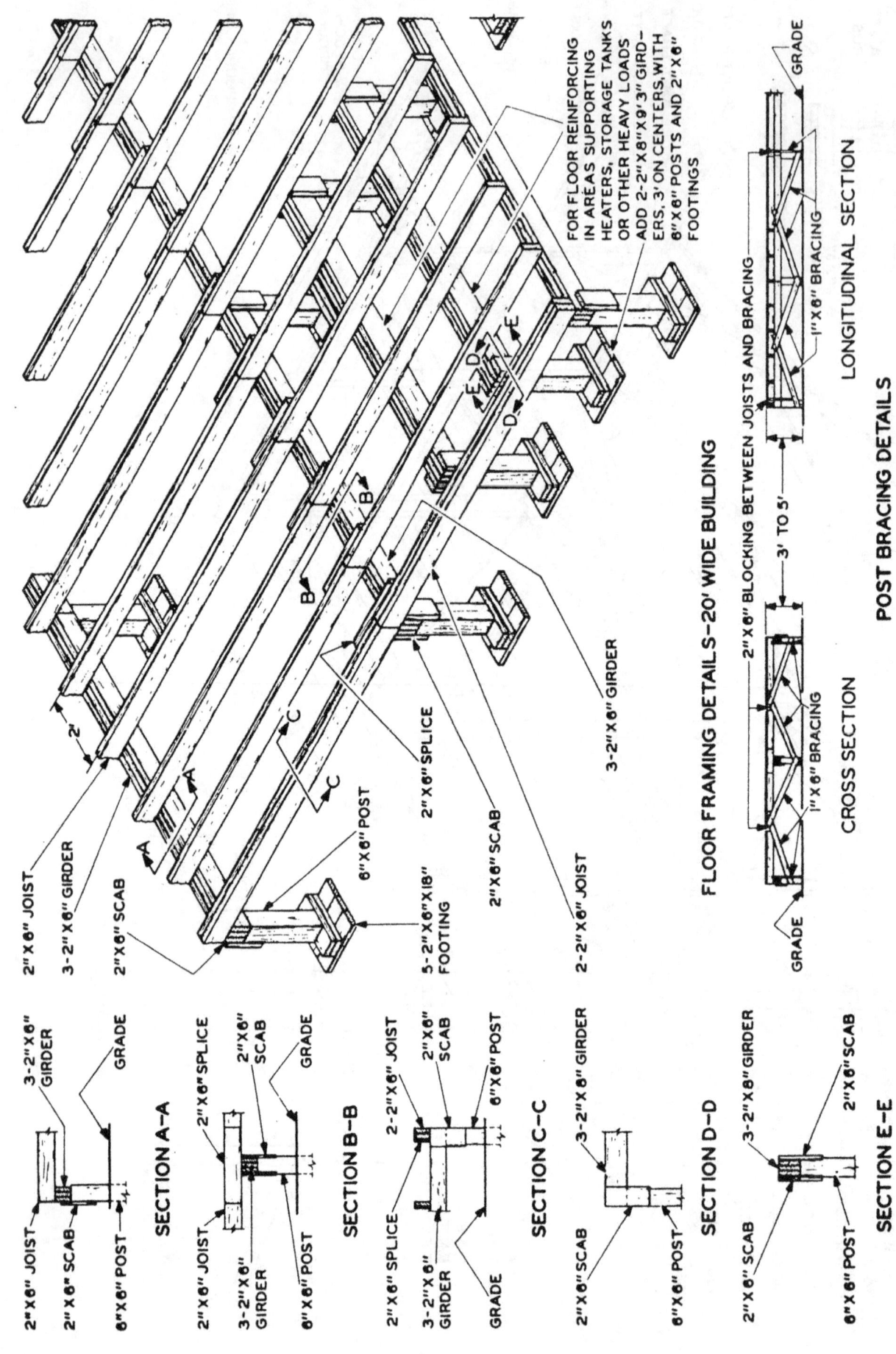

Figure 13. Floor framing details.

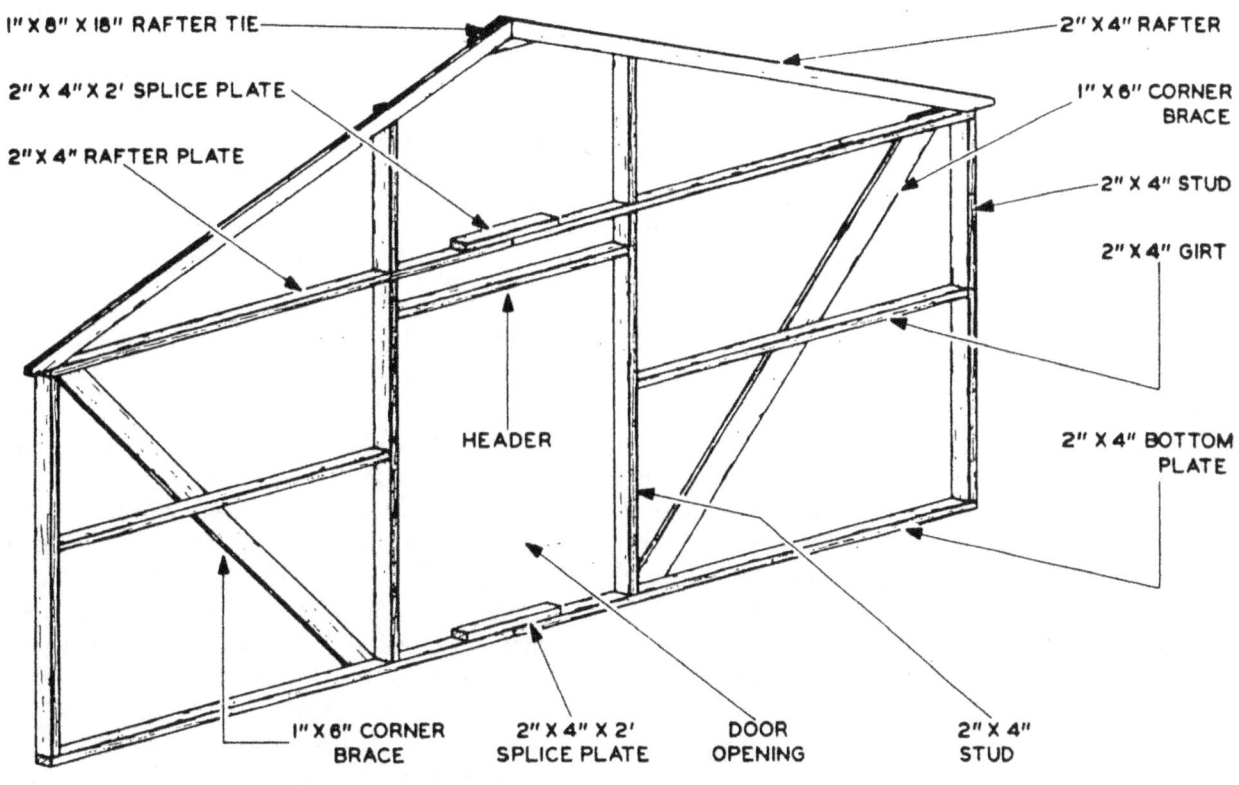

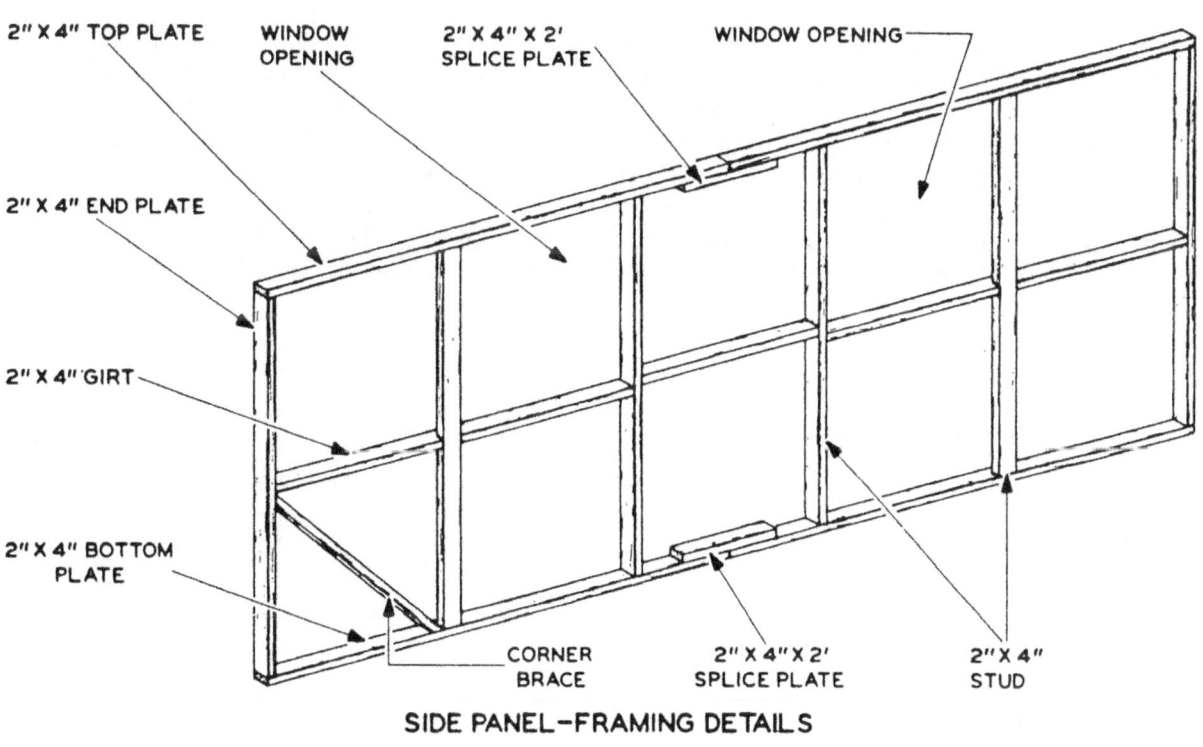

Figure 14. Typical wall panels—framing details.

ings, and similar structures.

a. The types of foundation walls, footings, and girder details normally used in standard theater of operations type construction are shown in figure 11. The various details for overall framing of a 20-foot-wide building showing ground level and including window openings, braces, splices, and nomenclature of framing are shown in figure 12.

b. Figure 13 illustrates floor framing details showing footings, posts, girders, joists, reinforced section of floor for heavy loads, section views covering makeup of certain sections, scabs for joining girders to posts, and post bracing details as placed for cross sections and longitudinal sections. On a construction print the type of footings and size of the various members are shown. In some cases the lengths are given while in others the bill of materials which accompanies the print specifies the required lengths of the various members.

c. Wall framing details for end panels are shown in ①, figure 14. The height of panels is usually shown and from this height the length of wall studs is determined by deducting the thickness of the top or rafter plate and the bottom plate. The space between studs is given in the drawing as well as height of girt from bottom plate, type of door opening, if any, and window opening. Details for side panels, ②, figure 14, cover the same type of information as listed for end panels. For window openings, the details specify whether the window is hinged to swing in or out or whether it is to be a sliding panel. Studs placed next to window openings may be placed either on edge or flat depending upon the type of window used.

d. The makeup of various trussed rafters is shown in figure 14. A 40-foot trussed rafter showing a partition bearing in the center is shown in ①, figure 15. This figure shows the splices required, bracing details, stud and top plate at one end of rafter, and size of members. The typical 20-foot truss rafter is shown in ②, figure 15. The use of filler blocks to keep the brace members in a vertical plane is needed since the rafter and bottom chord are nailed together rather than spliced. The rafter tie is placed on the opposite side from the vertical brace. Usually the splice plate for the bottom chord, if one is needed, is placed on the side on which it is planned to nail the rafters so that it can also serve as a filler block. A modified truss rafter is shown in ③, figure 15. This type of truss is used only when specified in plans for certain construction. It will not be used in areas subject to high wind velocities or moderate to heavy snowfall. In this type of trussed rafter, the bottom chord is placed on the rafters at a height above the top plate.

9. Heavy Wood Framing

Heavy wood framing consists of framing members at least 6 inches in dimension (timber construction). Examples of this type of framing can be found in heavy roof trusses, timber trestle bridges, and wharfs. The major differences between light and heavy framing are the size of timber used and the types of fasteners used. Fasteners for both light and heavy framing will be covered in a later chapter. Figure 16 shows the framing details for a heavy roof truss.

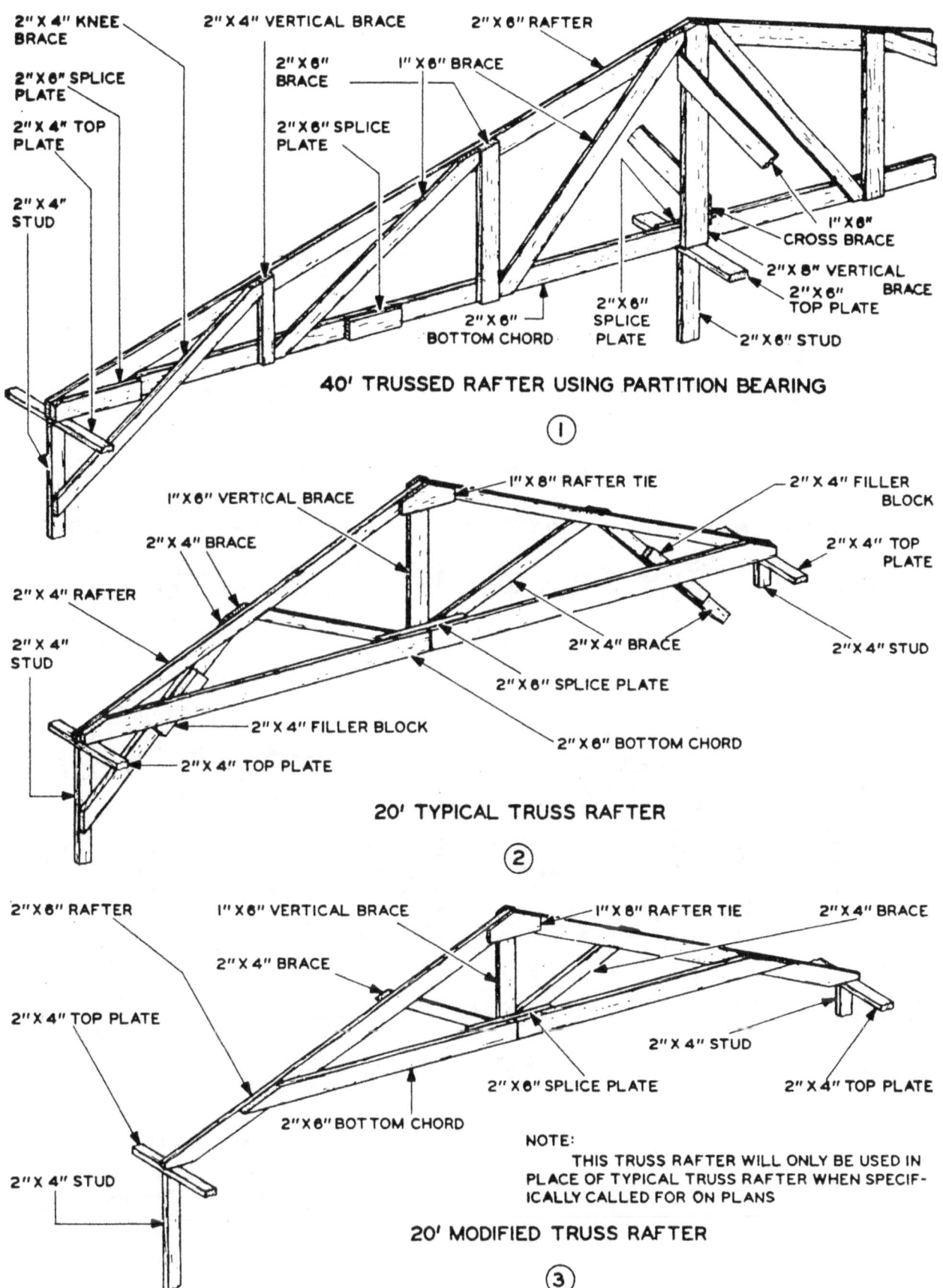

Figure 15. Trussed rafter details.

① TYPICAL LIGHT ROOF TRUSS

② TYPICAL HEAVY ROOF TRUSS

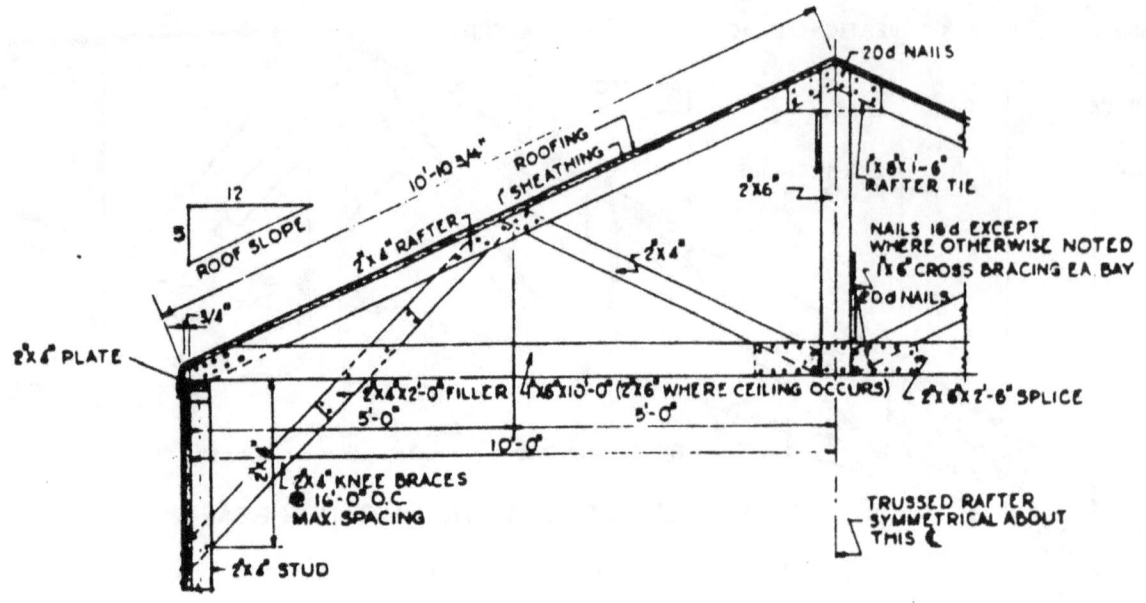

Figure 16. Typical heavy roof trusses.

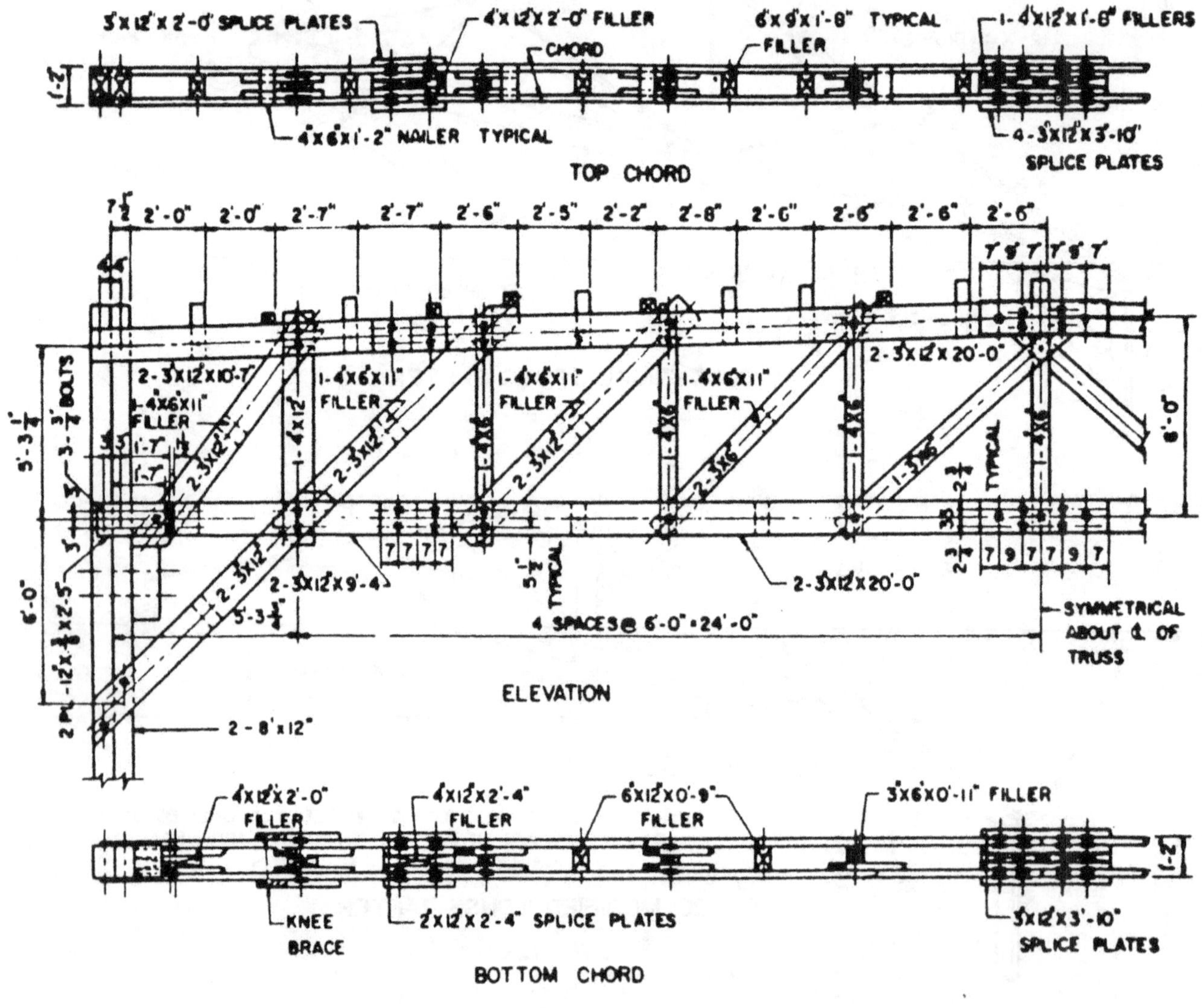

GLOSSARY OF HOUSING TERMS

TABLE OF CONTENTS

	Page
Airway ... Beam	1
Bearing Partition ... Butt Joint	2
Cabinet ... Coped Joint	3
Corner Bead ... Doorjamb, Interior	4
Dormer ... Flat Paint	5
Flue ... Gable	6
Gloss (Paint or Enamel) ... Insulation Board, Rigid	7
Insulation, Thermal ... Lintel	8
Lookout ... Millwork	9
Miter Joint ... Preservative	10
Primer ... Riser	11
Roll Roofing ... Shingles	12
Shingles, Siding ... Square	13
Stain, Shingle ... Termites	14
Termite Shield ... Varnish	15
Vent ... Weatherstrip	16

Glossary of Housing Terms

A

AIRWAY
A space between roof insulation and roof boards for movement of air.

APRON
The flat member of the inside trim of a window placed against the wall immediately beneath the stool.

ASPHALT
Most native asphalt is a residue from evaporated petroleum. It is insoluble in water but soluble in gasoline and melts when heated. Used widely in building for such items as waterproof roof coverings of many types, exterior wall coverings, and flooring tile.

ATTIC VENTILATORS
In houses, screened openings provided to ventilate an attic space. They are located in the soffit area as inlet ventilators and in the gable end or along the ridge as outlet ventilators. They can also consist of powerdriven fans used as an exhaust system. (See also LOUVER.)

B

BACK-FILL
The replacement of excavated earth into a trench or pier excavation around and against a basement foundation.

BALUSTERS
Usually small vertical members in a railing used between a top rail and the stair treads or a bottom rail.

BASE OR BASEBOARD
A board placed around a room against the wall next to the floor to finish properly between floor and plaster or dry wall.

BASE MOLDING
Molding used to trim the upper edge of interior baseboard.

BASE SHOE
Molding used next to the floor on interior baseboard. Sometimes called a carpet strip.

BATTEN
Narrow strips of wood used to cover joints or as decorative vertical members over plywood or wide boards.

BEAM
A structural member transversely supporting a load.

BEARING PARTITION
A partition that supports any vertical load in addition to its own weight.

BEARING WALL
A wall that supports any vertical load in addition to its own weight.

BED MOLDING
A molding in an angle, as between the overhanging cornice, or eaves, of a building and the sidewalks.

BLIND-NAILING
Nailing in such a way that the nailheads are not visible on the face of the work. Usually at the tongue of matched boards.

BLIND STOP
A rectangular molding, usually 3/4 by 1 3/8 inches or more in width used in the assembly of a window frame. Serves as a stop for storm and screen or combination windows and to resist air infiltration.

BOILED LINSEED OIL
Linseed oil in which enough lead, manganese, or cobalt salts have been incorporated to make the oil harden more rapidly when spread in thin coatings.

BOLTS, ANCHOR
Bolts to secure a wooden sill plate to concrete or masonry floor or wall or pier.

BOSTON RIDGE
A method of applying asphalt to wood shingles at the ridge or at the hips of a roof as a finish.

BRACE
An inclined piece of framing lumber applied to wall or floor to stiffen the structure. Often used on walls as temporary bracing until framing has been completed.

BUCK
Often used in reference to rough frame opening members. Door bucks used in reference to metal door frame.

BUILT-UP ROOF
A roofing composed of three to five layers of asphalt felt laminated with coal tar, pitch, or asphalt. The top is finished with crushed slag or gravel. Generally used on flat or low-pitched roofs.

BUTT JOINT
The junction where the ends of two timbers or other members meet in a square-cut joint.

C

CABINET
A shop-or job-built unit for kitchens or other rooms. Often includes combinations of drawers, doors, and the like.

CASING
Molding of various widths and thicknesses used to trim door and window openings at the jambs.

CASEMENT FRAMES AND SASH
Frames of wood or metal enclosing part or all of the sash, which may be opened by means of hinges affixed to the vertical edges.

COLLAR BEAM
Nominal 1- or 2-inch-thick members connecting opposite roof rafters. They serve to stiffen the roof structure.

COMBINATION DOORS OR WINDOWS
Combination doors or windows used over regular openings. They provide winter insulation and summer protection. They often have self-storing or removable glass and screen inserts. This eliminates the need for handling a different unit each season.

CONCRETE, PLAIN
Concrete without reinforcement, or reinforced only for shrinkage or temperature changes.

CONDENSATION
Beads or drops of water, and frequently frost in extremely cold weather, that accumulates on the inside of the exterior covering of a building when warm, moisture-laden air from the interior reaches a point where the temperature no longer permits the air to sustain the moisture it holds. Use of louvers or attic ventilators will reduce moisture condensation in attics. A vapor barrier under the gypsum lath or dry wall on exposed walls will reduce condensation in walls.

CONDUIT, ELECTRICAL
A pipe, usually metal, in which wire is installed.

CONSTRUCTION, DRY-WALL
A type of construction in which the interior wall finish is applied in a dry condition, generally in the form of sheet materials or wood paneling, as contrasted to plaster.

CONSTRUCTION, FRAME
A type of construction in which the structural parts are of wood or depend upon a wood frame for support. In building codes, if masonry veneer is applied to the exterior walls, the classification of this type of construction is usually unchanged.

COPED JOINT
Fitting woodwork to an irregular surface. In moldings, cutting the end of one piece to fit the molded face of the other at an interior angle to replace a miter joint.

CORNER BEAD
A strip of formed sheet metal, sometimes combined with a strip of metal lath, placed on corners before plastering to reinforce them. Also, a strip of wood finish three-quarters round or angular placed over a plastered corner for protection.

CORNER BOARDS
Used as trim for the external corners of a house or other frame structures against which the ends of the siding are finished.

CORNER BRACES
Diagonal braces at the corners of frame structure to stiffen and strengthen the wall.

CORNICE
Overhang of a pitched roof at the eave line, usually consisting of a facia board, a soffit for a closed cornice, and appropriate moldings.

COUNTERFLASHING
A flashing usually used on chimneys at the roofline to cover shingle flashing and to prevent moisture entry.

COVE MOLDING
A molding with a concave face used as trim or to finish interior corners.

CRAWL SPACE
A shallow space below the living quarters of a basementless house sometimes enclosed.

D

d
See PENNY.

DADO
A rectangular groove across the width of a board or plank. In interior decoration, a special type of wall treament.

DECK PAINT
An enamel with a high degree of resistance to mechanical wear, designed for use on such surfaces as porch floors.

DENSITY
The mass of substance in a unit volume. When expressed in the metric system (in g. per cc.), it is numerically equal to the specific gravity of the same substance.

DIMENSION
See LUMBER, DIMENSION.

DOORJAMB, INTERIOR
The surrounding case into and out of which a door closes and opens. It consists of two upright pieces, called side jambs, and a horizontal head jamb.

DORMER
A projection in a sloping roof, the framing of which forms a vertical wall suitable for windows or other openings.

DOWNSPOUT
A pipe, usually metal, for carrying rainwater from roof gutters

DRESSED AND MATCHED (TONGUED AND GROOVED)
Boards or plans machined in such a manner that there is a groove on one edge and a corresponding tongue on the other.

DRIER, PAINT
Usually oil-soluble soaps of such metals as lead, manganese, or cobalt, which, in small proportions, hasten the oxidation and hardening (drying) of the drying oils in paints.

DRIP CAP
A molding placed on the exterior top side of a door or window frame to cause water to drip beyond the outside of the frame.

DRY-WALL
See CONSTRUCTION, DRY WALL.

DUCTS
In a house, usually round or rectangular metal pipes for distributing warm air from the heating plant to rooms, or air from a conditioning device, or as cold air returns. Ducts are also made of asbestos and composition materials.

E

EAVES
The overhang of a roof projecting over the walls.

F

FACE NAILING
To nail perpendicular to the initial surface or to the junction of the pieces joined.

FACIA OR FASCIA
A flat board, band, or face, used sometimes by itself but usually in combination with moldings, often located at the outer face of the cornice.

FLASHING
Sheet metal or other material used in roof and wall construction to protect a building from seepage of water.

FLAT PAINT
An interior paint that contains a high proportion of pigment, and dries to a flat or lusterless finish.

FLUE
The space or passage in a chimney through which smoke, gas, or fumes ascend. Each passage is called a flue, which, together with any others and the surrounding masonry, make up the chimney.

FLUE LINING
Fire clay or terracotta pipe, round or square, usually made in all of the ordinary flue sizes and in 2-foot lengths, used for the inner lining of chimneys with a brick or masonry work around the outside. Flue lining in chimneys runs from about a foot below the flue connection to the top of the chimney.

FLY RAFTER
End rafters of the gable overhang supported by roof sheathing and lookouts.

FOOTING
A masonry section, usually concrete in a rectangular form wider than the bottom of the foundation wall or pier it supports.

FOUNDATION
The supporting portion of a structure below the first floor construction, or below grade, including the footings.

FRAMING, BALLOON
A system of framing a building in which all vertical structural elements of the bearing walls and partitions consist of single pieces extending from the top of the foundation sill plate to the roofplate and to which all floor joists are fastened.

FRAMING, PLATFORM
A system of framing a building in which floor joists of each story rest on the top plates of the story below or on the foundation sill for the first story, and the bearing walls and partitions rest on the subfloor of each story.

FRIEZE
In house construction, a horizontal member connecting the top of the siding with the soffit of the cornice or roof sheathing.

FROSTLINE
The depth of frost penetration in soil. This depth varies in different parts of the country. Footings should be placed below this depth to prevent movement.

FURRING
Strips of wood or metal applied to a wall or other surface to even it and usually to serve as a fastening base for finish material.

G

GABLE
The triangular vertical end of a building formed by the eaves and ridge of a sloped roof.

GLOSS (PAINT OR ENAMEL)
A paint or enamel that contains a relatively low proportion of pigment and dries to a sheen or luster.

GIRDER
A large or principal beam of wood or steel used to support concentrated loads at isolated points along its length.

GRAIN
The direction, size, arrangement, appearance, or quality of the fibers in wood.

GRAIN, EDGE (VERTICAL)
Edge-grain lumber has been sawed parallel to the pith of the log and approximately at right angles to the growth rings, i.e., the rings form an angle of 45 or more with the surface of the piece.

GUSSET
A flat wood, plywood, or similar type member used to provide a connection at the intersection of wood members. Most commonly used at joints of wood trusses. They are fastened by nails, screws, bolts, or adhesives.

GUTTER OR EAVE TROUGH
A shallow channel or conduit of metal or wood set below and along the eaves of a house to catch and carry off rainwater from the roof.

H

HEADER
(a) A beam place perpendicular to joists and to which joists are nailed in framing for chimney, stairway, or other opening.
(b) A wood lintel.

HEARTWOOD
The wood extending from the pith to the sapwood, the cells of which no longer participate in the life processes of the tree.

HIP
The external angle formed by the meeting of two sloping sides of a roof.

HIP ROOF
A roof that rises by inclined planes from all four sides of a building.

I

INSULATION BOARD, RIGID
A structural building board made of wood or cane fiber in and 25/32" thicknesses. It can be obtained in various size sheets, in various densities, and with several treatments.

INSULATION, THERMAL
　　Any material high in resistance to heat transmission that, when place in the walls, ceiling, or floors of a structure, will reduce the rate of heat flow.

J

JACK RAFTER
　　A rafter that spans the distance from the wallplate to a hip, or from a valley to a ridge.

JAMB
　　The side and head lining of a doorway, window, or other opening.

JOINT
　　The space between the adjacent surfaces of two members or components joined and held together by nails, glue, cement, mortar, or other means.

JOINT CEMENT
　　A powder that is usually mixed with water and used for joint treatment in gypsum-wallboard finish. Often called "spackle."

JOIST
　　One of a series of parallel beams, usually 2 inches thick, used to support floor and ceiling loads, and supported in turn by larger beams, girders, or bearing walls.

K

KNOT
　　In lumber, the portion of a branch or limb of a tree that appears on the edge or face of the piece.

L

LANDING
　　A platform between flights of stairs or at the termination of a flight of stairs.

LATH
　　A building material of wood, metal, gypsum, or insulating board that is fastened to the frame of a building to act as a plaster base.

LEDGER STRIP
　　A strip of lumber nailed along the bottom of the side of a girder on which joists rest.

LIGHT
　　Space in a window sash for a single pane of glass. Also, a pane of glass.

LINTEL
　　A horizontal structural member that supports the load over an opening such as a door or window.

LOOKOUT
A short wood bracket or cantilever to support an overhanging portion of a roof or the like, usually concealed from view.

LOUVER
An opening with a series of horizontal slats so arranged as to permit ventilation but to exclude rain, sunlight, or vision. See also ATTIC VENTILATORS.

LUMBER
Lumber is the product of the sawmill and planning mill not further manufactured other than by sawing, resawing, and passing lengthwise through a standard planing machine, cross cutting to length, and matching.

LUMBER, BOARDS
Yard lumber less than 2 inches thick and 2 or more inches wide.

LUMBER, DIMENSION
Yard lumber from 2 inches to, but including, 5 inches thick, and 2 or more inches wide. Includes joists, rafters, studs, plank and small timbers. The actual size dimension of such lumber after shrinking from green dimension and after machining to size or pattern is called the dress size.

LUMBER, MATCHED
Lumber that is dressed and shaped on one edge in a grooved pattern and on the other in a tongued pattern.

LUMBER, SHIPLAP
Lumber that is edge-dressed to make a close rabbeted or lapped joint.

LUMBER, YARD
Lumber of those grades, sizes, and patterns which are generally intended for ordinary construction, such as framework and rough coverage of houses.

M

MASONRY
Stone, brick, concrete, hollow-tile, concrete-block, gypsum-block, or other similar building units or materials or a combination of the same, bonded together with mortar to form a wall, pier, buttress, or similar mass.

MEETING RAILS
Rails sufficiently thicker than a window to fill the opening between the top and bottom sash made by the parting stop in the frame of double-hung windows. They are usually beveled.

MILLWORK
Generally all building materials made of finished wood and manufactured in millwork plants and planing mills are included under the term "millwork." It includes such items as inside and outside doors, window and doorframes, blinds, porchwork, mantels, panelwork, stairways, moldings, and interior trim. It normally does not include flooring, ceiling, or siding.

MITER JOINT
　　The joint of two pieces at an angle that bisects the joining angle. For example, the miter joint at the side and head casing at a door opening is made at a 45 angle.

MOISTURE CONTENT OF WOOD
　　Weight of the water contained in the wood, usually expressed as a percentage of the weight of the ovendry wood.

MOLDING
　　A wood strip having a curved or projecting surface used for decorative purposes.

MORTISE
　　A slot cut into a board, plank, or timber, usually edgewise, to receive tenon of another board, plank, or timber to form a joint.

N

NATURAL FINISH
　　A transparent finish which does not seriously alter the original color or grain of the natural wood. Natural finishes are usually provided by sealers, oils, varnishes, water-repellent, preservatives, and other similar materials.

NONLOADBEARING WALL
　　A wall supporting no load other than its own weight.

NOTCH
　　A crosswise rabbet at the end of a board.

O

O.C. ON CENTER
　　The measurement of spacing for studs, rafters, joists, and the like in a building from center of one member to the center of the next.

P

PLYWOOD
　　A piece of wood made of three or more layers of veneer joined with glue and usually laid with the grain of adjoining plies at right angles. Almost always an odd number of plies are used to provide balanced construction.

PLUMB
　　Exactly perpendiular; vertical.

PORCH
　　A roofed area extending beyond the main house. May be open or enclosed and with concrete or wood frame floor system.

PRESERVATIVE
　　Any substance that, for a reasonable length of time, will prevent the action of wood-destroying fungi, borers of various kinds, and similar destructive life when the wood has been properly coated or impregnated with it.

PRIMER
The first coat of paint in a paint job that consists of two or more coats; also the paint used for such a first coat.

PUTTY
A type of cement usually made of whiting and boiled linseed oil, beaten or kneaded to the consistency of dough, and used in sealing glass in sash, filling small holes and crevices in wood, and for similar purposes.

Q

QUARTER ROUND
A small molding that has the cross-section of a quarter circle.

R

RAFTER
One of a series of structural members of a roof designed to support roof loads. The rafters of a flat roof are sometimes called roof joists.

RAFTER, HIP
A rafter that forms the intersection of an external roof angle.

RAFTER, VALLEY
A rafter that forms the intersection of an internal roof angle. The valley rafter is normally made of doubled 2-inch-thick members.

RAIL
Cross members of panel doors or of a sash. Also the upper and lower members of a balustrade or staircase extending from one vertical support, such as a post, to another.

RAKE
The inclined edge of a gable roof (the trim member is a rake molding).

RIDGE
The horizontal line at the junction of the top edges of two sloping roof surfaces.

RIDGE BOARD
The board placed on edge at the ridge of the roof into which the upper ends of the rafters are fastened.

RISE
In stairs, the vertical height of a step or flight of stairs.

RISER
Each of the vertical boards closing the spaces between the treads of stairways.

ROLL ROOFING
Roofing material, composed of fiber and saturated with asphalt, that is supplied in rolls containing 108 square feet in 36-inch widths. It is generally furnished in weights of 45 to 90 pounds per roll.

ROOF SHEATHING
The boards or sheet material fastened to the roof rafters on which the shingle or other roof covering is laid.

ROUTED
See MORTISED.

RUN
In stairs, the net width of a step or the horizontal distance covered by a flight of stairs.

S

SASH
A single light frame containing one or more lights of glass.

SATURATED FELT
A felt which is impregnated with tar or asphalt.

SCAB
A short piece of wood or plywood fastened to two abutting timbers to splice them together.

SEALER
A finishing material, either clear or pigmented, that is usually applied directly over uncoated wood for the purpose of sealing the surface.

SEMIGLOSS PAINT OR ENAMEL
A paint or enamel made with a slight insufficiency of nonvolatile vehicle so that its coating when dry, has some luster but is not very glossy.

SHAKE
A thick handsplit shingle, resawed to form two shakes; usually edge grained.

SHEATHING
The structural covering, usually wood boards or plywood, used over studs or rafters of a structure. Structural building board is normally used only as wall sheathing.

SHEATHING PAPER
See PAPER, SHEATHING

SHINGLES
Roof covering of asphalt, asbestos, wood, tile, slate, or other material cut to stock lengths, widths, and thicknesses.

SHINGLES, SIDING
Various kinds of shingles, such as wood shingles or shakes and nonwood shingles, that are used over sheathing for exterior sidewall covering of a structure.

SHIPLAP
See LUMBER, SHIPLAP.

SIDING
The finish covering of the outside wall of a frame building, whether made of horizontal weatherboards, vertical boards with battens, shingles, or other material.

SIDING, BEVEL (LAP SIDING)
Wedge-shaped boards used as horizontal siding in a lapped pattern. This siding varies in butt thickness from 1/2 to 3/4" and in widths up to 12 inches. Normally used over some type of sheathing.

SIDING, DROP
Usually 3/4" thick and 6 and 8" in width with tongued-and-grooved or shiplap edges. Often used as siding without sheathing in secondary buildings.

SIDING, PANEL
Large sheets of plywood or hardboard which serve as both sheathing and siding.

SILL
The lowest member of the frame of a structure, resting on the foundation and supporting the floor joists or the uprights of the wall. The member forming the lower side of an opening, as a door sill, window sill, etc.

SOFFIT
Usually the underside covering of an overhanging cornice.

SOIL COVER (GROUND COVER)
A light covering of plastic film, roll roofing, or similar material used over the soil in crawl spaces of buildings to minimize moisture permeation of the area.

SOIL STACK
A general term for the vertical main of a system of soil, waste, or vent piping.

SOLE OR SOLE PLATE
See PLATE.

SPAN
The distance between structural supports such as walls, columns, piers, beams, girders, and trusses.

SQUARE
A unit of measure - 100 square feet - usually applied to roofing material. Sidewall coverings are sometimes packed to cover 100 square feet and are sold on that basis.

STAIN, SHINGLE

A form of oil paint, very thin in consistency, intended for coloring wood with rough surfaces, like shingles, without forming a coating of significant thickness or gloss.

STAIR CARRIAGE

Supporting member for stair treads. Usually a 2-inch plank notched to receive the treads; sometimes termed a "rough horse."

STOOL

A flat molding fitted over the window will between jambs and contacting the bottom rail of the lower sash.

STORM SASH OR STORM WINDOW

An extra window usually placed on the outside of an existing window as additional protection against cold weather.

STORY

That part of a building between any floor and the floor or roof next above.

STRING, STRINGER

A timber or other support for cross members in floors or ceilings. In stairs, the support on which the stair treads rest, also stringboard.

STUD

One of a series of slender wood or metal vertical structural members placed as supporting elements in walls and partitions. (Plural: studs or studding.)

SUBFLOOR

Boards or plywood laid on joists over which a finish floor is to be laid.

T

TAIL BEAM

A relatively short beam or joist supported in a wall on one end and by a header at the other.

TERMITES

Insects that superficially resemble ants in size, general appearance, and habit of living in colonies, hence, frequently called "white ants." Subterranean termites do not establish themselves in buildings by being carried in with lumber, but by entering from ground nests after the building has been constructed. If unmolested they eat out the woodwork, leaving a shell of sound wood to conceal their activities, and damage may proceed so far so to cause collapse of parts of a structure before discovery. There are about 56 species of termites known in the United States; but the two main species, classified from the manner in which they attack wood, subterranean (ground-inhabiting) termites, the most common, and drywood termites, found almost exclusively along the extreme southern border and the Gulf of Mexico in the United States.

TERMITE SHIELD
A shield, usually of noncorrodible metal, placed in or on a foundation wall or other mass of masonry or around pipes to prevent passage of termites.

THRESHOLD
A strip of wood or metal with beveled edges used over the finished floor and the sill of exterior doors.

TOENAILING
To drive a nail at a slant with the initial surface in order to permit it to penetrate into a second member.

TREAD
The horizontal board in a stairway on which the foot is placed.

TRIM
The finish materials in a building, such as moldings, applied around openings (window trims, door trim) or at the floor and ceiling of rooms (baseboard, cornice, picture molding).

TRIMMER
A beam or joist to which a header is nailed in framing for a chimney, stairway, or other opening.

TRUSS
A frame or jointed structure designed to act as a beam of long span, while each member is usually subjected to longitudinal stress only, either tension or compression.

TURPENTINE
A volatile oil used as a thinner in paints, and as a solvent in varnishes. Chemically, it is a mixture of terpenes.

U

UNDERCOAT
A coating applied prior to the finishing or top coats of a paint job. It may be the first of two or the second of three coats. In some usage of the word, it may become synonymous with priming coat.

V

VAPOR BARRIER
Material used to retard the movement of water vapor into walls and prevent condensation in them. Usually considered as having a perm value of less than 1.0. Applied separately over the warm side of exposed walls or as a part of batt or blanket insulation.

VARNISH
A thickened preparation of drying oil or drying oil and resin suitable for spreading on surfaces to form continuous, transparent coatings, or for mixing with pigments to make enamels.

VENT
A pipe or duct which allows flow of air as an inlet or outlet.

VERMICULITE
A mineral closely related to mica, with the faculty of expanding on heating to form lightweight material with insulation quality. Used as bulk insulation and as aggregate in insulating and acoustical plaster and in insulating concrete floors.

W

WATER-REPELLENT PRESERVATIVE
A liquid designed to penetrate into wood and impart water repellency and a moderate preservative protection. It is used for millwork, such as sash and frames, and is usually applied by dipping.

WEATHERSTRIP
Narrow or jamb-width sections of thin metal or other material to prevent infiltration of air and moisture around windows and doors.

www.ingramcontent.com/pod-product-compliance
Lightning Source LLC
Chambersburg PA
CBHW081802300426
44116CB00014B/2206